The Politics of Italy

This innovative text offers a completely fresh approach to Italian politics by placing it in its historical, institutional, social and international contexts. Students will get to grips with the theories and concepts of comparative politics and how they apply specifically to Italy, while gaining real insight into more controversial topics such as the Mafia, corruption and the striking success of Berlusconi. The textbook uses clear and simple language to analyse critically Italy's institutions, its political culture, parties and interest groups, public policy, and its place in the international system. Often regarded as an anomaly, Italy is frequently described in terms of 'crisis', 'instability' and 'alienation'. Sceptical of these conventional accounts, Newell argues that, if understood in its own terms, the Italian political system is just as effective as other established democracies. With features including text boxes and further reading suggestions, this is an unbeatable introduction to the politics of Italy.

JAMES L. NEWELL is Professor of Politics in the School of English, Sociology, Politics and Contemporary History at the University of Salford. He is the author of *Italian Politics: Adjustment under Duress* (with Martin Bull, 2005) and *Parties and Democracy in Italy* (2000), as well as numerous journal articles and book chapters on Italian politics.

CAMBRIDGE TEXTBOOKS IN COMPARATIVE POLITICS

Series Editors

Jan W. Van Deth, *Universität Mannheim, Germany*
Kenneth Newton, *University of Southampton, United Kingdom*

Comparative research is central to the study of politics. This series
offers accessible but sophisticated materials for students of
comparative politics at the introductory level and beyond. It comprises
an authoritative introductory textbook, *Foundations of Comparative
Politics*, accompanied by volumes devoted to the politics of individual
countries, and an introduction to methodology in comparative politics.
The books share a common structure and approach, allowing teachers
to choose combinations of volumes to suit their particular course. The
volumes are also suitable for use independent of one other. Attractively
designed and accessibly written, this series provides an up-to-date and
flexible teaching resource.

Other books in this series:

RICHARD GUNTHER & JOSÉ RAMÓN MONTERO
The Politics of Spain

KENNETH NEWTON & JAN W. VAN DETH
Foundations of Comparative Politics

The Politics of Italy

Governance in a Normal Country

JAMES L. NEWELL

CAMBRIDGE UNIVERSITY PRESS
Cambridge, New York, Melbourne, Madrid, Cape Town, Singapore,
São Paulo, Delhi, Dubai, Tokyo

Cambridge University Press
The Edinburgh Building, Cambridge CB2 8RU, UK

Published in the United States of America by Cambridge University Press, New York

www.cambridge.org
Information on this title: www.cambridge.org/9780521600460

First published 2010

Printed in the United Kingdom at the University Press, Cambridge

A catalogue record for this publication is available from the British Library

ISBN 978-0-521-84070-5 Hardback
ISBN 978-0-521-60046-0 Paperback

Contents

Contents

IV
Policies and performances

IV Policies and performances — 251

8 Economic policy — 253

9 Welfare and rights — 283

10 Foreign policy — 318

Appendix: The electoral system for the Chamber of Deputies and the Senate — 352
References — 358
Index — 373

Figures

Maps

Tables

Boxes

Acknowledgements

Most authors incur multiple debts in the process of writing a book and this one is no exception. Debts of gratitude are owed to the Leverhulme Trust for the Study Abroad Fellowship that provided the time spent in Italy where the bulk of the book was written, and to the University of Salford for agreeing to the sabbatical leave the funding of which the Leverhulme Fellowship made possible. My thanks go to Susan Senior for generously providing me with the office space I used for most of the actual writing and to the staff of the various libraries in and around Siena and its university. The stock of research materials contained in these libraries is second to none. Finally, thanks are owed to all the colleagues with whom I have been in contact during the period of the book's writing, and with whom, at various points, I have had occasion to discuss ideas, developed in the following pages or sometimes discarded: Daniele Albertazzi, Felia Allum, Geoff Andrews, Luciano Bardi, Roberto Biorcio, Martin Bull, Donatella Campus, Maurizio Carbone, Nicolò Conti, Aldo Di Virgilio, Mark Donovan, Ilaria Favretto, Stefano Fella, Giovanna Antonia Fois, Paul Furlong, Mark Gilbert, Carlo Guarnieri, David Hine, Jonathan Hopkin, Salvatore Lupo, Wainer Lusoli, Alfio Mastropaolo, Paola Mattei, Duncan McDonnell, Caterina Paolucci, Adriano Pappalardo, Gianfranco Pasquino, Martin Rhodes, Franca Roncarolo, Marco Tarchi, Alberto Vannucci, Luca Verzichelli. The usual disclaimers apply.

Abbreviations

ACP	African, Caribbean and Pacific
AFSOUTH	Allied Forces Southern Europe
AN	National Alliance (Alleanza Nazionale)
ASL	Local Health Company (*Azienda sanitaria locale*)
BP	British Petroleum
CAP	Common Agricultural Policy
CCD-CDU	Christian Democratic Centre–Christian Democratic Union (Centro Cristiano Democratico–Cristiani Democratici Uniti)
CdL	House of Freedoms (Casa delle Libertà)
CFSP	Common Foreign and Security Policy
CGIL	Italian General Confederation of Labour (Confederazione Generale Italiana del Lavoro)
CIG	Ordinary Wage Supplmentation Fund (*Cassa integrazione guadagni ordinaria*)
CIGS	Special Wage Supplementation Fund (*Cassa integrazione guadagni straordinaria*)
CIPE	Joint Ministerial Committee for Economic Planning (Comitato Interministeriale per la Programmazione Economica)
CISL	Italian Confederation of Workers' Trade Unions (Confederazione Italiana dei Sindacati dei Lavoratori)
CLN	Committee for National Liberation (Comitato per la Liberazione Nazionale)
CSM	High Council of the Judiciary (Consiglio Superiore della Magistratura)
DC	Christian Democratic Party (Democrazia Cristiana)
DE	European Democracy (Democrazia Europea)
Dpef	Economic and Financial Planning Document (*Documento di programmazione economica e finanziaria*)
DS	Left Democrats (Democratici di Sinistra)
ECB	European Central Bank
EDC	European Defence Community
EEC	European Economic Community
EMU	European Monetary Union
ENI	National Hydrocarbon Corporation (Ente Nazionale Idrocarburi)

EU	European Union
FI	Go Italy! (Forza Italia)
FIFA	International Federation of Football Associations (Fédération Internationale de Football Association)
FRY	Former Republic of Yugoslavia
GDP	Gross Domestic Product
GIP	Judge for the preliminary investigations (*Giudice delle indagini preliminari*)
GNP	Gross National Product
GUP	'Judge of the preliminary hearing' (*Giudice dell'udienza preliminare*)
ICI	Local property tax (*Imposta comunale sugli immobili*)
ICT	information and communication technology
IdV	Italy of Values (Italia dei Valori)
IGO	intergovernmental organisation
ILOR	Local income tax (*Imposta locale sul reddito*)
IMF	International Monetary Fund
INPS	National Social Security Institute (Istituto Nazionale della Previdenza Sociale)
INVALSI	National Institute for Evaluation of the Education System (Istituto Nazionale di Valutazione del Sistema Educativo)
IRAP	Regional Tax on Enterprises (*Imposta regionale sulle attività produttive*)
IRI	Institute for Industrial Reconstruction (Istituto per la Ricostruzione Industriale)
ISTAT	National Statistical Institute (Istituto Nazionale di Statistica)
ITANES	Italian National Election Study
LN	Northern League (Lega Nord)
MSFT	Social Movement – Tricoloured Flame (Movimento Sociale – Framma Tricolore)
MSI	Italian Social Movement (Movimento Sociale Italiano)
NATO	North Atlantic Treaty Organisation
NIC	newly industrialising country
Nioc	Iranian National Oil Company
OECD	Organisation for Economic Co-operation and Development
OMC	Open method of co-ordination
PCI	Italian Communist Party (Partito Comunista Italiano)
PCM	Prime Minister's Office (Presidenza del Consiglio dei Ministri)
PD	Democratic Party (Partito Democratico)
Pd'A	Party of Action (Partito d'Azione)
PdCI	Party of Italian Communists (Partito dei Comunisti Italiani)
PdL	People of Freedom (Popolo della Libertà)
PDL	Democratic Party of Labour (Partito Democratico del Lavoro)
PDS	Democratic Party of the Left (Partito Democratico della Sinistra)

PLI	Italian Liberal Party (Partito Liberale Italiano)
PLO	Palestine Liberation Organisation
PNF	National Fascist Party (Partito Nazionale Fascista)
PPI	Italian People's Party (Partito Popolare Italiano)
PPP	Purchasing Power Party
PRI	Italian Republican Party (Partito Repubblicano Italiano)
PSDI	Italian Social Democratic Party (Partito Socialista Democratico Italiano)
PSI	Italian Socialist Party (Partito Socialista Italiano)
PSIUP	Italian Socialist Party of Workers' Unity (Partito Socialista di Unità Proletaria)
PSLI	Italian Socialist Workers' Party (Partito Socialista Lavoratori Italiani)
PSU	Unified Socialist Party (Partito Socialista Unificato)
QMV	qualified majority voting
RC	Communist Refoundation (Rifondazione Comunista)
RI	Italian Renewal (Rinnovamento Italiano)
RMI	Minimum Insertion Income (*Reddito minimo di inserimento*)
RnP	Rose in the Fist (Rosa nel Pugno)
RSC	regional security complex
RUI	Income of Last Resort (*Reddito di ultima istanza*)
SA	Rainbow Left (Sinistra l'Arcobaleno)
SD	Democratic Left (Sinistra Democratica)
SDI	Italian Democratic Socialists (Socialisti Democratici Italiani)
SIRIP	Iranian–Italian Oil Company (Société Irano-Italienne des Pétroles)
TAR	Regional Administrative Tribunal
TI	Transparency International
UD	Democratic Union (Unione Democratica)
UdC	Union of the Centre (Unione di Centro)
UDC	Union of Christian Democrats and Centre Democrats (Unione dei Democratici Cristiani)
UDEUR	Union of Democrats for Europe (Unione dei Democratici per l'Europa)
UIL	Italian Workers' Union (Unione Italiana dei Lavoratori)
UN	United Nations
USL	Local Health Unit (*Unità sanitaria locale*)
USSR	Union of Soviet Socialist Republics
WEU	Western European Union
WTO	World Trade Organization

Chronology

Date	Event
18 February 1861	Count Camilo di Cavour of Piedmont-Sardinia declares the creation of the Kingdom of Italy and Victor Emmanuel assembles the deputies of the first Italian parliament in Turin.
17 March 1861	Italian parliament proclaims Victor Emmanuel II the first king of Italy.
29 February 1868	Pope Pius IX issues 'Non Expedit' decree enjoining Catholics to abstain from participation in general elections.
9 January 1878	Victor Emmanuel dies, to be succeeded by his son, Umberto I.
7 February 1878	Pope Pius IX dies.
16 May 1891	Pope Leo XIII issues the encyclical *Rerum Novarum*. The document rejects communism and affirms the right to property while supporting the rights of labour to form unions and calling for amelioration of the condition of the working class.
14 August 1892	Party of Italian Workers founded at a congress in Genoa: it will take the name Italian Socialist Party from January 1895.
29 July 1900	Umberto I assassinated in Monza by the anarchist Gaetano Bresci. He is succeeded by his son Victor Emmauel III.
20 June 1903	Pope Leo XIII dies.
11 June 1905	Pope Pius X issues the encyclical, *Il fermo proposito* allowing Catholics to vote when doing so is necessary to help prevent the election of socialist candidates.
26–29 April 1914	Austria-Hungary declares war on Serbia, thus initiating the process that will lead to the First World War. At the outset, the Italian socialists are strongly opposed to participation – but at the cost of severe internal tensions.
20 August 1914	Pope Pius X dies.
26 April 1915	Italy comes into the First World War on the side of the Triple Entente – Britain, France and Russia.
5 May 1919	Italian delegates return to the Paris peace conference. This follows a walk-out over the refusal of Britain, France and the United States to honour the pledges concerning territory that had brought Italy into the war.

Date	Event
August 1920	Blackshirts used to break the general strike which had started at the Alfa Romeo factory in Milan.
21 January 1921	At the Italian Socialist Party congress in Livorno Amadeo Bordiga and Antonio Gramsci lead a split that gives birth to the Italian Communist Party (PCI).
7 November 1921	National Fascist Party (PNF) founded in Rome from the fusion of the Fasci Italiani di Combattimento (founded by Mussolini, 23 March 1919) and the Italian Nationalist Association (founded in Florence in 1910).
22 January 1922	Pope Benedict XV dies.
27–29 October 1922	Fascists march on Rome, as a consequence of which Mussolini is invited by King Victor Emmanuel III to form a government.
21 July 1923	Acerbo Law passed. Gives two-thirds of the seats in Parliament to the party or coalition winning 25 per cent of the vote.
6 April 1924	At the general election, the PNF obtains two-thirds of the seats in accordance with the Acerbo Law, allowing Mussolini to establish a dictatorship.
10 June 1924	The socialist politician Giacomo Matteotti is kidnapped and killed, allegedly by members of Mussolini's PNF.
11 February 1929	The Lateran Treaty, bringing about the mutual recognition of the Kingdom of Italy and the Vatican City state, is signed at the Palazzo Lateranense in Rome.
3 October 1935	100,000 Italian troops begin the Fascist regime's invasion of Ethiopia.
9 May 1936	Italy annexes Ethiopia.
1 June 1936	Ethiopia, Eritrea and Italian Somaliland are united into Italian East Africa.
10 February 1939	Pope Pius XI dies.
7 April 1939	Italy invades Albania.
22 May 1939	Italy signs the 'Pact of Steel' with Germany: the countries commit themselves to follow a similar foreign policy and to aid the other country immediately in the event of war being declared.
10 June 1940	Italy declares war on France and Great Britain.
3 August 1940	Italy begins occupation of British Somaliland in East Africa.
13 September 1940	Italy invades Egypt.
28 October 1940	Italy invades Greece.
5 May 1941	Addis Ababa taken by the Allies.
22 June 1941	Italy joins Germany in declaring war on USSR.
2 December 1942	Enrico Fermi sets up an atomic reactor in Chicago.
16 December 1942	Italian troops defeated by Soviet forces on the river Don.
13 May 1943	German and Italian forces surrender in North Africa.
9 July 1943	Allied invasion of Sicily begins.
25 July 1943	Mussolini voted out of power by Fascist Grand Council and arrested upon leaving a meeting with the King.

Date	Event
8 September 1943	Victor Emmanuel III makes public the armistice with the Allies without first ordering the royal army to defend Rome. Left without orders, the Italian army disintegrates.
12 September 1943	Germans launch 'Operation Oak' rescuing Mussolini from prison and enabling him to establish a new fascist state in Northern Italy, the Italian Social Republic.
13 October 1943	Italy declares war on Germany.
27 March 1944	PCI leader, Palmiro Togliatti, returns from exile and promotes the so-called *svolta di Salerno* (after the city that is the seat of Italian government until the Allied liberation of Rome on 4 June 1944) that will bring his party into government.
4 June 1944	Victor Emmanuel passes most of his constitutional powers to his son, Umberto, who assumes the title Lieutenant General of the Realm.
9 June 1944	The Pact of Rome, signed by Giuseppe De Vittorio of the PCI, Emilio Canevari of the Italian Socialist Party (PSI) and Achille Grandi of the Christian Democrats (DC), gives birth to the Confederazione Generale Italiana del Lavoro (General Confederation of Italian Workers).
28 April 1945	Mussolini is executed by partisans after being discovered attempting to escape to Switzerland as part of a German convoy.
8 May 1945	Victory in Europe (VE) Day.
9 May 1946	Victor Emmanuel III formally abdicates in favour of his son. Umberto II thus becomes the last king of Italy and is nicknamed *il Re di maggio* (the May king).
2 June 1946	Constituent Assembly elections and referendum on the future of the monarchy. 54 per cent vote in favour of a republic.
28 June 1946	Liberal Party politician Enrico de Nicola elected provisional head of state by the Constituent Assembly.
10 February 1947	Paris Peace Treaty signed.
1 May 1947	Portella della Ginestra massacre: eleven people killed and thirty-three wounded during May Day celebrations in Sicily. Presumed killers are the bandit and separatist leader Salvatore Giuliano and his band, though their motives and intentions remain unclear.
1 January 1948	Post-war Italian Constitution comes into force.
18 April 1948	At the first post-war general election, the DC obtains 49 per cent of the vote and the Popular Front (Communists and Socialists) 31 per cent.
11 May 1948	Luigi Einaudi, of the Italian Liberal Party, elected second President of the Italian Republic at the fourth round of voting, with 518 votes out of 872.

Date	Event
14 July 1948	An attempt on the life of Palmiro Togliatti, by the law student Antonio Pallante, leaves the PCI leader severely wounded and provokes widespread violent demonstrations with several casualties.
4 April 1949	Italy signs the North Atlantic Treaty to become, along with eleven other countries, a founding member of the North Atlantic Treaty Organization (NATO).
5 March 1950	Unione Italiana del Lavoro (Italian Workers' Union) founded. Inspired by social democratic and republican ideals, its aim is to provide a trade union confederation for those workers whose outlooks are neither communist nor confessional in nature.
30 April 1950	Confederazione Italiana Sindacati Lavoratori (Italian Confederation of Workers' Trade Unions) founded. Its largest component is the Libera CGIL: Catholic workers who had seceded from the CGIL a few days after the attempt on Togliatti's life. They had been prompted to their action by the general strike the CGIL's leaders called in response to the attempt.
18 April 1951	Italy signs the Treaty of Paris to become a founder member, along with France, Germany and the Benelux countries, of the European Coal and Steel Community.
11 March 1953	Law no. 87 finally provides the enabling legislation necessary to give life to the Constitutional Court – five years after the 1948 Constitution had provided for such an institution.
31 March 1953	So-called swindle law (providing majority premium for the list or coalition of parties obtaining 50 per cent) promulgated.
7 June 1953	At the general election the DC and allies obtain 49.85 per cent of the vote thus narrowly failing to obtain the majority premium provided for by the 'swindle law'.
31 July 1954	Swindle law abrogated.
29 April 1955	Christian Democrat Giovanni Gronchi elected President of the Republic at the fourth round of voting with 658 votes out of 833.
14 December 1955	United Nations Security Council Resolution 109 recommends Italy for membership of the UN.
23 October – 10 November 1956	The Hungarian Revolution creates considerable difficulties for the PCI whose official position of support for the Soviet armed intervention results in the loss of over 200,000 members.
25 March 1957	Italy signs the Treaty of Rome to become a founder member, along with France, Germany and the Benelux countries, of the European Economic Community.
24 March 1958	Law no. 195 finally provides the enabling legislation necessary to give life to the Consiglio Superiore della Magistratura (High

Date	Event
	Council of the Judiciary) – ten years after articles 104–107 of the 1948 Constitution had provided for it.
25 May 1958	At the general election, the DC is confirmed as the largest party, increasing its share of the vote from 40.1 per cent to 42.4 per cent. Meanwhile, the PCI advances fractionally (from 22.6 to 22.7 per cent).
9 October 1958	Pope Pius XII dies.
25 March 1960	Minority DC government headed by Tambroni takes office with the external support of the Italian Social Movement (MSI).
30 June 1960	The MSI's national congress in Genoa provokes street demonstrations and clashes with the police.
19 July 1960	Tambroni forced to resign as Prime Minister thus closing the door on any further possibilities that governments might rely on the support of the MSI to sustain them in office.
6 May 1962	Christian Democrat politician Antonio Segni elected President at the ninth round of voting, the votes of the MSI and the Monarchists being decisive to the outcome.
11 October 1962	Pope John XXIII opens the Second Vatican Council.
27 October 1962	ENI president, Enrico Mattei is killed in an air crash during a flight from Sicily to Linate airport, Milan.
28 April 1963	At the general election, the DC's share of the vote declines to 38.3 per cent, while the PCI increases its share to 25.3 per cent.
4 December 1963	For the first time the PSI becomes part of the governing majority – by joining a coalition headed by Christian Democrat Aldo Moro.
3 June 1963	Pope John XXIII dies, just two months after completion of his encyclical, *Pacem in Terris*.
15 July 1964	As part of the process leading to the formation of a new executive to replace the Moro government (which had fallen in June), President Antonio Segni takes the unprecedented step of calling the head of the Carabinieri, General Giovanni de Lorenzo, for consultations.
6 December 1964	Antonio Segni resigns as President of the Republic following illness.
28 December 1964	The Social Democrat Giuseppe Saragat is elected President of the Republic at the twenty-first round of voting, with 646 votes out of 937, thanks to the decisive support of the Communists and the Socialists.
24 January 1966	The first occupation of an Italian university takes place when students occupy the faculty of Sociology of the University of Trento.
19 May 1968	At the general election, the DC sees its support rise slightly to 39.1 per cent, while the PCI's vote increases to 26.9 per cent.
20 August 1968	Soviet invasion of Czechoslovakia condemned unequivocally by the PCI, underscoring how far it had changed since 1956.

Date	Event
12 December 1969	Bomb explodes at the Banca Nazionale dell'Agricoltura in Piazza Fontana, Milan, killing seventeen people and wounding eighty-eight.
28 January 1970	The institutions of government of the 'ordinary-statute' regions finally become operative – twenty-two years after regions were provided for by article 131 of the 1948 Constitution.
20 May 1970	Law no. 300, known as the Workers' Statute, introduces a series of important measures designed to enhance conditions of employment. It is destined to become the cornerstone of the Italian system of labour law.
24 December 1971	Christian Democrat Giovanni Leone elected President of the Republic at the twenty-third round of voting with 518 votes out of 996.
7 May 1972	At the general election, the DC's support declines slightly – to 38.7 per cent – while the PCI's increases slightly – to 27.1 per cent.
12 May 1974	Referendum on a proposal to abrogate the 1970 Fortuna–Baslini Law, providing for divorce, is decisively defeated, with 59.3 per cent of the votes against.
20 June 1976	At the general election, the PCI makes spectacular gains, increasing its share of the vote to 34.4 per cent, while the DC remains stationary at 38.7 per cent.
11 March 1977	Police kill Lotta Continua activist Francesco Lo Russo, provoking a series of violent demonstrations. The event symbolises 'the Movement of '77', a spontaneous protest movement of students and the extra-parliamentary left against the authoritarianism and repressive attitudes of the trade unions and the established parties of the left.
16 March 1978	Aldo Moro kidnapped by the Red Brigades.
9 May 1978	Aldo Moro's body found in a car parked symbolically halfway between the headquarters of the DC and the PCI.
28 May 1978	Against the will of the DC and the Vatican, Parliament legalises abortion by enacting the most liberal abortion laws in Europe: any woman over eighteen is free to seek a termination during the first ninety days of pregnancy.
15 June 1978	Giovanni Leone resigns as President following allegations of his involvement in the Lockheed corruption scandal.
8 July 1978	Socialist Sandro Pertini elected seventh President of the Republic at the sixteenth round of voting, with 832 votes out of 995.
6 August 1978	Pope Paul VI dies.
28 September 1978	Pope John-Paul I dies after one of the shortest reigns in papal history. In Italy he is known affectionately as the 'smiling Pope'.
23 December 1978	Law no. 833 establishes new national health service.

Date	Event
3 June 1979	At the general election, the PCI's vote declines substantially – to 30.4 per cent – while that of the DC again remains essentially stationary at 38.3 per cent.
2 August 1980	Bombing of Bologna railway station, linked to right-wing extremists, kills eighty-five.
23 November 1980	Earthquake in Irpinia leaves 3,000 dead, tens of thousands injured and incalculable infrastructural damage – the repair of which would still be incomplete in the early years of the new millennium.
17 March 1981	Police raid the Arezzo office of Licio Gelli and discover the P2 masonic membership list, which includes 4 cabinet ministers, 3 under-secretaries, 38 parliamentarians, 195 military officers, as well as industrialists, bankers, diplomats, civil servants, judges, journalists, secret service officers and police officials.
26 June 1983	At the general election, the DC's vote declines spectacularly – to 32.3 per cent – while the PCI declines slightly – to 29.9 percent.
4 August 1983	Bettino Craxi becomes Italy's first Socialist prime minister.
24 June 1985	Christian Democrat Francesco Cossiga elected eighth President of the Republic at the first round of voting, with 752 votes out of 977.
10 October 1985	Stand-off between US and Italian armed forces at the Sigonella air base in the wake of the Achille Lauro hijacking.
14 June 1987	At the general election, the DC makes some gains (rising to 34.3 per cent of the vote), while the PCI suffers a third successive decline (to 26.6 per cent). Meanwhile, the PSI makes significant gains (rising to 14.3 per cent).
9 November 1989	Berlin Wall comes down. This leads PCI leader, Achille Ochetto, to announce, on 12 November, that his party will change its name, its symbol and its political programme.
3 June 1990	Referenda held on the issues of hunting, and pesticides in agriculture. The referenda fail for the lack of a quorum – the first time this has happened in the history of the Republic.
3–4 February 1991	Twentieth congress of the PCI in Rimini puts the seal on the party's transformation into a non-communist party with a new name: the Democratic Party of the Left (PDS).
9 June 1991	Referendum proposal to reduce the number of preference votes in Chamber of Deputies elections to one only achieves the support of 95.6 per cent of the votes.
17 February 1992	Carabinieri burst into the offices of Mario Chiesa, director of the old people's home, the Pio Albergo Trivulzio, catching him in the act of taking a bribe, and so initiate the investigations that lead to the great *Tangentopoli* corruption scandal.

Date	Event
12 March 1992	Giulio Andreotti's ally and 'proconsul' in Sicily, the DC politician Salvatore Lima is killed by the Mafia.
5 April 1992	At the general election (which sees the Northern League (LN) take 8.7 per cent of the vote) support for the DC falls to 29.7 per cent – while the PDS's share of the vote fails to rise above 16.1 per cent.
23 May 1992	Public Prosecutor and anti-Mafia investigator Giovanni Falcone is killed by Cosa Nostra along with his wife and three of his bodyguards.
25 May 1992	Christian Democrat Oscar Luigi Scalfaro elected ninth President of the Republic at the sixteenth round of voting, with 672 votes out of 1,002.
19 July 1992	Public Prosecutor and anti-Mafia investigator Giovanni Falcone killed by a Cosa Nostra car bomb.
2 September 1992	Socialist Deputy, Sergio Moroni, having become caught up in the *Tangentopoli* scandal and accused of numerous acts of corruption, commits suicide.
29 October 1992	Italian parliament ratifies the Maastricht Treaty.
15 December 1992	Bettino Craxi receives from the judicial authorities the first of the *avvisi di guaranzia* notifying him that he is under investigation for corruption as a result of allegations arising from the *Tangentopoli* scandal.
15 January 1993	Mafia boss Salvatore 'Toto' Riina arrested.
10 February 1993	Having received an *avviso di guaranzia* notifying him that he is under investigation for fraudulent bankruptcy, Claudio Martelli resigns as Minister of Justice.
11 February 1993	Thoroughly compromised by the *Tangentopoli* scandal, Bettino Craxi resigns his position as General Secretary of the Socialist Party.
25 February 1993	Having received an *avviso di garanzia* for presumed violations of the law on the public funding of political parties, Giorgio la Malfa resigns as General Secretary of the Italian Republican Party.
16 March 1993	Caught up in the *Tangentopoli* scandal, Renato Altissimo resigns as Secretary of the Italian Liberal Party.
25 March 1993	Parliament approves a new majoritarian electoral law for municipalities with up to 15,000 inhabitants.
18–19 April 1993	Referendum proposal to abrogate parts of the Senate electoral law (with the aim, thereby, of introducing a majoritarian system) is supported by 82.7 per cent of the votes.
28 April 1993	The first 'technocratic' prime minister in the history of the Republic, Carlo Azeglio Ciampi, publishes his list of cabinet ministers including three drawn from the ex-Communist PDS.
29 April 1993	Chamber of Deputies refuses judicial requests for the lifting of Bettino Craxi's parliamentary immunity, as a result of which the three PDS ministers resign from the Ciampi government.

Date	Event
20 July 1993	Ex-president of National Hydrocarbon Corporation (ENI), Gabriele Cagliari, commits suicide in San Vittore prison where he has been held since 9 March.
23 July 1993	Caught up in the *Tangentopoli* scandal, the industrialist, Raul Gardini, commits suicide.
4 August 1993	Parliament approves law nos. 276 and 277 providing for new electoral systems for the Senate and the Chamber of Deputies.
5 December 1993	The Progressive Alliance makes major gains at the municipal elections, taking the mayoralties of Rome, Naples, Venice, Genoa and Trieste.
27–28 March 1994	At the general election, Silvio Berlusconi's centre right wins with 42.8 per cent of the vote and 360 Chamber seats, while Forza Italia (FI) becomes the largest single party with 21.0 per cent.
22 December 1994	Berlusconi government falls following the LN's withdrawal from the coalition.
25 January 1995	At its congress held in Fiuggi, the MSI takes a further step to distance itself from its Fascist heritage, by merging fully with the recently formed Alleanza Nazionale (National Alliance, AN).
21 April 1996	At the general election the centre-left Ulivo coalition emerges victorious but is dependent for survival in office on the votes of twenty Communist Refoundation (RC) deputies.
26 September 1997	Earthquake in Umbria and Marche leaves ten people dead, thousands without homes and grave damage to the regions' artistic heritage.
21 March 1998	Ex-'*Mani pulite*' investigator, Antonio di Pietro, founds the new party, Italia dei Valori (Italy of Values, IdV).
25 March 1998	Italy officially included among the eleven countries which, from 1 January 1999, will adopt the euro.
2 June 1998	Final breakdown of negotiations between centre left and centre right to save the process of constitutional reform that is taking place through the work of the Bicameral Commission.
9 October 1998	Romano Prodi resigns as Prime Minister following the loss of a confidence vote.
11 October 1998	Party of Italian Communists (PdCI) founded as the result of a split in RC arising from the role of RC deputies in bringing about the fall of the Prodi government.
21 October 1998	New executive, under DS politician Massimo D'Alema replaces the fallen Prodi government, relying for a majority on the support of the PdCI and a number of parliamentarians originally elected as part of the centre right.
18 April 1999	Referendum on a proposal to remove the proportional component from the electoral law achieves a large majority in favour but is declared void owing to the narrow failure of turnout to reach the legally required minimum of 50 per cent.

Date	Event
13 May 1999	Ex-Governor of the Bank of Italy, Carlo Azeglio Ciampi, elected tenth President of the Republic at the first round of voting, with 707 votes out of 990.
13 June 1999	At the European elections, FI is confirmed as the largest party (with 25.2 per cent of the vote). The Democrats and the radicals perform well (with 7.7 and 8.5 per cent respectively).
28 June 1999	In local and provincial elections, the centre left performs disappointingly losing control of the symbolic 'red' city of Bologna for the first time in the history of the Republic.
23 December 1999	A new D'Alema government achieves the second of the two votes of confidence made necessary by a brief governmental crisis earlier in the month.
17 April 2000	Massimo D'Alema resigns as Prime Minister following poor performances for the centre left in the regional elections held the previous day. He is replaced by the law professor and former PSI politician Giuliano Amato.
21 May 2000	Voters called to the polls to decide on eight referendum questions including a proposed modification of the electoral law. With a turnout (32.8 per cent) far below the minimum of 50 per cent legally required, all are declared void.
25 September 2000	Giuliano Amato announces withdrawal of his candidature to lead the centre left at the forthcoming general election. Mayor of Rome, Francesco Rutelli, is thus chosen to take on Silvio Berlusconi.
13 May 2001	At the general election, Berlusconi's House of Freedoms (CdL) emerges victorious, obtaining secure majoirties in both the Chamber (with 368 seats) and the Senate (with 176 seats).
7 October 2001	For the first time in the history of the Republic, voters are called to the polls to decide whether to confirm changes to the Constitution. The changes in question (concerning the powers of the regions) are supported by 62.4 per cent of the voters on a turnout of just 34 per cent.
1 January 2002	Euro notes and coins circulate for the first time, with the old currency ceasing to be legal tender on 28 February.
6 January 2002	Foreign Minister Renato Ruggiero resigns following disagreements with the Eurosceptical views of right-wing cabinet colleagues.
24 March 2002	Founding conference, in Parma, of the Margherita, bringing together the Italian People's Party (PPI), the Democrats and Italian Renewal (RI).
10 October 2002	Chamber of Deputies passes the so-called Cirami Law (allegedly designed to help Berlusconi avoid trial on corruption charges) after a debate which almost sees parliamentarians coming to blows.

Date	Event
17 June 2003	In court on corruption charges, Berlusconi claims that he is the victim of a campaign to discredit him on the part of politically motivated judges and prosecutors.
2 July 2003	During his presentation to the European Parliament at the start of Italy's EU presidency, Berlusconi compares the German MEP Martin Schulz to a Nazi concentration-camp commander, provoking a diplomatic row with Germany and the Parliament.
25 July 2003	Seven-time prime minister Giulio Andretti is acquitted on charges of conspiring with the Mafia.
12 November 2003	Nineteen Italian servicemen are killed in a suicide bomb attack on their base at Nassiriya in southern Iraq.
24 November 2003	On an official visit to Israel, AN leader, Gianfranco Fini, condemns Mussolini's Italian Social Republic as among the most shameful episodes in human history.
27 December 2003	President of Parmalat, Calisto Tanzi, is arrested in Milan. The event leads to revelations of a multi-billion euro fraud and an eventual declaration of insolvency for the food giant.
13 June 2004	At the European elections, FI suffers a retreat in support (to 21.0 per cent) to the advantage of the UDC (5.9 per cent) and AN (11.5 per cent). The United Olive-tree Alliance (Ulivo) achieves 31.1 per cent.
4 March 2005	Italian military intelligence officer Major General Nicola Calipari killed by American troops in Iraq while escorting recently released hostage, Giuliana Sgrena, to Baghdad international airport.
2 April 2005	Pope John-Paul II dies.
19 April 2005	Cardinal Joseph Ratzinger elected Pope. Takes the name Benedict XVI.
22 April 2005	Berlusconi receives a presidential mandate to form a new executive following the governmental crisis and his resignation that followed the tension provoked by the centre right's poor performance in the regional elections of 5 April.
12–13 June 2005	Referendum proposals designed to relax the laws on embryo research and artificial insemination fail for the lack of a quorum following Church appeals to voters to abstain.
16 October 2005	More than 4 million people participate in the primary elections to choose the leader of the centre-left Unione coalition. Romano Prodi wins handsomely with 74.6 per cent of the vote.
16 October 2005	The vice-president of the Calabrian regional council, Francesco Fortugno, is assassinated at Locri.
14 December 2005	Parliament approves new proportional electoral law, replacing the majoritarian system introduced in 1993.

Date	Event
19 December 2005	Governor of the Bank of Italy, Antonio Fazio, resigns in the wake of allegations of illegal interference in the takeover of a bank, the Banca Antonveneta.
9–10 April 2006	At the general election, the centre-left Unione wins a secure majority in the Chamber of Deputies, thanks to the majority premium, but in the Senate, where it is behind in terms of votes, its majority is just two seats.
26 June 2006	Called to the polls to decide whether to confirm thoroughgoing constitutional changes promoted by the outgoing Berlusconi government, voters reject them, with 61.7 per cent voting against.
11 April 2006	Mafia boss, Bernardo Provenzano arrested.
10 May 2006	Ex-Communist Giorgio Napolitano elected eleventh President of the Republic at the fourth round of voting, with 543 votes out of 990.
21 February 2007	Government defeat on an important foreign-policy resolution leads to the resignation of Prime Minister Prodi.
2 March 2007	Government wins the second of the two confidence votes arising from the President's decision to require verification of the continued existence of a government majority.
14 October 2007	More than 3.5 million people participate in the primary elections to choose the leader of the new Partito Democratico, born of the merger of the Left Democrats (DS) and Margherita. Mayor of Rome and DS politician Walter Veltroni wins by a landslide taking 75.8 per cent of the vote.
24 January 2008	Romano Prodi resigns as Prime Minister following his defeat on a confidence motion in the Senate.
6 February 2008	Parliament is dissolved by the President of the Republic following the failure of an 'exploratory mandate' for the formation of a government, given to Senate president Franco Marini.
13–14 April 2008	At the general election, Berlusconi's Popolo della Libertà wins comfortable majorities in both the Chamber (with 344 seats) and in the Senate (with 174 seats), while the parties of the radical left fail to win any seats whatsoever.

Map 1 Italian regions and major cities

Introduction

In 2006, Italy saw a general election which resulted in the incumbent
centre-right government being ousted in favour of the alternative coalition
of the centre left. It saw the defeat of wide-ranging proposals for constitutional reform in a popular referendum. It saw Italy win the FIFA world cup.
All three of these things bore witness to the fact that Italy is a normal
country.

If the normal pattern of party politics in European countries is left–right
alternation in office sustained by bipolar competition, then the April general
election showed that Italian party politics conformed to this pattern: the
centre-right Casa delle Libertà (CdL) coalition of parties, under Silvio
Berlusconi, had won the election held in 2001. For the 2006 election to the
Chamber of Deputies, the centre-left Unione, under Romano Prodi, came from
3.8 per cent behind to stake out a position 0.3 per cent ahead of the CdL, in the
process taking over the reins of government with a majority of sixty-six seats.[1]
If a 'normal' country is one in which constitutional arrangements provide
political integration by offering fixed and enduring points of reference for
the large majority of players, then it had to be of significance that in June
voters decisively rejected wide-ranging proposals for change, in the process
ruling out the likelihood, for the foreseeable future, of major alterations to the
constitution that had been adopted in 1948. If a normal country is one for
whose citizens expressions of 'national pride' are something natural, then, as
Prime Minister Prodi pointed out a couple days after the world cup victory, the

celebrations suggested that the people had 'finally reclaimed [the national flag], wresting it back from the separate world of officialdom'. He continued: 'The same thing, if you look closely, has also happened in Germany, the other country which, like us, is most restrained in terms of national sentiments. We have turned the page, achieved and internalised a national spirit that is strong, healthy and positive, and free of nationalistic ideologies' (Mauro, 2006).

By the term 'normal country', then, I here mean one that is fully comparable (within the limits of comparative analysis itself) with other countries belonging to the category of 'developed industrial democracies'. I mean too that in terms of the quality of its democracy, Italy is in most respects no worse than other countries in the category and is in some respects much better.

The reasons why I have chosen to emphasise this point, beyond the obvious one of needing to explain the choice of a potentially obscure subtitle, are essentially twofold.[2] In the first place, until recently, it is unlikely that the claim I have just made about Italian politics would have found much support among mainstream political scientists, Italian or foreign. On the contrary: Italy tended to be viewed as a 'democratic anomaly', the party system and political culture in particular being thought of by many as falling short of what was required to sustain a healthy participatory democracy. Since the early 1990s, the consensus on this has begun to break down somewhat. This, as will become apparent from the following chapters, has been due partly to objective changes – in particular, the party-system upheavals that followed the collapse of the Berlin Wall in 1989 and their (long-term) institutional and policy consequences – and partly to the beginnings of a reassessment of what went before 1989. Once, the so-called First Republic and its principal actors were analysed almost exclusively in terms of their supposedly negative concomitants, notably, a lack of political accountability and policy-making inefficiency. Now, increasing emphasis is being placed also on the impressive contribution they made to the consolidation of democracy in international conditions whose pressures almost all worked in the opposite direction.

The second reason, then, for choosing to emphasise the point about normality is that the reader has a right to be told explicitly about the perspective (and possible biases) of the author. Though there is a world that has an objective existence independently of our perceptions of it, it remains the case that no description of that world can ever reflect its nature with complete accuracy; for perception always and inevitably takes place from a given 'angle of vision' that emphasises *this* at the expense of *that* aspect and so on. This was implicitly recognised in the Italian First Republic practice of dividing control of the then three principal television channels between the main political parties. Giving the viewer a choice of news bulletins, each with differences of emphasis, strikes the author as having been a rather better, because more honest, way of bringing current affairs to the citizen than is the way of broadcasting that is more rigidly governed by principles of party-political neutrality. Leaving aside lies and conscious distortion, there is no such thing as completely objective reporting. But precisely for this reason, the reader needs to be told about the angle of vision of the author whose work s/he is reading in order to be empowered to make an independent assessment of it.

My angle of vision is such that I claim for Italian politics the status of 'normality' as I have defined this term above. This does not mean that I wish to deny the reality of some of the obvious problems of Italian democracy – for example, fragmentation of the party system (though in this respect the 2008 election brought the system, at least in Parliament, well within the range of 'normality' for European democracies). Depending on party-political developments in the aftermath of the 2008 election, fragmentation could continue to pose significant conundrums, especially for the prospects of a stable centre-left alternative to the present government. Oreste Massari (2005: 448) was surely correct to point out that Italy's bipolar coalitions cannot be regarded as the 'functional equivalent' of the British 'two-party' system or of the German or Spanish bipolar systems. Or, to give another example, it is true that anti-political sentiments are widespread in Italy – and so on. But what I do wish to claim is two things; first, that if the attempt were made to draw up some kind of 'balance sheet' in order to compare Italian democracy with that of other European countries, then one would be forced to the conclusion that other countries have similar problems or, if free of one or the other of the problems affecting Italy, have other problems Italy does not have. Second, and more importantly, I want to claim that phenomena that are often adduced to compare Italy unfavourably with other democracies are too often interpreted, and evaluated, in terms of categories imposed on them from the outside and that this blocks understanding of their significance and therefore of the country's politics: see Newell (2004) and Mastropaolo (2006). So the claim that Italy is a normal country is also an invitation to the student to avoid interpretations in terms of external categories, and to seek, instead, to interpret phenomena in their own terms through the effort to appreciate the meanings that actors themselves attach to their actions; for ultimately, this is the only way in which the social and political life of others can be explained and understood, the only way in which – by definition – it can cease to appear mysterious and abnormal to us. The point goes beyond the question of Italy and is relevant for the study of comparative politics in general: a sympathetic understanding of the points of view of those whom one is studying is indispensable if one wishes to achieve knowledge such that 'the characteristics attributed to [the] foreign culture … differs from the folklore or prejudices about the foreign country which already exist in his own society' (Scheuch, 1967, quoted by Dogan and Pelassy, 1990: 70).

▪ Plan of the book

With the aim of offering something that allows the reader to acquire understanding, and that is *insight* into Italian politics, I have sought to present the chapters, though they can be read independently, in a way that reflects a clear underlying logic.

Since current arrangements and events have the shape that they do because past arrangements and events have conspired to give them that shape, chapter 1 seeks to offer a historical perspective on Italian politics, focusing on the main threads underlying the formation of the Italian state and its subsequent passage from liberal to Fascist to post-war republican regimes.

Chapter 1's observations about the failure of attempts, in the 1990s, at thoroughgoing reform of the republican constitution then provide the basis for the analysis, in chapter 2, of the Constitution's basic principles and the institutional framework it establishes and sustains. Chapter 3 proceeds to put flesh on the constitutional bones by considering how the institutions actually interact in the multi-level governance that is a central feature of the policy-making process in Italy as in all other democracies. Since the institutions of central government – Parliament, the executive and the bureaucracy – remain, despite polycentrism, those with the greatest influence over the substance of public policy, chapter 4 is devoted to an analysis of their working and interactions. The following three chapters then move beyond the institutional corridors of power to explore the social and political environment within which the institutions are embedded and with whose demands they must come to terms. Thus chapter 5 explores aspects of the political culture driving and expressed by political actors' behaviour, while chapter 6 explores how political demands are expressed through pressure-group activity – looking, in the process, at the organisations of capital and labour, promotional groups and the Catholic Church, and asking about their contribution to the quality of Italian democracy. For the vast majority of Italians as for the citizens of most other democracies, the most significant channel for the expression of political demands is, however, the one given by elections and parties – topics to which chapter 7 is consequently devoted.

The final part of the book then moves on to look at the nature of the policy outputs that are the product of the institutional interaction and the behavioural inputs described and analysed in the preceding two parts. Starting from the recognition that successful economic management is an essential prerequisite for success in every other area of policy-making – and therefore for governments' capacities to remain in office – chapter 8 looks at the record in terms of Italian governments' experience with economic policy in recent years. It, and the subsequent chapter, devoted to welfare and rights policy, adopt the same basic approach, exploring first the policy context, next the problems and constraints this has thrown up, and finally, the ways in which Italian governments have in recent years sought to respond to these problems and constraints. Finally, chapter 10, which explores foreign policy, offers a 'rounding off': while the first chapter placed the Italian polity in its temporal context, chapter 10 places Italy in its spatial context, describing the most relevant characteristics of the global environment within which the country is located, the implications these have had for Italian politics and how Italian policy-makers have reacted to them.

▪ Notes

1. In the Senate contest the Unione had a majority of two seats and was behind the Cdl by 124,273 votes. This placed the Senate contest alongside the outcomes of two British general elections and one US presidential election in the post-war period, all of which saw the loser in terms of votes nevertheless emerge as the winner in terms of seats.

2. It should also be noted that the subtitle is not being offered in some kind of polemical contrast with Geoff Andrews' (2005) book, *Not a Normal Country: Italy after Berlusconi* whose material is, in my opinion, well written, very insightful and yes, moving in places: see for example, chapter 2.

I

Historical background

1 History

▪ Introduction

It is conventional among writers on Italian politics to divide its history from the birth of the Italian state in 1861 into three main types of regime – the liberal, the Fascist and the republican. The republican era is often divided into two, the first running from the promulgation of the republican constitution after 1948 up to the early 1990s, and the second from the early 1990s to the present. In each of these, those in government tended to see the forces of political opposition as inherently illegitimate. In each case they saw their mission as being less to 'govern' than to defend the state against the forces of opposition, which they saw as 'usurpers'. The ultimate failure of those in power to contain the forces of opposition led to a crisis of the regime itself (Salvadori, 1994). The latest of these was prompted by a number of factors including, most notably, the fall of the Berlin Wall in 1989, the signing of the European Union's Maastricht Treaty in 1991, and revelations of widespread political corruption that emerged after the Italian general election of 1992. The result of this combination of political circumstances was that the parties that had been in power in the first republican period began to disintegrate, to be replaced by new and different parties and political forces. However, a regime transition of modern Italy is yet far from complete because there is still no fundamental constitutional change. Nevertheless, the Italian political system is no longer as 'unique' or 'anomalous' as it was in its early periods, and

Italian politics are now more like those of the countries in other parts of Western Europe.

With this in mind, we begin with a brief account of Italian political history from the birth of the state in 1861. The chapter covers:

- The liberal regime, 1861–1924
- The Fascist regime and its aftermath, 1924–46
- The first republican period, 1946 – early 1990s
- The second republican period, early 1990s to the present.

The liberal regime, 1861–1924

The processes that led to the genesis of liberal Italy are complex. However, the state's birth sprang from convergence of the goals of liberals and nationalists, with the international ambitions of Piedmont Sardinia. Prior to 1859, the

Figure 1.1. Giuseppe Garibaldi (see Box 1.1)

Italian peninsula was divided into ten separate states, whose existence had been underwritten by the Treaty of Vienna of 1815.[1] The overriding purpose of the treaty was to contain French expansionism and the revolutionary social and political ideas identified with it. Therefore it was designed to enable the Austrian Habsburgs to dominate the peninsula. This was achieved through Austria's direct control of one state (Lombardo-Venetia), while members of the House of Habsburg governed two others (Tuscany and Parma) and an Austrian was the ruling duke of a fourth (Modena). Austrian ambitions were counter-posed by the Kingdom of Sardinia (consisting of Piedmont and the island of Sardinia) and the Kingdom of the Two Sicilies (the southern half of the peninsula plus the island of Sicily). All these states were governed by conservative, absolutist rulers. However, economic and political changes had begun to feed a search for political liberty within the peninsula:

- First, while most of the peninsula was economically backward, in Lombardy silk production had spawned the emergence of commercial capitalists. These wanted liberal reforms as a means to advance their interests in general and to achieve specific economic goals – in particular, the removal of tariff barriers between the peninsula's states.
- Second, French occupation of the peninsula between 1796 and 1815 had shown that constitutional government there was feasible and that Italy could become a single state. This helped link demands for liberal reform to **nationalism** (Box 1.2). Meanwhile, people were aware that the achievement of reform would necessarily require independence because so many absolutist rulers depended on Austrian bayonets to sustain them (Gooch, 1989: 2).

The unification of Italy

Uprisings in 1820–1 and in 1831 that were easily crushed by Austria reinforced this awareness. Then, the argument for looking to Piedmont Sardinia to provide assistance in ousting Austria was strengthened by two things. The first of these was the wave of European revolutions of 1848 which led the Piedmontese king, Charles Albert, to grant a constitution. The second was the revolutions' aftermath, which left Piedmont as the only Italian state in which constitutional government survived. In this situation, Charles Albert's successor, Victor Emmanuel II (Box 1.1), was prepared to assist anti-Austrian revolutionaries for motives of dynastic aggrandisement. Piedmont's Prime Minister, Camillo di Cavour, was prepared to do the same because of the contribution he thought expansionism would make to Piedmontese economic and social development.

However, Cavour's aims did not encompass unification of the entire peninsula. Also, while he opposed absolutism, he also opposed democracy and republicanism. Therefore, the fact that democratic and republican Italian nationalists nevertheless embraced the cause of Piedmont against Austria owed much to the argument that independence had to be won first, before the ultimate goal of

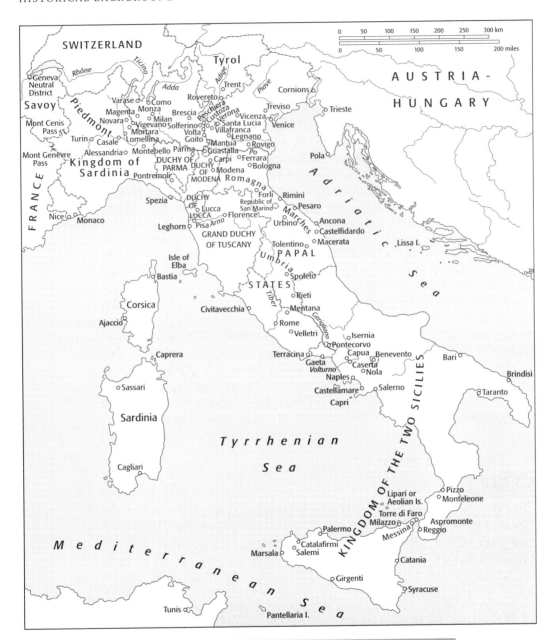

Map 2. The Italian states at the time of the Treaty of Vienna, 1815
Source: Shepherd, William. *Historical Atlas.* New York: Henry Holt and Company 1911

liberty could be achieved. As a result of the war of 1859, Piedmont acquired
Lombardy, Parma, Modena and the Romagna area of the Papal State. Further
expansion was potentially threatening to France. However, British pressure
helped induce the latter to accept the idea of a single state of central and

northern Italy. In September 1860 Cavour was allowed to annex the remainder of the Papal State, except the area around Rome.

When the Kingdom of Italy was proclaimed in March 1861, it was an outcome that Cavour had not planned. In May the previous year, the radical Italian nationalist Giuseppe Garibaldi had landed in Sicily. Here, swollen by peasant unrest, his famous army of a thousand succeeded in conquering first the island and then the mainland territories of the Kingdom of the Two Sicilies. Cavour accepted Garibaldi's expedition reluctantly. He was fearful of the impact of its possible success on the international balance of power and thus of its possible diplomatic consequences. Then, when the pressure of Piedmontese public opinion made it clear that he would be unable to prevent the expedition, he was fearful that the *Garibaldini*, would, as radical democrats, use their military victories as a political bargaining counter with Piedmont (Procacci, 1973: 319). He managed to dash this hope by arranging for plebiscites for annexation to be held immediately in Sicily and the South. In this he was assisted by the southern landowners. They were convinced that order in the countryside was better entrusted to a legitimate king and a regular army than to a dangerous group of democratic agitators (Procacci, 1973: 321). Consequently, 'Under the vigilant eyes of the local nobleman and his agent, the southern peasants went to place in the urn their "yes" to the unity of Italy' (Procacci, 1973: 321). However, the most fundamental reason for Cavour's reservations was that annexation of the South would alter the whole nature of the problem that Italian governments would have to face. The South was economically and socially far behind the North and plans for gradual capitalist development could not be applied to it (Procacci, 1973: 318–19).

Box 1.1

The protagonists of Italian unification: Victor Emmanuel II, Camillo di Cavour, Giuseppe Garibaldi

Victor Emmanuel was born in 1820 and died in 1878. He succeeded his father, Charles Albert, as King of Piedmont Sardinia in 1849 when the latter suffered a humiliating defeat in a battle against the Austrians at Novara. He became a figurehead of the *Risorgimento*, the term used to refer to the movement for Italian unification and which literally means 'Resurgence'. His greatest achievement, then, was his contribution to Italian unification, which he made through his appointment of Camillo di Cavour as the Piedmontese prime minister, and through his support for liberal reforms. His greatest political mistake was probably his insistence on retaining the title 'Victor Emmanuel II' rather than becoming 'Victor Emmanuel I' when he became King of Italy in March 1861 – a mistake because it symbolised the way in which unification was more about the imposition of Piedmontese rule on the entire peninsula than about a 'new beginning' driven from the 'bottom up'. Victor Emmanuel was married twice, having eight children by his first wife, two by his second, and six children by three mistresses.

Camillo di Cavour was born in 1810 and died in June 1861, just three months after becoming Prime Minister of the newly united Italy. He first became Prime Minister of Piedmont Sardinia in 1852. This followed a brief career in the army, then as a political journalist, and then finally as a cabinet minister. In this capacity he distinguished himself by commencing a vast programme of railway expansion, one that resulted in Piedmont acquiring 800 kilometres of track by 1860, a very large quantity by the standards of the day. This was intimately linked to the Unification theme; for Cavour was of the view that while political unification was unfeasible as things stood (though he was resentful of the role of Austria in the affairs of the peninsula), a customs union together with the promotion of technological development and railway expansion would allow engagement with the more developed states of Europe on terms of equality. An economic liberal, in politics his guiding principle was 'reform that you may conserve', and he was responsible for a style of governing – known as *connubio* ('marriage' or 'union') bringing together the moderate left and right – that could in many respects be seen as a forerunner of the kinds of parliamentary practices that, in the united Italy, would be referred to as *trasformismo*.

Giuseppe Garibaldi was born in 1807 and died in 1882. The renowned historian, A. J. P. Taylor apparently once described him as 'the only wholly admirable figure in modern history'. Garibaldi's early experience as a merchant marine captain brought him into contact, in a seaport inn in Russia, with Giovine Italia (Young Italy), the political movement founded in 1831 by Giuseppe Mazzini, with the aim of achieving a united Italy on liberal and republican lines. In 1834 Garibaldi was sentenced to death for his part in a Mazzinian insurrection, fled to Marseille and eventually ended up in South America where his military exploits on behalf of republican and independence causes led him and his followers to be hailed as heroes in Europe and Italy. The revolutions of 1848 led him to return to Italy. Here his ultimately unsuccessful military efforts on behalf of the republic which had been declared in the Papal States forced him once more into exile, which included a period of residence in New York and a month-long visit to Tyneside in Britain. Back in Italy in 1854, he bought, with a small legacy from his brother, half the island of Caprera, off the north coast of Sardinia where he devoted himself to agriculture. The exploit for which he is most famous, the landing in Marsala with 1,000 volunteers and his subsequent victorious march on Naples, took place in the spring and summer of 1860. Known as the 'sword' of Italian unification (Cavour being the 'brain' and Mazzini the 'soul'), Garibaldi continued his military and political involvements following declaration of the new kingdom. In 1862 he led a struggle against the Pope's temporal domains and in 1866 against the Austrians in Venetia. He was a member of the Italian parliament and in 1879 founded the League of Democracy, advocating universal suffrage.

A legacy of unification

The 'Southern question'

The first legacy, then, of the new regime was what became known 'Southern Question'. It is an issue that has persisted to this day. Wh North–South disparity preceded Unification, it grew larger after it. For late-nineteenth century industrialisation in Italy was a northern phenomenon – which increased the economic distance between it and the South. An area that is already relatively more industrialised than another is likely, by virtue of that fact, to enjoy better infrastructural resources, such as a good transportation system. Therefore, it will attract, in preference to the other area, still further industrial investment – and so forth. Meanwhile, the relative and absolute poverty of the South was exacerbated by three developments:

- Unification entailed the removal of internal tariff barriers and thus left southern silk manufacturers unable to compete with more efficient northern producers (Robson, 2000: 19).
- Agricultural investment in the South was discouraged by the system of landholding. This was based on the *latifondi*. These were very large estates belonging to absentee landlords, who leased them to middlemen, who in their turn had the land worked by day labourers. Though yields per acre were low, profits were high owing to the low levels of the labourers' wages. Landlords thus made substantial sums, despite low levels of productivity, simply in virtue of the size of their holdings. Given that land-ownership conferred respectability and power (Clark, 1996: 18), they preferred to reinvest their profits in the acquisition of still further land rather than in technological improvements.
- In the immediate aftermath of Unification, the state found that the cost of the independence war and of the resources required to provide the essential apparatus of a modern state left it heavily indebted (Seton-Watson, 1967: 19). This led to high levels of taxation and sales of the demesne lands inherited from the old states.[2] Poor southern peasants could rarely escape their poverty by buying this land; for the impossibility in bad years of meeting repayments of loans and paying the land taxes meant that they were forced to sell out. They then saw the land acquired by the wealthy and were aware that privatisation of the demesne lands entailed the loss of ancient grazing rights. These two things meant that the southern peasants could have little love for the new political and social order (Clark, 1996: 16–17).

The weakness of the state

Such conditions throw a spotlight on the second legacy of the new regime – the weakness of the state. To call a state 'weak' is to imply that it enjoys low levels of legitimacy and therefore finds it difficult to enforce public policy. At least five factors contributed to this weakness:

15

- By underlining how little Unification had done to reduce the peasants' oppression, their conditions ensured that they would have little commitment to the new regime.
- The fact that three-quarters of the population were illiterate meant that the ideals of national unity had never engaged the enthusiasms of more than very small minorities.[3]
- Unification itself had essentially been an elite-driven process of annexation by Piedmont. This was underlined by the fact that no provision was made, in the territories acquired, for discussing the constitution of the new state. Rather, the Piedmontese constitution, along with its legal system and bureaucracy, were simply imposed on the country as a whole. For the vast majority of the population, therefore, Unification meant little more than that 'the oppression of Piedmontese tax collectors was added to that of the local landlord' (Hine, 1993: 13). Unable, therefore, to identify with the new state, the population's allegiances remained parochial – centred on their own towns or villages.
- The creation of a national allegiance was also deliberately obstructed by the Church. The Pope feared that his territorial losses would undermine his worldwide spiritual authority by bringing him under the control of the Italian state. He was also ideologically opposed to the **liberalism** (Box 1.2) associated with it. Therefore he set out to deprive the new state of legitimacy by repeatedly forbidding Catholics to vote or to stand as candidates in elections.
- But in any case, voting was confined to no more than 2 per cent of the population. Therefore, elections failed to act as channels for the legitimate expression of grievances and so strengthened the sense of alienation from the state still more.

Parliamentary politics

Franchise restrictions underlay the third legacy of liberal Italy, namely the character of parliamentary politics:

- The absence of a mass electorate restricted the development of well-organised political parties.
- By ensuring that parliamentarians represented a narrow social circle, limited suffrage meant that left–right divisions within Parliament were neither clear-cut nor stable.

For these two reasons, Parliament's activities were governed by loosely organised factions built up around charismatic individuals unable clearly to distinguish themselves from the leaders of other factions in terms of programmes or ideology. Coalitions within Parliament therefore lacked cohesion and were constructed and reconstructed on the basis of log-rolling and the trading of jobs and favours.[4] Under these circumstances, the individual deputy

Box 1.2

Key terms: nationalism and liberalism

Nationalism is the doctrine that a 'nation', usually defined in cultural or ethnic terms, has the right to its own autonomous political organisation usually in the form of an independent state. As such, it has both universalistic and particularistic implications – universalistic in as much as it proclaims the right of *all* nations to independent statehood; particularistic in so far as given nationalist claims may, and often do, come into conflict with each other. The political science literature on nationalism and its manifestations is rather vast and has been preoccupied by two issues among other things. One is the question of which came first: nations or nationalism. Some have traced the idea of nation and a sense of national identity back several centuries; other have seen it as an essentially modern development, one that required industrialisation to give life to it by making technologically possible anything more than local loyalties. Another issue concerns the criteria according to which one nation may be distinguished from another and, relatedly, the different ways in which nationalism may express itself. One distinction often made is between 'ethnic nationalism' (where membership of the nation is hereditary) and 'civic nationalism' (where membership of the nation is voluntary and entails a commitment to the established political institutions as embodying the 'will of the people').

Liberalism is the doctrine according to which the good society is one whose arrangements give pride of place to individual freedom and equality of opportunity. Liberals thus emphasise laissez-faire principles in economics, and the idea that political rule must always be with the consent of the governed. They thus stress the importance of universalistic and transparent political procedures based on norms of due process. Liberalism also involves a strong commitment to reason and rationality and thus sets its face against the idea that there is any inherent value in tradition, and against any role for hereditary or religious criteria in political institutions or decision-making. For some liberals, 'freedom' is an entirely negative matter, implying freedom *from* coercion and thus the minimalist state; for others, 'freedom' also has positive connotations and would allow state intervention to give individuals, through welfare and other measures, freedom *to* realise their potential. While this brand of liberalism, commonly known as 'social liberalism', tolerates some of the restrictions on economic competition that would be advocated by socialists, in the nineteenth century liberalism defined itself in *opposition* to socialism as well as to the authoritarianism of the ancien régime.

was highly amenable to inducements to shift his support from faction to faction depending on the favours that might be on offer. This in turn provided the basis for what became known as *trasformismo*, the practice of governments seeking to maintain themselves in office on the basis of constantly shifting majorities through the offer and distribution of rewards to potential supporters.

The practice had two important consequences:

- It allowed governments to escape proper parliamentary accountability by preventing the emergence of clearly defined governing and opposition roles.
- By bringing about the inclusion of deputies of conflicting opinions within single governing coalitions, it ensured that the centre of gravity of the latter would always lie in the centre of the political spectrum.

In some quarters the practice of *trasformismo* was considered a virtue because it brought together 'moderates' opposed to radical republicans and reactionary Catholics alike. In this way it served, so the argument went, to defend and to strengthen the unified state and its constitution. In other quarters the practice was decried. It brought together politicians whose views on many important issues were opposed to each other, being seen as necessary for the survival of the coalition of the moment. It was therefore seen as conducive to the avoidance of contentious issues and thus to inaction. A very similar style of parliamentary politics would later characterise the period from the fall of Fascism to the early 1990s.

■ The Fascist regime

The growth of Fascism and the demise of liberal Italy were the two sides of a coin manufactured, at the end of the nineteenth and the beginning of the twentieth centuries, by the growth of forces unleashed by franchise extensions and the appearance of a mass electorate.

- In 1882, a lowering of the property qualification and a reduction in the minimum voting age from twenty-five to twenty-one increased the size of the electorate to about 7 per cent of the population.
- In 1912, abolition of the property qualification and of the literacy test for men over thirty increased the electorate's size to 24 per cent.
- In 1919, extension of the vote to all men over twenty-one gave the country universal male suffrage.

Meanwhile, industrialisation and urbanisation had seen the emergence and growth of socialism. There were 16 socialist deputies in 1897; 33 in 1900; 41 in 1909; 79 in 1913 and 156 in 1919. This led the Church to modify its attitude to the state. From 1904 it allowed the electoral participation of Catholics where abstention might result in the election of a socialist. The mass franchise permitted both socialism and Catholicism to establish themselves as political forces to be reckoned with. On the one hand, it gave the vote to the growing number of industrial workers most likely to vote for the socialists. On the other hand, it made possible the so-called 'Gentiloni Pact'. This was the insistence of Count Gentiloni, in 1913, that candidates for election sign their agreement to a number of policy positions in return for the Catholic vote.

Antecedents of Fascism

In these circumstances, the building and maintenance of governing coalitions became more difficult. In 1919, for instance, the liberals found themselves without a majority and in need of either socialist or Catholic support. The socialists would not collaborate, while the Catholic People's Party's deputies, numbering 100, 'were both too many to be comfortable partners in a coalition and too few to form a government on their own' (Seton-Watson, 1967: 551).

The growing difficulties of *trasformismo*, combined with the compromising, indecisive style of government to which it apparently led, contributed to the growth of nationalism, especially among middle-class Italians. This was because nationalists demanded not only greater assertiveness abroad, but also a firmer attitude towards labour unrest and the socialists at home. In this context, the nascent Fascist movement was able to gain a hearing through a unique mixture of violence on the one hand and a political programme combining nationalism and social reform on the other:

- On the one hand, the assistance of Fascist squads willing to attack socialists and beat up trade unionists appealed to the propertied classes. These felt they had been abandoned by governments whose *trasformismo* entailed attempting to avoid the alienation of both left and right through a policy of strict neutrality in industrial disputes.
- On the other hand, a programme of nationalism and social reform tapped the hostility of both the right and the left towards governments unwilling either to crush protest or to grant major reform.

The Fascist seizure of power

Mussolini was able to gain a foothold in Parliament with thirty-five deputies at the election of 1921. He managed this by seeking to legitimise Fascist violence as a painful necessity if the country were to be saved from Bolshevism, and more positively as the expression of a commitment to strong government. At the same time, appeals were made to those for whom Fascist violence remained unacceptable. These appeals were couched in terms of expediency: only Mussolini could curb the worst excesses of violence; a share in power would turn the Fascists into a respectable party. Underpinned by the conviction that, like other parties before them, the Fascists too could be 'transformed', the invitation was eventually issued to them to join the government, with Mussolini as Prime Minister.

From such a position, Fascism was able to establish itself in power through a combination of legal methods and violence (Hine, 1993: 17). In 1923, the so-called Acerbo Law (after the economist and Fascist politician who drafted it) provided that the party obtaining the most votes in an election would be allocated two-thirds of the seats, as long as it obtained 25 per cent. The law was passed with the support of a cross-section of deputies who believed that it would put an end to weak coalition governments. Meanwhile, Mussolini

Box 1.3

Mussolini and Fascism

Born on 29 July 1883, Benito Amilcare Andrea Mussolini led the authoritarian political movement that ruled Italy between 1922 and 1943 and that provided the original model for German Nazism and other fascist movements throughout the world.

Mussolini was originally a revolutionary socialist and his initial profile on the national political stage was as editor of the Socialist Party newspaper *Avanti!* (Forward). This meant that, in common with other socialists, he was opposed to Italian intervention in the First World War when it broke out in August 1914. However, Mussolini's politics were more than anything fuelled by opportunism. Thus, when the war began fanning the flames of nationalism he advocated intervention on the side of the Allies, his position being that the war in Europe could have revolutionary consequences. Expelled from the Socialist Party as a result, he volunteered for combat when Italy joined the war in 1915. If this experience gave him an attachment to violence and to grandiose projects, then his political position at this time underwent less of a volte-face than a metamorphosis. That is, he continued to advocate 'heroic action' – but this was now military action rather than workers' revolution; he continued to champion the cause of the underdog – but now saw this in terms of an improvement in the position of Italy, a 'proletarian nation', against the pretensions of the stronger imperialist powers such as Britain.

Fascism became an organised political movement in March 1919, having as its newspaper *Il Popolo d'Italia* (the People of Italy), which Mussolini had founded in October 1914. The party's symbol – the ancient Roman fasces – was highly significant: easily broken on their own but almost unbreakable when bound together, the fasces at one and the same time reflected Fascism's intellectual debt to socialism and the new Roman empire that Mussolini promised to bring about.

If this established aggressive nationalism as a central component of Fascism, its other components were corporatism, totalitarianism, militarism and anti-communism. *Corporatism* was professed as an alternative form of representation to that implicit in representative democracy (where what are represented are essentially undifferentiated individual citizens). It instead provided for the representation of economic, industrial and occupational groups in a body called the Camera dei Fasci e delle Corporazioni. By allowing for class collaboration under the tutelage of the state, corporatism reflected Fascism's opposition both to liberalism and socialism and its view that (as Mussolini himself famously put it in the 1932 edition of the *Enciclopedia italiana*) outside of the state 'no human or spiritual values can exist, much less have value'. Thus put, it expressed the *totalitarianism* professed by Fascism – although the regime's success in realising its ambitions in this area was in practice incomplete. *Militarism* arose from the Fascist attachment to social Darwinism and the link it forged between the idea of the nation and the notion of 'survival of the fittest' – peaceful nations being seen as inevitably doomed to succumb to more vigorous ones. Finally, anti-communism was linked to the elitist strain in Fascist thinking and to its rejection of reason; for in rejecting the equality and rational planning of the former, Fascism emphasised obedience to the leader and the creativeness of the will.

Figure 1.2. Benito Mussolini (see Box 1.3)

already held the position of Minister of the Interior as well as Prime Minister; and he had obtained the conversion of the Fascist squads into a national, publicly funded, militia (Robson, 2000: 64). This helped to ensure that his would be the party to benefit from the new law and to emerge with an overall majority following the election of 1924.

■ The Fascists' loss of power

Mussolini entered the war on 10 June 1940 on the side of Germany. The reason he entered the war was very similar to that leading to Italy's involvement in the First World War. For it was driven by the conviction that the war was at that point drawing to an end and that entry would secure a place at the peace conference table at which foreign-policy concessions could be extracted. But as on the earlier occasion, unpreparedness led to early heavy losses, and involvement quickly turned into a seemingly endless series of military disasters. By the end of 1942, the sense of defeat was general (Procacci, 1973: 443). With Allied bombs raining down on Italian cities, the search was on among ruling circles for a way to extract the country from the war. This necessarily entailed

Table 1.1. Governments of the democratic transition, 1943–1948

Government	Dates	Composition	Duration (in days)
Provisional governments			
Badoglio I	25 July 1943 – 17 April 1944	Military government	
Badoglio II	22 April 1944 – 8 June 1944	Government of national unity	
Bonomi I	18 June 1944 – 10 Dec. 1944	DC, PCI , PSI, PLI , PRI , PDL, Pd'A, PSIUP	
Bonomi II	12 Dec. 1944 – 19 June 1945	DC, PCI , PLI, PdL, Pd'A, PSIUP	
Parri	21 June 1945 – 8 Dec. 1945	DC, PCI , PSIUP, PLI, Pd'A, PdL	
De Gasperi I	10 Dec. 1945 – 1 July 1946	DC, PCI, PSI, PLI, PdL, Pd'A	203
Constituent Assembly (election: 2 June 1946)			
De Gasperi II	13 July 1946 – 20 Jan. 1947	DC, PCI, PSI, PRI	191
De Gasperi III	2 Feb. 1947 – 13 May 1947	DC, PCI, PSI	100
De Gasperi IV	31 May 1947 – 12 May 1948	DC, PSLI, PRI	347

Source: Adapted from Bull and Newell, 2005, table 3.1.

removing Mussolini from power, since the Allies would not offer peace as long as he remained. It necessarily entailed, too, that people looked for the initiative to come from the King as legitimate sovereign. When it did so, '[i]t all passed off very quickly and successfully – but then a *coup d'état* is not all that difficult if king, army, police, populace and even most governing politicians are all on the side of the rebels' (Clark, 1996: 299). With Mussolini arrested, the King appointed Marshall Badoglio to head a military-technocratic government (Table 1.1).

■ The legacy of Fascism

Fascism's legacy is in one sense straightforward. By replacing the nationalism of Unification with an aggressive and expansionist strain, Fascism brought war and destruction. This, in reaction, brought a new republican, democratic and anti-fascist constitution. But from another point of view the legacy is more complex, for rather than a dramatic caesura, there was – from the King's dismissal of Mussolini on 25 July 1943 to the entry into force of the post-war Constitution on 1 January 1948 – a process of continuous political evolution. Consequently, alongside reaction against what had been the defining characteristics of the regime – aggressive nationalism and authoritarianism – it is possible to identify certain lines of continuity.

▨ The aftermath of Fascism

The Badoglio government lasted until April 1944 but proved unable to extract the country from the war. For it failed to make peace quickly enough or secretly enough to avoid arousing the suspicions of the Germans who poured in divisions from the north. Consequently, the Badoglio government became a puppet of the Allies who had invaded Italy from the south:

- announcement of the armistice, on 8 September, led to an immediate German take-over of Rome; and therefore to
- the flight of king and government to avoid capture; and thus to
- reinstallation of king and government in Allied-controlled southern Italy where they initially had direct sovereignty only over Puglia and Sardinia.

The efforts of the Allies to broaden the base of a government now a 'co-belligerent' against Germany were resisted by the anti-Fascist parties. These were organised from 9 September in the Committee for National Liberation (CLN). They wanted the King's abdication, given his complicity with Fascism, and to take over power themselves – while the Allies wanted restoration of the status quo ante.

The deadlock was broken by Palmiro Togliatti, leader of the Communist Party, which had been founded as a breakaway from the Italian Socialist Party in 1921. Aware of Stalin's aim of dividing Europe into spheres of influence, and having obtained a compromise whereby the King would hand over powers to his son, his party joined a second Badoglio government. The other anti-Fascist parties could not afford to stay aloof without risking a huge increase in Communist influence. Then, having joined the government, the Communists were hardly able to resist when in June the other anti-Fascist parties demanded a new government under a civilian. This gave life to the government of Ivanoe Bonomi which continued until December.

A second Bonomi government took office that month – but without the support of the Socialists or the Party of Action (a democratic, republican party, in favour of a reformed capitalism, founded in 1942). This was unhappy that the government saw its legitimacy as deriving, not from the CLN, which had brought it into being, but from the Crown. The issue was significant, for it symbolised the shift in the balance of power that was taking place away from the forces working for innovation and renewal, in favour of those working for conservatism and the maintenance of continuity in Italian government:

- On the one hand, there was the CLN, which drew its strength from the Resistance movement. This was the movement consisting of northern-based partisan militia groups, many of which were affiliated to the anti-Fascist parties, especially the Communists. From September 1943, they carried on a popular armed struggle against the Nazi occupation.
- On the other hand there were the Allies. They were concerned that the military and political successes of the movement were allowing it to lay claim to the status of being the legitimate political authority in liberated areas of the North.

The movement's requests for technical and military assistance in November 1944 enabled the Allies politically to disarm it by obliging it to agree that it would disband its units and surrender its arms at liberation. They thereby forced it, in effect, to acquiesce in the Allied refusal to accord recognition of any of its claims to power or to legitimate political authority.

The CLN parties had agreed, for the sake of unity, to postpone institutional questions until after liberation, which came in April 1945. But though they now demanded, and obtained, a new government (under Ferrucci Parri) more representative of the northern Resistance, the possibilities of a break with the past were undermined by three factors.

(1) The laying down of arms deprived the Resistance leaders of an important political bargaining counter.
(2) The government's most influential and change-oriented component, the Communist Party, was in any case constantly outmanoeuvred as a result of its own insistence that assertion of its social and political goals had always to be subordinated to an overriding need for anti-Fascist unity.
(3) The government found itself at the head of a state administration whose Fascist elements it was unable to purge effectively simply because of its dependence on it for the acquittal of the ordinary business of government.

In November 1945, Prime Minister Parri's government was forced to resign in the wake of popular protest at the perceived injustices of the purge efforts. It was replaced by a government under Alcide de Gasperi, leader of the moderate Catholic party, the Christian Democrats (DC). Many of the DC's leading figures had been active in the pre-war People's Party. The government ended the purges and replaced virtually all of the Prefects and police chiefs who had been appointed in the North by the CLN. In this way it completed the process of securing the continuity of the state machine and its triumph over the Resistance.

It was in this context that the agreement reached by the anti-Fascist parties in 1944 was finally put into effect: 2 June 1946 saw elections to the Assembly that would draw up the 1948 Constitution. It also saw a referendum that resulted, by a narrow margin, in a decision to abolish the monarchy. Both abolition of the monarchy and the new constitution powerfully symbolised the strange combination of continuity and change left by Fascism and its collapse:

- Voting in the referendum revealed that the monarchy had lost thanks to the North: in the South where there had been no Resistance and no popular insurrections, and where old economic and political structures had remained intact, majorities in favour of the Crown were in some areas overwhelming.
- The new Constitution enshrined a new series of fundamental rights and liberties but was in practice unable to block courts' continued enforcement of Fascist penal codes. Courts were able to do this by virtue of an early legal decision that the constitutional articles in question were merely programmatic statements, without direct legal effect, designed to guide future legislative action, not the basis for the judicial enforcement of rights.

On the one hand, then, the process of political evolution that bridged Fascism and the post-war regime ensured that, here and there, pockets of authoritarianism would remain – both in terms of mass attitudes and the level of the state (see, in particular, chapter 6). For at no time did the process escape the control of the traditional elites. On the other hand, the elimination of royal power and the promulgation of a new republican and democratic constitution were in no sense token achievements. Rather, they represented real and significant institutional changes. They established democracy. In so doing, they embodied the anti-Fascist ideals of the Resistance and of the parties that were responsible for them. This ensured that the values of the Resistance and of anti-fascism acted as 'founding ideals', underpinning the Constitution. It ensured that the values would make an inestimable contribution to the preservation and enhancement of democratic government in the post-war period.

■ The first republican period, 1946 – early 1990s

The most significant characteristics of the post-war regime emerged in the wake of the first general election to be held (April 1948) under the new constitution. By then the Cold War was well under way, and its development over the years served to sustain the electoral strength of the DC and the Communists (PCI). These were the two largest parties, which regularly took some 64 per cent of the vote between them (Box 1.4). Their electoral domination owed much to the circumstances immediately following the fall of Fascism and Nazism, which left the Church and the Resistance movement as the only points of political reference for many ordinary Italians (Ginsborg, 1990). On the one hand, the Christian Democrats, founded in 1942, had the backing of the Church, which had deep roots in civil society through its parishes and its voluntary associations. On the other hand, the Communist Party acquired considerable authority and legitimacy from the dominant role it had played in the Resistance movement.

The growth of political participation which arose from the Resistance turned these two parties into mass-based organisations. This allowed them to consolidate their influence. They were also helped to consolidate their influence by (1) the part they played in the post-Fascist reconstruction of social organisations and interest groups (such as free trade unions) and (2) the development of 'flanking organisations' (such as the DC's powerful Coldiretti, for small peasant proprietors). These organisations were designed to establish social networks that would shore up feelings of partisan solidarity, especially in the parties' strongholds (the north-east in the case of the DC; the central regions in the case of the PCI). The two regions came to acquire the characteristics of territorially based, 'white' and 'red', political subcultures. Consequently, as the Cold War developed, the subcultures nourished and reflected a very profound ideological division running through Italian society. The subcultures also nourished a paradoxical mutual dependence of the parties on each other. For, if deeply held anti-communist attitudes almost automatically drove voters into the arms of the DC as the PCI's largest opponent, then the DC's anti-Communism served to consolidate the partisanship of PCI supporters.

■ Permanent exclusion of the left and right extremes

The Cold War was also the fundamental determinant of coalition formation in the post-war period. It led to the development of the so-called *conventio ad excludendum* – the taken-for-granted understanding between the DC and the smaller parties that the PCI would be excluded permanently from office by refusing it any offers of alliance. A similar policy of exclusion was practised against the parliamentary party lying at the opposite end of the political spectrum – the neo-fascist Italian Social Movement (MSI). This party's vote averaged around 5 per cent in the period to 1992. It was formed in 1946 by a group of young fascists who had served Mussolini as junior government officials. The left and the right extremes were hardly in a position themselves to ally with each other. This, and the refusal of any of the remaining parties to ally with them, had as its consequence that the DC was able to sustain itself permanently in office. For, it was the largest party and it was a party whose ideological profile placed it at the centre of the left–right spectrum. This enabled it to retain office in alliance with shifting combinations of the smaller parties of the centre – Liberals, Republicans, Social Democrats – and (from 1963) the Socialists.

This in turn had profound consequences for the quality of Italian government.

(1) The DC and its allies knew that their agreement to exclude left and right extremes virtually guaranteed them a place in government regardless of election outcomes. The collapse of any government (there were over fifty between 1945 and 1992: tables 1.1 and 1.2) would be followed by a new government composed of a similar combination of parties. This meant that they were under little or no pressure to enact coherent legislative programmes and therefore that they were under little pressure to construct governments with any real power vis-à-vis the legislature. Consequently, senior party leaders with the power to impose discipline on their followers tended not to be cabinet ministers. Rather, they would delegate these positions to secondary figures. And the fact that it was not they, but the powerful party secretaries who chose their cabinet colleagues, meant that prime ministers had little authority.

(2) The weakness of prime ministers and executives meant not only that they were under little pressure to enact coherent legislative programmes but also that they had little power to do so either. Consequently, the main basis of competition between the governing parties and the main party of opposition was ideological (that is, anti-communism). Meanwhile, competition between the governing parties themselves rested on small-scale distributive measures. In other words, the governing parties' preferred means of mobilising and retaining electoral support in competition

Box 1.4

Main parties of the first republican period

Christian Democratic Party (Democrazia Cristiana, DC)
The Christian Democratic Party was founded in Milan in September 1942 by anti-Fascist Catholics and ex-leaders of the pre-Fascist Partito Popolare Italiano. From the beginning, the DC's programmes were founded on explicitly cross-class appeals designed to allow the party to pursue a catch-all strategy that would reach beyond the ranks of the Catholic faithful and allow it successfully to act as the main bulwark against communism. Ever the largest party in post-war Italy, the DC was the mainstay of every governing coalition from the end of the war until the resignation of the Amato government in 1993.

Italian Communist Party (Partito Comunista Italiano, PCI)
Italy's principal party of the left during the period spanning the Second World War and the party's transformation and change of name, in 1990–91, to the Partito Democratico della Sinistra. Consistently the second-largest party in terms of votes and seats, the PCI was kept permanently in opposition as a result of the so-called *conventio ad excludendum*, the agreement between the DC and its allies never to admit it to government because of its presumed anti-system nature.

Italian Social Movement (Movimento Sociale Italiano, MSI)
Party founded in December 1946 by a number of former officers in Mussolini's Repubblica di Salò. Though careful to avoid explicit statements of a desire to restore Fascism (reconstitution of the Fascist Party being banned by the post-war Constitution) the MSI's nationalism and authoritarianism marked it out clearly as a party of the neo-fascist variety.

Italian Liberal Party (Partito Liberale Italiano, PLI)
Party formally constituted in 1922 but with organisational and political roots in the ruling elites which governed Italy following Unification. The traditional defender of the interests of the employing class, the PLI was unable to turn this to its advantage in the post-war world in competition with the DC whose understanding of the need for an appeal to a wider audience than the urban bourgeoisie offered to big business greater electoral guarantees. Espousing a doctrinaire combination of free-market liberalism and political authoritarianism, the PLI was one of the three smaller parties of the secular democratic centre that traditionally formed the DC's minor coalition allies – the other two being the PRI and the PSDI. Its vote averaged 3.5 per cent at elections between 1948 and 1992.

Italian Republican Party (Partito Repubblicano Italiano, PRI)
Founded in 1895, when it re-emerged after the fall of Fascism, it expressed an outlook combining anti-monarchsim, anti-clericalism and anti-fascism, together with a pro-market and transatlantic stand. One of the three smaller parties of the secular democratic centre (see above) the PRI's vote averaged 2.8 per cent at elections between 1948 and 1992.

Italian Socialist Party (Partito Socialista Italiano, PSI)
Party founded in 1892. The loss of its position as the principal party of the left in the immediate aftermath of the fall of Fascism created for the PSI a fundamental strategic dilemma that it would have to face throughout the fifty-year period separating the armistice from the party's effective collapse in 1993, namely, that it could only escape subordination to the PCI at the cost of subordination to the DC and vice versa. It appeared to have found an independent role for itself in the 1980s when its indispensability in coalition formation allowed it to set the agenda of political debate, but precisely because this drew it ever more closely into the web of power-broking and corruption woven by the DC, it would prove ultimately to be the cause of the party's collapse.

Italian Social Democratic Party (Partito Socialista Democratico Italiano, PSDI)
Party born, in 1947, of a split in the Socialist Party as a consequence of the latter's 'Unity of Action' pact with the PCI. While lending to DC-based governments of the 1950s a reformist, socialist colouring, the PSDI was virulently anti-Communist and rapidly became a party of mere power-brokers and clientelistic interests. One of the three smaller parties of the secular democratic centre (see above) the PSDI's vote averaged 4.4 per cent at elections between 1948 and 1992. Swept away by *Tangentopoli* it had all but ceased to exist by the end of 1993. Some of its parliamentarians, led by the MEP Enrico Ferri, were included, under the name Unione dei Democratici e dei Socialisti (Union of Democrats and Socialists), in the Alliance for Good Government. However, it failed to secure the election of a single candidate in 1994.
Source: Taken from Newell, 2000: 201–14.

among themselves was through establishing clientele relationships with their followers. Thus the negotiations leading to the formation of governments were usually about little more than who could control government positions and the patronage they brought. Thus did the parties penetrate vast areas of the state bureaucracy – something dubbed *partitocrazia* or 'partyocracy' – where possession of the right political contacts, rather than qualifications and objective needs became the criteria for citizens' access to jobs and other resources.

(3) The Communists' exclusion meant, paradoxically, that their legislative behaviour tended to be 'responsible'. 'Responsible' here means an only partly visible tendency to collaborate in the functioning of *partitocrazia* and the patronage system. On the one hand, the depth of the ideological divide separating the Communists from other parties meant that the PCI was engaged in a perpetual search for its own legitimacy. This was the only means of extending its electoral support. On the other hand, the precariousness of government coalitions often meant that the passage of legislation depended on the support or abstention of one or more of the non-governing parties. Moreover, article 72 of the Constitution enables

Table 1.2. Governments of the first republican period, 1948–1994

Government	Dates	Composition	Duration (in days)
1st legislature, 8 May 1948 – 4 April 1953 (general election: 18 April 1948)			
De Gasperi V	23 May 1948 – 12 Jan. 1950	DC, PLI, PSLI, PRI	599
De Gasperi VI	27 Jan. 1950 – 16 July 1951	DC, PSLI, PRI	535
De Gasperi VII	26 July 1951 – 29 June 1953	DC, PRI	704
2nd legislature, 25 June 1953 – 14 March 1958 (general election: 7 June 1953)			
De Gasperi VIII	16 July 1953 – 28 July 1953	DC	12
Pella	17 August 1953 – 5 Jan. 1954	DC	141
Fanfani I	18 Jan. 1954 – 30 Jan. 1954	DC	12
Scelba	10 Feb. 1954 – 22 June 1955	DC, PSDI, PLI	497
Segni I	6 July 1955 – 6 May 1957	DC, PSDI, PLI	670
Zoli	19 May 1957 – 19 June 1958	DC	396
3rd legislature, 12 June 1958 – 18 February 1963 (general election: 25 May 1958)			
Fanfani II	1 July 1958 – 26 Jan. 1959	DC, PSDI	209
Segni II	15 Feb. 1959 – 24 Feb. 1960	DC	374
Tambroni	25 March 1960 – 19 July 1960	DC	116
Fanfani III	26 July 1960 – 2 Feb. 1962	DC	556
Fanfani IV	21 Feb. 1962 – 16 May 1963	DC, PSDI, PRI	449
4th legislature, 16 May 1963 – 11 March 1968 (general election: 28 April 1963)			
Leone I	21 June 1963 – 5 Nov. 1963	DC	137
Moro I	4 Dec. 1963 – 26 June 1964	DC, PSI, PSDI, PRI	205
Moro II	22 July 1964 – 21 Jan. 1966	DC, PSI, PSDI, PRI	548
Moro III	23 Feb. 1966 – 5 June 1968	DC, PSI, PSDI, PRI	833
5th legislature, 5 June 1968 – 28 February 1972 (general election: 19 May 1968)			
Leone II	24 June 1968 – 19 Nov. 1968	DC	148
Rumor I	12 Dec. 1968 – 5 July 1969	DC, PSU, PRI	205
Rumor II	5 August 1969 – 7 Feb. 1970	DC	186
Rumor III	27 March 1970 – 6 July 1970	DC, PSI, PSDI, PRI	101
Colombo	6 August 1970 – 15 Jan. 1972	DC, PSI, PSDI, PRI	527
Andreotti I	17 Feb. 1972 – 26 Feb. 1972	DC	9
6th legislature, 25 May 1972 – 1 May 1976 (general election: 7–8 May 1972)			
Andreotti II	26 June 1972 – 12 June 1973	DC, PSDI, PLI	351
Rumor IV	7 July 1973 – 2 March 1974	DC, PSI, PSDI, PRI	230
Rumor V	14 March 1974 – 3 Oct. 1974	DC, PSI, PSDI	203
Moro IV	23 Nov. 1974 – 7 Jan. 1976	DC	410
Moro V	12 Feb. 1976 – 30 April 1976	DC	78
7th legislature, 5 July 1976 – 2 April 1979 (general election: 20–21 June 1976)			
Andreotti III	29 July 1976 – 16 Jan. 1978	DC	536
Andreotti IV	11 March 1978 – 31 Jan. 1979	DC	326
Andreotti V	20 March 1979 – 31 March 1979	DC, PRI, PSDI	11

Table 1.2. (*cont.*)

Government	Dates	Composition	Duration (in days)
8th legislature, 20 June 1979 – 4 May 1983 (general election: 3 June 1979)			
Cossiga I	4 Aug. 1979 – 19 March 1980	DC, PLI, PSDI	228
Cossiga II	4 April 1980 – 27 Sep. 1980	DC, PSI, PRI	176
Forlani	18 Oct. 1980 – 26 May 1981	DC, PSI, PSDI, PRI	220
Spadolini I	28 June 1981 – 7 Aug. 1982	DC, PSI, PSDI, PRI, PLI	405
Spadolini II	23 Aug. 1982 – 13 Nov. 1982	DC, PSI, PSDI, PRI, PLI	82
Fanfani V	1 Dec. 1982 – 29 April 1983	DC, PSI, PSDI, PLI	149
9th legislature, 12 July 1983 – 28 April 1987 (general election: 26 June 1983)			
Craxi I	4 Aug. 1983 – 27 June 1986	DC, PSI, PSDI, PRI, PLI	1,058
Craxi II	1 Aug. 1986 – 3 March 1987	DC, PSI, PSDI, PRI, PLI	214
Fanfani VI	17 April 1987 – 28 April 1987	DC, independents	11
10th legislature, 2 July 1987 – 2 February 1992 (general election: 14 June 1987)			
Goria	28 July 1987 – 11 March 1988	DC, PSI, PSDI, PRI, PLI	227
De Mita	13 April 1988 – 19 May 1989	DC, PSI, PSDI, PRI, PLI	401
Andreotti VI	22 July 1989 – 29 March 1991	DC, PSI, PSDI, PRI, PLI	615
Andreotti VII	12 April 1991 – 24 April 1992	DC, PSI, PSDI, PLI	378
11th legislature, 23 April 1992 – 16 January 1994 (general election: 4 April 1992)			
Amato I	28 June 1992 – 22 April 1993	DC, PSI, PSDI, PLI	298
Ciampi	28 April 1993 – 16 April 1994	DC, PSI, PSDI, PLI	353

Source: Adapted from Bull and Newell, 2005, table 3.1.

Parliament to speed the passage of legislation by give law-making authority to its committees – and to override the 'committee only' route when
such a request is made by just one tenth of the members of the house in
question. In such cases the bill concerned *must* be referred back to the
plenary session. Both of these features – the precariousness of governing
coalitions and article 72 – gave the Communist opposition considerable
'hidden' power to block the patronage-based legislation of which it rhet-
orically disapproved. Declining to do so gave it a valuable means of
providing proof of its 'responsible' intentions.

All of this served to perpetuate the nineteenth-century legacy of popular
hostility towards the state, just as it nourished dissatisfaction with the performance of the parties, especially those in government. Governing parties
were, however, initially protected from the worst electoral consequences of
alienation by (1) the strength of Catholicism, (2) the strength of the parties'
subcultures and (3) the clientelistic distribution of resources.

This began to change in the mid-1970s when the electorate was increasingly
composed of voters who were brought up in the period of record economic

growth and social change that had started in the early 1950s. In essence, rising living standards, rising standards of education, urbanisation and growing social and geographical mobility, all weakened the influence of the party subcultures and the Church on voters' political outlooks. Meanwhile, increasingly frequent reports of political and administrative corruption, which appeared to be intimately connected to clientelistic practices, undermined the latter's effectiveness as a generator of votes. As a result turnout at elections went down, electoral volatility went up, and the period saw the emergence of new, 'protest parties' – especially the Radicals, Greens and, from the late 1980s, the Northern League (LN).

■ The end of the first republican period

Against this background of electoral unrest, the fall of the Berlin Wall in 1989 led to the transformation of the PCI into a non-communist party with a new name. This, in turn, unleashed processes that would finally lead, between 1992 and 1994, to the complete electoral collapse and organisational disintegration of the traditional governing parties.

The end of the Communist Party

In the first place, the Berlin Wall's collapse brought to a head the growing conflict within the PCI. The party needed to maintain its Leninist heritage as the means to party unity, but at the same time, it also needed to abandon this heritage as the means of overcoming its political isolation. Thus when the party leader, Achille Occhetto, announced the transformation of the party into the Democratic Party of the Left (PDS), a not insignificant proportion of the party's membership decided to break away to form a new party, Communist Refoundation (RC).

The Christian Democratic Party and the Northern League

Besides weakening the left by dividing it, the split also weakened the DC; for the fact that by far the largest of the two parties of the left had renounced communism fatally undermined the DC's ability to mobilise support on the basis of its *anti*-communism.

This was of direct benefit, especially in the DC's north-eastern strongholds, to the Northern League. In the 1992 election its percentage of the vote grew to 8.7 per cent and it thus acquired, for the first time, a significant parliamentary presence. The Northern League capitalised on the conflicts that had arisen at the heart of the DC's electoral strategies. The DC's reliance on clientelism was particularly important to its electoral following in the South, but clientalism required high and growing levels of public expenditure, financed from tax revenues provided mainly by the richer North. And by undermining the coherence of public policy-making as we have seen, it acted as a brake on the efficient provision of public services and infrastructure. So clientelism was particularly harmful to the interests of northern small businesses, the growth of which from the 1960s provided a fertile source of support for the League. Arguing that the tax-and-spending activities of the *partitocrazia* were regionally biased against the North, it demanded a federal reform of the state that would give the northern regions greater autonomy from the central state, and reduce its powers to tax the North in order to subsidise the poor South.

Corruption

The collapse of the Berlin Wall thus compounded the traditional parties' electoral difficulties. It also provided direct encouragement to a series of judicial investigations of political corruption. These began in February 1992 and within a short space of time proved fatal to the parties. The spread of corruption in post-war Italy was a gradual process, resting on three developments.

(1) In the first instance it was an intrinsic part of the clientelist system (see in particular, chapter 5) that offered personal favours in exchange for votes.
(2) It was encouraged, from the 1970s, by the growing costs of political activity, and thus politicians' growing need for financial resources. At the same time, foreign funds began to dry up when the Cold War began to decline in intensity and Italy was less vital as an ally in the fight against Communism. In such circumstances, entrepreneurs' lack of trust in the efficiency and impartiality of public action led them to offer bribes in exchange for public works contracts and for other scams.
(3) Through the self-generating mechanisms inherent in it, corruption appears to have spread to the point where it became systemic in the late 1980s. Public prosecutors had periodically exposed cases of corruption before the 1990s, but the effectiveness of their investigations had been limited. It had been limited by connivance between individual politicians and members of the judiciary (involving the exchange of political for judicial favours). More importantly, it had been limited by the awareness that an excessively thoroughgoing exposure of the misdeeds of the governing class directly enhanced the fortunes of the Communist Party. For, the PCI had made the so-called 'moral question' one of its own great battle cries. In the early 1990s, however, judicial investigators were aware that they could expose established politicians without the risk of bringing the Communist Party to power.

Once under way, the 1992 investigations (which became known as the '*Mani pulite*' or 'clean hands' investigations) quickly proliferated with defendants implicating others, whose confessions, in their turn, implicated still others. Central to this process was the inherent fragility of the trust underlying corrupt exchanges, together with judicial investigators' success in using preventative custody laws (see, in particular, chapter 9). What seems to have happened is that suspects, held *incommunicado*, would be offered the choice of remaining in prison or release, if they confessed and named others. Accomplices, knowing that they too would be picked up in the event of a confession but not knowing exactly how much had been revealed, thus had an incentive to tell 'their side of the story' as soon as possible, before the confessions of those in prison led them into even greater trouble.

By the end of 1993, no fewer than 251 members of Parliament were under judicial investigation, including 4 former prime ministers, 5 ex-party leaders, and 7 former cabinet ministers. Ten suspects had killed themselves (Bull and Newell, 1995: 74; Nelken, 1996: 109). As each day brought news of increasingly well-known names being caught up in the tidal wave of scandal – which became known as *Tangentopoli*[5] – the traditional parties of government faced organisational collapse:

(1) By reducing the amounts available from illegal sources of financing to just a trickle, the investigations pushed all the traditional parties fairly quickly towards bankruptcy.
(2) By so thoroughly infecting the internal life of the parties, corruption had encouraged the growth of memberships whose motives were predominantly venal, while discouraging the participation of more ideologically committed potential members. By thus rendering parties' organisations inherently fragile, corruption ensured that when exposed, the consequent lack of money would lead rank-and-file members to melt away.

National electoral reform

It was in this context that a range of cross-party organisations now came together in a movement for reform that sought to change the way in which the two chambers of Parliament – the Chamber of Deputies and the Senate – were elected. The reform movement's chosen political instrument was the constitutional provision that allows proposals for the annulment of laws and parts of laws to be decided upon by popular referenda. Such referenda can be called when they are demanded by at least half a million signatures. In 1993 the movement obtained a referendum on a proposal to annul an apparently insignificant part of one of the clauses of the law governing elections to the Senate. The part was actually very significant because its annulment would bring about a de facto change in the electoral system for the Senate. Instead of proportional representation, it would provide for three-quarters of the seats to be elected on the basis of the single-member, simple plurality ('first-past-the-post') system.[6]

Reformers were driven to their action by two thoughts.

(1) By engineering a change in the electoral law for the Senate, they would thereby force Parliament to introduce a similar change for the Chamber of Deputies as well. Both chambers, which are elected at general elections on the same day, have co-equal legislative powers. In other words, legislative

proposals, if they are to become law, must be approved by both chambers and either can veto the proposals of the other. This means that both must have similar electoral systems if the risk is to be avoided of legislative paralysis caused by different party compositions.

(2) It was reasonable to hope that a new electoral system might put an end to the corrupt, inefficient administrations of the past – with a consequent significant improvement in the quality of Italian government.

The reasoning was based on the political incentives facing parties and voters under single-member, simple plurality systems. Such systems put parties that are close together on the ideological spectrum under pressure to reach a series of mutually agreeable stand-down arrangements across the constituencies. They put the parties under this pressure because it is only by means of such arrangements that the parties can reduce or eliminate the possibility of other parties, further away on the political spectrum, taking seats at their joint expense with less than 50 per cent of the vote. On this basis, reformers thought that a changed electoral law would encourage parties to organise themselves into two broad electoral coalitions, one of the centre left and one of the centre right. Each would have common coalition candidates as the means of maximising their combined seats while minimising the chances of victory of the opposing coalition.

On the voter side of the calculation was the general tendency of single-member, simple plurality systems to put voters under pressure to confine their choices to the two best-placed candidates, each casting his or her vote for the candidate he or she dislikes least. This makes it reasonable to expect that under most ordinary circumstances, elections will result in an overall majority of parliamentary seats going to one or other of the main centrist coalitions – with the result that each coalition's leader becomes, in effect, its candidate for the post of Prime Minister. It is then reasonable to assume that in virtue of their popular mandate prime ministers will enjoy sufficient authority to impose discipline on the governing coalition. It is reasonable to assume too, that prime ministers would use that discipline to ensure coherent policy-making. This would also maximise the coalition's chances of being returned to office at the next election. Consequently, reformers hoped that in place of the old system of governance, based on unstable coalitions decided by 'behind-the-scenes' negotiations after the votes had been counted, the new voting system would allow the electorate direct choice over the Government and Prime Minister. It might also result in fewer changes of government and greater levels of popular accountability.

The referendum of 18 April 1993 was almost universally regarded as judgement of the performance of the traditional parties of government. Turnout was 77 per cent, and the reform was passed with 83 per cent of the poll. The Prime Minister at the time was the law professor and socialist, Giuliano Amato. Since the election of 1992, he had headed a four-party coalition in which the DC as usual, was the largest component: Table 1.2. He had personally opposed the referendum as 'incostituzionalissimo'. Meanwhile, the 1992 legislature had been thoroughly deligitimised by *Tangentopoli*. Amato therefore now resigned to make way for a government of technocrats under ex-Governor of the Bank of Italy, Carlo Azeglio Ciampi. By common consent, the remit of this government was to introduce proposals for a new electoral law for the Chamber of Deputies, to be followed by fresh elections. These were held in March 1994.

Local electoral reform

In the meantime, reformers had also managed, in March 1993, to force a change in the way in which local council mayors were elected. Proportional representation was replaced by a new system based on the double ballot method. If no candidate managed to get 50 per cent +1 (an absolute majority) of the poll, then the strongest two would go into a 'run-off' ballot. The effects of such a system are similar to those of the predominantly 'first-past-the-post' system that was to be used for parliamentary elections. It too places parties under pressure to form electoral coalitions with 'like-minded' parties in opposition to parties that are ideologically more distant.

Mayoral elections held in December 1993 revealed that, with the traditional governing parties continuing to disintegrate under the weight of the corruption scandals, the PDS and other parties of the left were far more successful in forming coalitions and in winning contests than were parties of the right (principally the MSI and the Northern League, LN). With the DC and its traditional governing allies now definitively compromised and weakened, the elections appeared to be a portent of the general election to come.

Berlusconi and Forza Italia

It was in this context that the media magnate, Silvio Berlusconi, announced his intention of joining the political fray with a new party, Forza Italia (FI), in order to forge an alliance capable of 'saving Italy from communism' (Box 1.5). FI was less a political party in any conventional sense than a sophisticated marketing organisation designed to further the political ambitions of its rich leader. However, it promised a centre-right political home to the large pool of voters orphaned by the collapse of the traditional parties of government. The charisma of its self-made leader, with his promises to 'do for Italy what he had done for himself' further enhanced its electoral appeal by giving it novelty value. There were good reasons to be sceptical. Berlusconi's economic success had relied heavily on his contacts with the old political class, particularly with disgraced former Socialist prime minister, Bettino Craxi. Berlusconi's own economic interests were left exposed and vulnerable by the old parties' extinction, but this also raised the possibility of a grandiose project – that of taking their place with a new party or coalition of his own (Fiori, 1995: 203).

The seemingly excellent prospects of the new party were fulfilled in the 1994 elections. The neo-fascist MSI and the LN – the principal parties of the right other than Berlusconi's own – would not ally with each other. The first

Box 1.5

Berlusconi and Forza Italia

Born on 29 September 1936, Silvio Berlusconi is among the top handful of Italy's wealthiest individuals, if not the wealthiest. His fortune has been made on the back of a business career that in the popular imagination reflects his talents as a sales-man, these talents having had evident application in his political style and activities.

He began his business career in the early 1960s following a degree in law and, famously, various stints as a crooner on cruise ships and in nightclubs. One of his early projects was development of the garden city known as Milano 2. This featured the later development, for the residents, of a local cable-television station, Telemilano, which subsequently evolved into Italy's largest media empire, Mediaset, giving Berlusconi ownership of the country's three largest private tele-vision networks.

Mediaset's growth illustrates well Berlusconi's position in first republic Italy. Keen to overcome the state's monopoly on national television advertising for which there was huge pent-up demand, he was obstructed by the state's exclusive control of nationwide broadcasting. Finding a way round this by having the local stations in his orbit broadcast the same programmes at the same time, but facing legal challenges, he was able to use his relationship with Socialist prime minister, Bettino Craxi, to secure the passage (even at the cost of shameless manipulation of Parliament's standing orders) of legislation that regularised his position in exchange for generous party contributions. In this way he illustrated both that the border separating the activities of politicians and business people in first republic Italy was an ill-defined one, and that long before his launch of Forza Italia (FI) in 1994, he was no stranger to the world of politics and its parties – without which he would hardly have been able to make his fortune.

From this perspective, the emergence of FI can be seen as representing not just an attempt to occupy the political space that was left vacant by the collapse of the traditional governing parties, but an attempt by its founder to secure and enhance his own interests through the grandiose project of an organisation that would take their place.

FI's most distinctive characteristics are threefold:

1) the extent to which it is controlled by Berlusconi personally (mechanisms of internal democracy found in other parties being all but non-existent).
2) the unusual degree to which its image is bound up with the characteristics of its leader whose flamboyance and supposedly extraordinary personal qualities have been central to the party's appeal. Both this and the first characteristic have led observers to express doubts about the likelihood of the organisation's survival, at least in its existing form, once Berlusconi leaves the poltical scene.
3) its role as 'coalition maker' – its popularity and its ideological positioning having allowed Berlsuconi to bring together the parties of the centre right, under his own leadership, in opposition to the centre left.

Since FI's emergence, Berlusconi's career as a politician has been marked by four features above all others:

(1) his extraordinary success. He was nominated as Prime Minister for the fourth time in 2008 following a handsome election victory. His second government holds the post-war record for longevity, surviving uninterruptedly in office for 1,413 days before, in April 2005, he was obliged to resign and construct a new cabinet following a brief government crisis.

(2) the strong populist strain of his political approach. Populism is a rhetorical style that pits 'a virtuous and homogeneous people against a set of elites and dangerous 'others' who are together depicted as depriving (or attempting to deprive) the sovereign people of their rights, values, prosperity, identity and voice' (Albertazzi and McDonnell, 2007: 3). It therefore carries a heavy dose of impatience with procedures limiting the free exercise of power.

(3) Berlusconi's irritation with the debate that has taken place surrounding the conflict of interests involved in his being both Prime Minister and the owner of Italy's three largest private television channels (which is an expression of this impatience).

(4) the variety of criminal proceedings brought against him on charges ranging from corruption to false accounting and illegal party funding during his time as a politician. None of the cases have been successful, but they have under-lain centre-left charges that significant items of legislation introduced after 2001 were essentially *ad personam* measures designed to help him solve his personal legal difficulties.

stood for strong central government and a welfare state of greatest benefit to the South; the other stood for decentralisation and the interests of the North. But they would, given his electoral prospects, ally with Berlsuconi. Thus it was that Berlusconi was able to forge an alliance with the LN in the North (where the MSI was uncompetitive) – an alliance that became known as the 'Freedom Alliance'. In the South (where the LN was non-existent) he formed an alliance with the MSI that become known as the 'Alliance for Good Government'.

Berlusconi's victory at the 1994 election was short-lived. He had formed a government with the MSI and the LN, but then fell from office in December. In that month the LN leader, Umberto Bossi, withdrew his support because he feared that the similarities between its ideological profile and that of Forza Italia might impact negatively on his party's identity and organisational integrity. This event put Berlusconi and the centre right in opposition for the next six-and-a-half years. For the government was replaced by a government of technocrats, under Berlusconi's former Treasury Minister, Lamberto Dini, before fresh elections were held in April 1996 (Table 1.3). These elections were won by a coalition of the centre left largely because of the inability of Berlusconi and Bossi to repair their broken alliance. Yet in the longer term, the elections brought Berlusconi and Bossi back together. For, in 1996 Bossi had failed to capture the balance of

Table 1.3. Governments of the second republican period, 1994–2008

Government	Dates	Composition	Duration (in days)
12th legislature, 15 April 1994 – 16 February 1996 (general election: 27 March 1994)			
Berlusconi I	10 May 1994 – 22 Dec. 1994	FI, LN, AN, CCD, UdC	226
Dini	17 Jan. 1995 – 17 May 1996	Independents	486
13th legislature, 9 May 1996 – 9 March 2001 (general election 21 April 1996)			
Prodi	18 May 1996 – 9 Oct. 1998	PDS, PPI, Dini List, UD, Greens	876
D'Alema I	27 Oct. 1998 – 18 Dec. 1999	Ulivo, PdCI, UDEUR	423
D'Alema II	22 Dec. 1999 – 19 April 2000	DS, PPI, Democrats, UDEUR, PdCI, Greens, RI	119
Amato II	25 April 2000 – 11 June 2001	DS, PPI, Democrats, UDEUR, SDI, PdCI, Greens, RI, independents	398
14th legislature, 30 May 2001 – 27 April 2006 (general election: 13 May 2001)			
Berlusconi II	12 June 2001 – 23 April 2005	FI, AN, LN, CCD-CDU, independents	1,413
Berlusconi III	23 April 2005 – 17 May 2006	FI, AN, LN, CDU, independents	372
15th legislature, 28 April 2006 – 6 February 2008 (general election: 9 and 10 April 2006)			
Prodi II	17 May 2006 – 8 May 2008	DS, Margherita, RC, PdCI, Greens, RnP, UDEUR, IdV	
16th legislature, 29 April 2008 – (general election: 13 and 14 April 2008)			
Berlusconi IV	8 May 2008 – in office	Pdl, LN	

Source: Bull and Newell, 2005, table 3.2; www.governo.it/Governo/Governi/governi.html.

power in Parliament by running independently and he was now rapidly losing support. In February 2000, therefore, Bossi once more embraced Berlusconi. This meant that the centre-right alliance that fought the 2001 elections, a coalition called the Casa delle Libertà (House of Freedoms), in essence consisted of four formations: Forza Italia, the LN, and two others. One of these was the National Alliance. This was the name which the MSI had decided to adopt for itself in 1994, dropping MSI from its title altogether in January 1995. In this way it hoped to distance itself from its Fascist heritage and so consolidate the newly won legitimacy which the alliance with Berlusconi had given it. The other was the Christian Democratic Centre-Christian Democratic Union, one of a number of groupings consisting of former Christian Democrats.

The Olive-tree Alliance

Meanwhile, the second of the two main alliances contesting the 2001 elections was a coalition of the centre left known as the Ulivo, or 'Olive-tree Alliance'. This brought together nine formations of which the largest was the Left Democrats (DS), as the ex-Communists now called themselves. In 1996, the Ulivo had won an absolute majority of seats in the Senate and a relative majority in the Chamber. Here, it had been dependent for its hold on office on the support of RC – the most left-wing of the parliamentary parties. Unable, in 1998, to produce a finance law that could win the support of a sufficiently large number of RC Deputies, the first Ulivo government, under Romano Prodi, fell at the end of that year. It was replaced by another government of the centre left, under Left Democrat Massimo D'Alema, sustained in office by the support of a small number of Deputies who had originally been elected as part of the centre right.

The Ulivo went into the 2001 election with a creditable record. Most notable was its success in ensuring that Italy met the convergence criteria laid down in the 1991 Maastricht Treaty and was able to adopt the euro in 1999. The Ulivo suffered, however, from an image of disunity. This image was enhanced by the fact that its record was not, in fact, that of a single government that had been in office since 1996, but of four governments. The government that replaced Prodi's towards the end of 1998 had lasted a little over a year and then fallen because of diversity in the long-term strategic outlooks of some of its components. Though a second D'Alema government had been put together without difficulty, D'Alema resigned in the wake of the regional elections of April 2000 and their less-than-positive outcome for the centre left. A fourth government had been installed under the authoritative ex-Socialist, Giuliano Amato. Finally, it was decided that if the coalition was to have any chance of beating the centre right in 2001, it needed to have a leader capable of competing effectively with Berlusconi in terms of novelty and personal image. Mayor of Rome, Francesco Rutelli, thus became the coalition's leader in September 2000.

▪ A 'Second Republic'?

The victory of Berlusconi and the House of Freedoms in May 2001 came at the end of a decade of unprecedented change in Italian politics and, after five years of centre-left governments, resulted in a clear alternation in power from left to right. That is, for the first time since the war, an opposition united in supporting its leader's candidacy for the premiership ousted an incumbent government seeking a new term of office – and won a large overall majority in the process. For the first time since the founding of the Republic therefore, it seemed more likely than not that the government taking office would last for an entire legislative term of five years (Allum and Newell, 2003). The election outcome thus powerfully suggested the possible end of one of the characteristics (unstable governments) that had set Italy apart from other West European polities. Thereby it led observers to reflect even more intently on the sense in which the years leading up to the election could – or could not – be held to have witnessed a transition from a 'First' to a 'Second' Republic.

What seems clear is that the 1990s saw a complete transition – or, better, transformation – of the post-war *party system*, which has changed in three fundamental respects:

(1) The parties that once occupied the positions furthest to the left and the right on the political spectrum – the PCI and the MSI – had, by distancing themselves from their pasts and acquiring new names, managed to shed their pariah status.
(2) As a consequence of this, the non-governing parties no longer lay on both sides of the political spectrum but on one side only (that is, opposition was no longer bilateral but unilateral).
(3) Therefore, there no longer existed a centre party able to maintain itself permanently in office by excluding left and right extremes. In short, Italy's party system now had a bipolar, rather than a tri-polar format.

All of these changes were interconnected. The disappearance of bilateral oppositions was inseparable from the disappearance of a centre party able to maintain itself permanently in office. In turn, the latter change was both cause and consequence of the transformation of the two parties at the ends of the political spectrum. On the one hand, the collapse of the DC and its role as a dam against the opposing extremes removed the most fundamental, and hitherto insurmountable, obstacle in the way of the MSI's overriding ambition of finding a partner or partners in the construction of a conservative, anti-left pole. On the other hand, it had been the PCI's transformation that had removed the last of the three pillars (Catholicism, clientelism and anti-communism) on which electoral support for the DC had traditionally rested, thus hastening that party's demise in the first place.

A bipolar party system, then, gradually consolidated itself over the two elections after 1994 (Box 1.6). By 2001, there were two coalitions, each competing for overall majorities of seats. This confirmed the hopes of the promoters of the 1993 change in the electoral system. Initially, however, it seemed that their hopes had been dashed. In 1994, Berlusconi, as we have seen, formed two coalitions, not one. The result was that nowhere could voters vote for or against the entire coalition that subsequently went on to form the government (Ignazi and Katz, 1995: 32). Moreover, this government turned out to be every bit as litigious and short-lived as those of the past. For these reasons, constitutional reform, which had been discussed in and outside of Parliament since the 1980s, now came to be regarded as a matter of priority; for the apparent failure of electoral reform to deliver the clear electoral choices and stable government that had been the reasons for pursuing it in the first place suggested that far more thoroughgoing institutional change was needed. Adding to the pressures for such change were:

Box 1.6

Main parties of the second republican period

The numbers and identities of the parties, as well as the patterns of alliance between them, have been in a state of constant flux since the political upheavals of the early 1990s, with somewhat lesser stability shown on the centre left than on the centre right.

Here, the main party protagonists have been essentially four in number:

(1) **Forza Italia (FI)**: see box 1.5.
(2) **The Northern League (Lega Nord, LN)**, founded in December 1989 by the leader of the Lombard League, Umberto Bossi, as a means of bringing together a number of northern regional autonomy leagues under one umbrella. The Northern League combines a rigidly centralised form of organisation with an appeal based on a unique blend of populism and 'ethno-regionalism'.
(3) **The National Alliance (Alleanza Nazionale, AN)** founded in 1994 in order to further the growing legitimacy of its parent organisation, the neo-fascist Italian Social Movement, which had been founded in 1946 by a number of former officers in Mussolini's Repubblica di Salò. Since the party has sought to distance itself from fascism, its ideological profile has combined a commitment to traditional values with an emphasis on law and order and national cohesion.
(4) **The Union of Christian Democrats and Centre Democrats (Unione dei Democratici Cristiani, UDC)** formed in December 2002 as a result of the merger of three of the DC's 'successor parties': the Christian Democratic Centre (CCD), the Christian Democratic Union (CDU) and European Democracy (DE). Addition of the modest vote tally of the latter to that of the CCD-CDU drove hopes that, united as the UDC, the three forces might be able to build on their combined support to revive the tradition of Christian Democracy as a more-than-marginal force within the centre right.

On the centre left, the main party protagonists have been:

(1) **The PCI's successor parties** – which came into existence following the PCI's 1991 congress decision to transform itself into a non-communist party with a new name, the Democratic Party of the Left (Partito Democratico della Sinistra, PDS). Following its 1998 absorption of three smaller centre-left groups, the PDS took the name, 'Left Democrats' (Democratici di Sinistra, DS). Alongside them stood Communist Refoundation (Rifondazione Comunista, RC) which had come into existence at the same time as the PDS as the result of opposition, within the PCI, to the party's transformation. RC then spawned the Party of Italian Communists (Partito dei Comunisti Italiani, PdCI), which broke away in 1998 as a result of its opposition to RC's decision to refuse the then centre-left government support in the confidence motion that led to its downfall.

(2) **Parties born of the demise of the PSI** – which in 1998 came together as the Italian Democratic Socialists (Socialisti Democratici Italiani, SDI) with the aim of creating a single organisation of sufficient weight to be able to engage profitably with the emerging DS.

(3) **Parties born of the demise of the DC**. Besides those on the centre right (see above), the DC's successor parties included, on the centre left, groups with organisational and ideological ties to the old party (the Italian People's Party), and groups (Italian Renewal and the Democrats), variously influenced by its values. The three came together in 2002 to form the Margherita (or 'Daisy'). A fourth party – the Union of Democrats for Europe (Unione dei Democratici per L'Europa, UDEUR) – refused to join. UDEUR had been formed in 1999 originally as the result of an attempt to revive the fortunes of a political centre able to monopolise power by excluding left and right extremes and continued its independent existence following the emergence of the Margherita.

(4) **The Radicals**. Emerging originally from a split in the old PLI, the Radicals first came to prominence in the 1970s. Their emphasis on individual responsibility, combining staunch support for civil liberties with firm liberalism in matters socio-economic, makes them difficult to place in traditional 'left' / 'right' terms – so much so that it was not before the run-up to the 2006 elections that they allowed themselves to be unambiguously associated with parties on the centre left.

(5) **The Greens (Verdi)**, first acquired national significance in the 1980s. The appeal of their environmental concerns is seen by scholars as being closely tied to growing material affluence and therefore to the apparent growth in the *relative priority* given by Western electorates generally to so-called *post-material*, as opposed to *material* values (that is, values associated with 'quality-of-life' issues such as the environment, as opposed to values associated with economic security such as employment and inflation).

(1) the LN's demands for federalism (which, as a principle, had come to be accepted by most of the parties as a means of 'drawing the sting' from the issue) and

(2) the parties' awareness, given the overall context, that promises of political renewal, and 'turning one's back on the past' were necessary conditions of electoral success.

A parliamentary Commission for Constitutional Reform was set up after the 1996 election. However, it proved incapable of producing proposals able to win a sufficient degree of cross-party support. Such support was necessary if reforms were to have any chance of being enacted. In most democratic regimes, and here Italy is no exception, constitutional change requires more than a simple majority vote in favour if it is to pass.[7] The necessary broad base of support proved impossible to construct. In the final analysis this was due to two things:

(1) the sheer *number* of parties being called upon to participate in the reform
     process. The 1993 electoral law had stimulated the emergence of two large
     electoral coalitions, but in *Parliament* the party system lost none of its
     traditional fragmentation. Indeed, though the number of parties with
     more than just a 'handful' of seats (here arbitrarily defined as ten) did
     not rise, the *total* number in the Chamber of Deputies actually went up
     from fourteen in 1992 to twenty in 1994 and twenty-four in 1996.
(2) the *wide-ranging* nature of the reforms being sought. What was being
     attempted was a revision of the whole of part II of the Constitution,
     which outlines the entire institutional geography of the Republic.
     Ultimately, therefore, it proved impossible to produce a set of proposals
     that would be at once both workable and capable of avoiding the veto of
     this or that party against this or that aspect of them.

Therefore, more limited constitutional changes (described later in this volume) have been attempted since the Commission. In some cases, they have
even been enacted. However, anything that could reasonably be described as a
'constitutional overhaul' has not been achieved. And this, it is widely held,
argues against the view that the terms 'First' and 'Second' Republic can be used
to denote separate regimes between which there has been a transition.

On the other hand, the 1990s party-system upheavals have not been without
consequences for Italian governance. It is only natural to expect this. Parties
are central to the life of democratic polities. They are central to the way in
which their institutional incumbents interact with one another. It is even
more natural to expect it in the case of Italy. Here the parties had perpetuated
the weakness of the state and undermined the incisiveness of state action
through the mechanisms of *partitocrazia*. They had penetrated vast areas of
the state and thereby taken direct control of the nominations of its personnel.
As a consequence, they had become 'fertile ground for the activities and the
development of sub-party actors (factions, etc.) thus helping to reduce the
parties as such to mere agents of mediation between such actors' (Cotta,
1996: 23). For this reason they were complex constellations of interests, each
with a power of veto whenever policy change was considered. Much less were
they unitary actors endowed with clear programmatic agendas. As a consequence, they found it difficult to take decisive initiatives in the most significant areas of public policy. Hence their role in policy-making tended to be a
predominantly reactive one. And when external events made policy initiatives
on the part of governments necessary, the parties' made efforts to direct and
channel the policy response, seeking to limit, as much as possible, any consequent damage to the interests they represented. This meant that their
behaviour frequently came to acquire, in the public perception, the connotations of illegitimate interference in public affairs (Cotta, 1996: 22).

In the 1990s, the beginning of the parties' demise together with the signing
of the Maastricht Treaty seemed to bring about an unmistakable change in this
regard. The treaty required that if Italy were to qualify for membership of the

single European currency, she would have to achieve a wholesale restructuring of public finances. These had been brought to a parlous state by the clientelistic practices of the past. And there was widespread consensus that the country *had* to qualify for membership. Failure to do so meant the risk of her industries being placed in a situation of competitive disadvantage within the single market. Without membership of the currency, Italian industry would be unable to benefit from the reduction in interest rates, lower inflation and healthier public finances that the euro seemed likely to bring with it. In these circumstances, the demise of the traditional parties enabled governments to resist the penetration of state decision-making structures by the social and economic interests represented by these parties. Thus, they were able to introduce a series of stringent economic and financial measures that would have been unthinkable prior to 1992. This has led commentators such as Della Sala (1997) to argue that the period since the early 1990s has seen a 'hollowing out' and a 'hardening' of the state. This has left governments much better placed, than in the past, to resist the pressures of the constellation of interests and social forces which the old parties had been forced to appease.

There have been important changes in governance at the sub-national level as well. Prior to the 1990s, the parties' role in linking national and sub-national representatives meant that nothing like a genuinely distinct sub-national, or regional-level political system existed. The most powerful parties in the system had every incentive to ensure that the 1970 reform which set up the ordinary regions was such as to leave traditional political practices intact. Consequently, after the reform was introduced, the regions were taken over by established political elites so that they simply became additional components of the overall power apparatus to be bargained over. The demise of the traditional parties changed this situation radically, freeing sub-national politicians from their sub-ordination to the demands of national-level intra-party and inter-party power broking. At the same time, reforms of sub-national government, themselves the consequence of the party-system upheavals, have given sub-national politicians new powers. For example, included in the March 1993 reform, mentioned above, was a provision designed to strengthen the power of initiative of mayors by providing that councils passing votes of no confidence in them would, as a consequence, bring about their own automatic dissolution. The upshot has been the creation of a new class of regional and municipal politicians represented by such figures as Orlando in Palermo, Bassolino in Naples, Cacciari in Venice and Ruttelli in Rome (or Formentini in Milan and Guazzaloca in Bologna). Many of these have been successful in building independent power bases and bringing about something of a renaissance in the quality of sub-national government.

Finally, the government that took office in 2001 maintained a hold on power much firmer than any of the past. Berlusconi's tenure of the premiership became the longest lasting of any prime minister since the war. This was clearly due to what were the novel characteristics of his government at the time it took office. Its position was directly legitimated by the outcome of the election itself. Unusually for post-war Italy, each of the main party leaders were included within government or in positions very close to government. In this way, the prospects of any one of the parties individually were bound much more closely than normal to the success or otherwise of the Government as a whole. Thereby, Berlusconi succeeded in strengthening his own hand vis-à-vis his governing partners and that of the executive vis-à-vis Parliament.

For a number of reasons, then, the terms 'First Republic' and 'Second Republic' would appear to have much more than just journalistic value. It is to the political life of the 'Second Republic' that the remainder of this volume is devoted.

■ Summary

This chapter has covered the political history of Italy from unification in 1861 to the present day. It argues that:

- Italy has had three main regimes since 1861, namely, liberal, Fascist and republican. Each of these has left enduring legacies.
- Liberal Italy (1861–1924) passed on to later generations the 'Southern Question', a weak state and a style of politics that appeared in a new guise after the fall of Fascism in 1943. It was a style of politics that was unable to cope with a mass electorate, disciplined parties and the emergence of Catholicism, socialism and nationalism as organised political forces. The result was that the entire regime fell victim to Fascism.
- Fascist Italy's (1924–1943) nemesis came with the decision to enter the Second World War – a decision that led to foreign military disasters and domestic suffering on a scale such that the regime was overthrown by the same elites that had helped create it. The fact that transition to the post-war republican regime never escaped the control of the elites ensured that pockets of authoritarianism lived on under the republican constitution.
- The first republican period (1946–1992). In this period the main opposition parties were permanently excluded from power. The extreme right was discredited by the Fascist history, and the main opposition party of the left, the Communist Party, was neutralised by Cold War. This allowed the main centre party, the Christian Democrats, to maintain itself perpetually in office with the support of shifting combinations of various smaller centre parties. The electoral discontent provoked by their policies and style of governance (clientalism, patronage, and corruption) proved fatal to these parties. In the early 1990s, a combination of the collapse of communism, a series of corruption scandals and electoral law reform led to a transformation of the entire party system, and the start of the second republican period.
- The second republican period (1992 – the present) has been marked by two main electoral coalitions of the centre left and the centre right. The failure to underpin this with thoroughgoing constitutional change means that the political system has not been transformed into an entirely new regime type. Nevertheless, there is evidence of significant change having taking place in Italian governance at both the sub-national and at the national levels.

■ Further reading

A highly readable and entertaining history of the first republican period can be found in Paul Ginsborg, *A History of Contemporary Italy. Society and Politics 1943–1988* (Harmondsworth: Penguin, 1990), while Mark Gilbert (*The Italian Revolution: the End of Politics Italian Style?*, Boulder, CO and Oxford: Westview, 1996) provides an equally readable account of the political upheavals following the collapse of the Berlin Wall. See also Vittorio Bufacchi and Simon Burgess, *Italy since 1989: Events and Interpretations* (revised edition, Basingstoke: Palgrave, 2001). Dennis Mack-Smith is the most renowned historian of Italy from the *Risorgimento*. See, among his many books, *Modern Italy: A Political History* (Ann Arbor: University of Michigan Press, 1997). This covers the period of Unification through to the 1990s and offers an incisive account of the general tendencies underlying the events responsible for the distinctiveness of Italian political history. Martin Clark's *Modern Italy 1871–1995* (2nd edn, London: Longman, 1996), analyses the political, economic and social history of Italy with particular emphasis on society and its relationship with the state.

■ Notes

1. The ten were: Lombardo-Venetia, the Kingdom of Sardinia, the Duchy of Lucca, the Duchy of Massa and Carrara, the Duchy of Parma, the Duchy of Modena, the Grand Duchy of Tuscany, the Papal State, San Marino and the Kingdom of the Two Sicilies.
2. Demesne land was originally, under feudalism, land held back by the lord of the manor for his own use as opposed to being leased out to others. Serfs worked demesne lands in payment of their feudal obligations.
3. On the importance of elites in state and nation building see the core textbook of this series, *Foundations of Comparative Politics* (Newton and Van Deth, 2005: 13).
4. The term 'log-rolling' refers to the process whereby politicians agree to support measures strongly desired by other politicians in exchange for such politicians' support in passing measures that they themselves strongly desire.
5. The term is a combination of *tangente*, a colloquialism meaning 'bribe', and *metropoli*, meaning 'metropolis' or 'city'. It therefore translates as 'bribe city' and was initially a euphemism for Milan where the scandal first broke, being designed to poke fun at a city which had previously had a reputation for scrupulousness and honesty.
6. On electoral systems, see Newton and Van Deth: 203–5.
7. In the Italian case, amendments to the Constitution can be enacted only if they have the support of majorities of the two chambers' *members* (not just those *present*); and unless such majorities reach two-thirds, the proposed amendments may then be made subject to a popular, and binding, referendum.

II

The polity: structures and institutions of the regime

2   The constitutional framework

■ Introduction

The focus of this and of the following two chapters is on the structures and institutions of government: Parliament and the executive; the bureaucracy; subnational government structures; the international and supra-national organisations of which Italy is a member. These institutions lie at the core of the policy-making process which is itself 'the pivotal stage of the political process' (Almond and Bingham Powell, Jr, 1992: 91). Policy-making is 'the pivotal stage of the political process' in the sense that it is the link which connects the input of demands from political parties, pressure groups and so forth, to political outputs in the form of policies designed to respond to and to shape such demands. If policy-making is 'the pivotal stage of the political process', then government institutions 'lie at the core of' policy-making. They do so in the sense that in most societies they are the basic structures through which policy is made. In describing how these structures work and are related to each other, we shall highlight what is distinctive about them as compared to recognisably similar structures in other countries. Central to this will be the attempt to identify the actual as opposed to the formal locus (or loci) of power over policy-making in the Italian system. Before doing this, however, we begin by spelling out the basic features of the Italian Constitution; for if constitutions can be defined as sets of rules specifying how the political process is to be carried on, then they define what government structures exist in the first place.

The basic features of the Italian Constitution are described in the following section. The pressures for constitutional overhaul that came to a head in the 1990s are described in the section following. The penultimate section describes the attempts at reform that grew from these pressures and the perennial obstacles in the way of reform in Italy that caused the attempts to fail. In the light of this, the final section considers the future of the Italian Constitution.

The Constitution: fundamental characteristics

Constitutions establish the fundamental rules of the political game. They therefore tend to be drawn up in the immediate aftermath of major political upheavals such as wars or revolutions. The Italian Constitution is no exception. It was drawn up by the **Constituent Assembly** elected on 2 June 1946 (Box 2.1) and, though the enabling legislation necessary to give effect to several

---

Box 2.1

The Constituent Assembly

The Constituent Assembly met for the first time on 25 June 1946 in palazzo Montecitorio, the building that still hosts the Chamber of Deputies. Elected on the basis of proportional representation, the Assembly consisted of 552 members. Of these 207 were drawn from the Christian Democrats, 115 from the Socialists and 104 from the Communists, the remainder coming from a variety of smaller formations. Although its principal task was of course to draft the new constitution, it also elected Enrico de Nicola temporary head of state following the abolition of the monarchy resulting from the 2 June referendum outcome. It also had responsibility for approving budgetary laws and for ratifying international treaties. And although, in this transition period, legislative powers belonged to the Government, the latter had to retain the confidence of the Assembly. In practice, therefore, many of the most important of governments' legislative decisions at this time were subject to Assembly approval.

The task of actually preparing the new constitution was delegated to the so-called Commission of 75, which in turn subdivided the work among three smaller subcommittees to deal with 'citizens' rights and duties', 'the constitutional organisation of the State', and 'economic and social relations' presided over by a Christian Democrat, a Communist and a Socialist, respectively. The task of actually drafting the constitutional text was assigned to a fourth committee, the so-called Commission of 18, which co-ordinated and synthesised the work of the other three committees. With the draft thus prepared, 4 March 1947 saw the beginning of debate on the floor of the Assembly, which resulted in the document's final approval on 22 December. The contribution made by this document to national integration and the consolidation of democracy following the trauma of the Fascist experience is very difficult to overstate.

Figure 2.1. The Chamber of Deputies in the Palazzo di Montecitorio, showing: the semi-circular seating arrangements for the Chamber's members; the raised bench occupied by the Chamber's president, and the government benches immediately below (see Box 2.1)

of its provisions was delayed, it went into effect formally on 1 January 1948. Like other constitutions, the Italian Constitution speaks volumes to the historical conjuncture in which it was drafted. It does this in two main ways:

(1) by its inclusion of a wide range of economic and social rights;
(2) through the nature of its institutional arrangements.

Let us examine each of these in turn.

Economic and social rights

The Constituent Assembly's largest single component was the block composed of the Italian Socialist Party (PSI) and the Italian Communist Party (PCI). There had always been hopes, widespread among these parties' followers, that the anti-fascist struggle that had just been concluded would not limit itself to a re-establishment of the institutions of liberal democracy but would be extended to embrace the aim of social revolution as well. In order, perhaps, to draw the sting from these passions, members of the Constituent Assembly agreed to include in the Constitution, in addition to the traditional political freedoms (of speech, of assembly and so forth), an unusually large number of social and economic rights (outlined in part I of the Constitution entitled 'Citizens' Rights and Duties'). The effects of these have been the subject of extensive debate in the period since the Constitution's drafting.

The debate about the economic and social rights

This debate has revolved around the issue of the political significance to be attributed to these part I economic and social rights. On the one hand, their importance has been held to have been vitiated by at least three factors.

(1) A decision of the Court of Cassation in February 1948 to make a distinction between *norme precettizie* (preceptive rules) and *norme programmatiche* (programmatic rules). The consequence of this was to deprive the part I articles of impact. For the implication of the ruling was that they did not have direct effect. Therefore they could not be appealed to in order to annul legislation that apparently conflicted with them. In other words, they were merely a set of programmatic statements designed to guide future legislative action, not the basis for the judicial enforcement of rights (Newell, 2005).

(2) Though the Constitutional Court later overturned this judgement, it has been argued that some of the part I articles (such as article 9 which gives the state responsibility for promoting 'the development of culture and of scientific and technical research') are of a vagueness such that 'they are compatible with very different types of legislative backing' (Hine, 1993: 147).

(3) Others of the articles (such as article 46 which establishes a right of workers to participate in the management of their enterprises) specify that the rights in question are to be exercised 'in the manner and within the limits prescribed by law'. Again, therefore, they are compatible with a wide range of different *actual* states of affairs.

On the other hand, there are at least three factors arguing for a certain significance to be attributed to these articles.

(1) It was claimed at the time of the Constituent Assembly by the jurist Calamandrei that some articles risked undermining public confidence in future governments were they to be seen as failing to fulfil the obligations in question. A good example is article 32, which obliges the state to 'protect health as a fundamental right of the individual'. And Calamandrei's fear certainly found an echo in the results of later surveys revealing the considerable scepticism on the part of Italians concerning the general efficiency of their public institutions.

(2) However, it is possible to find plenty of examples of items of legislation that politicians have sought to justify as attempts to fulfil economic and social rights established by the Constitution. Therefore, these rights may in fact have inspired the legislation in question.

(3) As we shall see in chapters 6 and 9, like other established democracies, Italy has in recent years undergone a process that political scientists call 'the judicialisation of politics'. This means that courts and their judgements have become increasingly significant for processes of political decision-making. In Italy, this has been partly due to the part I provisions. They confer on the judiciary a de facto policy-making power, it is argued, since they are susceptible to a wide range of interpretations. This in turn means that judges are called upon, in the course of their activities, to formulate opinions about whether legislation is compatible with them and therefore whether the legislation itself is constitutionally valid.

The nature of the Constitution's institutional arrangements

The second way in which the Constitution reflects the circumstances in which it was drafted is that, in setting out the institutional geography of the republic, it reveals the anti-fascist concerns of its drafters. It does this through the limitations that it places on the possibilities of a centralised concentration of power. Two such limitations are especially important:

(1) The Constitution deliberately refrains from establishing any mechanisms that would allow the executive to protect itself against the erosion of its parliamentary majority (such as the German 'constructive vote of no-confidence', for example).
(2) The Constitution establishes a number of institutions designed to restrain the power of a cohesive parliamentary majority. Three such institutions stand out:
   i   the Constitutional Court: this exercises a restraining function in virtue of the fact that it is invested with the power to determine the constitutionality of ordinary legislation;
   ii sub-national units of government (more specifically, regions): these restrain by virtue of the fact that their existence is constitutionally guaranteed (and hence they cannot be abolished except by means of a change in the Constitution itself);
   iii **referenda** (Box 2.2): these counterbalance parliamentary majorities in virtue of the fact that, if invoked by the signatures of 500,000 electors or the request of five regional councils, they give the electorate the opportunity to repeal unwanted legislation.

Amending the Constitution

Besides reflecting the political breaks that are also, usually, responsible for them, constitutions typically have several further features in common. One is some provision for their amendment. Here, a distinction has grown up among students of such matters between 'flexible' constitutions, on the one hand, and 'rigid' constitutions on the other:

Box 2.2

Referenda in Italy

A referendum is a mechanism that allows voters to express opinions on specific issues, directly, without the intervention of intermediaries such as members of Parliament. It is therefore praised by some as being highly democratic, while others are sceptical. They say it makes it possible for the powerful to attain their goals more easily just by manipulating public opinion. The Italian Constitution takes a position some way between these two extremes in that it essentially provides for referenda of two types. One is the referendum that can be instigated by ordinary citizens, on a proposal to *abolish* a law or parts of a law *already* in force, if they can gather the support of half a million fellow citizens willing to put their signatures to a request for such a vote. The other is the referendum, instigated in a similar way, on *proposals* for constitutional change (unless these already have the approval of at least two-thirds of the members of Parliament): both mechanisms appear to be oriented more towards institutional conservation than towards legislative innovation.

Although there have been only two referenda of the second kind, there have been no fewer than fifty-nine of the first (abrogative) kind, making Italy the democracy that makes the most frequent use of the instrument after Switzerland. And despite the preoccupations of the constitutional founding fathers, abrogative referenda have been the drivers or concomitants, on at least two occasions, of very significant change in post-war Italy. The first was in 1974, with the referendum on the recently introduced legislation legalising divorce. This was in fact the very first of the abrogative referenda to be held and came about through an understanding among the parties in Parliament whereby the DC would not obstruct the legislation providing for divorce, in exchange for the enabling legislation that would allow the constitutional provision for abrogative referenda actually to be applied. The outcome was a sensational defeat for the proposal (that is, a vote in effect to *retain* divorce). The second was the set of referenda in 1993 on the electoral law and other matters, where in contrast, all the proposals in question received huge majorities in favour.

In recent years the institution of the abrogative referendum has lost a fair amount of its appeal owing to a whole series of votes, from 1997, all of which resulted in defeat for their instigators owing to their failure to bring to the polls the required minimum of 50 per cent of the electorate if the outcome was to be declared valid. This has led to the institution being attacked on two fronts. On the one hand there are those who take the large number of failed referenda as evidence that the institution is being (ab)used too readily and that access to it should be restricted (perhaps by raising the number of signatures required). On the other side are those who claim, on the contrary, that the relevant mechanisms are already loaded against those seeking change through the referendum since those opposed to change can win in two ways: either through a majority 'no' vote or else by encouraging a majority of the electorate to stay at home – as notoriously happened in 2005 with the referendum on artificial insemination and related matters.

(1) 'flexible' constitutions are those whose texts can be changed by means of the same procedures that are used for ordinary legislation (such would be the British case), while
(2) 'rigid' constitutions are those requiring some special procedure designed to make amendment relatively difficult.

Italy has a rigid constitution in this sense. In common with a number of other countries' constitutions, amendment requires a twice-recorded majority of the legislature. This can then be followed by a referendum if the majority is below a prescribed size. Specifically,

(1) proposed amendments must be passed by both chambers of Parliament at an interval of three months;
(2) on the second occasion, the majorities concerned must be of the chambers' members;
(3) less than two-thirds majorities on the second occasion will trigger a referendum if requested by a fifth of the members of either chamber, 500,000 electors or five regional councils (article 138).

Amendments have not often been made using these procedures[1] and referenda have at the time of writing only twice been used for this purpose.[2] However, this does not of course mean that the Constitution has remained substantially unchanged since 1948. Formal modifications to its text are only one way in which it may change. Another way is by means of variations in the way in which it is interpreted (in this case by the Constitutional Court). Yet a third way is by means of constitutional conventions. These, while not specified in the text of the Constitution itself, prescribe the way in which constitutionally conferred powers are to be exercised. For example, article 88 vests power to dissolve Parliament in the President of the Republic, and it has become a constitutional convention that presidents do all in their power to avoid premature dissolution. Vice versa, significant institutional change may take place even in the absence of constitutional change.

• The most obvious example concerns the 1993 and 2005 changes to the electoral law. The latter (discussed in chapter 7) in particular raised delicate political issues. The electoral system is not a constitutional matter, and therefore the governing majority was legally entitled to change the system by simple act of Parliament – as it did in 2005. However, it clearly did so in order to obtain a partisan advantage. In this it followed in the footsteps of the Acerbo Law, discussed in chapter 1, and the so-called swindle law of 1953.[3]
• Another example concerns processes of European integration. These, as we shall see in chapter 4, have led to significant changes in the way in which the cabinet and Parliament interact with each other. This is important since, as we shall see, the executive–legislature relationship lies at the heart of the most distinctive features of the policy-making process in Italy.

The division of political authority

A third feature that the Italian Constitution shares with the constitutions of most other liberal democracies is its tripartite division of political authority between executive, legislative and judicial agencies. As in other parliamentary regimes, so in Italy, the executive consists of a cabinet or Council of Ministers (*Consiglio dei Ministri*) which is responsible to the legislature and remains in office only as long as it enjoys the confidence of the latter. Unusually for a parliamentary regime, the cabinet in Italy must retain the confidence of both branches of the legislature (the Chamber of Deputies and the Senate); nor is there the usual constitutional requirement that ministers be members of Parliament. This fact has been of considerable importance since the 1992 elections. On the one hand, it has made a significant contribution to political stability. For example, it enabled President Scalfaro, in 1993 and again in 1995, to appoint governments led by 'technocrats' at moments when Parliament was unable to sustain in office governments led by party figures. On the other hand, the appointment to cabinet positions of outside experts has often been used by governments as a means of raising their authority. The most obvious examples here are the appointment of Renato Ruggiero to the post of Foreign Minister at the outset of the 2001 Berlusconi government (see chapter 10 for details) and, more recently, the appointment of the widely respected economist, Tommaso Padoa-Schioppa, to the position of Minister of the Economy and Finance in the centre-left government that took office in May 2006. This aside, the Italian executive shares most of the characteristic features of parliamentary executives elsewhere: ministers are individually and collectively responsible to Parliament and the executive is 'biscephalic' – in other words, there is a head of state (with the title of 'President' in the Italian case) in addition to the head of government (the Prime Minister).

The President of the Republic

The President is elected by an assembly that includes not only the members of the two branches of the legislature, but also three delegates from nineteen of the twenty regions and one from the Valle d'Aosta region. The rationale is to broaden, beyond Parliament, the base on which presidential legitimacy rests; for the incumbent is enjoined by the Constitution to represent, not just the state, but the entire nation. Election requires the support of two-thirds of the members of the assembly at the first three rounds of voting, a simple majority thereafter. The rationale is to ensure, as far as possible, that the winning candidate enjoys the support of forces extending beyond those of the government of the day. A government with a bare majority *can* elect a president on its own – but only if it is cohesive. In fact, high levels of fragmentation and majorities lacking in cohesion have nearly always rendered dialogue with non-governing forces essential in presidential elections. And, since a vote is cast simply by writing, in secret, the name of a person on a blank piece of paper (meaning that the choice of person for whom to vote is not in any way limited by any prior process of nomination of

Box 2.3

President of the Republic, Giorgio Napolitano

Italy's current President, Giorgio Napolitano, is a mild-mannered man who was born on 29 June 1925 and has the distinction – among others – of being the first former Communist to occupy the highest office of state. Prior to his election to the presidency, his most senior role had been as Interior Minister, a post he held between 1996 and 1998, again as the first former Communist to do so. Traditionally occupied by the Christian Democrats, the post carries responsibility for the police forces and other matters concerning domestic order, and so it would have been unthinkable for such a position to go to anyone with PCI connections prior to the collapse of the Berlin Wall. When it was eventually so assigned, the fact that it went to a man like Napolitano was revealing of his public profile. Gentlemanly and of the highest moral rectitude, Napolitano was best known for most of his political and parliamentary career (he served in ten legislatures following his election in 1953) for his position as leader of the *miglioristi* (literally, 'improvers', that is those within the PCI most closely wedded to the idea that the preferred path to the party's ultimate socialist goal was through the eschewal of revolution in favour of the gradual improvement of capitalism through reforms). All these qualities helped to increase the appeal of the nickname, 'the Red Prince' that was often applied to him because he was thought to look like Italy's last king. A well-respected intellectual who has given frequent lectures in the United States, Napolitano's other distinguished appointments include his period as president of the Chamber of Deputies, between 1992 and 1994, as member of the European Parliament between 1999 and 2004 and finally, in October 2005, a few months prior to his election as President, his nomination, by then President, Carlo Azeglio Ciampi, as a life senator.

candidates), the number of rounds of voting required has often been large.[4] The 2006 election of **Giorgio Napolitano** (Box 2.3) therefore represented something of an unusual case: his support was confined to the governing majority and his election came at the fourth round. Presidential terms last for seven years. The rationale is to free the incumbent from any form of dependence on those who elected him (presidents have all been men so far): since parliamentary terms cannot exceed five years, presidents can never be re-elected by the same assembly that elected them previously (Barbera and Fusaro, 2004: 266).

As in other parliamentary regimes, along with the usual ceremonial functions, the President is endowed with the power

- to appoint the Prime Minister and other members of the cabinet;
- to dissolve and convoke Parliament, and
- to promulgate laws.

Unlike the situation in most parliamentary systems, however, these powers are not circumscribed by constitutional provisions which make the cabinet in fact responsible for official acts of the President. The President's role therefore is by no means purely symbolic. Thanks to the lack of detailed specifications in the constitutional text, and to the great benefit of peaceful governance in Italy, the role is one whose significance varies depending on the specific circumstances.

With respect to the appointment of members of the executive, for example, when parties commanding a majority in Parliament have a clear preference, presidents have little choice in appointments bearing in mind that executives must retain the confidence of Parliament. On the other hand, when, as in the period between 1992 and 1996, the parties have lacked the authority to determine the composition of governments, presidential discretion has been greater. Effective governance actually *requires* presidential discretion in such circumstances. So it is not surprising that periodic attempts by the parties to reduce the presidential power to a mere formality have been consistently resisted. For example, drafters of the 2005 electoral law reform included the provision that party coalitions competing for government were required to nominate a leader. But they were careful to silence doubts about the constitutionality of their innovation by making the law state explicitly that 'presidential prerogatives [in the appointment of prime ministers] remain[ed] unaffected'.

Much the same can be said of the presidential power to dissolve Parliament. By common consent, the supreme function of the President is to mediate and regulate with the aim of ensuring that political processes are carried on without threatening national integration. (This means, incidentally, that the President's role is *not* simply juridical but also *political* in character.) Therefore, there is no question but that a president would be seen to be acting illegitimately were s/he to try to dissolve a parliament against the wishes of a government whose ability to command a majority was not in doubt. This does *not* mean, however, that actual power regarding dissolution has passed to the Prime Minister, as in the British case. That this has not happened was made very clear after the first Berlusconi government fell at the end of 1994. Then, the entrepreneur tried, unsuccessfully, to argue that he had received a 'Westminster-style' mandate that had not been respected by one of his coalition partners, and that therefore it should pass back to the electorate for re-conferral through fresh elections.[5]

Finally, the power to promulgate laws has a clear and obvious link with the President's supreme function; for it entails the power to refer proposed legislation back to Parliament for reconsideration (after which the President must pass it). And again, its significance varies. It gives the President a *suspensive* not an *absolute* veto. Precisely for this reason its impact must depend on the political circumstances in which it is exercised. There is more than one example of a government having concluded that though legally *possible*, defying the presidential veto was not politically *expedient*.[6] The recent shift to bipolarity in the party system has seen an increasing tendency for oppositions to try to 'co-opt' the President. In other words, they have tried to oblige him to act as a sort of protector of minority interests by calling on him to exercise the veto when faced with legislation they do not like. But clearly, as Fusaro (2003: 90) points out, presidents must be careful: referring back a law strongly desired by a government backed by a large majority might conceivably have no other effect than to undermine the authority of the presidency itself.

The legislature

Turning, then, to the legislature, this is bicameral – but it is also 'perfectly bicameral'. This means that each branch has legislative powers identical to those of the other branch. In this, Italy's parliamentary arrangements are highly unusual, and it is often claimed that their only effect is to make the legislative process lengthier and more cumbersome than it would otherwise be. In fact this is not their only effect: it could, indeed, be argued that they actually make legislating *more* efficient – certainly than it would be, were there only a single chamber. In that case only one bill could be considered at a time. Two chambers make it possible to consider two bills at the same time. They also have an obvious impact on the electoral system: identical authority and tasks means that the 630 members of the Chamber and the 315 members of the Senate have to be elected in accordance with very similar electoral laws for each house. Electoral laws that diverged too radically might result in houses with very different political complexions. This almost happened in 2006 when, as discussed in chapter 7, the centre left that emerged victorious in the April election had a narrow majority of votes and a comfortable majority of seats in the Chamber but was behind in terms of votes and had a very small majority of seats in the Senate. Contrasting majorities between the chambers would have serious consequences for the possibility of stable and effective governance. Theoretically, such contrasting majorities could come about even if the electoral systems for the two branches of the legislature were identical; for the Constitution (in article 58) restricts elections to the Senate to those aged twenty-five and over (the voting age for the Chamber is eighteen). It also stipulates (in article 59) that, besides being themselves entitled at the end of their terms to a senatorial seat for life, presidents have the right to nominate five life senators. These are to be nominated from among individuals who have distinguished themselves in the 'social, scientific, artistic and literary fields' (Box 2.4). Once of little practical political importance, this is another constitutional provision whose significance has changed with the shift to bipolarity in the party system. It was only thanks to the support of life senators that the 1994 Berlusconi government was able to obtain the confidence of the 'upper house', and the matter became unexpectedly delicate with the outcome of the 2006 election. The issue was this: prior to the presidency of Sandro Pertini (1978–1985), article 59 was interpreted to mean that the Senate could include a *total* of five 'presidentially nominated' life senators, while Pertini and his successor, Francesco Cossiga (1985–1992), interpreted it to mean that *each* president was entitled to nominate five. Carlo Azeglio Ciampi (1999–2006) also nominated five. Had Giorgio Napolitano decided to make nominations within the life of the parliament elected in 2006, then his choice(s) would have had a not insignificant impact on the stability of the Government. This is

Box 2.4

Italy's life senators

Besides the three former presidents, Francesco Cossiga, Oscar Luigi Scalfaro and Carlo Azeglio Ciampi, Italy's life senators currently include the former Christian Democratic politicians Giulio Andreotti and Emilio Colombo; the industrialist Sergio Pininfarina; and the neurobiologist Rita Levi-Montalcini. All are very senior figures in public life, as one would expect, with distinguished and extremely lengthy careers behind them. This is most concisely illustrated, perhaps, by the fact that of the seven, the youngest, Francesco Cossiga, is nevertheless eighty – while the most elderly is Nobel Prize-winner, Rita Levi Montalcini, who was born in 1909. Despite their advanced years and the limited political weight they can have as a group under normal circumstances, they retain, because of their status, a capacity to attract media attention far beyond that of the ordinary elected senator. Through their continued activity in public life, all have therefore been at the centre of high-profile stories of one kind or another in the recent past. Levi-Montalcini, for example, gained attention for her public refusal, on grounds of a conflict of interests, to vote on a Northern League-sponsored amendment to the 2008 Finance Bill. The amendment would have eliminated from the Bill the assignment of money to the European Brain Research Institute, of which Levi-Montalcini had been founder. Perhaps the most media savvy of the seven is Giulio Andreotti, well known for his dry sense of humour and his witty aphorisms, such as, 'To think ill of someone is to commit a sin, but it is to hit the nail on the head most of the time.'

because the Government had a majority of just two in the Senate. Even if they had had no party connections, anyone nominated by Napolitano would have influenced the stability of the Government, simply because they would have had to make decisions about how to vote in Senate debates. Finally, the Constitution seeks to prevent legislators from becoming errand boys for special or parochial interests by admonishing them to represent the nation as a whole and to perform their tasks 'without the ties of a mandate' (article 67); and, more practically, by stipulating that 'no new taxes or expenditures can be established by the law approving the budget' (article 81).

The judiciary

The judicial agency, like its counterpart in other liberal democracies, is intended by the Constitution to be independent of the other two agencies. This means that its authority is not subject to the authority of the other two, and that its members are not responsible to any or all of the members of the other two. Thus is it intended, in time-honoured fashion, that the individual be afforded a measure of protection against arbitrary action on the part of state officials and on the part of the state as a whole. Further protection against arbitrary action by the state as a whole is sought by means of the power vested in the Constitutional Court to pronounce definitively on the constitutionality of legislation. The independence of the judiciary is sought by means of a free-standing Consiglio superiore della magistratura (High Council of the Judiciary, CSM) having (almost) sole discretion in the appointment and dismissal of judicial personnel. It has consisted of twenty-four members since March 2002 (when law no. 44/02 brought the number down from thirty). Sixteen are elected by the judiciary from among members of the various branches of the judiciary itself; eight are chosen by Parliament, which must make its selection from among members of the academic law community and practising lawyers. In deference to the head of state's role of overseer of 'fair play' throughout the polity and its main branches, the CSM is presided over by the President of the Republic. Finally, the citizen is afforded a measure of protection against arbitrary action by the judiciary itself in the form of article 111 of the Constitution. This enshrines the right of the citizen to appeal sentences to the Court of Cassation (the highest appeal court for the ordinary judicial system) 'on grounds of violation of the law'; and, as discussed in chapter 9, was in 1999 reinforced in terms of the rights for defendants that its provisions seek to provide.

The geographical distribution of authority

A fourth, and final, dimension in terms of which the Italian Constitution may be compared with constitutions elsewhere is in terms of how it distributes authority geographically. Here a distinction is commonly drawn between '**federal** states' and 'unitary states' (Box 2.5). In the former the powers and the existence of the sub-national units of government are constitutionally safeguarded, while in the latter there are no such formal safeguards. In federal states, sovereignty is divided between national and sub-national government structures, each having exclusive powers within constitutionally stipulated areas of policy. In principle, it is possible for the 'powers' and 'existence' dimensions to vary independently. That is, the existence of sub-national units of government might be guaranteed while their powers are not – though clearly, a constitution with these features would not be one enshrining a decentralisation of any real substance. Still, falling in between the federal and unitary types are hybrid constitutions which have precisely this character-istic: that while they safeguard the existence of the sub-national units, they do not enshrine any specific division of authority between the central authorities and sub-national units.

Prior to the reform of title V, in 2001, the Italian Constitution was of just such a hybrid type. Articles 114, 115 and 131 stipulated a division of the country into given regions (of which there are twenty) and these into prov-inces, which are in their turn divided into communes. The regions were given 'their own powers' (article 115) and the authority to legislate in specified policy areas (article 117). Nevertheless, the Constitution also specified that such

> **Box 2.5**
>
> *Key terms: federalism*
> A system of government in which power is constitutionally divided between a central governing authority, on the one hand, and 'sub-central' authorities on the other, with each authority having sovereignty within its constitutionally prescribed area of competence. Since central and sub-central authorities alike owe their sovereign powers to a constitution to which they are equally subject, genuinely federal regimes require that proposals for constitutional change should have the assent of representatives of *both* levels if they are to come into effect. The Italian political system does not incorporate such a requirement and so cannot be regarded as genuinely federal in that sense. It is, perhaps, unlikely, too, that it will acquire such a characteristic any time soon, for the reasons that political scientist Gianfranco Pasquino (2000: 93–8) explains. For one thing, federalism requires convinced federalists, and these are currently few and far between. Public political debate in Italy often gives the impression that 'we are all federalists now'. However, this is only because the term is used in such debate to mean nothing more precise than more power and autonomy for the regions. Such imprecision derives from the Northern League itself whose central concern has in fact far less to do with a federal recasting of the Italian state as a whole, than with advancing the autonomy of just one part: the North. Second, therefore, genuine federalism, to be achieved, would require the emergence of demands from below, for the transfer of sovereign powers to some set of viable sub-national tiers of government – an unlikely prospect given the rivalries and conflicting interests among Italy's economically and politically very diverse regions. Alternatively, it might in theory, perhaps, be imposed from above. But if imposed from above, it is difficult to envisage it being genuinely federal.

legislative powers were to be exercised 'within the framework of the basic principles established by the laws of the State' (article 117). Moreover, article 127 made it possible for governments to challenge regional legislation on grounds of constitutionality (in which case the matter would be decided by the Constitutional Court) and on grounds of merit (in which case the matter would be decided by Parliament). In short, the powers of the regions were **concurrent** not **exclusive** (Box 2.6). The 2001 reform appeared to represent a radical change in this respect; for it introduced the novel principle that 'the regions have legislative powers in all areas not expressly reserved to the state' (article 117). It did not, however, render the state fully federal; for federalism implies not only a bipartite division of (exclusive) legislative powers, but also a situation of dual **sovereignty** (Box 2.6). This can only exist where constitutional change requires the assent of *both* the national *and* sub-national levels. (This is the reason that, in contrast to the Italian case, genuinely federal systems such as exists in the United States tend to provide for one of the two chambers of the

Box 2.6

Key terms: concurrent powers, exclusive powers, sovereignty, majoritarian democracy

Concurrent powers: powers, held by two or more tiers of government, which may be exercised simultaneously within the same territory in relation to the same body of citizens. Where the exercise of such powers results in conflicting or contradictory legislation, decisions have to be made as to which is to prevail. In Italy, such decisions are made by the Constitutional Court in light of the implications of the case in question for adherence to the principles of the Constitution generally.

Exclusive powers: powers held by one tier of government that are expressly denied to other tiers. In Italy, as in most liberal democracies, the central tier has exclusive competence in such areas as the state's foreign policy, control of the armed forces, immigration, the conferral of citizenship.

Sovereignty: the legal right and the actual capacity to make final decisions in the public sphere. The decisions are 'final' in the sense that they cannot be overruled by a higher authority. Two types of sovereignty are generally distinguished: internal and external sovereignty. The former refers to the issue of supremacy within a given territory – states being said to be sovereign in this sense when all other bodies within the territory have a freedom of action that is defined and circumscribed by the constitution of the state. It follows from this that the act of any entity retains a claim to legal validity only as long as it is not inconsistent with a law of higher legal standing, which, in the event of a conflict, always prevails. Thus the Constitution and constitutional law trump ordinary legislation, which trumps the regulations of local authorities and so on. 'External sovereignty' refers to the recognition, in international relations, of a state's independence and thus of its right to exercise sovereign power over its territory.

Majoritarian democracy: a political system in which, through free competition, majorities are able to acquire temporary monopolies on decision-making power. In parliamentary regimes, majoritarian democracy implies that an absolute majority of seats in the legislature is assigned to the party or group of parties receiving the largest number of votes in the country and thus that the composition of the executive reflects the votes cast by a relative majority of electors. The UK is therefore the classic example of a majoritarian democracy in that sense. Such democracies are usually contrasted with 'consensus' democracies where decision-making power is never monopolised by one party or party group but is shared. Therefore, in parliamentary regimes seats in the legislature are distributed proportionally and executives are grand coalitions reflecting the distribution of popular votes cast among the parties.

legislature to be representative of the sub-national levels and to have the same powers in constitutional matters as the other chamber.)

More will be said about sub-national government in the following chapter, for clearly, identifying the actual division of power and authority between centre and localities requires taking into account a wide range of factors in addition to what is specified in the Constitution. For the time being, let us note that the territorial division of authority in Italy once more throws a spotlight on the earlier point that constitutional provisions reflect the historical conjuncture in which they were born. This is because the quasi-federal characteristics of the Italian Constitution were originally due to the fear, on the part of the Christian Democrats (DC) and their allies, of the parties of the left with their perceived dedication to a nationalised economy under central control.

Ironically, once it became clear, shortly after the Constitution came into force, that the nature of the post-war party system would be such as to ensure the permanent exclusion from government of the PCI (and the concomitant permanence in office of the DC), the positions were reversed. That is, the constitutional provision for a reasonably robust tier of regional government rapidly lost its initial political *raison d'être* as far as the DC and its allies were concerned. Meanwhile, the PCI sought to compensate for its exclusion from government at national level by means of exemplary efforts to demonstrate its governing competence in those local administrations it was able to win control of. Among the towns and cities it governed in the central, 'red-belt' regions of Emilia-Romagna, Tuscany, Umbria and Marche, for example, the city of Bologna became a widely discussed model of what effective and innovative Communist government could achieve at sub-national level. As a result, from a position of opposition to a strong system of regional government, the PCI soon swung, instead, to a position of support for it. However, it was excluded from government at national level, and partly because of this the legislation necessary to give life to the regional structures provided for in the Constitution was delayed. In fact, it was not until 1970 that this legislation was passed.

▨ The pressure for constitutional reform

The geographical distribution of authority specified by the Constitution was the target of growing criticism from the late 1980s, and this contributed to putting 'root-and-branch' revision of the Constitution as a whole high on the agenda of Italian politics.

For the first two decades of its existence, however, the most prominent concerns were not with the Constitution's *modification* but with its *implementation*. That is, the concern was with the apparent unwillingness in some quarters to give effect to the Constitution's most important provisions through passage of the necessary enabling legislation. The regions were not the only structures that were delayed. Thus, it was not until 1956 that the Constitutional Court and not until 1958 that the CSM came into existence. Both bodies were long resisted by an alliance of conservative governments and senior members of the judiciary. The latter, in particular feared that these bodies would undermine their ability (a) to control the activities of junior judges and (b) to continue to apply Fascist legislation at odds with the principles set out in part I of the Constitution.[7] It was not until 1970 that provisions were made enabling the holding of the abrogative referenda mentioned above – and thus not until 1974 that the referendum concerning the legalisation of divorce in Italy could be held. And so the examples could be multiplied. Each contributed to the view that the Constitution was for a long time like an appendix to a book written in another language. In particular, those attached to the Constitution's anti-fascist and more innovative principles, felt that it was a document setting out a series of hopes rather than a set of principles informing actual conduct in more than a few areas of political and social life.

Demands for modification of the constitutional framework came later, growing in the 1980s to reach a crescendo in the following decade. Now, a range of dissatisfactions and trends came together to feed the idea that the entire constitutional framework needed superseding in a radical break with the past. The dissatisfactions and trends were many, their interactions complex, but four can be identified as having been especially significant.

Public dissatisfaction

From round about the mid-1970s, there were growing levels of general public dissatisfaction, with the speed and incisiveness of public policy-making. The dissatisfaction was connected to the political and social developments discussed in the last chapter, and it served to sustain, in the 1980s, growing calls for change to the 'form of government'. This is a technical term referring to the way in which political power is distributed among the various branches of the state, and it recalls the standard distinctions between presidential, semi-presidential and parliamentary forms. The loudest calls at this time came from the PSI, under its abrasive leader Bettino Craxi. His principal, and not more precisely specified, demand was that the President should be directly elected. It was a demand that chimed with the mood of the time. As Marco Tarchi (2003: 118) notes, the 1980s saw (a) a retreat from the political activism of the 1970s (manifested by, for example, the students' protests in Italy and elsewhere); (b) the resumption of high rates of economic growth; and (c) the emergence of the yuppie phenomenon. Increasingly significant, therefore, were values that (a) were impatient with the lengthy negotiations that seemed to precede every political decision of any importance; (b) extolled creativity and individualism; and (c) wanted rapid and efficient decision-making. A directly elected president, freed from the arcane procedures of parliamentary forms of government, who would be re-elected or not on the basis of an ability to get things done, seemed to respond to this mood.

As Onida (2004: 124) notes, it is difficult to escape the impression that demands for constitutional change in recent years have often been driven by sheerly instrumental concerns; for they have been at their loudest when parties have found themselves short of substantive ideas or unable to implement the ideas they do have. And in fact, the PSI's demand was consistent with the strategy it was trying to pursue in order to find a way out of the impasse it had reached. Able to escape subordination to the PCI only at the cost of subordination to the DC and vice versa, it had in the early 1960s chosen the latter. Having succeeded in becoming, in the following decade, numerically indispensable in coalition formation, it had, however, found itself unable to resist the slide towards becoming a party of office-holders and electoral opportunists, with few distinct ideals to pursue. Desperate to distinguish his party from his larger coalition partner, Craxi advanced the demand for direct election of the President as part-and-parcel of the reputation for decisiveness which he sought, with only partial success, to create for his party as Prime Minister from 1983. He also championed electoral reform of a kind that he hoped would have the effect of marginalising the PCI and allowing him to head a non-communist alternative to the DC.

The emergence and growth of the Northern League

The influence of the Northern League (LN) in the electoral and parliamentary arenas after 1992 was such that its demand for decentralising reform (or 'federalism', variously understood) rapidly ceased to be a position issue (that is, one on which parties take different positions) becoming instead a valence issue (one on which parties take the same position while claiming to have the best ideas about how to achieve it). It is this, ultimately, that explains the above-mentioned 2001 reform of title V. This is the single most wide-ranging constitutional reform to date. The reform was pursued in Parliament in 2000 and early 2001 by the then centre-left majority which was apparently driven to it, as Anna Cento Bull explains, by 'pressure from political events (such as the electoral success of the right in the April 2000 regional elections) and from public opinion in the North, including some of [its] own supporters and representatives'.

> By 2001 it had become almost impossible for political parties in Italy to reject the idea of federalism, given the high level of popular support it enjoyed, especially, but not exclusively, in the North, as various opinion polls consistently indicated. In addition, a constitutional law passed in November 1999 to strengthen the role of regional governments had greatly increased the visibility and political standing of regional presidents, many of whom, particularly those belonging to the centre-right coalition, used their enhanced role to keep up the pressure for a federalist reform of the state. In the light of the forthcoming May 2001 general elections, whose outcome was widely believed to be determined by the behaviour of the northern electorate, it was vital for the centre-left coalition not to hand federalism on a plate to its political opponents. There was also, presumably, a desire to make it difficult for the centre-right to introduce a radical version of federalism in case they formed a government.
>
> *(Cento Bull, 2002: 6)*

The notion of regime transition

Academics and other opinion leaders concluded that the political upheavals after the collapse of the Berlin Wall bore witness to the fact that Italy was undergoing a regime transition. By definition, this implied that the political system was passing through an interval of time separating one regime from another where a 'regime' consists of the rules, norms and procedures that govern the selection of the authorities and the functioning of political institutions, and that define the boundaries of the political community (Pasquino, 2000: 202). It was rarely made very clear on what *grounds* one was required to believe that a transition in this sense was actually under way; nevertheless, to the extent that this was believed to be the case and to the extent that the legal framework of a polity's regime is given by its constitution, it was quite naturally felt that a successful conclusion to the transition made the pursuit of constitutional overhaul essential.

The 1994 election and its aftermath

The circumstances associated with the 1994 election and its aftermath gave rise to pressures for constitutional overhaul from within all of the principal political parties. In the first place, the elections were fought in a context in which the demise of the traditional governing parties meant that the themes of 'novelty', renewal and freedom from connections with the past seemed likely to bring significant electoral gains. In these circumstances, the parties had a clear incentive to brandish institutional and constitutional reform as a means of associating these themes with themselves in the voters' minds (Newell, 2000: 137). In the second place, if, as Pasquino pointed out, 'institutional and constitutional reform [had] been discussed intensely for more than ten years' (1997: 35), 'then there was a general presumption that the demise of the parties whose mutual vetoes had paralysed reform for so long meant that early institutional changes aimed at removing the perceived deficits of responsiveness and accountability in Italian democracy could, and would, be enacted' (Newell, 2000: 137). In the third place, as we saw in the last chapter, the 1993 electoral law was itself expected to usher in a profound change in the system of governance by forcing parties to form electoral coalitions able to compete for overall majorities in Parliament. By this means it was expected, or at least hoped, that the new law would bring with it a shift from a system of governance based on unstable coalitions constructed through post-electoral negotiations to a new system providing greater stability, responsiveness and popular accountability. The 1994 election did produce electoral coalitions of sorts – but it in fact failed to give voters the opportunity to vote for or against the entire coalition of parties that subsequently went on to take office, so that the incoming centre-right government could not really claim to have received a direct popular mandate. Second, it was a litigious government whose life was rather shorter than the 300-day average for post-war Italy. Third, its fall forced the effective suspension of party government; for the President did not feel that he could sanction the formation of an alternative government majority made up of the LN, plus the centre-left coalition that had clearly *lost* the election. Italy was therefore forced to make do with a period of technocratic government. For these reasons, constitutional reform now came to be regarded as an absolute priority, a means of compensating for the apparent failure of the new electoral law to live up to the hopes placed in it. Early 1997 therefore saw the appointment of a parliamentary commission for Constitutional Reform – the third of its kind since 1983[8] – whose task would be to produce proposals for the reform of part II of the Constitution which sets out the institutional arrangements of the Republic.

The obstacles in the way of constitutional reform
The main issues underlying the commission's work were fourfold:

(1) how to devise a set of reforms that would, in accordance with the classic models of '**majoritarian**' or 'Westminster' **democracy** (Box 2.6), increase government stability, reinforce the authority of the Prime Minister, and allow executives to exercise greater control over the work of Parliament;
(2) how to devise a set of reforms that would re-cast the geographical distribution of power and authority in a federalist mould;
(3) how to reform the legislature (an issue that followed logically from the first two): if majoritarian democracy were genuinely to be achieved, then the executive had to be made to depend for its survival on the confidence of a single chamber rather than two; and such chamber had to have more legislative power than the second. If federalism were genuinely to be achieved, then the second chamber had to become a body providing representation for the regions and/or other sub-national levels of government;
(4) how to reform the system of justice. This issue had arisen because of controversies surrounding the ways in which public prosecutors had conducted the investigations into the *Tangentopoli* corruption investigations. It centred around the claim that Italy's judicial arrangements (described in more detail in chapter 9) left politicians vulnerable to unjustified persecution by judicial investigators motivated more by political concerns than by a concern to uphold the law. This was a claim that was pursued with particular vigour by Silvio Berlusconi who was under investigation on a variety of charges ranging from bribery, tax fraud and false accounting. His claim was that left-wing judicial investigators were (ab)using their positions to try to undermine him politically.

Few would want to argue that the proposals eventually produced by the commission excelled in terms of clarity and coherence. True, a number of proposals designed to reinforce majoritarian tendencies in the political system were made. Thus, there would be a directly elected president who would nominate the Prime Minister 'taking account of the election results'. The president would have an explicitly stated power to dissolve Parliament in the event of a government resignation arising either from a successful no-confidence motion or for any other reason. These arrangements were put forward together with proposals for further reform of the electoral law designed to consolidate party-system bipolarity. They seemed significant because if the president belonged to a party opposed to those in government, then his power to dissolve Parliament would create pressure on the governing majority to remain united in order to avoid such a threat. Meanwhile, if he belonged to the same coalition as the one staffing the Government, then the latter would be able to dominate Parliament's legislative agenda by using the threat of resignation to keep its followers in line.

The remaining proposals, however, were clearly the fruit of a compromise arising from the need to accommodate a range of competing views and interests. As a consequence they lacked incisiveness. The proposals regarding the Senate were, it is true, consistent with the aim of achieving arrangements embodying a majoritarian model of democracy: governments were to be freed of the requirement to retain the confidence of the Senate. This, except in certain specified areas such as constitutional matters, would lose its equality with the Chamber, retaining only a delaying power. However, the federalist requirement that the Senate be made representative of sub-national levels of government was not effectively addressed. Owing to the resistance of senators then in office, there was to be no fundamental change to the basis on which the body was elected. It was stipulated merely that when legislative proposals in areas such as local finance had to be considered, the 200 senators would be joined in 'special sessions' by an equal number of indirectly elected local, provincial and regional councillors.

Third, at least some of the proposals concerning the system of justice were of doubtful legitimacy. A good example was the proposal establishing the principle that 'A person who has committed an act which is defined in law (*previsto*) as an offence shall not be punished if the act has not resulted in concrete injury.' Such a principle might be considered particularly helpful to politicians facing charges of corruption – which is typically a crime without easily identifiable 'victims'. However, it was a principle allowing subjective judgements about the *consequences* of crimes, rather than the duly proved guilt or otherwise of their perpetrators, to be the ultimate determinant of the application of punishment. Such a principle was arguably undesirable in a society in which public trust in the even-handedness of the state and its laws was already very low.

Finally, the constitutional reform project ground to a halt when in June 1998 Silvio Berlusconi announced that his party would no longer support the commission's work. In the process he illustrated some of the very real obstacles in the way of constitutional revision under any historical circumstances in a country like Italy. These obstacles can be seen as threefold.

(1) Formal constitutional amendments normally require the backing of substantial majorities of legislators from across the political spectrum. In part this requirement arises from procedural considerations. Thus, as we have seen, constitutional amendments in Italy can be challenged by referendum unless they have the backing of two-thirds of both chambers of Parliament. But the requirement for substantial majorities also arises

from the fact that constitutional provisions must have support that is of a certain minimum degree of political breadth if they are to carry the authority necessary in order for them to survive.

(2) Substantial majorities have in any case been difficult to construct in Italy owing to the fragmentation of its party system. A large number of parties has meant a correspondingly large number of interests that have to be reconciled. ←

(3) Unfortunately the reconciliation of interests is especially difficult in the case of constitutional reform proposals. This is because they are typically 'zero sum' – that is, the advantages they confer on one party are ineluctably and immediately lost by another – rather than 'positive sum', allowing both parties to gain. For example, the Italian People's Party (PPI), a small centre party, was far less enthusiastic about the commission's search for majoritarian political arrangements than were the National Alliance (AN) on the right and the Left Democrats, (DS) on the left. Their interests were best served by attempts to preserve proportional principles as these tend to enhance the power of centre-placed parties which are thereby enabled to play a pivotal role, holding the balance of power between left and right. Both AN and the DS, on the other hand, had a strong interest in majoritarian arrangements as these would consolidate party-system bipolarity thereby diminishing the chances of the resurrection of the permanent exclusion from government to which they had been subject during the first fifty years of the post-war Republic's life.

The collapse of the commission reflected all three of these obstacles:

(1) The reason why the withdrawal of Berlusconi effectively brought the constitutional reform process grinding to a halt is because it was difficult to think that, without the support of the principle party of the centre right, the requirement for large majorities, could be achieved. The constitutional law establishing the parliamentary commission stipulated that its proposals, once passed by Parliament, would be subject to popular approval in a referendum. Berlusconi's withdrawal from the commission brought with it the withdrawal of his principal ally, AN.[9] With the likelihood that the two major opposition parties would thus be opposed to the commission's proposals in any referendum, it was difficult to see how, if they became law, the proposals would subsequently survive, even assuming the success of the referendum in the first place.

(2) Berlusconi was apparently interested in the work of the commission only in so far as it might produce reform of the judicial system of a kind such as to help him solve his personal legal difficulties. He thus withdrew when it became clear that this would not be forthcoming. The president of the commission, Massimo D'Alema (whose party, the DS, was then in government), was apparently willing to make concessions for the sake of the achievement of reform; however, in doing so he had to bear in mind the possible consequences for a government that depended on the goodwill of

a large number of parties each having considerable blackmail power owing to the slimness of the government's majority.

(3) To the extent that the reforms D'Alema got in exchange for concessions on justice might be of a majoritarian character, they would, as we have seen, have zero-sum implications for the distribution of power between parties. Therefore they would be in danger of failing to achieve the required broad majorities in the first place.

The failure of the commission, like the two that preceded it, revealed that attempts to achieve constitutional reform in Italy have hitherto always been subject to the reform paradox. This is the paradox that those actors whose support is most needed in order to achieve reform (the political parties) are precisely the actors least likely to be able to deliver it since it is they whose interests are most at stake. Awareness of this has led, in relation to several issues in recent years, to attempts to break out of the vicious circle by having recourse to the alternative road to reform provided by the possibility of holding abrogative referenda. In relation to efforts to achieve constitutional overhaul, the period after the commission's failure saw two attempts to achieve reform through abrogative referenda. These can be invoked only to strike down existing laws, not to consider proposals that have not already been passed by Parliament. However, following the 1974 divorce referendum (the first time the referendum instrument was used), it soon became apparent that, depending on *how* and on *what* questions were framed, popular initiatives could take on a quasi-propositional character. Partly because of this, it was recognised that the accepted political significance of referenda might not infrequently be far greater than the referenda questions *formally* considered. The 1993 electoral law referendum had had precisely these characteristics; for it was widely understood that the political significance of the vote in favour of electoral-law change was a vote of no confidence in the political class and in favour of an overhaul of the political system as a whole.

One immediate consequence of the failure of the parliamentary commission, therefore, was the revival of attempts to achieve reform by means of this alternative road. Thus, in both 1999 and 2000 there were referenda designed to abolish the remaining proportional features of the electoral system. As in the case of the 1993 consultation, it was felt that a referendum success would push the political system decisively in the direction of majoritarian democracy. First, in light of the commission's own failure to achieve reform, a referendum would, like the 1993 referendum, serve as a demonstration of public hostility to the apparent continuity of government 'of the parties for the parties' (Donovan, 2000: 74). Second, though not a constitutional issue in the legal sense of the term, electoral-law reform would, because of its real political effects, result in significant change in the so-called '*costituzione materiale*' (the constitution as interpreted and applied). However, following the disappointing results of the 1993 reform and then the failure of the parliamentary commission, an ingredient crucial to the success of the earlier referendum was now missing. This ingredient was a widespread conviction that real change could actually be had by this means. Consequently, both the 1999 and the 2000 referenda came to nothing for both failed to stimulate the participation of the minimum 50 per cent of the electorate that is required if referenda outcomes are to be recognised as legally valid.

Since then, there has been one further attempt at major constitutional overhaul. This was the attempt that came when, in 2005, the Berlusconi government obtained parliamentary approval for a far-reaching proposal touching on almost all aspects of part II of the Constitution. This differed from previous attempts in that it turned its back on the notion that reform had to have backing from across the political spectrum. It sought, instead, to follow the precedent set by the previous centre-left government when it reformed title V, of pursuing change unilaterally. Since the proposal was opposed by the centre left, it failed to pass with the support of two-thirds of Parliament's members. This made it possible to insist that the proposal be subject to the referendum provided for by the Constitution's article 138. The referendum was held on 25 and 26 June 2006. On a turnout of 53.6 per cent, it resulted in the proposal being rejected by 61.3 to 38.7 per cent.

▪ The future of constitutional reform

How are we to interpret the attempts at constitutional transformation that have been made in recent years? First, the June 2006 referendum could be interpreted as implying that the electorate had decisively turned its back on the idea of establishing any radically new institutional framework for the Republic in the immediate term. The referendum had, after all stimulated the participation of a clear majority of the electorate (something that had not happened in a referendum for eleven years), and it had produced an unambiguous outcome. The parliamentary commission for constitutional reform began its work almost five years after the 1992 election had revealed the first major cracks in the old 'regime'. Already, therefore, much of the enthusiasm for large-scale reform had passed its peak. Opinion polls regularly indicated very low levels of awareness of, and even lower levels of concern for, the commission's activities. 'Partly because of this there was an absence of any really deeply held vision – either within or common to the parties – of the essential nature of the polity the reforms ought to be designed to achieve' (Newell, 2000: 140). In turn, this ensured that debates over constitutional overhaul became 'progressively reduced to a technical question' (Follini, 1997: 681). It ensured, too, that reforms could never be pursued for reasons other than expediency. For example, Berlusconi's lack of real interest in reform, unless for specific partisan advantage, is notorious. The LN insisted on wide-ranging reform after 2001, opposing the centre left's reform of title V (which it dubbed as a 'minifederalism of the left') – even though a number of observers (Cento Bull, 2002; Luciani, 2002; Parker and McDonnell, 2003) expressed doubts about how much the centre right's proposals really added to the degree of sub-national autonomy that the centre left's reform had granted already. As the proposals were making their way through Parliament, the centre left opposed provisions that they had supported at the time of the earlier parliamentary commission (Vassallo, 2005). For both of these reasons – the lack of popular support and the instrumental approach politicians have taken to them – reform proposals have never really been able to build up significant quantities of political energy behind them. This makes it reasonable to ask about the sense in which the Italian polity is still undergoing a 'regime transition' – in the sense of passage from one constitutional set-up to another – if ever it really was so. If transition implies a lack of consensus in favour of the existing 'rules of the game', it surely also implies support for an alternative set of rules on the part of a group of actors at least potentially capable of bringing it into existence and making it stick.

Such a group does not appear to exist in Italy today – though it did appear to exist for a very brief period following the general election of 2008 (see chapter 7). The consequence of the vote was to reduce considerably party-system fragmentation – at least in Parliament. There, just two groups – the People of Freedom (PdL) led by Silvio Berlusconi, and the Democratic Party (PD), led by Walter Veltroni, commanded 78 per cent of the seats between them. Both leaders had a specific interest in constitutional overhaul. As far as Veltroni was concerned, perceptions of the need for a revolution in the mode of functioning of the party and political systems lay at the very heart of what, in 2007, had driven the emergence of his party in the first place.[10] As far as Berlusconi is concerned, he, as we have suggested, has something of a reputation for being rather indifferent to institutional questions.[11] However, now seventy-two, he is reputed to want to crown his career at the end of his current term as Prime Minister with election to the presidency. Successful reform arguably offered the opportunity of a place in Italian political history as one of the fathers, along with Veltroni, of a new constitutional settlement. This would indirectly strengthen Berlusconi's candidature for the presidency.

It was not surprising, then, that in the immediate aftermath of the 2008 election, the Prime Minister and leader of the opposition seemed intent on a regular set of meetings with a view to finding mutually acceptable institutional reforms that they might then be able to pass by virtue of the combined proportion of parliamentary seats they controlled. In subsequent months, however, the likelihood of this coming to pass faded; for the conflict of interests involved in Berlusconi's position as Prime Minister and owner of Italy's three largest TV stations once more rose to the top of the political agenda. Veltroni was outflanked by Italy of Values (Italia dei Valori, IdV) – a small party led by the former '*Mani pulite*' public prosecutor, Antonio Di Pietro, who made of Berlusconi's conflict of interests one of his major battle cries. Therefore, Veltroni was obliged to take the kinds of positions in opposition to Berlusconi that made the possibility of agreement on constitutional reform much slighter than had at first seemed. This made it seem likely that any constitutional changes that were attempted might once again be legislated for by the centre-right majority on the basis of its parliamentary strength alone. This invites two comments.

(1) Passing constitutional reforms by simple majorities would appear to carry with it the danger of weakening the Constitution as a whole; for it carries the risk that the Constitution 'ceases to be the fixed and enduring point of reference for all players and becomes terrain at the disposal of temporary majorities and of inevitably partial and precarious measures supported by such majorities' (Cammelli, 2003: 91). The reform of title V may therefore have set an unfortunate precedent.

(2) The foregoing suggests that 'the process of modifying the Constitution seems destined to have an incremental and, as it were, "pendular" character' (Vassallo, 2005), with each coalition seeking to graft its own proposals onto a text already modified by the other. This in turn makes it legitimate to wonder about the likely effects on the overall coherence of the document as a whole. From this point of view, it may be regarded as fortunate that, in the immediate aftermath of the June 2006 referendum, the then Prime Minister, Romano Prodi, asked the Minister for Relations with Parliament, Vannino Chiti, to make contact with all the political forces with a view to achieving reform by means of dialogue. In this way, Prodi appeared to turn his back on the idea of unilateral reform. On the other hand, if Vassallo's thesis is correct, then wide-ranging or incisive reform would appear to be an unlikely prospect.

Does it matter? The answer one gives to this question depends on the balance of likely costs and benefits one sees as being associated with constitutional overhaul.

● On one side are those who argue that in the search for institutional mechanisms that would best guarantee the survival of democracy in a society as profoundly divided as Italy was at the time, the framers of the 1948 Constitution were inevitably led to favour principles promoting dialogue and guaranteeing the rights of minorities over the unfettered exercise of majority rule. It was this that led the Constituent Assembly to reject a presidential system of government. Now, the argument continues, it is necessary to shift the constitutional emphasis away from these guarantees in the direction of guarantees of decision-making efficiency. For the passing of the old divisions has made possible the emergence and gradual consolidation of a bipolar party system. This has enabled the formation of governments whose composition directly reflects the distribution of votes. However, hitherto the party system has been highly fragmented, and it is difficult to be certain that the very recent reduction in fragmentation will survive future electoral contests. Therefore, reforms are needed that would free directly elected governments from the blackmail power of minority forces in Parliament. This would increase the likelihood of governments lasting an entire legislature. Those who take this view point out that even the 2001 Berlusconi government failed to last for an entire term. Instead, it was forced, in the wake of the 2005 regional elections (see chapter 7), to resign and to seek a fresh vote of confidence on the basis of a new coalition agreement. Consequently, of the ten governments that have been sworn in since the 1994 election, only three – those that took office in June 2001, in May 2006 and in May 2008 – have come into being as the direct result of an election outcome rather than post-election negotiations in the parliamentary arena; and sometimes they have even relied on changes of allegiance by members of the opposition. This was true of the three governments that held office between 1998 and 2001. It was for these reasons that reforms proposed by the centre right during the 2001–6 legislature included provisions designed to strengthen prime ministers against members of their coalitions and make impossible the assumption of office of coalitions based on majorities other than those indicated by the electorate.

(i) In the first place, dissolution was to have been the automatic consequence of a successful vote of no confidence or failure to approve a bill designated by the government as a matter of confidence.

(ii) In the second place, dissolution was also to have been the automatic consequence of a prime-ministerial decision to resign, unless within twenty days a number of members belonging to the coalition victorious at the preceding elections and at least equal to an absolute majority of the Chamber's members voted in favour of a motion confirming the government's programme and electing a new prime minister.

On the other side stand the 'constitutional conservatives', more lukewarm towards the idea of thoroughgoing change. Their argument is essentially twofold.

(i) In spite of the inhospitable circumstances created by the Cold War and the profound ideological divisions by which Italian society was torn, the 1948 Constitution played a significant role in ensuring that democracy was maintained and consolidated.

(ii) The problems in Italian governance that put constitutional revision on the political agenda in the first place were the result of specific historical and political circumstances, and above all the nature of the political parties and the party system, rather than constitutional shortcomings as such. This argues in favour of continuity: by upholding shared values whose strength grows with time, constitutional stability has an important role to play in securing national integration (Pizzorusso, 1996: 67–8). It argues, too, that the likelihood of change actually delivering the increases in decision-making efficiency that are promised for it is doubtful. On the one hand, there is nothing in existing arrangements to prevent this if only governing majorities can find the necessary cohesion. On the other hand, to the extent that shortcomings in this regard are mainly the consequence of party-system fragmentation, it is not at all clear to what extent changing the rules of the game can actually compensate for this. For instance, Vassallo (2005) notes that though the centre right's constitutional reform proposals were supposedly designed to strengthen prime ministers against coalition partners, the *only* situation in which the power of dissolution given to executive heads could credibly be used against an allied party is one in which that party's parliamentary support is larger than its electoral base *and* unlikely to affect the victory of the governing coalition. Moreover, given the proposals, it is perfectly possible to imagine situations in which, far from being empowered, prime ministers in effect become prisoners of their parliamentary majorities (Pasquino, 2008: 31). This was precisely the situation which, because of its party-system characteristics and not the Constitution, had been typical of the 'First Republic'.

■ Summary and conclusion

- The Italian Constitution reflects the historical circumstances of its drafting in including a variety of economic and social, as well as political, rights, and by virtue of the limitations it places on the possibilities of a centralised concentration of power.
- Besides the historical circumstances of its drafting, there are three other features in terms of which the Italian Constitution may be compared with those of other liberal democracies:
  - the provisions for its amendment;
  - its tripartite division of political authority between executive, legislative and judicial agencies;
  - the geographical distribution of power which it embodies.
- Italy has a rigid constitution providing for a parliamentary regime and a geographical distribution of power that makes the country neither a fully federal nor a fully unitary state.
- From the 1980s, popular dissatisfaction with the efficiency and incisiveness of public policy-making gave rise to growing pressures for a complete constitutional overhaul. These pressures came to a head as a result of the circumstances surrounding the party-system changes of the following decade.
- A number of constitutional-reform proposals were made designed to push the political system decisively in the direction of majoritarian democracy.
- The proposals were ultimately not implemented due to certain obstacles in the way of constitutional overhaul in Italy, that is, the need for large majorities which are especially difficult to construct when it comes to constitutional reform proposals because of the nature of constitutional reform as such.

- With the failure of these proposals, of two subsequent electoral-law referenda in 1999 and 2000, and of a second set of proposals in 2006, many
analysts have concluded that two decades of parliamentary and extra-
parliamentary activism in the cause of constitutional reform have now
come to an end. With it, they conclude, has also come to an end the
possibility of establishing any radically new institutional framework for
the Republic in the immediate term.
- Having reached its sixtieth birthday, the Italian Constitution is now among
the oldest in the world. This, together with the values and ideals it embodies
ensures that, notwithstanding the pressures for change in recent years, the
Constitution continues to be effective in securing the rights and freedoms of
Italian citizens within a framework of stable democratic governance.

Further reading

Through an account that is concise and simplified, without being in any sense
superficial or simplistic, *Political Institutions in Italy* (Oxford: Oxford University
Press, 2007), by Maurizio Cotta and Luca Verzichelli, argues that though comprehensive reform of the country's institutions has not yet taken place, we
have nevertheless seen a large number of 'uncoordinated' changes. The cumulative impact of these, the authors argue, has been the emergence of a political
and institutional system that may be qualitatively different from that of the
past. The following book chapters provide analysis of the three most significant constitutional-reform initiatives of recent years, the 1997 Bicameral
Commission, the 2001 reforms, and the reforms proposed by the centre right
in the 2001–6 legislature: Gianfranco Pasquino, 'A postmortem of the
Bicamerale', in David Hine and Salvatore Vassallo (eds.), *Italian Politics: The
Return of Politics* (New York and Oxford: Berghahn, 2000); Anna Cento Bull,
'Towards a federal state? Competing proposals for constitutional revision', in
Paolo Bellucci and Martin Bull (eds.), *Italian Politics: The Return of Berlusconi*
(New York and Oxford, Berghahn, 2002); Martin J. Bull, 'The Constitutional
Referendum of June 2006: end of the "grande riforma" but not of reform itself',
in Jean-Louis Briquet and Alfio Mastropaolo (eds.), *Italian Politics: The Center-Left's
Poisoned Victory* (New York and Oxford: Berghahn, 2007). Though it does not,
obviously, include discussion of the 2001 changes, chapter 5 of David Hine's
book *Governing Italy: the Politics of Bargained Pluralism* (Oxford: Oxford University
Press, 1993) provides a concise and clearly written overview of the Constitution and its most important provisions.

Notes

The first part of this chapter draws extensively on material I wrote for chapter 7 of
the book co-authored with Martin Bull: *Italian Politics: Adjustment under Duress* (2005).
1. The most important changes concern the powers and the number of members
    of the Constitutional Court; intervals between elections to the Senate; the right

     to vote of Italians living abroad; the powers and functions of sub-national levels of government.

2. The first occasion was on 7 October 2001 in relation to changes to the powers and functions of regions, approved by Parliament in March of that year. The second was on 25 and 26 June 2006 in relation to a complex series of reforms to part II of the Constitution and which, unlike the 2001 amendments, failed to meet with the voters' approval.

3. This stipulated that a 'majority premium' of 65 per cent of the seats in the Chamber of Deputies would be given to the party or coalition that achieved 50 per cent plus 1 of the votes. The narrow failure of the DC and its allies to reach the required threshold in the 1953 elections led to the law being abolished the following year.

4. The record was set by the election of Giovanni Leone in 1971, which required twenty-three rounds of voting.

5. In refusing dissolution, President Scalfaro rejected this reasoning and was correct to do so: Berlusconi had not received a 'Westminster-style' mandate. As he had presented two electorate coalitions, not one, in 1994, he led a government that owed its position to post-election negotiations among parties in the parliamentary arena not to the unmediated choices of a majority of voters. Moreover, it is not true that dissolution is required when a government loses its majority in the Westminster system.

6. One of these concerned the first president, Luigi Einaudi, who sent back to Parliament a law concerning the retention of a system of salary supplements for public employees (Fusaro, 2003: 90–1), another the decision of President Ciampi, in 2003, to send back the so-called Gasparri Law, which sought to circumvent anti-trust legislation and a number of rulings of the Constitutional Court apparently for the personal benefit of the Prime Minister.

7. For details see Bull and Newell, 2005, chapter 8.

8. The other two being the so-called Bozzi Commission, which sat between November 1983 and January 1985, and the De Mita-Iotti Commission, which sat between September 1992 and January 1994.

9. The ostensible reason for Berlusconi's withdrawal was his inability to win the commission's approval of an amendment to the proposals concerning the President's powers of dissolution. While AN did not wish to risk a breakdown of the commission over the issue, it did not want to risk a split with its principal ally either.

10. As Veltroni (2007: 20) puts it: 'the Democratic Party was born in order to move beyond the idea that what counts is to win elections, that is, to beat the opposing line-up by fielding the broadest coalition possible regardless of its actual capacity to govern the country'.

11. This is an attitude that would seem to chime rather closely with his populist style of politics; for one of the hallmarks of populism (see chapter 5) is precisely an intolerance of institutional and procedural restrictions on the use of power by the popularly chosen leader. After all, such a leader presents him- or herself as being both *of* the people and *uniquely qualified* to lead the people.

3   Multi-level government

▦ Introduction

In the last chapter we looked at the institutional framework as laid out by the Constitution, that is, we looked at the principal institutions of government. By contrast, in this chapter and the next we look at how these and other institutions function and interact in the processes by which policy is made and administered. What will hopefully be apparent by the time the reader reaches the end of this chapter is the extent to which policy and its implementation is the product of the interaction of a large number of institutions at the national, sub-national and supra-national levels. In other words, far from policy being the product of autonomous decision-making by those at the apex of Italy's political institutions, it is, rather, something that emerges from consultation and nego-tiation between decision-makers located in a wide range of institutional set-tings. This has become increasingly the case in recent decades, partly as the consequence of processes of *globalisation*, so that political scientists talk about government having given way to governance. In other words, 'the overall administration of social affairs which must take place in any society' (that is, governance) 'is said to be slipping away from national governments to be partially re-located at sub-national or supra-national levels' (Barrett, 1996: 6). It is for this reason, then, that in looking at the structures through which governance is carried on in Italy, this chapter and the next look at a range of institutions, including but going beyond the institutions of central government.

In this chapter the analysis moves across three levels.

- First, we explore the role of the institutions of sub-national government.
- Then we look at the range of institutions associated with central government and the ministries. In concerning themselves with administration, these institutions 'are the tools for transforming political intentions into policy output' (Hine 1993: 225).
- Finally, we look at the part played by Italy's membership of international and supra-national organisations (such as NATO, the IMF, the UN and especially the EU).

Throughout this analysis we shall be concerned to describe the means and mechanisms of conflict resolution between institutions and levels of government. For the fact that there is no one institution able to make enforceable decisions for Italy as a whole in conditions of complete autonomy inevitably means that disagreements over 'due process', as well as over the substance of policy, feature significantly in modern governance.

■ Territorial decentralisation: regions, provinces and local government

The central–local axis has been a salient issue ever since the beginning of Italy as a unified state. As we saw in chapter 1, one of the difficulties faced by the new state in the immediate aftermath of Unification arose from the fact that the process of unification itself had provided no room for discussion, popular or otherwise, about constitutional arrangements: Piedmont's Statute was simply imposed on the rest of the territory. Moreover, it was a statute which, as far as the territorial distribution of power was concerned, embodied Napoleonic conceptions. That is, power was centralised and uniformly applied. It was little wonder, then, that with the creation of the Italian state out of a heterogeneous group of independent kingdoms, the problem of how to generate feelings of identification with, and loyalty to, the new state institutions was especially keenly felt. More than one hundred years later, as parties such as the Northern League (LN) agitated for a regional autonomy that was at times little short of independence, it was clear that the problem of national integration was still very much a live one.

Prior to the advent of the 1948 Constitution, the key figures in sub-national and local politics were the provincial prefects. These were Rome appointees whose sweeping powers enabled them, in conjunction with mayors, to ensure the return of government candidates at each general election. By the same token, they were also able to ensure that local government remained in the hands of dominant elites:

- On the one hand, the weakness of the Italian state meant that prefects were effectively obliged to rely on local 'notables' when it came to recommending the appointment of mayors (who were unelected prior to 1896).

- On the other hand, in return for leaving municipalities 'free' in this way, prefects were able to rely on mayors to use their powers (to draw up electoral rolls and to issue passports, trading documents and so forth) to ensure that the right candidates were returned at general elections (Clark, 1996: 58–61).

Under Fascism, central government tutelage of local government became all but complete. In fact, in 1926, all mayors were dismissed along with their councils and replaced, in each municipality (*comune*), by a *podestà*. 'The *podestà* was appointed by the Prefect; he could be dismissed at any time by the Prefect; and he could be transferred to another *comune* by the Prefect' (Clark, 1996: 235). In looking for a reliable *podestà*, the prefect usually chose elderly conservative gentlemen, finding that retired colonels were ideal as they had plenty of time and needed no pay (Clark, 1996: 236).

The 1948 Constitution, then, represented a *caesura*. Prior to its entry into force, the liberal and Fascist regimes had been able to intervene with impunity in local government since the latter had no constitutional recognition. This now changed: as constitutionally recognised elements in the national system of government, the *comuni* could appeal to the courts if the centre took action corrosive of their constitutional status (Norton, 1994: 9). As we saw in the previous chapter, the geographical distribution of formal authority inherent in Italy's constitutional arrangements is not federal – but neither is it that of a purely unitary state.

- On the one hand, provided that they can muster enough support within the two chambers of Parliament, the central authorities can change the constitution to which the sub-national units are subject and can do so against the wishes of these units.
- On the other hand, sub-national units in Italy have general competence within the law. This means that the onus is on Parliament to show that they have acted in ways that are *ultra vires*, not on them to show that their actions are sanctioned by some specific piece of parliamentary legislation. This differs radically from the situation in a genuinely unitary state where sub-national units have no powers other than those explicitly given to them in acts of Parliament.

The Constitution specifies four tiers of government below the national level: regions, metropolitan cities, provinces, *comuni* (that is, municipalities).

The regions

Regions (twenty in all) are of two types: ordinary regions (fifteen) and the *regioni a statuto speciale*, or 'special statute' regions: Sicily, Sardinia, Trentino-Alto Adige, Friuli-Venezia Giulia, Valle d'Aosta. The fundamental difference between the two is that the statutes of the latter, unlike those of the former, have the status of constitutional legislation. Constitutional legislation is legislation which, having been expressly provided for by the Constitution, has the same legal status as the articles of the Constitution themselves. The practical consequence is to enable the special statute regions but not the ordinary ones to deviate from principles established elsewhere in the Constitution. And since it is the Constitution that establishes the legislative powers and financial arrangements for the ordinary regions, this meant that from the beginning, the special statute as compared to the ordinary regions had powers in a wider range of areas, exclusive powers in some areas and greater financial autonomy.

The establishment of the special statute regions was a way of providing official acknowledgement of the claims of certain areas that they had particular needs and interests. These areas are located on Italy's borders and on the two islands. At times they have been threatened by separatism and ethnic problems. The special statute regions were thus established early on precisely in order to defuse such threats. (Of the special regions, Friuli-Venezia Giulia had to wait upon resolution of the Trieste dispute with Yugoslavia and was established in 1963; the other four came into existence in 1948.) For the reasons discussed in the previous chapter, the ordinary regions had to wait until 1970 before the enabling legislation giving life to them could be passed.

Besides drawing the distinction between ordinary and special statute regions, the Constitution also establishes the basic internal structures and their functions of each region. Originally, the ordinary regions' statutes had had to be sent to Parliament for approval and passage. This enabled uniformity to be imposed from the centre. With the constitutional reform of 1999 this changed. Now, each region was empowered, subject to the observance of certain broad constitutional principles, to adopt its statute on its own authority. This enabled some diversity in the regions' internal institutional arrangements. The principles are four.

(1) Each region must have:
  i an elected council with legislative power;
  ii a *giunta*, with executive power;
  iii a president, with responsibility for leading the *giunta*, for appointing its members and for representing the region externally;
  iv a standing committee to enable consultation with the local authorities.
(2) Regional presidents are directly elected unless the statute in question stipulates otherwise.
(3) In the former case, a presidential resignation or a vote of no confidence in the president by the council leads automatically to dissolution and fresh elections of president and council. In the latter case, the same thing happens in the case of a presidential resignation, whereas a vote of no confidence gives the council the option of choosing an alternative president.
(4) The region's electoral system must conform to principles established by parliamentary legislation. The most significant of the principles currently in force is that all the regions' elected bodies have five-year terms.

As amended by the reform of 2001, article 117 divides legislative powers three ways establishing:

(1) matters (such as foreign policy, defence and environmental protection) concerning which legislative competence is reserved exclusively to the state;

(2) a longer list of matters concerning which the regions and the state enjoy concurrent powers;

(3) that the regions have residual legislative competence in all remaining areas.

Though apparently simple, this threefold division masks considerable ambiguity and complexity concerning the division of powers. Not surprisingly, therefore, it has given rise to a considerable volume of litigation before the Constitutional Court. As a result of the Court's successive judgements, clarity and accepted conventions have begun to emerge. For example, the Court has established that 'environmental protection' is not a 'matter' in the strict sense, but rather a 'function' that thus allows the state to take measures touching on matters otherwise subject to the legislative competence of the regions. However, the process of acquiring greater clarity cannot yet be said to be 'complete'.

The 2001 reform also effected the following changes:

- It abolished the post of regional Commissioner. Through this appointee the Government had exercised an *ex-ante* power of control over regional legislation.
- It also abolished the Government's *ex-post* power of control of regional legislation, a power that it had exercised by bringing offending legislation before Parliament for a judgement of its merits. The only grounds on which it remains open to governments to challenge regional legislation are those of legal legitimacy, before the Constitutional Court.
- It raised the potential for diversity still further by giving regions an explicit option of requesting the passage of parliamentary legislation conferring upon them legislative powers in areas additional to those set out in article 117.

Legislative powers are not worth very much if unaccompanied by any autonomous revenue-raising powers. The Constitution therefore

(1) enables regions to incur debts (for investment expenditure) but prohibits the state from underwriting them (meaning that the regions must rely entirely on their own creditworthiness);

(2) allows the regions to levy their own taxes but insists that these powers must be exercised in such a way as to allow the effective coordination of public expenditure and the tax system as a whole;

(3) gives the regions a right to share in the proceeds of state taxes attributable to their areas.

THE POLITY: STRUCTURES AND INSTITUTIONS

The two remaining constitutionally established sources of regional income are:

(4)   the state's equalisation fund (disbursements from which cannot be tied to specific uses and must be used to provide additional resources for areas with lower tax bases);

(5)   central government grants made available for specific, socially desirable purposes.

Finally, since it is open to the state, through ordinary legislation, to impose administrative and other tasks on the regions and other sub-national tiers, the Constitution imposes on the state an obligation to ensure that the money available to these tiers from sources (2), (3) and (4) is sufficient to enable them actually to meet their state-imposed obligations.

Lastly, the options available to regions to interact with other institutions beyond their borders reveal the principle of multi-level governance in all its glory. The 2001 amendments give the regions concurrent powers to entertain relations and stipulate agreements with foreign and EU bodies with regard to matters in which they have legislative competence. The so-called 'state–regional conference' established in 1988 brings together representatives of the Government and the regions. Over the years it has established itself as an authoritative forum for negotiation between Government and the regions on all aspects of government policy impinging on regional competences. It has been especially significant when it comes to negotiations concerning public expenditure and the annual budget. The regions have a constitutionally guaranteed right to establish, for the better exercise of their functions, legal agreements with other regions including agreements establishing inter-regional bodies.

Metropolitan cities, provinces, municipalities

Although these are all 'sub-regional' tiers, the Constitution reserves the specification of their electoral systems, their internal institutions and their functions not to regional, but to parliamentary legislation. The relevant legislation is currently the 'single text on the framework of local authorities' established, in August 2000, by legislative decree 267. This sought to rationalise and consolidate a disparate range of previous measures.

Provinces and municipalities differ in terms of their geographical extent and the substance of their functions, but not in terms of much else. Both are contained within the boundaries of regions. Municipalities (of which there are 8,103) are contained within the boundaries of provinces (of which there are 103). In other words, they do not cross each other's boundaries and neither cross the boundaries of regions.

- The single text gives the provinces administrative responsibilities in areas that include environmental protection, water and energy sources, artistic

heritage, highways, flora and fauna, hunting and fishing, waste disposal, school buildings, data collection and the provision of technical-administrative assistance to the municipalities.
- The single text gives the municipalities administrative responsibilities in the areas of personal and public services for their residents, town planning and economic development, as well as various functions, such as the maintenance of electoral registers, that they are required to perform on behalf of the state.

Provinces and municipalities carry out their administrative responsibilities by issuing regulations which – in deference to the principle that legal norms are given their legitimacy by other norms of greater legal force – must be consistent both with regional and parliamentary legislation and with the statutes of the provinces and municipalities themselves.

These statutes, like those of the regions, are adopted by the provinces and municipalities on their own authority. They thus enable some diversity in the authorities' internal arrangements, subject to the limitation that they are consistent (a) with parliamentary legislation and (b) with certain broad principles set out in the single text. These principles are similar to those constitutionally established for the regions and, again, are four in number.

(1) Each authority must have:
  i an elected council (with responsibility for adopting regulations; approving the authority's budget and taking related decisions; supervising the work of the authority's executive bodies);
  ii a *giunta* (with competence in all areas not expressly reserved by the statute or by law to other bodies);
  iii a mayor in the case of municipalities, and a president in the case of provinces.
(2) Mayors and presidents are directly elected for five-year terms and must achieve absolute majorities. In the absence of such a majority there is a run-off ballot between the two best-placed candidates. In municipalities of fewer than 15,000 inhabitants, a relative majority is sufficient.
(3) Mayors and presidents are responsible for appointing and leading the *giunta* and representing the authority in its external relations. Mayors are also empowered, in cases of emergency, to issue regulations to ensure public safety; for they are representatives of the government in the locality as well as being representatives of the locality in government circles.
(4) A vote of no-confidence by the council in mayor or president leads automatically to dissolution of the authority and to fresh elections of both council and mayor (or president) – as does an autonomous decision of mayor or president to resign.

The financial resources to enable provinces and municipalities to carry out their functions derive formally (that is, in terms of what the Constitution specifies) from exactly the same five sources as the funds accruing to the regions. In practice, however, one of these sources is unavailable to the provinces and municipalities; for they do not have tax-raising powers. The reason is that the Constitution also stipulates, as one of the fundamental rights and freedoms in part I, that 'Nobody may be obliged to perform personal services or to make any kind of payment unless otherwise established by law' (article 23). And since neither the provinces nor the municipalities have law-making powers as such, this means that they cannot levy their own taxes.

Finally, metropolitan cities were first provided for by law no. 142 of 1990. They only gained a mention in the Constitution with the reform of 2001. None have yet been established, but we mention them here for the sake of descriptive completeness. Essentially, the metropolitan cities were conceived to allow local authorities to respond more effectively to the social and economic developments of the post-war decades by coming together to offer a co-ordinated delivery of services through bodies of the same name. Specifically, law no. 142 denoted specific large cities as 'metropolitan areas'. Within these the single text makes it possible, on the initiative of the local authorities and subject to a popular referendum, to set up metropolitan cities. The idea is that, having the functions of both provinces and municipalities, such structures should be in a position to meet the strategic and co-ordination needs not always adequately met by existing divisions of competence between the two.

The centre–periphery relationship

The previous subsection should have made clear that it is difficult to specify the role of sub-national politics within the national political system in any very precise or simple way. This should become even clearer when we look at the political context within which the sub-national structures have had to operate in recent years. Besides the formal/legal context described above, four political factors have significantly affected the national/sub-national interaction:

(1) the nature of the party system;
(2) financial politics;
(3) geographical inequalities in the distribution of economic, organisational and other resources;
(4) the conflicting political ideals to which central/local arrangements have sought to respond.

The impact of the party system

Prior to the 1990s, the institutional arrangements governing central–local relationships were heavily overlaid by the political parties. That is, the constitutional and legal arrangements created the potential for distinctive, sub-national systems of politics; but this was in practice suffocated by the parties. These had a tendency to subordinate all institutional dynamics to the requirements of **clientelistic** power-broking within and between them (Box 3.1). This meant that centre and locality were linked together by means of informal

Box 3.1

Key terms: clientelism

A form of social organisation based on the provision of personal protection in return for loyalty and support. Clientelistic relationships are thus a response to inequality in the distribution of resources, and they may take a variety of concrete forms, depending on the specifics of the social context in which they arise. In the context of electoral politics, politicians (the patrons) use their influence in the state machine to secure a variety of forms of protection, from favourable bureaucratic decisions of various kinds, to access to jobs and welfare benefits, for their voting supporters (the clients). In return, these voters are expected to cast their ballots the way they are told to – either for the patron, or for another politician by whom the patron is him- or herself protected clientelistically. For this reason, clientelism rarely takes the form of a single exchange relationship but rather gives rise to entire clientele chains running from the top to the bottom of the political and social hierarchy; and it represents an individualistic alternative to collective action as a potential solution to the common problems faced by clients.

channels within the main parties. Consequently, only with difficulty was it possible to speak of a sub-national or local level of government that had any effective autonomy from clientelistic processes of power-broking working from the top downwards.[1]

This is not to say that the parties were always able rigidly to control sub-national politics from the centre. On the contrary, the interlocking vetoes existing at the heart of central government (and thus the difficulties involved in taking united stands on issues) made such control difficult. These interlocking vetoes meant that the sub-national units could sometimes count on the fact that to veto their initiatives was not a worthwhile proposition for a party. Since parties' aims were to manipulate as many contractual resources as possible '[c]entral direction then had to be clever enough not to disclose a more global design' and (by refraining from showing too great a capacity for control of local tensions and conflicts) to 'use as a resource the very opposition of their own local groups to the party line' (Graziano, Girotti and Bonet, 1984: 435). Nevertheless, it remained the case that sub-national units of government and their performance were as much subject to the shortcomings of party domination as were politics at the national level.

For example, if governments were unstable at national level, the same was true at local level. Prior to 1993, both mayors and *giunte* were chosen by, and responsible to, their municipalities' councils. Since national-level coalitional dynamics almost inevitably had local-level consequences, mayors and *giunte* were subject to frequent party vetoes within the councils. This ensured that the stability of local *giunte* was on average very low. In fact, Baldini (2002a: 368–9) points out that between 1972 and 1989, of 904 *giunte* formed in the ninety-five provincial capitals, less than 1 per cent lasted for their entire

Box 3.2

Achille Lauro

Born on 16 June 1887 into a small ship-owning family, Lauro was himself to become a ship-owner – but of much more significant proportions – and one of the most colourful figures in Italian, and especially Neapolitan, politics of the early post-war period. His initial contact with shipping came at the age of fourteen when he was sent away to sea by his father as punishment for keeping the company of one of the family's maids. Starting with a small coastal vessel in 1912, he gradually built up a fleet of ships, only later to see them requisitioned for the war effort. Starting again from scratch, he was able to rebuild his business with the assistance of contacts in the Fascist Party, which he joined in 1933. Arrested in 1943 and detained for twenty-two months by the Allies for aiding and abetting Fascism, Lauro was eventually acquitted but forced to start from scratch for a third time. By the early 1950s he had become a multi-millionaire, having gone into the booming field of passenger shipping with its lucrative market for the transport of Italian immigrants to Australia and New Zealand and the transport of tourists from these parts to Italy. Elected mayor of Naples in 1951, Lauro was re-elected in 1956 and again in 1958 and became immensely popular, partly due to the lavish and flamboyant style of his election campaigns. These would see him giving out free packets of pasta and offering voters a left shoe – with the promise that they would get the right shoe once they could demonstrate that they had voted the right way. Opinions about Lauro were rarely tepid or neutral. Rather, he tended either to be feted as the pragmatic man responsible for rebuilding Naples after the devastation of the Second World War, or condemned as the unprincipled man responsible for the rampant building speculation of the 1950s and the corruption that went with it. A member of Parliament in the 1960s and 1970s, there is no doubt that, whatever else he was, Lauro was a courageous businessman: he went into the oil tanker business in 1973 at the age of eighty-six; and in 1976, at the age of eighty-nine, he founded Canale 21, Europe's first private television station. He died on 15 November 1982 aged ninety-five.

(five-year) terms. A majority of them failed to survive for more than a year. Or, to give a more colourful example: **Achille Lauro**, monarchist mayor of Naples from 1952 (Box 3.2), was given a free hand to commit all kinds of irregularities because the votes of monarchist parliamentarians were occasionally necessary to ensure the survival in office of the Christian Democrats (DC) at national level. Later, DC general secretary, Amintore Fanfani, was fearful of the spectre of Lauro's movement spreading beyond its Neapolitan stronghold. He therefore got Interior Minister, Fernando Tambroni, to dissolve the Neapolitan council for administrative irregularities and set about dismantling Lauro's party by enticing his councillors to abandon him. This was made possible by virtue of the fact that the councillors were businessmen whose need for credit facilities required them to turn to banks controlled by the DC. Thus they had to seek the intervention of local DC leaders (Allum, 1973b: 274–89).

In these respects, the 1990s, with their party-system changes and consequent institutional changes at sub-national level, represented a watershed.
The 1993 reform of municipalities (law no. 81) was especially significant. It
gave the municipalities the internal institutional arrangements that we have
described above. These included placing membership of the *giunta* in the
hands of a directly elected mayor while stipulating that a council passing a
vote of no confidence in the latter would bring about its own demise. In
making these stipulations, the reform considerably strengthened the position
of the mayor and local executive; it also thereby ensured that the disintegration of the traditional governing parties was accompanied by a veritable
renaissance of local government in Italy. This renaissance could be seen in at
least three ways.

(1) There appears to have been a significant increase in the stability of local
     authorities (Baldini, 2002a: 368–9).
(2) The 1993 reform has undoubtedly given mayors significant resources
     with which, potentially, to establish power bases independent of the
     dictates of the political parties.[2]
(3) Greater powers and greater direct exposure to the winds of public opinion
     have considerably increased the significance, for success in heading
     municipalities, of leadership and managerial skills. This has made a
     significant indirect contribution to improving the quality of local
     government.[3]

The impact of changing financial arrangements

The room the sub-national levels of government have for independent initiatives is heavily dependent on the financial context in which they must carry on
their activities: without money, they can do nothing; with few resources, they
can do very little. This is of particular significance in relation to the municipalities and suggests that local government finance lies at the heart of the quality
of Italian democracy:

* most of the public services most directly impinging on the individual
   citizen are provided, or organised, by the municipality;
* the municipality is the government structure with which citizens have the
   most frequent direct contact;
* aside from the duties imposed on them by legislation, the municipalities
   have a responsibility, in the wider political environment, for protecting
   and representing their communities in relation to all remaining matters.

So external financial constraints imposed on the municipalities diminish or
enhance the quality of the citizen's experience of public governance, directly.

   Prior to the 1990s, by far the largest proportions of the local authorities'
incomes came from central-government transfers; for in 1971, most local taxes
were abolished and replaced by a local income tax, ILOR (*imposta locale sui redditi*).
Despite the tax's title, the rates at which it was imposed were decided centrally

and its proceeds went to central government to be redistributed to the localities (Paoloni and Cesaroni, 1998: 214–15). In and of itself, this did not necessarily imply high-level constraints on the authorities' freedom. On the contrary, it enabled a transfer of resources from richer to poorer areas and thus necessarily enhanced what authorities in these poorer areas could do for their citizens. It also had the advantage that, by centralising fiscal policy, it potentially stream-lined processes of national-level macroeconomic management. The problem was that there were no clear prior limits on overall spending levels. This made it difficult to control public expenditure effectively and to ensure that funds were spent efficiently. The period since 1990 has therefore witnessed a change in the funding regime. In essence this change involves two elements:

(1) There has been a move in the direction of a limited degree of fiscal autonomy for the local authorities. In 1994, for instance, ICI (*imposta comunale sugli immobili*, or local property tax) was introduced. This did not amount to a grant to the local authorities of independent tax-raising powers: ICI is a nationally imposed tax whose rates individual local authorities can vary within narrow limits (and which, since May 2008, has been abolished as far as the tax-payer's main residence is concerned). Its significance, rather, is that the proceeds remain with the municipality within whose boundaries they are raised and they are expected to be the principal source of finance for local authority spending decisions. The role of central-government transfers meanwhile has been limited to 'picking up the slack' by topping up, in accordance with a range of demographic and socio-economic parameters, the funds available to poorer areas.

(2) There has been a greater insistence on the principle that spending deci-sions be made only *after* it has become clear to the municipality what will be the total income (from local taxation, central-government transfers and user charges) available to it. In these ways, it is expected that local authorities will become more accountable to their electorates than in the past since they are encouraged to maximise the efficiency and effective-ness of spending and will have to look to increases in local taxation to finance additional spending they may decide upon. On the other hand, the tightening of control over central-government disbursements implied by the new regime inevitably brings a loss of autonomy for the author-ities. This loss is the greater the greater is the proportion of the author-ities' income that comes from central-government transfers.

The impact of inequalities in economic and organisational resources

The foregoing throws a spotlight on the third of the factors affecting the nature of the sub-national units' interactions with the national level; for variations in the sizes of the former have combined with the awesome economic dispar-ities across the country (especially the North–South divide) to create real differences in the institutions' abilities to make use of their powers (Box 3.3).

Box 3.3

Regional diversity in Italy

The extent of regional diversity in Italy – demographic, economic, social and cultural – can hardly be overstated, as the following figures show. In a very real sense, the residents of Calabria at one extreme and those of Lombardia at the other live in very different worlds, the various political concomitants having been analysed in Robert Putnam's acclaimed book, *Making Democracy Work* (discussed in greater detail in chapter 5). The figures given below allow the reader quickly to perform the calculations necessary for comparison. Thus one can see, for example, that in Lombardia, household incomes are 51 per cent above those in Calabria, while the rate of unemployment is just 15 per cent of the rate in the latter region. The rate of church attendance in Sicily is almost double that in Toscana.

Region	Resident population (January 2007)	Inhabitants per square kilometre (2005)	Average household income (€) (2003)	Rate of unemploy-ment (2003)	Per cent aged 6 and over attend-ing church at least once per week (2005)	Per cent aged 6 and over read-ing a news-paper at least once per week (2005)	Homicides and attempted homicides per 100,000 inhabitants (2003)
Piemonte	4,355,352	170.92	27,474	4.80	30.6	66.0	2.54
Valle d'Aosta	124,886	37.99	27,474	4.06	24.7	70.9	4.12
Lombardia	9,551,750	397.07	30,095	3.60	36.6	64.6	2.76
Ligura	1,607,804	296.99	24,355	6.02	23.1	65.2	4.25
Trentino-Alto Adige	995,417	72.40	29,353	2.44	38.3	74.6	1.67
Veneto	4,775,853	257.53	28,044	3.41	36.4	63.1	2.00
Friuli-Venezia Giulia	1,213,017	153.76	28,025		26.6	67.9	1.84
Emilia Romagna	4,226,247	189.33	29,895	3.06	23.6	64.7	2.61
Toscana	3,640,552	157.43	29,190	4.70	23.1	63.7	2.34
Umbria	873,514	102.63	27,340	5.17	27.8	53.1	2.38
Marche	1,537,078	157.71	27,908	3.78	38.8	56.2	2.27
Lazio	5,497,177	307.77	28,157	8.71	28.0	61.1	3.57
Abruzzo	1,311,791	121.28	25,303	5.37	35.6	52.3	1.95
Molise	320,008	72.31	23,603	12.28	36.6	45.4	2.49
Campania	5,789,933	426.11	23,011	20.20	42.2	44.6	6.67
Puglia	4,069,773	210.33	22,382	13.78	41.9	44.1	5.65
Basilicata	591,143	59.44	20,778	16.06	37.6	41.2	5.19
Calabria	1,998,145	132.91	19,835	23.42	39.8	50.9	8.16
Sicilia	5,017,282	195.14	19,847	20.13	43.7	45.6	5.21
Sardegna	1,659,783	68.73	24,984	16.88	28.4	68.3	5.61
Italy	59,156,505	194.97	26,521	8.68	34.3	58.1	3.79

Source: Data taken from the website of the Istituto Nazionale di Statistica, www.istat.it.

Table 3.1. Municipalities in Italy

Inhabitants	No. of municipalities	Cumulative total	Percentage of total	Population (1991 Census)	Percentage of national total
Below 100		21	0.26	1,704	0.003
100–500	798	819	10.00	254,658	0.450
501–1,000	1,140	1,959	24.00	851,571	1.950
1,001–3,000	2,721	4,680	58.00	4,963,970	10.690
3,001–5,000	1,223	5,903	73.00	4,709,235	18.980
5,001–10,000	1,156	7,059	87.00	8,034,942	33.130
10,001–15,000	408	7,467	92.00	4,915,716	41.790
15,001–30,000	350	7,817	96.00	7,093,813	54.290
30,001–50,000	150	7,967	98.00	5,547,164	64.060
50,001–100,000	90	8,057	99.00	5,983,846	74.600
100,001–250,000	34	8,091	99.00	4,862,771	83.160
250,001–500,000	6	8,097	99.00	2,048,302	86.770
500,001–1,000,000	3	8,100	99.00	2,339,834	90.890
Over 1,000,000	3	8,103	100.00	5,170,504	100.000
Total	8,103			56,778,031	

Source: Vandelli, 2005, table 1, p. 10.

This is especially so in the case of the municipalities, whose dimensions vary from under 100 inhabitants to over 1 million (Table 3.1). Clearly, in seeking to gain attention and in pressing the centre for resources, the small, rural, southern municipality operates within a completely different set of parameters from the large, wealthy northern city.

The origins of this state of affairs are to be sought essentially in the French Revolution and its principles of equality. These sought to replace varying and arbitrary local privileges with the same rights and obligations for all local institutions. Consequently, uniformity was imposed on pre-existing structures whose capacity to manage the rights and obligations involved was actually very varied. In an age in which the responsibilities of the state at all levels were relatively limited, this was not necessarily a problem. At the beginning of the twenty-first century, it is no longer unproblematic to treat the local authorities as abstractly homogeneous entities.

Faced with this issue, governments in recent years have reacted in two ways.

(1) They have come to treat the local authorities according to the principle not of uniformity but of diversity:

    i It was this that underlay the provisions of law no. 142 of 1990, which first gave the local authorities the above-mentioned power to adopt, within broad parameters, their statutes on their own authority, according to their own needs.

    ii This was followed by the so-called Bassanini laws of 1997. These sought to marry a process of administrative decentralisation with one of administrative simplification. They thereby embodied the principle that responsibilities would be devolved to regions and local authorities in accordance with their demographic, territorial and organisational characteristics.

    iii Finally, the constitutional reform of 2001 stipulated that administrative responsibilities were to be distributed among the various levels of government according to the principles of 'subsidiarity, differentiation, and adequacy'. That is responsibilities were to be allocated to the level of government closest to the citizen, consistent with the need to ensure their effective exercise. Therefore they were not to be allocated to the same level uniformly.

(2) They have sought, with less success, to act directly on sub-national structures. In particular, they have encouraged amalgamations and the creation of consortia to deal with the diseconomies of scale arising from municipalities that are too small; and they have encouraged the setting up of sub-municipal structures to deal with the remoteness arising in those municipalities that are too large.

Law no. 142 of 1990 contained a variety of incentives designed to encourage the amalgamation of smaller municipalities but met with no success. Consequently, legislative decree 112 of 1998 (pursuant to the provisions for administrative decentralisation contained in the first of the Bassanini laws) adopted a more directive approach. It stipulated that the regions were to identify the most appropriate levels for the exercise of the functions to be devolved. Further, they were to assist local authorities too small to exercise the functions on their own to find ways of exercising jointly the functions to be allocated to them. Where the local authorities failed to come up with the required solutions, the regions were empowered to impose solutions of their own. These provisions added to a series of older statutes providing for the autonomous creation of inter-municipal structures. Such structures include:

(1) consortia and conventions (to enable the participating municipalities to provide one or more services);

(2) unions (for the provision of a plurality of services and potentially leading to fusion);

(3) mountain communities. Originally conceived as bodies that would have predominantly planning functions, these were designed to deal with the particular difficulties created by the geographical characteristics of areas where municipal fragmentation has traditionally been very high. As they are governed by regional legislation, they come in various sizes and with a wide variety of functions.

This is also true of the *circoscrizioni*. These are compulsory subdivisions of municipalities of over 100,000 inhabitants, optional subdivisions of municipalities having between 30,000 and 100,000. As their organisation and functions are determined by the municipalities' own statutes, they may be directly elected, indirectly elected by their governing municipalities or elected from among the members of local associations. They may have consultative, administrative and governing powers or some combination of the three.

The impact of conflicting political ideals

Finally, the role of sub-national units of government, and their power within the national political system have been significantly affected by the changing balance legislators have sought to strike between conflicting political ideals.

- On the one hand, legislators in the established democracies generally have always had to come to terms with the need to tread a path between uniformity and diversity. That is, they need to impose a degree of uniformity in administration and task allocation across the state in order to meet citizens' legitimate claims for equal access to public resources regardless of where they happen to reside. At the same time, legislators must also allow local authorities sufficient scope to decide the *manner* in which their centrally allocated tasks are to be executed. Otherwise the authorities will be unable either to respond to local variation in citizens' demands or to perform their role as general representatives of their communities within the national collectivity.

- On the other hand, the path that legislators have found between these two imperatives has varied over time. In the early post-war decades, until round about the mid-1970s, policy-makers' horizons, in Italy as elsewhere, were dominated by theoretical presuppositions according to which processes of industrialisation and economic development went hand in hand with social changes bringing a growing standardisation, within and between countries, of lifestyles and cultural patterns, and thus a gradual withering of local distinctiveness. Convinced, as they were, that territorial diversity was a thing of the past, policy-makers' approaches to regions and localities tended to be 'top down' in conception, aimed above all at helping more 'backward' peripheries catch up with more developed centres. The period since round about the mid-1970s has seen a change in this approach. There has been a growing awareness of the shortcomings of policies based on assumptions of inevitable convergence (for example, the problems for high unemployment areas of Keynesian macroeconomic policies designed to counteract 'overheating' in the economy as a whole). This has combined with a growing awareness of the significance of local social fabrics as factors of production in the competition to attract inward investment, to give rise to a growing celebration of local and regional diversity.

It is an attitude that today appeals both to those on the left (attracted by the potential of local autonomy to enhance the opportunities for grass-roots participation) and by those on the right (attracted by the potential for autonomy in fiscal matters to act as an effective control on overall levels of public expenditure). Nevertheless, left–right differences remain, and these are likely to combine with the inevitable ambiguities in legislation and constitutional arrangements to ensure that the line between uniformity and diversity also bends as governments alternate in Italy's bipolar party system. For example, the clause in the 2001 constitutional reform that attributes to the state the power to ensure that minimum standards of services are guaranteed across the peninsula is susceptible of being interpreted in many different ways (Cammelli, 2003: 88): it could be used by the state to minimise, in the interests of national equality, the legislative powers granted to the regions, or it could be branded as justification for reducing to a bare minimum the transfer of resources from the richer to the poorer regions (Cento Bull, 2002).

■ Functional subdivisions: ministries, departments and agencies

At the national level, the substance of public policy is significantly influenced

(1) by all those institutions associated with central government and the ministries – that is, by the bureaucracy linked by hierarchical structures of authority to the ministerial summits;
(2) by the 'para-state' agencies – that is, a wide range of public bodies with a varying degree of autonomy from the central administration.

'The 50,000 officials of the Italian central administration at the end of the nineteenth century have increased fortyfold and today number almost 2 million' (Mény, 1990: 238). Dimensions such as these make the administration the largest part of government; and from the fact of size, a considerable degree of bureaucratic power over the nature of policy is often deduced. Practically, bureaucrats do not simply implement the policies decided upon by politicians. At senior levels they are in most countries closely involved with politicians in the formulation of policy: they provide advice on what is 'practical' and 'impractical', and they 'help to determine the substance of policy decisions

95

by drafting bills conceived or accepted by the political authorities' (Mény, 1990: 240). At lower levels, the execution of policy requires taking decisions about the substance of policy, so that in practice, the conceptual distinction between policy-making and policy-execution cannot really be sustained.

At the apex of the administrative system lies the cabinet with its departmental ministers and ministers without portfolio. The numbers of both types of minister vary slightly from government to government: a single individual may be given responsibility for more than one department, and/or new posts without portfolio may be created. New ministries may be created only by law. At present there are twelve ministries (see Table 3.2).[4] Posts without portfolio, of which there are usually between six and eight in each government, exist within the Prime Minister's Office (Presidenza del Consiglio dei Ministri, PCM) and are created – ostensibly at least – either to entrust an individual with a specific task (for example, the co-ordination of European policy) or to give them charge of an agency (such as the Development Fund for Southern Italy).

The Prime Minister's Office

The PCM has the dual (and overlapping) function of assisting the Prime Minister in carrying out his job of co-ordinating the policy of government and of providing machinery for co-ordinating the work of cabinet. Ultimately responsible for this task are the three individuals in closest contact with the Prime Minister:

- his general secretary – who is drawn from the most prestigious levels of the public administration and who acts as the PCM's chief administrator;
- the *sottosegretario di stato* (under-secretary to the PCM), an elected politician who has four tasks: to monitor the detailed legislative work of the Government as a whole; to represent the Government in the Chamber of Deputies; to negotiate with parliamentary committees over government bills; to act as secretary to the cabinet (Hine 1993: 209);
- the *segretario particolare* (personal secretary) whose task is to manage the Prime Minister's personal political arrangements.

Below this top triumvirate are the departments into which the PCM is organised. These are of essentially three kinds: the Prime Minister's offices (consisting of his personal office, press office, diplomatic office, military office), administrative offices and the departments headed by the ministers without portfolio. With a few exceptions, all have traditionally been subject to periodic reorganisation. The most important of the departments from the point of view of the core function of policy co-ordination are probably the Department for Implementation of the Government's Legislative Programme and the Department for Judicial and Legislative Affairs. The principal task of the former is essentially strategic. That is, its task is to assist its minister in carrying out all the initiation, co-ordination, monitoring, verification and evaluation tasks associated with the processes of implementing and updating the Government's

Table 3.2. Composition of the Italian Government, December 2008

Prime Minister (President of the Council of Ministers)
Silvio BERLUSCONI

*Under-secretaries to the Presidency of
    the Council of Ministers*
Gianni LETTA
Paolo BONAIUTI   (Information, communication
                                                and publishing)

Gianfranco MICCICHÈ   (CIPE)
Carlo GIOVANARDI   (Families, drugs and service to
                                                the community)

Michela Vittoria BRAMBILLA   (Tourism)
Aldo BRANCHER   (Federalism)
Roco CRIMI   (Sport)
Maurizio BALOCCHI   (Legislative simplification)
Guido BERTOLASO   (Solution for the refuse
                                                emergency in Campania)

Ministers without portfolio
Raffaele FITTO   Relations with the regions
Gianfranco ROTONDI   Implementation of the
                                                Government's programme

Renato BRUNETTA   Public administration and
                                                innovation

Mara CARFAGNA   Equal opportunities
Andrea RONCHI   European policies
Elio VITO   Relations with Parliament
Umberto BOSSI   Federal reform
Giorgia MELONI   Youth
Roberto CALDEROLI   Legislative simplification

Ministers with portfolio		*Under-secretaries*
Franco FRATTINI	Foreign affairs	Stefania Gabriella Anastasia Craxi Alfredo Mantica Enzo Scotti
Roberto MARONI	Interior	Michelino Davico Alfredo Mantovano Nitto Francesco Palma
Angelino ALFANO	Justice	Maria Elisabetta Alberti Casellati Giacomo Caliendo

Table 3.2. (*cont.*)

Ignazio LA RUSSA	Defence	Giuseppe Cossiga Guido Crosetto
Giulio TREMONTI	Economy and finance	Alberto Giorgetti Daniele Molgora Nicola Cosentino Luigi Casero Giuseppe Vegas
Claudio SCAJOLA	Economic development	Ugo Martinat Paolo Romani Adolfo Urso
Luca ZAIA	Agriculture, food and forests	Antonio Buonfiglio
Stefania PRESTIGIACOMO	Environment, seas and territorial protection	Roberto Menia
Altero MATTEOLI	Infrastructure and transport	Roberto Castelli Bartolomeo Giachino Mario Mantovani Giuseppe Maria Reina
Maurizio SACCONI	Health, work and social security	Pasquale Viespoli Ferruccio Fazio Francesca Martini Eugenia Maria Roccella
Mariastella GELLMINI	Universities, education and research	Giuseppe Pizza
Alfredo BONDI	Heritage and cultural activities	Francesco Maria Giro

Note: Under-secretaries assist ministers in fulfilling their remits. The functions shown in brackets indicate the areas of responsibility delegated to them.

Source: www.governo.it/Governo/Ministeri/ministri_gov.html.

programme. The Department for Judicial and Legislative Affairs, on the other hand, is concerned with co-ordination in terms of legislative detail. Its tasks, in other words, are to promote 'inter-departmental co-ordination in the process of drafting proposed legislation and regular monitoring of existing legislation for incoherence, over-complexity and, most significantly, inconsistency with current government policy' (Hine and Finocchi, 1991: 92–3).

Ministries

Ministries vary enormously in size – from well over a million in the case of Education to well under five hundred in the case of Environment and Territorial Protection. This is a range that reflects a corresponding diversity in the ministries' structures. Prior to the reform of 1999 (discussed in the following chapter), the structural features common to most of the ministries were their division into a number (ranging from two to twelve) of *direzioni*. Each of these had responsibility for a particular area of the ministry's activity and was headed by a *dirigente generale* directly responsible to the minister. (Only Defence and Foreign affairs have single heads along the lines of the British permanent secretaries.) This feature was introduced by Prime Minister Crispi in the late 1880s and was intended to forestall the emergence of an independent centre of power by preventing the development of a single unified view at the apex of the ministry. However, it also creates obvious problems of administrative co-ordination and efficiency. The latter suffers also as a consequence of inter-ministerial divisions and overlap of responsibility between ministries (Furlong, 1994: 101).

Neither the division of responsibilities nor the structure of the ministries reflect any overarching design apparent at the time of the Republic's foundation. Moreover, any thoughts of rationalising the structure – for instance through amalgamations of the kind that were proposed by the Piga Commission in 1981 – were in subsequent years effectively vanquished by the realisation that to do so would upset the delicate balance of power subsisting between the governing parties. The problem was twofold.

- On the one hand, the formation of each new government would be accompanied by lengthy negotiations among the coalition partners over the division between them of the twenty-odd ministerial positions and eighty-odd positions as under-secretary.
- On the other hand, the positions so divided were in no sense regarded as being all of equal weight. Some were regarded as more desirable than others, this because of the unequal opportunities for the exercise of political power that they carried. Some – for instance, the ministries of the Interior or of Foreign Affairs – carried power because of their high visibility and prestige. Others, such as the ministries of Transport and of Public Works, were valued for the opportunities for the exercise of patronage which they offered. Yet others – for example, Industry – were considered important because of the opportunities for policy-initiatives that they

offered. And the precise value of each ministry would tend to vary over time. For example, ministries with high patronage potential might be considered particularly valuable just before an election.

So the process of distributing ministries and under-secretarial positions among parties and factions tended to be an extremely delicate and complex one – so much so that it was for long a matter of folklore that there existed a manual – the *Manuale Cencelli*, named after its supposed originator, a director of the personal office of the Christian Democrat leader Mariano Rumor (Furlong, 1994: 116) – designed to guide the participants to the negotiations. This being the case, it is easy to appreciate why rationalisation of the structure of ministries was never forthcoming: any reform proposal would not only have had to find a majority in a highly fragmented parliament but would also have had to be successful in dealing with the complexities just described in order to obtain that majority in the first place.

In any industrialised democracy, ministers will need senior officials to assist them in the making of policy by providing information, advice and operational solutions to the problems posed by policy objectives. On the other hand, such a need leaves ministers vulnerable to 'bureaucratic capture', that is, to the danger that they are unable to resist accepting officials' views about what policy should be in the area in question. This danger has been potentially great in post-war Italy given the weakness of governments and high turnover of ministers. Prior to the 1990s when, as described in the following chapter, the situation began to change somewhat, the danger was effectively neutralised by means of an unwritten agreement between politicians and senior officials. In exchange for officials' acceptance of an essentially marginal role in most major policy decisions, politicians undertook not to use their discretionary power to interfere with established patterns of promotion based on seniority, thus refraining from attempts to use an American-style spoils system as the means to avoid bureaucratic capture.

Consequently, in the design and operationalisation of policy objectives, ministers have traditionally received assistance, not from senior officials but from ministerial cabinets. These are composed of outside advisers and, through their legislative offices, are sometimes able to play a role in co-ordinating the activities of the *dirigenti generali*. In this way they help compensate, to some degree, for the absence of a single administrative head of the ministry in question. Nevertheless, formally speaking, the cabinets are expected to provide advice to the minister, not to attempt to manage or control the day-to-day activities of the ministry. Most members of the cabinet come and go with the minister.

Agencies

A second means by which the political class has historically sought to achieve the subordination of administrators to its designs has been through the creation of a variety of special agencies, collectively known as the *para-statali*. These have not been subject to the 'self-restraint' agreement effectively limiting the freedom of ministers to hire and fire. Therefore, they have provided ministers with a more pliable stratum of senior officials than were available through the central ministries.

The *para-statali* have traditionally been divided into three broad groups:

- *amministrazioni autonome* covering organisations that derive a substantial part of their revenue from the provision of commercial services. They are effectively independent in terms of day-to-day management but are at the same time responsible to a given ministry. The largest of these 'autonomous administrations' in terms of personnel are the National Forestry Commission, the National Aviation Authority, the State Monopolies Board. Until recently they included the railways (which became a private company with the birth of Trenitalia in 2000) and the National Road Building Agency (which became a private company in 2002).
- the *enti pubblici*, which are even harder to define and of which there are somewhere in the region of 54,000. They should probably be regarded as a residual category. Most of them have even greater autonomy than the 'autonomous administrations'. Many are organised on a local level and are ultimately responsible to a sub-national unit of government (as would be the case of a local bus service, for example). Most arose to provide welfare and other services to a limited sectional group. To a large extent, therefore, the group can be seen as consisting of bodies providing, in a piecemeal fashion, services associated with the growth of the welfare state from the 1920s on and whose provision has still to be rationalised.
- Finally, there is the group consisting of the state holding companies which, following the example of the Institute for Industrial Reconstruction (Istituto per la Ricostruzione Industriale, IRI) established in 1933, emerged in order to manage state-owned shareholdings in private companies which could thereby be used as tools of industrial policy. By being made to invest in areas where private industry was slow to act, the companies could be used to stimulate commercial activity in such areas and thus provide for public direction of industrial development. The state stands at considerable remove from day-to-day operations. The typical arrangement is for a state holding company to own further, subsidiary holding companies, while the individual enterprises at the base of the pyramid operate in accordance with their legal status as private companies. Meanwhile, the shares of these operating companies may be only partly owned by the state.

The size of the state holdings sector has been greatly reduced since the early 1990s as the result of a policy of privatisation. This policy was launched half-heartedly at first, but with growing conviction from 1992: then, the grip of the traditional governing parties on the state machine began gradually to be loosened; and doubts began to grow about the ability of Italy to meet the so-called 'convergence criteria' laid down in the Treaty of Maastricht. The latter

101

specified that the achievement of monetary union required each signatory state to have a budget deficit no larger than 3 per cent of Gross Domestic Product (GDP) and a public-sector debt no larger than 60 per cent of GDP. Italy's shortfalls were in both cases considerably in excess of these figures. Moreover, in accordance with a traditional attitude of enthusiasm for European integration, the country's governing class had a particular fear of being left in the 'slow lane' of monetary union. It was therefore clear that radical measures were required in the arena of public finance.

▨ Membership of international and supra-national organisations

The conviction of Italian governments of the 1990s that efforts to join the single currency were essential to the country's future economic wellbeing meant that the EU-established membership criteria would thereby be enabled to exert a decisive influence on the basic contours of the Government's economic policy. And Italy's membership since then provides a particularly good example of the degree to which central government must share authority in policy-making with decision-makers located elsewhere. Paradoxically, in fact, European Monetary Union (EMU) has led to a shift of policy-making authority away from Italian state structures while increasing their capacity for autonomous decision-making vis-à-vis societal interests within the country.

As we saw in the previous chapter, the First Republic was characterised by weak executives and prime ministers.

- The authority of such prime ministers was rendered fragile by their positions as heads of coalition governments whose members were chosen not by themselves but by negotiations between the leaders of the parties of which the governments were composed.
- The parties, for their part, were, as we saw above, unable to compete on alternative policy programmes and used, as an alternative basis of voter mobilisation, the sharing out of positions of influence for the purposes of patronage and the distribution of favours.

These two features combined left the state open to the penetration of its decision-making structures by a wide range of social and economic interests which in turn made it weak, with policy-makers unable to set clear economic objectives and then to use the instruments of the state to achieve them. Since economic policy-making served a broad range of micro-sectional interests, it could only be incremental and so not surprisingly levels of public debt began to grow.

Levels of growth of the public debt were particularly significant in the 1980s so that by the time Italy agreed to the convergence criteria set out in the Maastricht Treaty, the ratio of debt to GDP was of the order of 100 per cent (della Sala, 1997: 22). Membership of the single currency was felt by Italian policy-makers to be essential for at least three reasons:

(1) The growing strength of international financial markets had made it impossible for single governments to pursue autonomous monetary policies that might be rejected by the markets themselves.

(2) A single currency was required in order to complete the internal market which Italy had already signed up to.

(3) Not being in the currency meant the risk of being placed in a situation of disadvantage in the single market and of being marginalised in Europe.

At the same time, the membership criteria themselves held out the prospect that, were Italy to be successful in meeting them, the economy might perform better; for they would force governments to reduce public debt which in turn would bring lower interest rates. There thus developed a broadly based consensus on the need to seek to meet the criteria, and this served to augment governments' authority vis-à-vis the political and social forces that it had previously been forced to appease. Efforts to meet the convergence criteria required a wholesale restructuring of public finances. These included privatisation, a restructuring of the welfare state and a reform of the tax system. And every time this or that group seemed likely to challenge its choices, the Government was able to immobilise opposition by pointing to the need to catch the European train as the force dictating budgetary policy (della Sala, 1997: 27).

Thus it is that Italy's membership of the EU and the constraints emanating therefrom have led to what della Sala (1997) has called a 'hollowing out' and 'hardening' of the state in recent years:

- On the one hand, European integration has led to significant shifts of the state's authority upwards to the institutions of the EU.
- On the other hand, these very shifts have set up pressures from the EU to create more coherent policy-making that makes it more difficult for societal interests to penetrate state structures.

This situation is set to continue, with the EU assuming an ever-increasing profile as a level of Italian governance. EMU itself has meant that the central authorities have surrendered power over such basic levers of macroeconomic management as control of interest rates, exchange rates and the money supply. Meanwhile, more generally the Growth and Stability Pact adopted in 1997 sets out a combination of legal and political instruments designed to ensure the co-ordination of member states' economic policies, particularly in the matter of budget deficits. These instruments are necessary if EMU is to work properly. EMU 'was largely a spill-over from the single market programme … In its turn EMU is now prompting a further spill-over, with many EMU participants pressing for the further development of macroeconomic policies including fiscal policy' (Cram, Dinan and Nugent, 1999: 356).

Meanwhile, the EU is likely to ensure that Italian governance becomes even more multi-level as growing integration interacts with the slow process of decentralisation on which Italy has embarked. The Bassanini Laws mentioned earlier widened the administrative remit of the regions. In doing so, they represented a recognition that in a Europe with a single currency, tough rules on state aid to private enterprise and a common legal framework, extensive, centralised bureaucratic procedures were likely to represent a significant competitive disadvantage (Gilbert, 2000: 140). As we have seen, the 2001 constitutional reforms gave the regions new powers to intervene in the legislative processes of the EU in cases where the EU laws in question concerned matters over which the regions had legislative powers. In short, in common with the other member states, Italy will find domestic politics and European politics increasingly intermeshed with fewer and fewer political actors and actions without a European dimension.

Meanwhile, membership of international organisations such as NATO, the IMF and the UN provide additional levels of Italian governance whose capacity to have a direct impact on the everyday lives of ordinary citizens was graphically illustrated by the circumstances surrounding the Group of Eight (G8) meeting in Genoa in July 2001. In that month, whole areas of the city were closed off to host the summiteers, and the city itself was the scene of violent street demonstrations. In fact, Italy has in the post-war period been a country whose position in the international system of alliances has had an especially strong influence on her internal governance given that her second largest party and main party of opposition, until the collapse of the Berlin Wall, was also the largest communist party in the West. This meant that her party politics directly mirrored the geopolitical conflict between the United States and the Soviet Union, and that the internal authority of her governments was accordingly limited. The freedom of her national-level politicians in coalition formation was, as we have seen, subject to the limitations imposed by the *conventio ad excludendum*. This was underwritten by the United States which, consequently, would periodically remind Italian governments, in subtle and not-so-subtle ways (as described in greater detail in chapter 10), that whatever the electorate thought, America was the ultimate authority in matters of coalition formation.

NATO membership meant that the United States also had ultimate authority over the basic contours of Italian foreign policy. Italy and the other European countries that were members of the alliance knew that they would be unable to defend the United States in the event of a Soviet attack, but that the United States would be able to defend them. Consequently, in common with the other European countries, Italy was bound to the United States by ties of mutual assurance. That is, the United States agreed to defend Italy's national security in the event of a crisis involving the Soviet Union. In exchange, Italy acceded to US control of the nuclear arsenal and of arms-limitation negotiations. In so doing, it surrendered to the United States, when it came to dealings with the Eastern bloc, two of the classic instruments of foreign policy: force and diplomacy (Colombo, 1994).

These instruments were not always deployed according to the highest standards of due process. *Gladio*, for example, was a secret, armed, anti-Communist organisation set up in 1956 by the Central Intelligence Agency and the Italian government without the knowledge of Parliament. The constitutional lawyer, Zagrebelsky argued that the formation and operation of *Gladio* amounted to high treason (Ferraresi, 1992: 90). For it was a secret military organisation, serving political ends, controlled by a foreign power and formed through an international treaty kept secret from Parliament. In this it conflicted with article 80 of the Constitution, which places in Parliament the responsibility for ratifying international treaties. When it came to light in 1991, the *Gladio* affair served to provide the public with yet another reminder of the weakness of the Italian state referred to above. Specifically, it reminded them of the difficulties experienced by the state in exercising proper control over its many parts. On 3 February 1992, the head of the Rome Prosecutor's Office requested that the *Gladio* case be closed (*archiviato*). This office had long been known as the 'foggy port' for the large number of judicial proceedings it had succeeded in 'burying' over the years without the accused in such proceedings being brought properly to trial.

The end of the Cold War has thrown a question mark over the purpose of NATO; and the role of it and of the United States in the processes of Italian governance are now less clearly definable. This is not to say that these entities are, or are likely to become, less *significant*; for one of the features that has until recently distinguished Italian foreign policy from that of a number of the liberal democracies is that it has tended not to be the subject of cross-party consensus. This has meant that domestic political alignments have been unusually heavily exposed to the repercussions of international politics. This was apparent in 1997, for example, when the effect of the institution of an Italian-led international peace-keeping force in Albania was actually such as to weaken the Government because of the divisions provoked within the parliamentary majority. Other intergovernmental organisations (IGOs) too will retain a not marginal role in Italian governance. Few, with the obvious exception of the EU, are supra-national. That is, few of them have the power to make decisions binding on the member states even if unanimity has not been achieved (Papp, 1991: 59). On the other hand, IGOs provide a wide range of services for their members. These range from regulative functions (for example, the World Health Organization) to distributive functions (for example the IMF). Therefore, it is difficult to deny that they add significant additional levels to the governance of states despite their lack of clear authority to enforce their decisions on their members.

◼ Conclusion

In this chapter we have sought to provide a feel for the degree to which governance in Italy is a multi-level phenomenon with no single type of institution having overwhelmingly more influence over public policy than any other type, far less being in a position to make policy in conditions of autonomy. Policy is the product of multiple pressures deriving from a large number of institutions existing in a state of interdependence. Though hardly original, this is an observation whose meaning, like much that is obvious, is not necessarily clear. What we have therefore sought to do in this chapter is to provide an overview of some of the most important government structures at sub-national, national and international levels, describing how they are related to each other, as well as some of the ways in which they affect each other. What will hopefully have been conveyed by this description, then, is a clear sense of the degree to which Italian governance, like that of most countries, is not something that is provided by sovereign institutions for a country conceived as a distinct and insulated unit. Rather, it is something that emerges from processes of negotiation and interaction between institutions whose terms of reference and capacities to act are in a state of perpetual change.

That said, it is important to avoid overstating the case. Public policy *is* the product of multiple influences deriving from actors and institutions at a range of levels of governance. However, it remains the case that some actors and institutions are more influential than others. The institutions of central government, in Italy as in most other democracies, have significance that is *at least* equal to that of other institutions in shaping the public circumstances of citizens' lives; and, as we argued in the previous section, in Italy their power has grown, not diminished, in recent years. For this reason, we devote the whole of the following chapter to them.

■ Further reading

Sidney Tarrow, in *Between Center and Periphery: Grassroots Politics in Italy and France* (New Haven: Yale University Press, 1977), provides the classic account of central–local relations in Italy and does so from a comparative perspective. Though dated now, the book repays close attention by providing significant insights into how local politicians engage with the institutions of government and seek to mobilise resources for their areas. Another classic account is Percy Allum's study, *Politics and Society in Post-War Naples* (Cambridge: Cambridge University Press, 1973), providing rich insights into the operation of clientelism at the local level. Meanwhile, Simona Piattoni's edited collection, *Clientelism, Interests and Democratic Representation* (Cambridge: Cambridge University Press, 2001), allows a comparison of Italy with other countries while offering a novel perspective on clientelism as a tool of governance. Fabio Rugge provides insights into Italy's bureaucratic traditions by comparing them with those of other European countries in 'Administrative traditions in Western Europe'. This can be found in B. Guy Peters and Jon Pierre, *Handbook of Public Administration* (London: Sage, 2003). Insights into some of the ways in which governance in Italy was affected by the processes leading up to European Monetary Union (EMU) are to be found in Vincent della Sala 'Hollowing out and Hardening the State: European Integration and the Italian Economy' (in Martin J. Bull and Martin Rhodes (eds.), *Crisis and*

Transition in Italian Politics, London: Frank Cass, 1997) and in Mark Gilbert, 'The Bassanini Laws: a half-way house in local government reform' (in David Hine and Salvatore Vassallo (eds.), *Italian Politics: The Return of Politics*, New York and Oxford: Berghahn, 2000).

Notes

1. See, for example, Tarrow, 1977.
2. Mayors and councils are elected at the same time, and each mayoral candidate is obliged, in announcing his or her candidature, to declare an affiliation with one or more of the party lists containing the names of candidates for the council. The resources are therefore threefold: the threat of resignation; the threat of standing for election against their supporting parties: this is unlikely to result in victory for the mayor (Baldini, 2002b) but has the potential at least to cause the parties to *lose*; the threat of refusing to stand (thus depriving the parties of any electoral 'added value' the mayoral candidate may have).
3. These points are explained in greater detail in Newell, 2007.
4. Between ministers with and without portfolio, deputy ministers and under-secretaries, the current government numbers sixty-three people. This contrasts with the 105 members of the previous Prodi government, which was necessarily larger owing to the larger number of parties belonging to that coalition.

4   Policy-making and policy implementation: executives, legislatures and bureaucrats

■ Introduction

The purpose of this chapter is to explore

(1) how, in the process of policy-making, the legislature, the political executive and the bureaucracy interact in the Italian case, and

(2) how **power** (Box 4.1) to influence the content of policy is distributed between them.

Political scientists usually think of legislatures as being the least influential of the three types of institution. As we shall see, Italy is a somewhat unusual case in this respect.

    Largely because of the scope and complexity of modern government in mass democracies, parties compete for office on the basis of programmes of policies. In parliamentary regimes, the enactment of these policies requires party leaderships to be able to rely on stable and disciplined majorities. Under normal circumstances, such discipline is forthcoming because those who want to be members of Parliament usually require the support of party organisations in order to be elected. Without such support, their chances of election are slim indeed, and this in effect subordinates them to party leaders. For these

Box 4.1

Key terms: power, globalisation, supra-national organisations, policy communities

Power: the ability of a person or group to control the environment around them, power both constrains action and makes it possible. Inherent in the nature of social interaction itself (all parties to a relationship have *some* power), power cannot be meaningfully conceived apart from the social interaction through which it manifests itself. Measuring its exercise and distribution is, however, problematic because not only does it reveal itself in action we resist having to take, but also, by acting on our values and beliefs, it effects what we do freely, by ourselves. Consequently, empirical observation of what *does* happen may mislead us – while on the other hand, we cannot measure what *does not* happen. Thus, the observation that a government has a 100 per cent success rate in passing its bills – for example – may be indicative, not of great power of the executive vis-à-vis the legislature but of great weakness if what is really going on is that the government is refraining from introducing all but those bills it feels certain will be successful.

Globalisation: the process whereby what goes on in any one part of the world is decreasingly subject to the constraints of physical geography. Viewed as being driven by economic and technological change (especially that associated with development of the information and communications technologies), globalisation is seen as leading to various forms of homogenisation and thus the greater integration of economies, societies and polities on a world scale.

Supra-national organisations: these are international organisations, like the EU, with the power to enforce compliance with their decisions, even on the part of members who oppose them. They are to be contrasted with intergovernmental organisations, whose decisions can only have effect on all members if all agree to sign up to them.

Policy community: a group of individuals with an interest – whether as legislators, lobbyists or experts – in a particular area of public policy. Because they share a unified body of knowledge, the members of a policy community, though having their own specific goals, come to develop shared perspectives on the problems at hand and hence come to embrace many of the same policy objectives.

two reasons, electorates have come to view the onus for formulating or 'making' public policy as lying with the political executive (governments), and this has in turn reinforced the desire and ability of the latter to dominate legislatures through disciplined majorities. On the other hand, the scope and complexity of public policy mean that governments are frequently dependent on the expertise of interest-group representatives in the framing of legislation. These representatives are thus in a position to exert pressure over the content of proposals as the price of their co-operation. Therefore, given disciplined parties, they and governments are together effectively able to determine the content of legislation before the process of legislative enactment has even begun.

Meanwhile, **globalisation** (Box 4.1) has brought to the fore a range of problems beyond the control of individual nation-states. These problems include environmental damage, terrorism and the international movement of refugees. This has encouraged the growth of international and **supranational organisations** (Box 4.1), such as the UN and the EU, with powers to make an increasing range of decisions binding on member states. Thereby governments (the only players in international arenas) have been placed under new obligations. In turn, they have been placed under new pressures to seek to bend legislatures to their will because their international obligations must often be met through national legislation. Globalisation, then, has accentuated the subordination of legislatures to executive branches of government.

At the same time, groups within the bureaucracy have policy-making resources that are unavailable in the legislative and executive arenas. These include the following considerations:

(1) The power to implement policy. This confers a de facto power to make policy since it necessarily entails an irreducible minimum of discretion.
(2) As compared to plenary sessions of the legislature, arenas within the bureaucracy are relatively private and specialised. This brings relative insulation from public pressure, and privileged access to information and intellectual resources.
(3) To a greater extent than actors in the legislative and executive arenas, departments within the bureaucracy work in close daily contact with interest groups whose co-operation is essential for the successful implementation of policy. This enables the departments, with the groups, to form **'policy communities'** (Box 4.1) engaged in detailed and relatively secretive policy-making on the basis of shared interests (for instance, the interest of farming groups and ministries of agriculture in obtaining ever larger public subsidies).

The above factors invite the assumption that, in terms of sheer influence over the content of legislation, bureaucracies are at least on a par with executives, with legislatures occupying a decidedly marginal position. On the other hand, in parliamentary democracies, bureaucracies are legally accountable to their executive masters, and political executives are constitutionally accountable to legislatures. This prompts the suggestion of a simple model depicting a two-way flow of power in policy-making: 'downwards' from bureaucracies and executives to legislatures, and 'upwards' from legislatures to executives and bureaucracies. As we shall see, in Italy, policy-making through legislature, executive and bureaucracy is captured imperfectly by this model. The distribution of power within and between the three institutions is, instead, much more polycentric in the Italian case than the simple two-way flow implies.

The remainder of the chapter is divided into three sections in each of which we explore the interface, in the policy-making process in Italy, between

- Parliament and the executive,
- the executive and bureaucracy,
- the bureaucracy and Parliament.

In each case, our concern is with the nature of interaction between them and how each influences the behaviour and functioning of the other. They are not the only public institutions that play a significant role in the formulation and implementation of policy at the national level. Of growing significance in recent years, and in this reflecting a transnational phenomenon, have been the judicial authorities. These are considered in chapters 6 and 9.

■ Parliament and executive

Three interrelated sets of factors have traditionally made it difficult for Italian governments to wield the kind of power over their parties' followers that in other liberal democracies allows executives to subordinate the legislature to their will.

The Influence of history

The first of these is history. That is, in the Constituent Assembly, the Christian Democrats (DC) and the Communists (PCI) were each keen to avoid constitutional arrangements that would make it easy for the other party to steer the legislative activity of Parliament in the event that it won an overall majority. The arrangements that were made also reflect awareness of the deep ideological division running through the polity at the time. The problem was that the PCI was associated with a geopolitical power block in competition with the block to which Italy belonged. Therefore, it could never be admitted to government. On the other hand, excluding the PCI permanently from office had a potentially significant cost. The cost was that a not inconsiderable proportion of the electorate might come to feel that it had no stake in the system whatsoever. The solution that was found for this dilemma lies in the second factor that accounts for the relative inability of executives to dominate Parliament, namely the legal rules and structures governing its procedures; for these allowed the PCI to participate in legislation but without the need for it formally to be associated with the government and its majority.

Legal rules and structures

The Constitution

Legal rules and structures did this first and foremost through the constitutional provision guaranteeing to each chamber's committees a role in the drafting of legislation (Box 4.2). That is, the Constitution stipulates that bills, once presented, *must* be considered in committee. Here they may be amended or combined with other bills so that the text referred for decision to the plenary session may differ considerably from the original. Thereby, the Constitution decentralises processes of internal decision-making within each chamber. It creates arenas where, away from the public gaze, the formation of 'anomalous' majorities, combining governing and opposition parties, is much easier than on the floor of either chamber (Box 4.3). By the same token, however, the constitutional provision places a significant obstacle in the way of attempts by the executive to dominate; for it gives the committees a constitutionally guaranteed sphere of autonomy which may not be infringed by any other body. That is, proposals emerging from committees may be amended or thrown out during the course of subsequent plenary debate; but until such time, committee decisions may not be overturned. This makes these bodies, constitutionally speaking, fully independent powers.

Second, the Constitution establishes a parliament of the symmetrically bicameral type. In doing so, it gives groups of parliamentarians power to resist executive pressure that is greater than it would be if Parliament were monocameral or the powers of its chambers asymmetrical. This is because symmetric bicameralism entails that until such time as the two chambers are able to agree identically worded texts, bills are condemned to shuttle back and forth between them as they each debate the latest version produced by the other.

Third, the Constitution gives the power of legislative initiative to individual parliamentarians as well as to the Government. This is unusual from a comparative perspective. By giving this power to each actor on exactly the same terms, the Constitution erects a barrier against the marginalisation of backbench initiatives as compared to those of the Government.[1] Thus, Parliament's standing orders may establish different procedures for the consideration of different categories of bill. They may also allow priority to be given, in the parliamentary timetable, to particular categories of bill. What they cannot do, while remaining within the Constitution, is to allow the Government to choose, on its own authority, the procedure to which its bills will be subject. Nor can they allow the Government to decide, on its own authority, the priority its bills will be given in the parliamentary timetable.

The standing orders

A second source of the legal rules and structures governing Parliament's procedures is its standing orders. Despite various amendments over the years, planning is still managed according to rules that protect it from the impositions of simple majorities. The standing orders thus prevent governments from controlling the parliamentary timetable. In 1948, the Chamber of Deputies decided simply to adopt the standing orders that had been in force prior to the advent of Fascism. Meanwhile, the Senate decided to adopt very similar standing orders. This made it possible for parties, the deep divisions among which directly reflected those of the Cold War, to avoid conflict over the drafting of fresh regulations – which would have required a number of difficult decisions about the distribution, within the parliamentary arena, of

Box 4.2

Inside the Italian parliament: making law

The legislative process:

- Each member of Parliament, and the Government, can make legislative proposals on the same terms.
- Once the proposal is printed, the president of the chamber in question assigns it, for consideration, to one of the chamber's standing commissions.
- These consider the proposal either in *sede referente* or in *sede legislativa* (a third procedure, *sede redigente* being rarely used). In the former case, the commission uses the proposal as a 'first draft' to produce a 'final' version – possibly amalgamating it with other, similar proposals, or dividing it into two or more separate proposals – for subsequent debate by the chamber. In the latter case, the commission considers the proposal and passes it – or a modified version – into law on its own authority without need for further reference to the chamber.
- Proposals ready for consideration by the chamber are then given a place in the parliamentary timetable by the Committee of Group Leaders, with initial debate focusing on the proposal's general outlines.
- At this stage, the proposal may fall altogether if one or more parliamentarians successfully propose that the bill not be discussed for reasons of merit (that is, for reasons having to do with the substance of the proposal) or for reasons of constitutionality (that is because the proposal is claimed to be unconstitutional).
- Proposals that succeed in getting over these hurdles are then subject to discussion of their individual articles and of any amendments to them that may be proposed. Each proposed amendment is voted upon, those proposing the larger changes being voted upon first, in accordance with the principle of preclusion: thus, once the chamber has voted to delete an article altogether, any proposals to modify that article fall automatically.
- The text as amended is then voted upon in its entirety before being transmitted to the other chamber for consideration.
- If amended by the other chamber, the text must go back to the first chamber for the amendments (not the entire text) to be considered by it – and the text shuttles between the two chambers until identically worded texts can be agreed.
- This requirement for two – or possibly even more – 'readings' is commonly thought of as a source of inefficiency in law-making, but this view is too simplistic. In practice, more than two readings are rarely required owing to similarity in the political composition of the two chambers, and in any case the chambers' presidents are in a position to facilitate the reaching of political agreements designed to avoid the process becoming too drawn out. And the existing arrangements arguably speed up the legislative process: they enable each chamber to deal with different bills at the same time and thus, together, to work more quickly than would be possible did a single chamber have to deal with the same number of bills.

rights and obligations between them (Lippolis, 2001: 616). But it also meant that until 1971, the standing orders made no provision for planning at all in so far as agendas were set on a day-to-day basis, by each chamber's president. With the reform of 1971, the planning of activities was entrusted to each body's Committee of Parliamentary Group Leaders. This, however, could decide only on the basis of unanimity. The 1997 amendment cut to two-thirds the majority required in the Committee of Parliamentary Group Leaders. The change reduced but did not eliminate the obstacles in the way of control of the parliamentary timetable. Failing agreement, planning is done by the chambers' presidents. True, in carrying out this task, they are obliged to take account of the 'priorities outlined by the government'. But they are also obliged to take account of the proposals of each parliamentary group.

Over the years, opportunities to resist executive dominance by various types of obstructionism have progressively been closed off. This has occurred because of the common interest of parliamentarians, whether of the governing majority or not, in preventing the work of the institution being paralysed by the exploits of small minorities (notably the Radicals, who entered Parliament for the first time in the 1970s).

- Thus, the times available for individual speeches, and the opportunities to present amendments, have been increasingly severely restricted.
- Most importantly, the provision that the final vote on bills had to be secret – making it possible for government supporters to sabotage, without risk of being discovered, parts of bills with which they disagreed – was abolished in 1988.

These changes have arguably increased the efficiency of decision-making through Parliament. However, they have been balanced by the retention or introduction of provisions that have sought to protect the interests of minorities. Thereby, the difficulties faced by governments in seeking to steer the work of the chambers have been perpetuated. Thus:

- while secret voting has largely ended, it continues to be available for decisions concerning the standing orders, constitutional rights and electoral laws;
- while there is a rigorous system of 'time rationing', all the matters on which the secret vote is available remain excluded from it;
- while opportunities to amend legislation have been limited, the 1997 reforms guarantee to each parliamentary group the opportunity to present a minimum number of amendments to each article of government proposals.

The party system

This set of facts throws a spotlight on the third set of factors that make life difficult for governments in seeking to legislate through Parliament, namely the characteristics of the party system. In so doing, it reveals the way in which

Box 4.3

Inside the Italian parliament: the chambers' standing commissions

The Chamber of Deputies	The Senate
Constitutional affairs	Constitutional affairs
Justice	Justice
Foreign affairs	Foreign affairs and emigration
Defence	Defence
The budget	The budget
Finance	Finance and the treasury
Cultural affairs	Education and heritage
The environment	Public works and communication
Transport	Agriculture and food production
Industry	Industry, commerce and tourism
Employment	Employment and social security
Social affairs	Health and hygiene
Agriculture	Land, environment and environmental heritage
The European Union	European Union policies

the three sets of factors we have referred to are interrelated. That is, legal rules and structures (a) are a product of history, and (b) do little to assist governments in directing the work of the chambers, and (c) would not have been a big problem if party-system characteristics had enabled governments to count on cohesive majorities. This, however, is the dilemma: Parliament's procedures reflect an historical absence of governing majority cohesion – which they have then helped to perpetuate.

The difficulties in acting in concert faced by majorities headed by the DC were described in detail in chapter 1. Governments frequently sought to escape from the consequences of indiscipline among their own followers by co-opting the support of the PCI. The party was willing to allow itself to be co-opted in this way because it saw the royal road to power and policy-making influence as being admitted, by the other parties, to the executive. Therefore, it had no alternative but to behave 'respectably'. This meant that for much of the period prior to the 1990s, the PCI in reality opposed very little but rather was embroiled in a series of pacts, often hidden, with the parties of government. This situation was often referred to using the term '*consociativismo*'. In exchange for assistance in the passage of legislation, the communist opposition acquired – especially in the 1970s when it was at its strongest – both substantive policy concessions and access to certain key positions within Parliament. These positions included, most notably, the chairs of a number of permanent committees and the presidency of the Chamber of Deputies.

It was a style of policy-making whose significance political scientists have traditionally highlighted by pointing to the proportion of bills approved on the floor of one or the other chamber as compared with the proportion approved by committees only. They have chosen this means of highlighting the issue because article 72 of the Constitution enables Parliament to give law-making powers to its committees. It also stipulates that the 'committee-only' route can be overridden at the request of one-tenth of the membership of the chamber, 'in which case the bill in question must be referred back to the plenary session' (Newell, 2000: 143). 'This gave the opposition considerable concealed power over the government since it could, if it so desired, choke the work of the whole chamber by demanding that all legislation be subject to the full legislative procedure' (Hine, 1993: 143). A high proportion of bills approved by committees only therefore becomes an indicator of the opposition's willingness to refrain from using its power. That is, it becomes an indicator of the opposition's willingness to collaborate in the passage of legislation.

The proportion of bills approved in committee fell considerably after 1992 when the party system began to take on increasingly bipolar characteristics. However, collaboration has simply shifted from the committees to the floor. This is revealed by the fact that the combined percentage of bills approved *either* in committee *or* by ample majorities on the floor has not changed substantially (Giuliani and Capano, 2001: 41–51; Capano, 2003: 23).[2] This points to the persistence of consensual styles of decision-making. In doing so it suggests that, even after the party system upheavals of the 1990s, governments still had difficulty in relying on clear and stable majorities in the passage of legislation. Two factors seemed to account for this difficulty.

(1) Coalitions of the centre left and centre right now compete for and win overall majorities of seats in Parliament. However, the coalitions are alliances whose cohesion is required in the electoral arena, but which are largely free of such pressures in the parliamentary arena. In other words, the parties form alliances, outside Parliament, for the strictly instrumental purpose of winning elections; but once elections have taken place, the party groups inside Parliament do not face the same imperatives. On the contrary, the numbers required to form a parliamentary group are small,[3] and fragmentation is given further encouragement by the laws concerning the public funding of parties (Capano, 2003: 18). After 1993, the winning of elections required parties belonging to the two coalitions to reach mutual stand-down arrangements across the single-member constituencies. *In between elections*, there was little to prevent parliamentarians abandoning their groups to form new parties: this was especially true if such parliamentarians calculated that they were likely to have sufficient blackmail power in the electoral arena to negotiate, for the subsequent election, stand-down arrangements with the remaining parties of the coalition. Unity and cohesion are public goods. The 2005 electoral-law reform did nothing to reduce the parties' powers to

negotiate and, if necessary, blackmail each other in processes of coalition formation. Not surprisingly, then, there was no noticeable impact of the 1990s party-system transformation on fragmentation within Parliament, which was on a clear upward trend well before this period.[4] The general election of 2008 brought a sudden reduction in fragmentation.[5] Further general elections will have to be fought before we can be certain whether the reduction is permanent or temporary.

(2) The consequence of growing fragmentation is to increase the number of veto players. That is, growing fragmentation increases the number of players whose consent is required, in decision-making, in order to bring about a shift away from the status quo (Tsebelis, 1999; 2002). Even though a majority of players may favour a shift from the status quo, they may disagree on the direction the shift should take, making reform impossible. Policy-making therefore continues to require bargaining and log-rolling involving ample majorities. By these processes, each actor agrees (as far as ideological and other considerations will allow) to support legislative projects desired by other players *now*, in the expectation that she will thereby maximise the likelihood of their support for his/her own projects in the *future*.

The most widely used measure of executives' capacities to get their way in legislatures has traditionally been the number of government bills passed as a percentage of the number presented. The assumption behind this measure is that the number of government bills presented indicates what governments *want*; while the proportion passed reflects their ability actually to *get* what they want. As the figures in Table 4.1 indicate, the rate of success of government bills declined markedly from the first to the twelfth legislature. It has not shown consistent signs of improvement since then. Rates remain well below the average for the legislatures elected before the 1990s.

A further sign of Parliament's continuing ability to constrain the activities of the executive has been the growing number of laws of delegation enacted since the early 1990s. The growth has led observers to see in such laws an attempt by governments, ' – urged into taking the lead in the field of legislation by the external pressure of European integration and by the legitimisation obtained under … new electoral rules – … to become more autonomous with regard to legislation by governing outside Parliament' (Capano and Giuliani, 2003). Laws of delegation give governments, in accordance with article 76 of the Constitution, authority to issue decrees having the force of law. As a percentage of non-reserved laws of government origin,[6] they amounted to 6.8% in the 1987–92 legislature, to 27.1% in the legislature that ran from 1992 to 1994, to 20.0% in the 1994–6 legislature and to 21.8% in the legislature that ran from 1996 to 2001 (Capano and Giuliani, 2001, table 1). In the legislatures that ran from 2001 to 2006 and from 2006 to 2008, the proportions were 39.9% and 48.5% respectively.[7] Qualitative evidence suggests that the laws of delegation have concerned important rather than minor matters (Capano and Giuliani, 2001; 2003).

Table 4.1. Success rate of government bills

Legislature		Presented to the chamber	Number approved	Proportion approved (as % of number presented)
1948–1953	I	2,199	1,996	92.8
1953–1958	II	1,564	1,439	92.0
1958–1963	III	1,484	1,340	90.3
1963–1968	IV	1,442	1,259	87.3
1968–1972	V	831	663	79.8
1972–1976	VI	1,133	941	83.1
1976–1979	VII	831	644	77.5
1979–1983	VIII	1,242	861	69.3
1983–1987	IX	1,175	769	65.4
1987–1992	X	1,369	922	67.3
1992–1994	XI	653	292	44.7
1994–1996	XII	819	318	38.8
1996–2001	XIII	1,222	695	56.9
2001–2006	XIV	1,471	729	49.5
2006–2008	XV	423	131	31.0

Source: Legislatures I to XII: della Sala, 1998, table 4.4a; legislatures XIII to XV, my own elaboration based on data available at www.senato.it.

New divisions of labour between legislature and executive

The increasing tendency of governments, under growing pressure from Europeanisation, to attempt to meet the resulting obligations by legislating outside of Parliament has been accompanied by a growing assiduousness of backbenchers generally in seeking to hold the executive to account (Box 4.4). The period since 1992 has seen the introduction of new instruments of control[8] and an upward trend in the frequency of use of such instruments (Table 4.2).[9] Moreover, 'whereas prior to the 1990s the instruments were exercised predominantly by opposition parliamentarians, over the past decade government backbenchers have become increasingly involved in their use' (Bull and Newell, 2005: 124; see Capano and Giuliani, 2003, table 2). This points in the direction of the emergence of a new 'division of labour' between legislature and executive. This new division of labour has involved Parliament accepting a 'downgrading' of its previously 'central' role in national governance while seeking to retain a significant role in the process. It has sought to retain this role by giving greater emphasis, in its activities, to the exercise of *ex-post* controls (questions and interpellations) and *ex-ante* guidance and direction (motions and resolutions).

A second change in the division of labour between executive and legislature that also seems to be related to processes of Europeanisation concerns the growing tendency towards *delegificazione* (deregulation). The tendency has arisen from the pressures for growing administrative efficiency if Italian industry was

Table 4.2. Oversight activity and laws of delegation

Legislature	Interpellations (monthly values in brackets)	Motions and assembly resolutions (monthly values in brackets)	Laws of delegation: number and as % of non-reserved government laws (in brackets)
1976–1979 VII	803 (22.3)	156 (4.3)	
1979–1983 VIII	3,169 (64.1)	452 (9.1)	
1983–1987 IX	1,706 (35.3)	456 (9.4)	
1987–1992 X	2,557 (43.7)	991 (16.9)	26 (6.8)
1992–1994 XI	1,654 (68.8)	459 (19.1)	16 (27.1)
1994–1996 XII	1,274 (50.7)	473 (18.8)	5 (20.0)
1996–2001 XIII	4,168 (67.7)	1,369 (22.2)	50 (21.8)
2001–2006 XIV	2,648 (45.7)	1,071 (18.2)	67 (39.9)
2006–2008 XV	1,216 (57.9)	542 (25.8)	16 (48.5)

Sources: for VII to XIII legislatures: Capano and Giuliani, 2001, table 1; 2003, table 2; for XIV and XV, my own elaboration based on data available at www.camera.it.

Box 4.4

Inside the Italian parliament: holding the Government to account

The instruments available to Parliament for ensuring that the executive remains accountable for what it does are of essentially two types: *ex-ante* (meaning 'before') and *ex-post* (meaning 'after'). By definition, therefore, *ex-ante* instruments enable Parliament to indicate what action it believes the Government should take in the future, to what end, with respect to what values, to the benefit of what groups. *Ex-post* instruments enable Parliament to acquire information about actions the Government has already undertaken.

Ex-ante instruments

- *Motions*: once presented, these give rise to a debate, with the possibility of amendment, etc., in much the way that legislative proposals do. They therefore give their proposers a means of inviting Parliament to take a position on the views expressed in the motion itself, where these views request that the Government take some particular stance rather than another on a given matter.
- *Resolutions*: these have the same function as motions but are presented at the end of a debate, such as one that – for example – may have taken place following a ministerial announcement of particular significance or gravity.
- *Orders of the day instructing the Government*: usually presented during the course of a debate on an item of proposed legislation, a resolution or a motion, these orders of the day demand that the Government interpret the text in

question in some specific way or that it implements the text's provisions in a given way or taking account of given factors.

While there are no formal, legal, consequences for governments that choose to ignore motions, resolutions or orders of the day, there may be *political* costs – which could in theory ultimately result in it having to face a vote of no confidence.

Ex-post instruments

- *Interrogations*: questions (which must be put in writing) to the Government (usually the relevant minister) in order to request information or to request confirmation of information already in the public domain. The member of Parliament raising the question can require an oral or a written response.
- *Interpellations* (which must also be put in writing) differ from interrogations in that they concern not specific, individual facts or situations but rather allow their presenters to ask the Government why it has conducted, or intends to conduct, itself in a certain way. They also provide more time for their presenters to explain their positions and to offer rejoinders to the Government's responses.
- *Hearings and investigations*: carried out by the commissions, they allow these bodies to ask ministers and other individuals to supply information or to appear before them to answer questions.
- *Commissions of inquiry* can be set up by either chamber on its own, or by means of the passage of a specific law (thus requiring the support of both chambers) – in which case it can be made to outlive the legislature in which it was established and/or be given special powers. In any case, these powers will be equivalent to those of the judicial authorities – meaning that the commission can legally compel compliance with its instructions (e.g. to individuals to appear and answer questions). The commissions are therefore set up to examine matters of considerable public interest, often under the pressure of public opinion, and to compel ministers or the entire government to take responsibility they are assumed to have, or actually have, for action in a given area.

to remain competitive within the single market. And it is a tendency that is bound up with article 70 of the Constitution, which gives legislative authority to the two chambers of Parliament *without qualification*. In doing this, article 70 removes the barriers that, in other polities, are usually placed in the way of law invading spheres dealt with by administrative action. Since matters regulated by law can only be changed by an act of at least equal legal standing, there is inherent in the absence of areas reserved to administrative action the potential for legislative proliferation (Di Palma, 1977: 40). Both the volume of legislative output and the spheres of action subjected to it are, in the Italian case, regularly among the largest in Europe. Since the early 1990s there have been increasingly frequent attempts to drive law out of the administrative sphere through legislation stipulating that the unwanted laws are to be abrogated with effect from the entry into force of regulations to replace them. In this way, the legislation has drawn upon the Government's power to issue regulations in pursuit of a given law. In this observers have seen an increasing division of labour between Parliament and the executive, with the former continuing to make broad policy decisions while leaving it to the executive to take the more specific and concrete decisions within the policy area concerned (Mazzoni Honorati, 2001: 153).

■ Executive and bureaucracy

In an efficiently functioning democracy, ministers and senior administrative officials work co-operatively to translate ministerial policy objectives into workable solutions. In turn, ministers seek constantly to reconcile the fulfilment of two, not entirely compatible, needs.

- One is the need to have officials who, because they are pro-active, are able to offer policy consultation and advice, and who in that sense 'make' policy, alongside their ministers. As David Hine (1993: 241) has pointed out, 'An administration which from the top down is the passive instrument of the politician's will is unlikely to serve him well.' After all, where else is the minister to go for advice?
- The other need is to avoid 'bureaucratic capture', or the risk that the minister ends up accepting the departmental conventional wisdom about what policy should look like.

Individually and collectively, members of the Italian executive have traditionally managed to avoid bureaucratic capture – but this, as we shall explain later, has been at the expense of being able to rely on proactive officials. And, as we shall explain now, success in avoiding bureaucratic capture has not generally been thanks to a clear collective purpose. Had this purpose existed, it would have enabled the executive decisively to steer the bureaucracy in the two crucial policy-making functions of drafting legislative proposals and then overseeing their implementation once enacted.

Prime-ministerial co-ordination

Under different circumstances, a clear collective purpose might have been provided by prime ministers leading from the front. However, Italian prime ministers have for most of the time in republican Italy found it difficult, if not impossible, to play such a role. In part, the difficulty has stemmed from the very same reasons that have made it difficult for executives effectively to steer the legislature. That is to say, for much of the post-war period, Italian prime ministers have lacked (a) the political resources and (b) the institutional/administrative resources that would have enabled them to play a strong leadership role in policy-making.

Prime ministers' political resources

Until the political upheavals of the 1990s, factionalised parties and unstable coalitions ensured that prime ministers were not usually authoritative leaders. Rather, they were mediators. Article 95 of the Constitution states that the Prime Minister 'conducts, and is responsible for, the general policy of the government'. However, prior to the early 1990s, successive prime ministers were rarely individuals with clearly distinct policy agendas of their own. Nor was a cabinet colleague's public expression of disagreement with a prime minister in itself threatening to the political fortunes of the colleague or his party. In the 1980s, Socialist Prime Minister, Bettino Craxi, turned out to be a forceful incumbent. As such, he was able to exert a degree of autonomous pressure and influence on the choices of his cabinet colleagues. But this only demonstrated that he was the exception that proved the rule. Craxi, who was one of only two non-Christian Democratic politicians to hold the office prior to the 1990s, became Prime Minister in August 1983. He thereupon set the record for the longest-lasting government (1,058 days) to that point. In fact, Craxi owed his power to two highly unusual circumstances:

(1) The fact that he, unlike most Christian Democratic prime ministers, had tight control over his party (after De Gasperi, Christian Democratic prime ministers were unable to combine that office with the office of party leader for any length of time).
(2) The Christian Democrats' reluctance, after their severe electoral setback in 1983, to challenge him.

Normally, prime ministers were Christian Democrat faction leaders. Their longevity in office was a function of their skills in reconciling internal differences within their own large party as well as the differences between the parties of their coalitions. And they had none of the powers of appointment that British prime ministers, for example, can use to impose policy and to reconcile policy differences. On the contrary, prime ministers were subordinate figures. Both cabinet appointments (including their own appointment!) and policy differences were normally decided by others. They were decided, that is, by the party and faction leaders. And they were frequently dealt with in what were called 'majority summits' (Criscitiello, 1993). That is, they were dealt with in arenas that were detached from the formal arenas of cabinet and cabinet committees.

In Italy, as in most parliamentary regimes, the role of Prime Minister is, in *constitutional* terms, very broadly defined. As a consequence, its *actual* powers – or the lack of them – become, as Hine and Finocchi (1991: 81) have pointed out, self-fulfilling. That is to say, prior to the 1990s the lack of precision in *formal* definitions of the role meant that *in practice* prime ministers could be challenged and checked. And 'such behaviour [fell] within the range of the politically acceptable. Voters expect[ed] it, and the taboo against doing so [was] permanently lowered' (Hine and Finnochi, 1991: 81). With the political upheavals of the 1990s, these mechanisms began to push in the opposite direction. In doing so, they started a trend towards more powerful prime ministers that culminated with the second Berlusconi premiership beginning in 2001. Election campaigns are now contests between two coalitions whose leaders are candidates for the premiership. Election campaigns are therefore now dominated by the leaders. Their personal characteristics and political styles play the most central role. This in turn has heightened the significance of choice of leader for the political fortunes of the coalition, and it has strengthened the position of leaders vis-à-vis the parties they lead in cases where the coalition has been victorious. That is to say, the fact of having been more or less decisive in bringing victory to the coalition gives leaders a degree of authority over their governments that 'First Republic' prime ministers could only dream of. This is not to say that prime ministers have acquired a degree of authority approaching that of their British counterparts: from the point of view of governmental survival long after the election, prime ministers remain exposed to the political manoeuvres of their coalition partners. Nor is it to say that prime ministers' authority is unvarying: prime ministers who are party leaders are stronger than those who are not leaders of one of their coalition's component parties. But what *is* new is

(1) that prime ministers are no longer simply obliged to accept the choice of ministers made for them by the parties supporting their governments,[10] and,

(2) that they attempt to pursue distinct policy agendas: though the election platform is the product of negotiation among the coalition's component parties, it is the leader who will be held responsible, by the voters, for its implementation. It was, as Campus and Pasquino (2006) note, Berlusconi's desire to spectacularise his acceptance of this responsibility that led to his famous signing, during the course of a television talk show, of a 'contract with the Italian people', at the time of the 2001 campaign.

Prime ministers' administrative resources

Changes in the prime-ministerial role have been reflected in changes in the institutional and administrative resources available to incumbents seeking to provide co-ordination. Prior to the 1960s, these resources were scarce in the extreme. The Presidenza del Consiglio dei Ministri (PCM), or Prime Minister's Office, lacked financial and organisational autonomy; for it was housed within the Ministry of the Interior, which provided much of its staff. This was small by later standards, amounting to about fifty in 1961 (Pajano, 2000: 48). There were three reasons for this state of affairs.

(1) It reflected – not unusually from a comparative perspective – a conception of prime-ministerial functions that antedated the twentieth-century growth of big government. It was a conception according to which such leadership and co-ordinating functions as needed to be performed could be performed simply by drawing on the resources of one or other of the ministries.

(2) The constitutional founding fathers had a conception of ministerial responsibility according to which, if ministers were to be effectively accountable

for the actions of their officials the latter had to ensure the precise and unvarying execution of political directives. But if execution really was to be so automatic, then logically, once the cabinet had reached its decisions, the resources required for co-ordination could not but be very few.

(3) In a context in which ministerial positions were distributed among parties keen to exploit them for patronage purposes, the parties themselves insisted on having a free hand when it came to the activities of the ministries entrusted to them.

For these reasons, prior to the reform of 1999, it was at least doubtful that the PCM could be accurately thought of as an institution enabling the prime minister to direct the work of government:

- For one thing, it tended to be overloaded with substantive responsibilities. That is, there was a habit of using it to house the machinery required for the carrying out of a wide range of ad hoc governing tasks that, periodically, showed themselves to be necessary. The habit appears not to have been entirely broken even today. From time to time, the decision will be taken to appoint ministers, without portfolio, but with responsibility for overseeing public intervention in some particular area. Each has a department based within the PCM.
- In the second place, traditionally within Italian public administration, statutes have played a very large role in defining rules and procedures. This means that such rules and procedures very often, if not most of the time, have the force of law. This in turn has been the consequence of:
  - the desire to ensure the 'mechanical' execution of political directives mentioned above;
  - adherence to principles of equality and impartiality in the state's dealings with citizens;
  - the absence of constitutional obstacles in the way of law invading the administrative sphere, discussed in the previous section.
  Such 'legalism' has tended to encourage an orientation to administrative activity dominated more by a concern for its formal correctness than its effectiveness in achieving defined substantive objectives. It has affected the PCM as much as any other sphere and has acted as an additional brake on the PCM's ability to provide effective co-ordination.
- Third, organisationally, the PCM embodied a fundamental ambiguity over whether its mission was primarily to serve the needs of the Prime Minister or, rather, those of the cabinet as a whole.

This ambiguity was, to some degree, addressed by the reform embodied in law no. 400 of 1988. This sought to replace the contingent quality of earlier measures regarding the PCM with a much more systematic approach to its functions and organisation. Thus the reform

- gave the PCM, for the first time, its own budget.
- placed most of the organisation's departments within the framework of a general secretariat. Its head, the general secretary, was to be personally

appointed by the Prime Minister and his/her term, unless renewed, was to cease automatically with arrival in office of the subsequent prime minister.

- introduced a kind of spoils system by enabling the heads of departments and offices to be appointed from outside the public administration and for fixed terms (Fabbrini and Vassallo, 1999: 157).
- added, alongside a permanent structure of departments and offices, a 'variable component' (Fabbrini and Vassallo, 1999: 156) by stipulating that prime ministers could establish departments and offices at their own discretion.

Observers seem agreed that, by allowing for reorganisation with each change of prime minister, the new system enhanced the potential for efficient and effective policy co-ordination (Fabbrini and Vassallo, 1999: 157; Barbera and Fusaro, 2004: 286).

However, the potential of the new law could not make itself fully felt as long as governments continued to be staffed by unstable coalitions. Likewise, it was not until the party-system changes of the 1990s (and the above-mentioned processes of Europeanisation requiring more forceful executive leadership) that further institutional and administrative reform could take place. When it came, the reform[11] sought to move decisively beyond the dual structure for the PCM (one serving the Prime Minister, the other the cabinet) envisaged by law no. 400. It also sought to move beyond the traditional conception of policy co-ordination. This, by equating policy co-ordination with the acquisition of structures and functions, had largely been responsible for the accumulation of a range of 'temporary', substantive responsibilities (Criscitiello, 2003: 167). In this way it had brought about that progressive overloading of the PCM mentioned above. Thus the responsibilities of most of the departments housed by the PCM were transferred elsewhere. Either they were transferred to those parts of the bureaucracy with sectoral responsibilities; or they were transferred to a new series of executive agencies. By this means it was anticipated that the PCM itself would be enabled to concentrate, the more effectively, on its core business of policy coordination under prime-ministerial direction.

The reform's sponsors were well aware that that effective performance of this function not only required paying attention to the PCM, but also depended on addressing the shortcomings of the broader machinery of government to which the PCM was connected (Pajno and Torchia, 2000: 30). It was therefore significant that the reform was introduced not in isolation but rather as part of a broader package that included the administration, to which we now turn.

The administration

In any parliamentary democracy, the capacity of the political executive to direct the activity of the bureaucracy depends on its control of a number of resources besides the Prime Minister's powers of co-ordination. Drawing on the analysis of Rosalba Chiarini (2003), we may list such resources as:

(1) the power to reorganise the bureaucracy;
(2) the power to determine the terms and conditions of employment of public officials;
(3) the power to appoint the most senior officials, and
(4) the power to control the budget.

The significance of the last of these four lies in what it implies for control of actual activity. If, for example, executives can transfer resources from one budget heading to another without having to obtain the prior approval of Parliament, the greater is the flexibility with which they can manage the administrative apparatus. In fact, almost all public activity presupposes the getting and spending of money. Thus, control of such getting and spending confers not just the power to manage and direct the activities of the administration but effective supremacy in relations with *all* of the other institutions involved in the process of policy-making.

The power to reorganise the bureaucracy

Traditionally, the executive's control of the first resource has been rather low. In 1904, law no. 372 vested in Parliament the authority to modify the organisation and deployment of civil servants. The aim was to prevent ministers using reorganisation as a means of pursuing clientelistic personnel policies (Melis, 2003: 26). In 1946, members of the Constituent Assembly had different concerns but were led to take similar action. Driven by the twin desire to erect as many institutional barriers as possible in the way of any future return to authoritarianism, and to assure to Parliament firm control of the state administrative apparatus, the Assembly wrote into the constitutional document article 97. This stipulates that 'Public offices are organised according to the provisions of the law.' It implies that governments may not establish, reorganise or abolish ministries through recourse to their own regulations alone. Nor may they alter the powers of public officials or organisations vis-à-vis external organisations and individuals (though they may use regulations to determine the *internal* organisational arrangements required for the effective exercise of such powers). In other words, they can only reorganise ministries or alter public officials' powers by getting the approval of Parliament first. But in addition to such legal obstacles in the way of executive control of the nature of administrative structures, there were political ones: until the 1990s, reform proposals that were more than incremental were vanquished in Parliament by party veto players aware that any radical change inevitably implied a major shift in the distribution of power between the governing parties.

The power to determine the terms and conditions of employment of public officials

The executive's control of terms and conditions of employment was likewise limited.

- Its freedom of action was heavily circumscribed by the tradition, stretching back to the nineteenth century, for rules of conduct, rights and duties to be codified in public law. This meant that the rules governing the employment of public officials could not be waived in this way unless through a change in the law that had given rise to them. (This represents a radical contrast to private law, from whose rules it is possible to derogate – as, for example, when the parties to a contract agree not to insist on the enforcement of its conditions.)
- An additional factor of inertia was the fact that, with the passage of time, the body of public law involved had become highly complex: by exerting pressure on members of Parliament (anxious to maintain and increase electoral followings through patronage measures), groups within the bureaucracy had succeeded in obtaining passage of the relevant microsectoral legislation.
- Finally, at the end of the 1960s, the trade unions were buoyed up by the explosion of worker militancy that characterised the period. This enabled them to win new collective bargaining rights in the areas of pay, pensions and duties of employment. All of these were then given the status of public law. For this reason, public employees were said to benefit from a system of 'double protection'; for terms and conditions of employment were underwritten *both* by collective bargaining arrangements typical of the private sector, *and* by a series of legally binding guarantees typical of the public sector. Both sets of guarantees circumscribed the exercise of managerial prerogatives and limited the degree to which working arrangements could be altered to respond to changed circumstances.

The power to appoint the most senior officials

But in any case, the civil service was, according to a well-known thesis advanced by Sabino Cassese (1984), in effect 'unavailable' for collaboration with the executive in making policy; for the *formal* power of appointment and dismissal of senior officials that was in the hands of ministers was not a *real* one. This power had been 'frozen' as the result of an unwritten understanding with officials that they would refrain from aspiring to a policy-making role in exchange for security of employment. The reasons for this exchange recall processes and trends stretching back to the nineteenth century. Industrialisation and extension of the franchise led to new forms of state intervention and a growth in size of the bureaucracy. A growing proportion of the members of this bureaucracy came from the South. Since alternative employment opportunities were scarce here, the tendency arose among civil servants towards a heightened sensitivity to personnel matters and issues of job security. And since governments often had recourse to expansions of civil service numbers as a means of buying social peace in the region (implying an ever finer division of decreasingly rewarding tasks), there also arose a tendency towards a lack of sensitivity to responsibilities and the achievement of work goals. Meanwhile,

Fascism, with its totalitarian pretensions, established the tradition of a clear line of demarcation between political and administrative roles, with access to the former reserved to members of the party and the Fascist movement. The social differences between administrative leaders (predominantly southern) and political leaders (predominantly northern), and the lack of 'osmosis' or interchange between them, fed mistrust. On the part of administrative leaders, there was the fear that political leaders might, in the pursuit of policy, interfere with established careers patterns and their powers in personnel matters. On the part of political leaders, there was the fear that administrative leaders might use their organisational resources to frustrate ministerial policy ambitions. Thus it was that senior civil servants exchanged policy influence for security:

- On the one hand, they got the illusion of power that came with being left free to manage the recruitment and co-optation of subordinates as they saw fit – while seeing the remainder of their responsibilities confined to routine tasks of execution.
- On the other hand, ministers got the guarantee of civil service neutrality, while being left free to have recourse to external personnel for advice and collaboration in the tasks more closely associated with policy-making. Such collaboration was most commonly achieved through reliance on the *gabinetto* (the minister's private secretariat) or on the ad hoc setting up of administrative bodies outside the ministerial apparatus. The situation was one in which governments were free from the risk of 'bureaucratic capture' – while being left without any effective means of guiding an administration that was in any case not highly motivated.

The power to control the budget

Finally, the executive's capacity to manage and steer the policy-making process was limited by its weaknesses in the fourth area, that of the annual budget. Here, scope for decision-making was heavily circumscribed by the provisions of article 81 of the Constitution. This stipulates that 'No new taxes or new expenditure can be established by the law approving the budget.' It also stipulates that 'In all other laws implying new or additional expenditures the means for covering them must be set forth' (Furlong, 1994: 209). It was taken by its original sponsors in the Constituent Assembly to imply that governments were effectively prohibited from engaging in deficit financing. The second of the two clauses just cited was successfully circumvented by allowing legislative proposals to specify that their implied expenditure would be covered by incurring debts. However, the first of the two clauses prevented governments from adjusting taxation and expenditure in a single exercise to pursue macroeconomic policy objectives. This meant, in effect, that the annual budget could amount to little more than a restatement of the taxation and spending decisions already embodied in other laws.

Law no. 468 of 1978 attempted to circumvent this restriction by stipulating that the annual budgetary process would include the passage of a Finance Law. Since, legally, this was a piece of legislation *separate* from the law approving the budget, the constitutional restrictions did not apply to it. Thereby, it would give the budget the function of changing revenue and expenditure for all practical purposes. The problem then was that the Finance Law rapidly fell victim to the clientelistic concerns of members of the two chambers of Parliament. Such members were aware that, given the micro-distributive opportunities opened up by this new instrument, the passage of even the tiniest article or amendment to the Finance Bill could have enormous implications for their political prospects (Verzichelli, 1999: 47). Thus it was that these finance bills came to assume vast proportions, being referred to as 'legislative omnibuses' that required endless hours of negotiation. Only twice in the period before 1988 were they approved within the statutory time limits that the 1978 reform had laid down for their enactment. It is therefore possible to say that the effects of the 1978 reform were the opposite of those intended. Deprived, by the Constitution, of the power to exercise effective control in the area of economic policy, the executive in the mid-1970s needed to establish such control both because of rising public-sector deficits and, more generally, because the structural dependence of governments on capitalist economies means that the ability to influence the latter is an essential prerequisite for control of policy-making in every other area of public activity. In fact what happened was that, rather than the Government being in a position to establish the financial parameters of finance bills in a top-down fashion, their drafting became a bottom-up process. In other words, *first* all the measures to be taken and the amounts to be allocated were agreed upon and only *then* were the financial limits decided: since passage of the Finance Bill was a legal requirement and therefore guaranteed, it offered from the point of view of distributive politics an opportunity that was simply too good to miss (Verzichelli, 1999: 56–7). Thereby, paradoxically, it helped actually to *worsen* the state of public finances in the 1980s.

Governments' scope for decision-making was further restricted by the rules on virement. Each year the budget document presented to Parliament contained a section known as 'global funds'. This referred to the resources to be used to cover the expenditure implied by bills being considered by Parliament but not yet approved. If a bill fell, then the funds set aside for it could be allocated elsewhere – but these were the only circumstances in which funds could be shifted between headings. In all other cases, such action was essentially impossible without Parliament's approval of fresh legislation, since all of the original spending decisions had been enshrined in laws and could therefore be overturned only through the passage of other laws.

Reform of the administration

Since the 1980s, the combination of growing public-sector deficits and party-system change has allowed the passage of reforms in all four of the areas we have discussed. The result, arguably, has been considerably to improve the executive's capacity to direct policy-making. One does, of course, need to be cautious in asserting this. Capano (2000), for example, argues that some of the new legislation may involve less of a 'paradigm shift' than appears at first sight, and certainly the passage of legislation is not the same as change on the ground: reforms, to be worthy of the label, have to be successful. Nevertheless, though it may be too early to draw up a 'balance sheet', we would argue that from an analysis of the content of the reforms, significant reinforcement of the executive vis-à-vis the bureaucracy is certainly what one is entitled to *expect*.

Reform of budget procedures

The first reform, law no. 362 of 1988, sought to render the annual budget cycle more effective as an instrument of financial planning, thereby reinforcing the position of the executive in that process. In the first place, the cycle was brought forward with the stipulation that by 15 May each year, the Government was to present, to the chambers of Parliament, an economic and financial planning document (*Documento di programmazione economica e finanziaria*, Dpef). This sets out, on the basis of various macroeconomic assumptions, the Government's estimates of tax yields and spending commitments given existing legislation. It also sets out the Government's budget targets and the tax and spending measures it thinks are necessary to achieve such targets. The Dpef, or an amended version thereof, must be approved by both chambers of Parliament by 31 July (that is, two months before the start of the so-called 'budget session' of Parliament, which begins on 1 October). The effect is to obtain Parliament's agreement to a set of financial limits *before* proceeding to consideration of new expenditure. The parliamentary resolutions by means of which the Dpef is approved are not laws. This means that the provisions of the Dpef are not as such legally binding. Therefore law no. 362 introduced two additional safeguards. Both were designed to restore to the Finance Law the purpose originally intended for it of an adjustment of the overall financial implications of past decisions:

(1) It provided that the Finance Law could in essence no longer contain new measures or modify existing ones; it could merely amend the sums made available by existing legislation.

(2) As a corollary, law no. 362 provided that all new substantive measures required to achieve budget targets were to be removed from the framework of the Finance Law and embodied in 'measures annexed to the Finance Law'. Although these annexes are presented to Parliament along with the Finance Bill, legally, each is a separate bill in its own right. Although, therefore, they are theoretically as much hostage to recalcitrant parliamentarians as any other government proposal, their approval is facilitated by the fact that their legislative passage takes place during the 'budget session'. During this 'season' the consideration of all other bills implying public expenditure is (in accordance with

changes to Parliament's standing orders introduced at the same time as law 362) suspended (Massai, 1992: 185). Such suspension remains in force until the budget proceedings have been completed. This ensures that Parliament is under pressure to expedite the latter as efficiently as possible.

Reform of public officials' terms of employment

The second set of reforms were law no. 421 of October 1992 and the 'Cassese reforms' of 1993. These concerned the terms and conditions of employment of public officials. The measures were intimately connected to the reform discussed in the previous paragraph; for, like the new budgetary procedures, they too were in many respects a response to (the same) financial emergency. The 1988 reform had been introduced after the level of public debt had topped 100 per cent of Gross Domestic Product, and the 1988 Finance Law was described as the incumbent government's 'Caporetto'.[12] Law no. 421, for its part, came in the wake of the Maastricht Treaty and Italy's September 1992 exit from the European Exchange Rate Mechanism. Both reforms sought a way out of the resulting financial straitjacket by attempting to raise the efficiency of the machinery of state.

Through legislative decree 29, which in January 1993 gave effect to the relevant provisions, law no. 421

(1)   removed the contracts of public employees from the realm of public law, subjecting them, instead, to private law;
(2)   centralised collective bargaining arrangements by providing that all negotiations were to take place through an Agency for Relations with the Trade Unions located in the Prime Minister's Office;
(3)   limited to questions of pay the matters reserved to the outcomes of collective bargaining.

The implications, from the point of view of control of the administrative apparatus, were

(1)   that posts would from then on be less secure;
(2)   that it would be possible to move labour between tasks unilaterally;
(3)   that senior administrators would be able to manage their units by calling on the same powers as those enjoyed by private employers.

The Cassese reforms, so-called after the minister who sponsored them, were introduced largely as provisions annexed to the 1994 Finance Law. They were driven by the desire to achieve financial savings through further measures of 'rationalisation' and 'simplification' within the public administration. They served to re-emphasise a view of the budget as an instrument of executive financial planning whose requirements would guide policy throughout the state apparatus.

Administrative reorganisation

The next major attempt to reform the administration came after the election, in 1996, of the Prodi government. As we have seen, the executive's capacity to direct the bureaucracy was effectively limited by the insistence of the constitutional founding fathers that administrative reorganisation could only take place through the passage of legislation. However, they made no stipulation about the kind of legislation that had to be involved. Thus, in 1997, through the passage of three very complex laws of delegation, the Government was able to persuade Parliament to give it power to carry out extensive reorganisation by issuing legislative decrees. These complex laws were known as the 'Bassanini Laws' after the minister who sponsored them. The most important of the reorganisation measures was brought about by means of legislative decree no. 300 of 1999. The measures were three in number.

(1) The decree reduced the number of ministries from eighteen to twelve (raised to fourteen by law no. 317 in 2001: see Table 4.3). In doing so, it set a virtual precedent in that this was the first time since 1853 that the ministries had been listed in a single statute and thereby established according to systematic criteria rather than incrementally (Torchia, 2000: 127). Proposals for a general overhaul had not been absent in the past, but this was the first time that reorganisation had been successfully pursued on the basis of an overall analysis of the distribution of functions and of how in their entirety, they could be most efficiently and effectively performed.

(2) The decree changed organisational arrangements within the ministries, doing so with the aim of obtaining both clarity and flexibility. That is to say, at the most general level, the decree laid down uniform arrangements for each of the ministries while leaving to normative sources of progressively more limited legal force (regulations, the discretion of individual managers) the arrangements to be made for subsequent levels. In this way, it was hoped that the new arrangements would make their own contribution to the process of deregulation referred to earlier, replacing a mass of diverse but rigid arrangements that had accumulated over time, with new, uniform, but flexible arrangements that would allow administrative structures to adapt to changing circumstances.

(3) The decree established eleven new agencies for the execution of technical and operational functions.[13] Though attached to specific ministries, the agencies were to be relatively autonomous organisations available to provide services to regional and local, as well as to national public bodies. In this way, it was anticipated that they would contribute to the elimination of duplication and overlap, organisational and functional, within and between different parts of the public administration. In each case, an agreement would be drawn up between the agency's director and the relevant minister setting out, for the agency, (a) objectives; (b) results to be achieved within specified time periods; (c) the financial resources to be

Table 4.3. Ministries of the Italian Republic

Ministries prior to legislative decree 300/1999	Ministries following legislative decree 300/1999 and law 317/2001	Functions and remit of ministries
Foreign Affairs	Foreign affairs	Foreign policy and international relations, diplomatic and consular representation
Ministry of the Interior	Ministry of the Interior	Civil administration, public safety and police forces
Justice	Justice	Organisation and functioning of the judicial system, the administration of prisons
Treasury, Budget and Economic Planning	Economy and Finance	Macroeconomic policy, public expenditure and taxation, state holding companies
Finance		
Defence	Defence	Armed forces, defence and military security of the state
Education	Education, Universities and Research	Schools, universities, technological and scientific research
Universities, Technology and Scientific Research		
Public works	Infrastructure and Transport	Road and rail networks, public works relating to navigation, transport and traffic
Transport and Navigation		
Agriculture and Forests	Agriculture and Forests	Co-ordination and EU representation in relation to policy concerning agriculture and forests
Communications	Communications[*]	Postal and telecommunications services, information technology, broadcasting
Industry, Commerce and Artisan Activities	Productive Activities	Industry, artisan activities, energy, commerce, tourism, foreign trade
Foreign Trade		
Work and Social Security	Work and Social Security [**]	Social security and employment policies
Health	Health [**]	Co-ordination of the national health service, veterinary services, health and safety at work, food safety and hygiene

Table 4.3. (*cont.*)

Ministries prior to legislative decree 300/1999	Ministries following legislative decree 300/1999 and law 317/2001	Functions and remit of ministries
Heritage and Culture	Heritage and Cultural Activities	Theatrical and sporting activities; care and management of the nation's artistic, archaeological, landscape and architectural heritage.
Environment	Environment and Territorial Protection	Ecological and territorial equilibria; the care of land and seas; protection from flooding; protection of wildlife.

Notes: The number of ministries was raised to eighteen, shortly after the centre left's election victory in April 2006, as the consequence of decree law no. 181/06 (converted into ordinary law as the result of law no. 233 of 17 July 2006): Education, Universities and Research was divided into Education, and Universities and Research, respectively; Infrastructure and Transport was divided into Infrastructure on the one hand and Transport on the other; Work and Social Security was divided into Work and Social Security, on the one hand, and Welfare, on the other; Productive Activities was abolished and replaced by two new ministries: Economic Development, and Foreign Trade.

* Following the election of the Berlusconi government in 2008, this ministry was abolished and its functions transferred to the Ministry for Economic Development.

** Amalgamated by the Berlusconi government elected in 2008 into a single ministry: Health, Work and Social Security.

Source: www.senato.it/leg/Governi/gov24.htm and Barbera and Fusaro, 2004: 333–4.

made available to the agency; (d) strategies for improving the provision of services; (e) the procedures for verifying results achieved.

The reform of senior appointments

Finally, taking its cue from the first Bassanini law, legislative decree no. 80 of 1998 provided for the creation of senior administrative positions whose incumbents would provide direct collaboration with ministers and linkage with the bureaucracy. The positions were to be open not only to 'insiders' but also to candidates from outside the administrative apparatus. Appointees would be employed on fixed-term contracts. Directors and directors-general were also to be employed on fixed-term contracts, with ministers being given the option of filling with external experts up to 5 per cent of the available positions. Contracts would run for renewable terms of two to seven years and would be revocable with each change of government. In this way the reform introduced a kind of spoils system for senior administrative officers. The terms of the system were rendered even more uncompromising with the passage of law no. 145 of 2002.[14] Thereby, the law has brought about a radical reversal, in

the name of the executive's right to govern, of that historic tendency, referred
to above, towards the separation and isolation, one from the other, of political
and administrative spheres (Melis, 2003: 101).

◼ Bureaucracy and Parliament

As well as the interface between Parliament and executive, and between
executive and bureaucracy, analysed in each of the two preceding sections,
there is also an interface between bureaucracy and Parliament. The bureaucracy–Parliament interface has acquired increasing significance in liberal
democracies generally in recent years thanks to the emergence and growth
of independent administrative authorities. These are associated, in the Italian
case, with processes of European integration (Giraudi, 2003: 264–5). The interface has also acquired increasing significance thanks to the emergence and
growth of executive agencies. These are associated with what has come to be
known as 'the new public management'. Both independent administrative
authorities and executive agencies pose significant questions concerning principles of accountability and can be regarded as corrosive of parliamentary
powers of oversight in the policy-making process.

   In view of the variety of their organisational and functional characteristics,
what in Italy are called the 'independent administrative authorities' (or else
'independent authorities', or simply 'authorities') are difficult to define. In
essence they are public bodies, established by Parliament. They are empowered by it to regulate the behaviour of private actors belonging to some specific
sector of activity. In carrying out their regulatory functions, the authorities
operate within a sphere of action that is essentially protected from parliamentary or government interference. The 1990s, which saw the addition of some
ten authorities to those already in existence (Table 4.4), were a boom time for
these bodies. Most operate in areas of public policy subject to strong pressures
towards Europeanisation. Their establishment offered governments a neat
way of avoiding the political costs arising from the requirement to enforce
EU decisions, on the one hand, and possible domestic resistance to the implications of such decisions, on the other (Giraudi, 2003: 264–5).

   From the point of view of our present concerns, what is most significant
about the independent authorities is that, with one or two variations as to
degree, their composition, organisation and remit are such that they have to
be considered as fully autonomous policy-makers in their own right:

(1)   Most have a membership appointed, not by the executive, but by some
      combination of government and parliamentary bodies; the members
      cannot be removed from office during the period of their tenure; their
      appointments cannot be renewed, or can be renewed only once. All this
      means that the capacity of government and Parliament to influence the
      members, once nomination has taken place, is minimal or non-existent
      (Giraudi, 2003: 252).

Table 4.4. Principal independent administrative authorities in Italy

Authority	Functions	Date established	No. of members	Term of office (years)	Appointed by
National Commission for Enterprises and the Stock Exchange (CONSOB)	Supervises the workings of financial markets and the stock exchange	1974	5	5	the Government on the advice of Parliament
Institute for the Supervision of Insurance Companies (ISVAP)	Regulates the activities of insurance companies	1982	7	5	the Government on the advice of Parliament
Italian Competition Authority	Acts to ensure free competition and the avoidance of restrictive practices, the abuse of monopoly power and unfair and misleading advertising	1990	5	7	the presidents of the chambers of Parliament
Commissione di garanzia dell'attuazione della l. 12 giugno 1990, no. 146	Regulates strikes in the essential public services with the aim of reconciling the right to strike with 'the personal rights guaranteed by the Constitution'	1990	9	3	the presidents of the chambers of Parliament
Authority for the Supervision of Public Works	Acts to ensure value for money and uniformity in the award of public works contracts	1994	5	5	the presidents of the chambers of Parliament
Electricity and Gas Authority	Regulates the electricity and gas industries with the aim of ensuring adequate levels of quality and service and a reliable and transparent system of pricing	1995	3	7	the Government on the advice of Parliament
Garante per la protezione dei dati personali	Acts to ensure that personal data are used in accordance with respect for fundamental rights and freedoms with particular reference to issues of privacy	1996	4	4	the Chamber of Deputies (2) and Senate (2)

Table 4.4. (*cont.*)

Authority	Functions	Date established	No. of members	Term of office (years)	Appointed by
Italian Communications Authority	Regulates the radio and television sector with the aim of ensuring pluralism and objectivity in broadcasting	1997	9	7	the Chamber of Deputies (4), Senate (4), the Government (1)

(2) The authorities have complete organisational autonomy from other political and administrative institutions in the sense that they are empowered to decide, without the need for any outside authorisation, how they will organise themselves in pursuing their remit.

(3) The power to regulate, within the terms of their remit, is absolute in the sense that no outside body has any legal authority whatsoever to change any of their decisions. It is this feature in particular that raises serious issues of accountability; for in supervising activities within the spheres for which they are responsible, they issue regulations, and in that sense make real policy decisions, that are every bit as legally binding as acts of Parliament. And yet, beyond the obligation to submit an annual report to Parliament and to submit, just like any other body, to the rule of law as interpreted by the courts, they are, in effect, free from the requirement to account for their decisions, to anyone.

The new public management represents a radical rejection of the classic Weberian model of bureaucracy whose key features are

(1) government by rules, where these rules establish a hierarchy of offices prescribing who can give orders to whom, criteria for admission and advancement, routines for the performance of work;

(2) the separation of person and position, requiring participants to interact in terms of the rights and duties embodied in their formal roles rather than in terms of their personal identities;

(3) the proliferation of formal communications and written records in order to collectivise memory;

(4) job security and advancement on merit in order to engender organisational loyalty.

The new public management represents a departure from Weberian principles in at least four respects. Thus,

(1) instead of being held responsible for the correct application of fixed rules to cases, the public official is held responsible for the achievement of substantive results. Therefore,

(2) instead of being required to adhere to routines for the performance of work, the official is given discretion in the performance of his or her duties. In order to help the official use such discretion to best effect, job security is

(3) replaced with fixed-term contracts, performance related pay and contract renewal dependent on the achievement of stipulated targets.

(4) Since contractualism separates 'principal' and 'agent', it implies that functions need no longer be performed 'in house', through a single hierarchy of offices and orders issued from the top downwards, but that executive or service-delivery functions can be hived off to autonomous agencies or even the private sector. This too helps the agent to achieve results, since the stipulation of a contract with the agency holds out the possibility of replacing it with another provider who is cheaper, and thus the possibility of competition between agencies.

It will be apparent that these ideas were reflected in many features of the reforms discussed in the previous section and especially in the arrangements for the agencies established by legislative decree 300 of 1999.

These too raise significant accountability issues in that, as the experience of similar agencies in other jurisdictions suggests, their working is likely to divorce even further the practical workings of ministerial responsibility from the theory. That is to say, in Italy, as in all or most parliamentary regimes, there are constitutional provisions that make ministers individually responsible to the legislature for everything that goes on within their departments. This does not always, or perhaps in most cases, mean that ministers are obliged to resign when things go wrong; for it has long been recognised that ministers cannot sensibly be held to have knowledge of everything that is done in their name. But it does mean that ministers are obliged to take all reasonable action to put things right when they do go wrong (and to prevent them happening in the first place). It means too that ministers are obliged to render an account, or to explain, to Parliament what has or has not been done. It means that ministers are liable to suffer *political* damage when things go wrong. It is this exposure to the threat of political damage, if not of the loss of their positions, that ensures that ministerial responsibility, in the sense of carrying out ministerial duties in accordance with parliamentary and public concerns, retains some substance. Yet executive agencies, because they sharpen the distinction between policy and operational matters, make it easier for ministers to steer clear of blame for operational failures, thereby weakening the pressures on ministers to act in ways that are responsive to public and parliamentary concerns. In that sense, they are corrosive of ministerial responsibility.

Summary and conclusion

In this chapter our objective has been to understand how, in the process of policy-making, Parliament, executive and bureaucracy interact with one another and how power to influence the substance of policy is distributed between them. What we have seen is that policy-making in Italy has tradition-ally been, and to a large extent remains, highly polycentric in the sense that it is difficult to argue with any conviction that any one actor or group of actors involved is clearly better placed than any of the others:

- For one thing, the making of policy is, as in any polity, a multifaceted activity (involving the drafting, deliberation and implementation of legis-lation and other rules having legal force, as well as oversight of the imple-mentation process).
- For another thing, in Italy a large number of checks and balances condition the interaction between Parliament, executive and bureaucracy.

It is partly because of these checks and balances that all three of the national-level institutions of policy-making we have examined in this chapter have been the object of criticism of political scientists. This criticism can be excessive. For example,

- scholars have traditionally judged negatively the difficulty of achieving deci-sive policy change through Parliament. As we describe in chapter 6, this has been widely held to reduce the predictability of decision-making processes and thus to increase, for civil-society actors, the risk associated with invest-ment decisions. Here we note that the opposite argument is plausible, namely, that the difficulty (and therefore the small likelihood) of bringing change represents an element of *certainty* for civil-society actors, which might in some circumstances *reduce* risk. From there one might advance hypotheses about the role of Parliament in the post-war economic miracle. Did certainty stemming from lack of change facilitate the high growth rates? And in this respect can one compare the Italian parliament favourably with parliaments such as that of the United Kingdom? Here, commentators very frequently complained that strong government and decisive policy-making were responsible for precisely the kinds of ills for which Italy's contrasting arrangements are held responsible! Frequent two-party alternation and con-sequent policy instability were, in other words, for long thought responsible for the country's less-than-glowing performance in economic terms.
- It is said that the separation and isolation of the executive from the senior administrative class have traditionally rendered the latter unavail-able for the most important tasks in the policy-making process. But one of the advantages of the separation has been that it has ensured for the executive 'a neutrality of the civil service that is not easily reached' (Cassese, 1984: 65).
- Public administration in Italy has often been accused of being bureaucratic and excessively bound by legal rules, thus making it inefficient. But it should be remembered that the bureaucratic model is one that empowers people by letting them work in co-ordinated ways. Rational legal systems embody values which people respect. Rules and regulations protect the members of

the organisation and its external clients (Jarvis, 2005). The bureaucratic model is founded on principles of honesty and integrity, of regular, predictable behaviour without which social life would be impossible.

The period since 1990 has been one of extensive changes in the organisation, powers and behaviour of the institutions of policy-making at national level. It is often said that the changes were possible only because financial emergencies and external constraints made it possible to overcome earlier forces of resistance, especially the interlocking vetoes of the parties in Parliament. This may be true, but internal or external pressures are necessary for change in any polity; and it may be said that the fact that resistance was overcome in Italy speaks to the virtues, rather than the drawbacks, of its political system. From the point of view of the quality of democracy, the most positive of the changes has been the success of executives, now directly legitimated by election outcomes, in overcoming some of their previous weaknesses in relation to the legislature and the administration. The change giving most cause for concern is the introduction of regulatory and executive agencies on the basis of models imported from other jurisdictions. What impact, if any, the changes may have had on Italians' traditionally negative views of the way democracy works in their country is a matter of political culture. This is the issue to which we direct our attention in the chapter that follows.

▓ Further reading

The first (and really the only) major study of the Italian parliament in the English language is Giuseppe Di Palma's, *Surviving without Governing: The Italian Parties in Parliament* (Berkeley, CA: University of California Press, 1977). Developments since Di Palma's book was published have been discussed in a fairly large number of journal articles, many in the *Journal of Legislative Studies*, among which Giliberto Capano and Marco Giuliani 'The Italian parliament: in search of a new role?' (vol. 9, no. 2, pp. 8–34, 2003). See also the special issue of *South European Society and Politics* (vol. 13, no. 1) published in March 2008, which examines changes in Italy's law-making processes from a range of perspectives including the role played by the bicameral structure of parliament; the effects and dynamics of the amendment process; levels of consensualism in the adoption of bills; the complex nature of the budgetary process. Annarita Criscitiello, in 'Majority summits: decision-making inside the Cabinet and out: Italy, 1970–1990' (*West European Politics*, vol. 16, no. 4, pp. 581–94, 1993), provides significant insights into the role of the poltical parties in cabinet decision-making in First Republic Italy. Sabino Cassese, currently a Constitutional Court judge, is the author who has done most to explore the place of the bureaucracy in the policy-making process in Italy. Among others, see his 'The higher civil service in Italy' (pp. 35–71, in Ezra N. Suleiman (ed.), *Bureaucrats and Policy Making: A Comparative Overview*, New York and London: Holmes and Meier, 1984).

Notes

1. Private members' bills currently constitute about 90 per cent of the total presented, this proportion being far higher than in most other European countries. The monthly average of such bills increased by about two-thirds over the course of the two legislatures that followed the introduction of the new electoral law in 1993, and it seems likely that the increase is at least partly to be explained by the new single-member constituencies established by the law (Giuliani and Capano, 2001: 19–21).

2. Giuliani and Capano's (2001, figure 3) data show that the proportion of bills approved in committee fell from about 80 per cent in the tenth, to under 40 per cent in the three subsequent legislatures. Meanwhile, the proportion approved by ample majorities (defined as those opposed on final reading by fewer than 30 of the 630 members of the Chamber of Deputies) went up. Thus, the proportion approved *either* in committee *or* by ample majorities remained at around 80 per cent.

3. Twenty in the Chamber and ten in the Senate, though the presidents of each branch are empowered to authorise the formation of groups of even smaller size.

4. In terms of the measure proposed by Laasko and Taagepera (1979), the effective number of groups in the Chamber of Deputies rose from 3.2 in 1976 to 6.2 in 1994 and 6.1 in 1996 and remained at 5.3 in 2001. (Calculated from the data given in De Micheli and Verzichelli, 2004, table A3, pp. 344–5.) It was 6.04 in the legislature that ran from 2006 to 2008. (Calculated from the data available on the Italian parliament website, www.parlamento.it.)

5. The effective number of groups in the Chamber of Deputies declined to 3.11. (Calculated from the data available on the Italian parliament website, www.parlamento.it.)

6. 'Reserved laws' are those – such as laws ratifying international treaties – whose initiation is reserved to the Government.

7. Calculated from data available on the Italian parliament website, www.parlamento.it. That is, for the 2006–8 legislature, government-initiated laws = 131 of which 'reserved laws' (laws ratifying international treaties (48), budgetary laws (12) and laws converting government decrees into ordinary legislation (38)) amount to 98. Laws of delegation = 16, or 48.5 per cent of the 33 non-reserved laws initiated by the Government.

8. Such as Prime Minister's question time and urgent interpellations.

9. The use of such instruments as motions, resolutions, questions, interpellations and so forth rose from approximately thirty instances per day during the 1987–92 legislature, to over fifty during the subsequent three legislatures to 2001. For a contrasting view, one which plays down the significance of this development, see Verzichelli and Cotta (2002).

10. As Campus and Pasquino (2006) note, this was not true of D'Alema or Amato who, having acceded to the office of Prime Minister during the course of the thirteenth legislature without any specific electoral mandate, therefore had less discretion in choosing their ministers.

11. In the shape of legislative decree no. 303 of 1999, giving effect to article 11 of law no. 59 of 1997.
12. 'Caporetto' refers to the First World War battle of Caporetto, which saw the Italian army routed by Austro-Hungarian and German forces. As a consequence, the term 'Carporetto' has come to be used in popular parlance to mean a terrible defeat.
13. These were the Agency for Defence Industries, the Agency for Technical Standards, the Agency for Industrial Property, the Environmental Protection and Technical Services Agency, the Agency for Terrestrial Transport and Infrastructure, the Public Revenues Agency, the Customs Agency, the Land Registry, the State Property Office, the Civil Protection Agency, the Agency for Vocational Education and Training.
14. Among other things, the law reduced to three years the duration of the contracts of directors-general and to five years the duration of the contracts of directors. The proportion of positions at the level of director-general potentially available to outsiders was raised to 10 per cent; the proportion of positions at the level of director, to 8 per cent.

III

Politics: citizens, elites and interest mediation

5　　Political culture and behaviour

■ Introduction

In the last chapter we looked at how policy is made through the institutions of Parliament, the executive and the public administration. A focus on **institutions** (Box 5.1) and how they function can provide insight into a wide range of political processes. This is because the rules and procedures embodied in institutions exercise a powerful influence on the behaviour of individuals. Political scientists see this influence taking place in one or other of two ways. That is, from what is known as the '**behaviouralist**' perspective (Box 5.1), rules and procedures influence individuals' behaviour because they define institutional roles and stipulate norms (which individuals internalise) concerning how role incumbents *ought* to act. Alternatively, from a '**rational choice**' perspective (Box 5.1), they do it by structuring (a) the alternative political goals that are available to individuals to pursue, and (b) the resources available to them.

However, a focus on institutions can only get one so far. In particular, if our attention remains confined to the *formal* properties of institutions, it is likely that we will come to understand little of how politics – the acquisition, retention and relinquishing of power – actually takes place through those institutions. Accordingly, the focus of our attention in this chapter shifts to another dimension of political behaviour, the cultural dimension. This means that our focus shifts from the straightforward world of rules and procedures to

Box 5.1

Key terms: institutions, behavouralism, rational choice

Institutions 'can be defined broadly as relatively stable collections of social practices consisting of easily recognized *roles* coupled with underlying *norms* and a set of *rules* or conventions defining appropriate behavior for, and governing relations among, occupants of these roles (cf. Young, 1989: 32; March and Olsen, 1998: 948). These norms and rules "prescribe behavioral roles, constrain activity, and shape expectations" (Keohane, 1988: 383)' (Jönsson, 2007: 5).

Behaviouralism is an approach to the study of politics based on the idea that it is possible to analyse political life objectively and in quantitative terms and on this basis to explain and predict political behaviour in a value-free way. Prior to the so-called behavioural revolution, it was thought that the study of politics could not be scientific and therefore could not but be qualitative and normative.

Rational choice is an approach to the study of political and other social phenomena that assumes them to be the consequence of the decisions of individual actors about how to maximize the achievement of their goals, at the least cost, given the constraints facing them. Rational choice theorists thus seek to account for phenomena by developing models of behaviour that allow us to predict what will happen *if* the actors involved had certain goals etc. They claim that the models stand or fall not according to the degree to which they describe how people *actually* behave, but rather according to the degree to which the hypotheses they generate are true or not.

the more elusive one of the values and beliefs people carry around in their heads (and to the impact of these values and beliefs on people's political behaviour). It means also that our focus undergoes a spatial shift. That is, our attention shifts from what goes on inside the institutions of government to the impact on all of this of the values, beliefs and behaviour of the citizens in the community outside.

The remainder of this chapter is organised as follows. In the next section we explore the meaning of political culture and how it may contribute to the understanding of a country's politics. Then, in the third and fourth sections respectively we consider two cultural phenomena that have had an especially high profile in discussions of Italian politics: national identity and the notion of 'social capital'. The discussion of social capital will enable us to shed light on four phenomena that have often occupied a prominent place in academic discussions of Italian politics: clientelism, corruption, the Mafia and the so-called Third Italy. The penultimate section considers the contribution that cultural phenomena can make to an understanding of some of the most significant party-political developments of recent years. The final section draws some conclusions.

▪ Political culture: meaning and significance

The term 'political culture' has been variously defined. According to the classic definition offered by Almond and Verba (1963: 13), it is a set of 'specifically political orientations'. These 'orientations' have cognitive, affective and evaluative dimensions, 'toward the political system and its various parts' and 'toward the role of the self in the system' (Almond and Verba, 1963: 13). The definition offered by Pye (1995: 965) really amounts to the same thing. Pye regards political culture as 'the sum of the fundamental values, sentiments and knowledge that give form and substance to political processes'. In this text we shall adopt a somewhat broader definition. That is, we shall view political culture simply as the patterns of beliefs and attitudes people have towards the world, as these pertain to politics.

The concept can make a useful contribution to the understanding of a country's politics provided that one avoids certain pitfalls associated with its use. Three such pitfalls are especially worth dwelling on.

'Political Culture' unable, on its own, to explain phenomena

The first pitfall one needs to be aware of is that by itself, political culture cannot provide satisfactory causal explanations of political phenomena. To appreciate this, consider the following points.

(1) 'Political culture' is something that is embodied in the desires and beliefs of individuals, and it has no existence apart from these desires and beliefs. The fact that cultures are objectified in works of art, etc. does not change this.

(2) Political phenomena (such as voting, pressure-group activity and so forth) are embodied in the action of individuals and have no existence apart from this action.

(3) 'Action' is behaviour that the actor controls in the sense of being able to act differently if s/he chooses. Therefore, we cannot identify a piece of behaviour as an action of this or that type without implicitly committing ourselves to the existence of certain desires or beliefs that produced it. In other words, 'we cannot describe an action' – carrying an umbrella, for example – 'without thereby committing ourselves to the existence of desires and beliefs that contain descriptions of that action'. Vice versa, we cannot describe a set of beliefs and desires – for example, the belief that carrying an umbrella will help keep me dry today – without referring to the actions that are supposedly their effects – carrying an umbrella – because 'description of the belief makes reference to the action itself' (Rosenberg, 1988: 38).

(4) Therefore, actions on the one hand and desires and beliefs on the other are logically, not contingently, connected;

(5) Because they are not contingently connected, they cannot be causally connected or identified as 'variables' that can be measured independently of one another.[1]

The very important concomitant of the above five points is that when scholars appeal to the supposed cultural characteristics of a group of people to explain its political behaviour or characteristics, the 'explanations' they give risk being tautological. To appreciate this, consider the following example. Almond and Verba (1963) ask about the cultural preconditions for stable democracy; and they suggest that stability pertains when the political culture of a polity is 'congruent' with its political structures. A political culture is then 'congruent' when there is a high frequency of awareness of the structures, and where affect and evaluation in relation to them tend to be favourable. Now, leaving aside the problem of knowing exactly *how many* citizens' orientations have to be congruent in order for there to be 'democratic stability', one wants to ask whether this concept is not already *implied* in the authors' notion of a 'congruent culture' itself. In what sense would we want to define a democratic system as 'stable' if not in terms of its citizens' orientations to it?

This is not to say that the notion of political culture has no role to play in understanding political phenomena. However, it can contribute to causal explanations of such phenomena only in so far as it is expressed in political behaviour that can be identified and measured *independently* of the phenomena to be explained. This then throws a spotlight on the second pitfall associated with use of the culture concept.

Evidence for the content of a political culture is often flawed

A political culture is, we have said, bound up with actors' desires and beliefs. This means that it is expressed in the meaning actors attach to their action (or, if one prefers, actors' reasons for action).[2] Therefore, in order to be able to understand the nature and significance of cultural traits correctly, one has to be able to appreciate the understandings that actors *themselves* have of their action. This means that one must interpret with considerable caution the type of evidence that is most frequently offered for the 'content' of a culture, namely, survey-based evidence. The latter involves a double process of inference: from respondents' replies to their reasons, and from their reasons to the nature of the culture expressed through them. However, it is well known that survey methods involve the very real danger that investigators, in applying them, impose their own framework of understanding on the reality they seek to study.[3]

Notion of the political culture of a country is doubtful

The third pitfall to be avoided is the uncritical assumption (a) that one can talk unproblematically of 'the' culture (as opposed to cultures) of an entire country and (b) that such culture has the same relevance for the whole community. As Loredana Sciolla (2003) has pointed out, the idea that there exist distinctly 'Italian', 'French', 'German' or 'British', etc., political cultures whose characteristics are homogeneous throughout the populations concerned seems implausible bearing in mind the complexity and internal differentiation of modern industrial societies. And she provides empirical support for this view by drawing on survey data to compare public attitudes in five European countries (Britain, France, West Germany, East Germany, the Netherlands) plus Italy. Her research highlights two things:

(1) Political attitudes do not vary consistently across the six countries. (For example, while Italy emerges in last place in terms of the presence of attitudes denoting trust in the principal political and social institutions, Italy is behind only Britain and France in terms of the presence of attitudes denoting interpersonal trust – and so forth.)
(2) Within all of the countries, attitudes vary significantly with such factors as age, educational attainment and social class.

In short, Sciolla's research contains little to suggest that it is possible to identify some configuration of cultural traits that would allow us to pinpoint an 'Italian' culture as distinct from a 'French', 'British' or 'German', etc. culture.

   This suggests that at most one can talk in terms of cultural traits that are, or have been presumed to be, more commonly found in Italy than elsewhere. In the remainder of this chapter, I shall explore the most debated of these. In doing so, I shall describe (a) their historical roots, (b) the political and social behaviour patterns thought to have been expressive of them and (c) the debates surrounding their interpretation and their political consequences.

▪ National identity

In the conclusion to her piece, Sciolla (2003: 111) notes that Italy falls behind the other countries in terms of the presence of (a) sentiments of national identity and (b) confidence in the institutions of government. It is likely that the two traits are linked. A nation is a politico-cultural community asserting a claim to statehood or self-government. Thus, if one is negatively, or not very positively, oriented to one's institutions of government, it is not very likely that one will be very positively oriented to themes associated with the nation. Vice versa, a weak sense of nation is unlikely to be able to sustain very positive feelings towards the institutions of government.

   Widespread feelings of indifference or diffidence in Italy towards patriotism and such symbols of nation as the flag, the national anthem and so forth thus have three sources:

(1) Relatively low levels of trust in the institutions of government, or the state.
(2) The consequences of Fascism.
(3) The type of national integration furnished by the principal party actors in the four decades following the war.

Let us examine each in turn.

Box 5.2

Path dependency
The notion of 'path dependency' draws attention to the obstacles that lie in the way of change as a result of decisions made in the past. The example most often given to explain the principle of path dependency is the QWERTY keyboard system. This was developed in 1873

> to solve the problem of jamming keys on typewriters. By spacing out the most commonly used letters, typing was slowed down enough to reduce key-jamming. But today's electronic keyboards do not suffer from this problem. There is no longer any reason to use QWERTY, especially since a better system, DSK, speeds up typing by 10 per cent. So why do we still use QWERTY? Because changing would require a massive change – the nation's typists would have to relearn an entirely new system. Keyboard manufacturers would have to retool their production lines and write off any reserve supplies or backlogs of QWERTY keyboards as a loss. Computer keyboards are easier to change; all a manufacturer needs to do is reprogram a computer chip. But no individual company wants to risk being the first one to change. What if they changed, and no one else did? It takes a group agreement of very large proportions to initiate the revolution. And this inertia keeps us tied to QWERTY.
>
> *(home.att.net/~Resurgence/Pathdependency.htm)*

So it is with cultural phenomena: since they are embodied in the taken-for-granted beliefs and assumptions that everyone 'knows' to be correct, the individual takes a risk in challenging them and is only successful in changing them in the unlikely event that there are other individuals prepared to take the same risk.

Low levels of trust in the institutions of the state

This has roots that stretch back to the circumstances surrounding the foundation of the state itself: see chapter 1. These circumstances retained their significance long after Unification owing to processes of socialisation. These processes enable cultural tendencies to be transmitted from one generation to the next. Thereby, they allow the tendencies to retain their force over time, long after the factors that originally gave rise to them have ceased to exist. And this means that cultural phenomena are highly '**path dependent**' (Box 5.2).

The experience of Fascism

The traumatic experience of Fascism and its aggressive nationalist rhetoric made it difficult, after the war, to deploy themes of nation and patriotism without evoking painful memories. In other words, the themes had been so closely tied to an anti-democratic and totalitarian discourse by a regime whose decision to enter the war had brought such disastrous consequences, that it was, afterwards, almost impossible to use the themes without arousing the suspicion that one harboured fascist or extreme right-wing sympathies. Thus, the abandonment of patriotic discourses by all except those on the extreme right came to be taken as evidence of anti-fascism, immunity to nationalist nostalgia, a commitment to the values of democracy (Cartocci and Piscitelli, 2003: 119).

The type of integration furnished by the parties

This requires some explanation.

First, consider that, by means of their campaigning and propaganda activities, political parties perform pedagogical functions. They do so because, to avoid the risk of civil war and thus the possibility of their own destruction, they must teach followers democratic norms and patterns of behaviour. One of the ways in which they can do this is by drawing on the theme of 'the nation'. This theme evokes such concepts as loyalty, allegiance, 'the national interest' and so forth. It therefore implies that parties belong to a community whose members have ties and obligations that are more important than the party-political issues and allegiances dividing them. In this way, political conflict is kept within bounds. It remains peaceful.

Second, though clearly committed to democracy and to making the 1948 constitutional settlement work, neither of the parties that emerged as by far the two largest after the war – the Communists (PCI) and the Christian Democrats (DC) – were able to make any use of this 'democratic patriotism'. For neither party drew inspiration from the *Risorgimento*; and the communities of reference of both parties were ones other than the national community. For the PCI it was the international working class; for the DC it was the worldwide Catholic Church. Both parties therefore had visions of 'the good society' in which the world-view of the other party could find no place.

For these reasons, neither party was able to afford, to the other, unconditional recognition as a fully legitimate actor. Consequently, the allegiance to democracy and the Constitution inculcated by the parties could only ever be an *indirect* one, through the parties themselves. In other words, citizens' primary loyalties were party-political, not 'national', in nature and it was thanks to this that allegiance to the Constitution was secured.

The operation was made possible by the parties' capacity to step into the power vacuum that came to be created with the fall of Fascism. This capacity was heightened by the popular authority of the Resistance Movement in the case of the PCI, by the authority of the Church in the case of the DC. It enabled the two parties to gain control of large numbers of interest groups. Thereby, the parties were able to create veritable political subcultures, whose hold and cohesion owed much to the very depth of the ideological divide between them.

The potentially disaggregating effects of the divide were initially held in check by the common objective of struggle against the Nazi occupation and

Mussolini's Repubblica di Salò. Therefore, agreement on anti-fascism became the fundamental politico-cultural ideal that it was felt should inspire the work of those undertaking the task of drafting a new constitution.

It was thus anti-fascism and not national identity that underpinned the restoration of democracy in Italy. It provided for a degree of mutual acceptance between the parties – and thus for peaceful interaction between them despite the depth of the ideological divide running through society. Thereby, it allowed the party system itself to act, in the area of national integration, as a functional equivalent to the missing sense of 'nation' (Nevola, 2003: 149).

Recent changes in the sense of national identity

Since the party-system transformation of the 1990s, there have been some signs that the theme of 'nation' may be acquiring a new degree of acceptance. Gaspare Nevola (2003) in particular has argued that the process that led to the disappearance or transformation of all the parties that gave birth to the Republican constitution led to a deficit in the area of national integration. The emergence and growth of the Northern League was a powerful indicator of this. The result has been to open up space for the emergence of a new 'constitutional patriotism' which Carlo Azeglio Ciampi, President of the Republic between 1999 and 2006, sought to promote.

President Ciampi's efforts could be seen in a variety of initiatives, including

- revival of the *Festa della Repubblica* – whose date (2 June) is designed to coincide with the date of the referendum on the monarchy and the election of the Constituent Assembly in 1946;
- restoration of the **Vittoriano** (Box 5.3) in Rome;
- the opening of the gardens of the presidential palace, the **Quirinale** (Box 5.3), to the public.

The aim was to contribute to efforts to overcome perceptions, at home and abroad, of Italy as a 'democratic anomaly'. It has been of considerable pertinence in the light of the tendency of the two main coalitions to compete by each denying the other recognition as a fully legitimate political actor.

Whether a sense of patriotism and collective solidarity can actually be generated by actions of the kind President Ciampi was seeking to promote (Cartocci and Piscitelli, 2003: 135) is a very real question. Our earlier point about the highly path-dependent nature – and therefore the persistence – of cultural phenomena might suggest that the President's actions were unlikely to succeed. However, poll evidence, along with impressionistic evidence based on levels of popular participation in the President's initiatives, suggest that the latter may have found a popular echo. In other words, they suggest that the initiatives may amount to *more* than just 'official rituals' (Nevola, 2003: 156–60). This should not surprise: it must be remembered that the evidence suggests that the sense of nation appears to be weakly rooted in Italy, not that

Political culture and behaviour

The Vittoriano and the Quirinale

Public space and the built environment often have enormous, but frequently unrecognised, impacts on political phenomena – this because of the symbols they contain and because of the way in which they organise and physically channel action.

The Vittoriano is a large white monument in the centre of Rome, erected between the end of the nineteenth and the early years of the twentieth centuries (though not finally completed until 1935) to honour Vittorio Emmanule II, the first king of Italy. An immense edifice, 70 metres high and 135 metres wide, it is built of marble. It houses the tomb of the unknown soldier and the Altare della Patria. Exploited as a backdrop by the Fascists for many of their political rallies and considered by many as in any case too pompous, it was as a consequence allowed to decay for a number of years after the war. Work to restore the monument began in 1987, and it was reopened to the public on 4 November 2000.

The Quirinale is the name of the official residence of the President of the Republic, and thus one of the principal buildings symbolising the Italian state. As happens in most well-established polities, the names of the buildings that provide homes to the principal state institutions often come to be used in media commentary to refer to the institutions themselves. Thus, while the term 'Quirinale' is often used to refer to the presidency, Montecitorio is often used to mean the Chamber of Deputies; Palazzo Madama, the Senate; la Consulta, the Constitutional Court; Palazzo Chigi, the Prime Minister's office; la Farnesina, the Ministry of Foreign Affairs, and il Viminale, the Ministry of the Interior. Begun in 1583, the Quirinale was the Pope's summer residence until 1870, when it became the official residence of the king.

it is non-existent. The complete failure of the League's secessionist rhetoric for a time in the 1990s was evidence of this.

Social capital

A weak sense of nation has been thought both to reflect and to contribute to a relatively low level of 'social capital' in some parts of Italy. This term refers to 'features of social organization, such as trust, norms, and networks that can improve the efficiency of society by facilitating coordination actions' (Putnam, 1993: 167). A variety of indicators are typically used to measure it including the proportions of a collectivity: that accord legitimacy to public institutions; that show a sense of belonging to a community, respect for rules, interpersonal trust, membership of voluntary associations and other social networks, and so forth. The importance of social capital is thought to lie in the contribution it makes to overcoming dilemmas of collective action, and thus to making

Figure 5.1. The Vittoriano monument in Rome (see Box 5.3)

Box 5.4

Public goods

Public goods (of which a clean environment, safety on the streets and national defence are examples) are ones that cannot be made available to single individuals to the exclusion of others, but can be made available to any one individual only if they are made available to the entire community. Their provision is therefore dependent on overcoming collective-action problems. These are said to exist when there are states of affairs that are sub-optimal for a group of people as a whole, brought about as the result of each person trying to achieve what is optimal for him or her individually. For example, the rational individual, Jane, realises that the amount of environmental damage caused by her own car use is minuscule. She realises too that the environment can be improved only if not merely she, but vast numbers of people, stop using their cars unnecessarily. Jane also realises that the best situation as far as she is concerned is one in which she continues to use her car while everyone else refrains from doing so. And she knows that if she gives up using her car, other people are unlikely to do so, because as rational beings they reason in exactly the same terms as she does. So, acting rationally, both she and everyone else continue using their cars – and the environment remains unclean despite the fact that everyone would like a cleaner environment.

available **public goods** such as economic growth (Box 5.4). The term itself appears to have entered the political science lexicon relatively recently. But closely related concepts have been used to explore political culture in Italy at least as far back as the 1950s. A very important example of such concepts is given in the work of Edward Banfield.

Edward Banfield's Work

The Chiaromonte study

Edward Banfield was an American sociologist who in 1958 published the results of his research into the social organisation of Chiaromonte, in the southern Italian province of Potenza:

- When he arrived there four years earlier, what he found was a town of about 3,400 inhabitants, the majority of whom were poor peasants and agricultural labourers. Besides the absence of a newspaper or of any local voluntary associations save one, Banfield noted that the nearest hospital was a five-hour drive away in Potenza. The only way in which a child could get any education beyond the elementary level was by taking a bus to another town. This was beyond the resources of most since the bus service did not allow the round trip to be made within one day.
- What struck Banfield most about these deprivations was that though the inhabitants of Chiaromonte had complained for years about the lack of a hospital, the local political parties had never made an issue of it. No organised pressure had ever been exerted on the Government to build a hospital. No one had ever suggested the organisation of an ambulance to transport urgent cases to Potenza. Likewise, though the peasants were very bitter about the absence of the educational opportunities that would allow their children to escape from their poverty, it had never occurred to any of the better-educated inhabitants to offer any teaching to their fellow inhabitants. No organised attempts had ever been made to get the bus timetable changed to enable the local children to attend secondary school.
- Banfield was therefore prompted to ask why, despite being keenly felt, the deprivations of the citizens of Chiaromonte did not give rise to any of the kinds of organised political action that would enable the town's inhabitants to address their common problems.
- The answer he developed was that the inhabitants were subject to an 'amoral familism' that prevented them from making the kinds of personal sacrifices and acquiring the degree of trust that would make possible effective organisation. In other words, the citizens acted as if they were following the rule: 'maximize the material, short-run advantage of the nuclear family; assume that all others will do likewise'. This meant that they were unable to make the kinds of immediate-term personal sacrifices necessary to achieve long-term collective improvement. On Banfield's account, Chiaromonte was clearly lacking in social capital as defined

above; and he thought that in a number of relevant respects Chiaromonte was typical of southern Italy as a whole.

Criticisms of Banfield

Banfield's book gave rise to an unusually large number of reviews and critical articles:[4]

- His work implied that one of the causes, if not the only one, of the peasants' poverty was their amoral familism; and yet, said the critics, the peasants' deprivations were such that it was already remarkable that they managed to make sacrifices for other members of their families, never mind the whole community.
- It was suggested that explaining the peasants' poverty did not require recourse to such obscure concepts as 'amoral familism' but could instead be done by referring to much more familiar structural factors such as those related to the system of social stratification, the pattern of landholdings, economic dependency, geographical isolation and so forth.
- It was recalled that despite the emphasis he placed on the importance of a change in the peasants' familistic ethos if their circumstances were to change, Banfield was forced to note, ten years later, that there had been considerable improvements in the facilities and public life of Chiaromonte. This had happened despite the apparent persistence of attitudes supposedly indicative of amoral familism (Masi, 1976: 28).

Yet no critic went as far as to claim that nothing like what Banfield called amoral familism actually existed in southern Italy.[5]

Robert Putnam's Work

For this reason it is not, perhaps, very surprising that almost four decades later, Robert Putnam (1993) sought to advance concerns having clear links to those of Banfield (and to those of Almond and Verba) by developing a concept that was clearly inspired by the notion of 'amoral familism'. Putnam noticed that regional administrations in the North have been consistently 'more efficient in their internal operations, more creative in their policy initiatives, more effective in implementing those initiatives' (1993: 81). He advanced the hypothesis that the difference could be explained in terms of the presence or absence of features of what he called 'the civic community'. The civic community, he tells us, is one that 'is marked by an active, public-spirited citizenry, by egalitarian political relations, by a social fabric of trust and cooperation' (Putnam, 1993: 15).

As thus described, all of the features of the civic community are the 'positive' counterparts of 'negative' attitudes and behaviours that, according to Banfield, we can expect to find in a society of amoral familists.[6] The civic community is one whose defining features are such as to allow it successfully to surmount collective-action problems, while the features of amoral familism prevent this from happening. Thus the two terms may be thought of as describing the end points of a single dimension defining different degrees of the presence of social capital.

Problems with the social capital concept

In essence, then, both Banfield and Putnam, in their different ways, advance a hypothesis that links the efficiency and effectiveness of political organisation in a community to its stock of social capital. It is a hypothesis that appears hard to refute if only because the variables involved are so closely linked conceptually. Try, for example, to imagine a community which, despite having citizens that are distinctly lacking in trust and a willingness to co-operate, nevertheless has institutions that are responsive to their constituents. Try to imagine a community which, despite having citizens without any public spiritedness, nevertheless has institutions that take creative policy initiatives – and so forth. Clearly, such a community is hard to imagine unless we can assume that ordinary citizens on the one hand, and those who staff the institutions on the other, belong to entirely different cultural realities. So one needs to be wary of deploying the concept of social capital in isolation, forcing it to do more explanatory work than it can bear. To repeat the point we made in the first section of this chapter: when scholars appeal to the supposed cultural characteristics of a group of people to explain its political behaviour or characteristics, the 'explanations' they give risk being tautological. The concept of social capital can, nevertheless, help us to understand four phenomena that have had a very high profile in analyses of Italian politics in recent years. These phenomena are clientelism, political corruption, the Mafia and the so-called 'Third Italy'.

Clientelism

Clientelism is a term that describes a situation in which inequality in the distribution of resources gives rise to the exchange, on a personal basis, of protection and material rewards, for political support. Where the quantity of social capital available is low, people have difficulty in protecting and advancing their interests on an organised basis and are therefore obliged to seek the necessary protection on an individual basis. Therefore, inequality is more likely to spawn clientelism where social capital is lower than where it is higher. In turn, social capital is likely to be lower where poverty is greater; for among other things, the more precarious existence is, the less people are able to trust one another.

It was for these reasons that, with the re-establishment of democracy in Italy after the war, electoral politics in large parts of the South came to be conducted on a clientelistic basis. First, the area was, and still is, one of the poorest

in Europe.[7] Traditionally, much private economic activity has been beholden
to the state for its implantation and development (Allum, 1973b: 166). 'The
elected politician thus found, on the one hand, that he controlled access to the
principal source of wealth and, on the other hand, that he was faced with a
mass of isolated individuals (electors) each in search of a protector' (Newell,
2000: 48).

While clientelism was one of the most significant ways in which the governing parties maintained themselves in power for much of the post-war period,
in the end it sowed the seeds of the parties' destruction:

(1) It undermined the parties' abilities to take decisive policy initiatives when
needed, thus weakening their long-run electoral support. Hierarchical
clientele chains, running from top to bottom within the parties, inevitably led to factionalism and to complex networks of vested interests. Each
of these had a power of veto whenever policy change was considered.
Thus, the parties' role in policy-making tended to be highly reactive.
Significant initiatives usually only arose because they were forced on
the parties by some major external event.
(2) It proved to be self-expanding. Political success required being able to
distribute favours to larger numbers of people. Competition with rivals
trying to achieve the same objective ensured that it was inherently inflationary. It was no accident, then, that levels of public indebtedness grew
inexorably, finally becoming unsustainable when Italy signed the
Maastricht Treaty in 1991.

It is therefore not surprising that political scientists have tended to view
clientelism in Italy with extreme disfavour. However, such disfavour must be
tempered by four points:

(1) The kind of clientelism that developed with the restoration of democracy
after the war must not be conflated with a more traditional kind that was
common in the agrarian South prior to the war. This was a clientelism
concerning which the peasant had very little choice as economic and
physical survival depended on submitting to it. And, since the logic of
clientelism itself undermined the possibilities of collective action, it reinforced the power of landlords to the point where it was possible to doubt
whether, in their relations with the peasants, the notion of 'exchange'
had any real place at all. With universal suffrage, with the rights of
citizenship, and with the emergence of official, bureaucratic channels
for the distribution of resources, the balance of power between patrons
and clients shifted considerably in favour of the latter. The ballot became
the medium of exchange whereby voters collectively were able to determine who, among patrons, would have control of state resources and
whether these would be distributed clientelistically or not.
(2) 'Clients' were as often as not collective actors (such as interest groups, as
we shall see in the following chapter). Therefore, the question of where,

exactly, one draws the line between clientelism, on the one hand, and on the other hand the lobbying activities and constituency services accepted as a routine part of politics in other countries becomes a very pertinent one (Piattoni, 1998: 488–93).

(3) Piattoni (1998) has argued that while clientelism has been one of the factors that has kept rates of economic growth in the South behind those of the North,[8] there is a kind of 'virtuous clientelism' that may promote, rather than hinder, economic growth. The relative power of patrons and clients will depend on the number and cohesion of patrons, and on the opportunities for exit and voice of clients. The presence in an area of a single politician with a large following combined with a strong opposition party is likely to oblige the politician to use resources obtained clientelistically from the centre to provide public goods that will conduce to economic growth.

(4) Clientelism arguably has the virtue of being a powerful source of political integration. By offering an individualistic alternative to collective action as a means of deciding questions of resource distribution, it ties masses to elites. By creating informal exchange hierarchies within political parties, it ties centre to periphery (Tarrow, 1977).

Political corruption

Political corruption is an illegitimate transaction. It can be defined as something that takes place when a politician or public official is bribed by someone to act in their favour against the preferences of the state or citizens. If, for example, I pay a local councillor to ensure that I win a building contract to which I would not be entitled under the rules, then that is an act of political corruption.[9]

The relationship between political corruption and social capital

As such, political corruption both reflects low levels of social capital and is destructive of it. This is because it implies a willingness to engage in behaviours that make possible an arbitrary and unequal distribution of precisely those resources whose distribution, by common consent, should rather be governed by normatively defined criteria (Bull and Newell, 2003: 4–5). Such resources include planning permission, licences and permits, public works contracts and so forth. Corruption thus undermines the trust and confidence of citizens in the impartiality of public institutions. Hence, it undermines society's capacity to engage in co-ordinated action, to act collectively. On the other hand, high levels of social capital tend to prevent corruption: in a world where honesty is the norm, corruptors will have difficulty finding persons willing to accept bribes and not report them to the police (Varese, 2000: 6).

Political corruption in Italy

From the mid-1970s, political corruption appeared to become more widespread in Italy than it had been previously. This can probably best be accounted for in terms of demand and supply factors influencing the incidence of corrupt trans-actions. On the supply side, the relevant factors were the drying up of party donations from abroad with the decline of the Cold War conflict, and the growing costs of party and election campaigning that took place round about this time. These factors meant that the political parties were short of money. On the demand side, what appears to have been important is the desire of entre-preneurs to reduce, in their dealings with the authorities, the unpredictability stemming from administrative inefficiencies and legislative uncertainty.

Once it has emerged, corruption tends to spread, its expansion fed by declining social capital in a vicious circle. Part of the social capital of a com-munity consists of a commitment to honesty such that the individual suffers moral costs when behaving dishonestly. Let us assume that corrupt exchanges will take place when the expected moral and material costs are outweighed, for the contracting parties, by the expected benefits. The likelihood that expected benefits outweigh expected costs will be the greater the more wide-spread corruption is already. If nothing else, widespread corruption means that the resources available to investigate it have to be spread more thinly than when it is less widespread. As each corrupt transaction takes place, so for each subsequently envisaged transaction does the likelihood of expected benefits outweighing expected costs go up.

As confirmed by the evidence that emerged at the time of the 'mani pulite' anti-corruption investigations in the early 1990s, a point is eventually reached where corrupt activities have become so routine that all sense that they involve anything reprehensible is lost. Enzo Papi recalled:

> When I was appointed Cogefar managing director I was given a booklet where all the 'obligations' and payment dates of the company were recorded: a list of names and numbers; an obligation that was to be rigorously honoured. Illegal dealings were so common that I did not feel I was perpetrating a criminal act. *(quoted by Varese, 2000: 7)*

The conflict over political corruption in Italy

It is by virtue of the beliefs that corruption generated, and that in turn under-pinned it, that the networks that came to light as a result of 'mani pulite' have since given rise to what today amounts to a generalised cultural conflict in Italy. In order to appreciate this, one needs to understand the following points:

- Where corruption is widespread, it comes to affect the content of social norms – as the above quotation illustrates.
- Social norms provide answers to questions of fairness, morality and justice. They thus indicate socially acceptable behaviour.
- One of the most important social norms is that which enjoins reciprocity: most if not all cultures seem to have such a norm.

- Therefore, where behaviour that is formally *illegal* is not perceived as morally *reprehensible*, it comes to be expected that the recipient of a favour will reciprocate by himself being willing to do something illegal when asked. It is expected that recipients of bribes will 'honestly' fulfil their side of bargains, that they will not cheat, and so forth.
- Under such circumstances, the intervention, in a given instance, by agents of law enforcement breaks norms of reciprocity; for it prompts the question on the part of those targeted: since everyone engages in illegal activities or is prepared to do so if necessary, why target me rather than someone else? (Varese, 2000: 12)

These points enable us to understand the nature of the cultural conflict over corruption. One side of this conflict can be represented by the thoughts expressed in the suicide note written by Socialist deputy Sergio Moroni after he had been accused, in 1992, of receiving numerous bribes for public works contracts:

> An enormous veil of hypocrisy (shared by all) has for many years shrouded the mode of functioning of the parties and the means whereby they have been financed. The establishment of regulations and laws that one knows cannot be respected is a typically Italian way of doing things – one that is inspired by the tacit assumption that at the same time it will be possible to agree upon the establishment of procedures and behaviours which, however, violate the very same regulations…
>
> *(Colaprico, 1996: 31–2, my translation)*

It was very similar thoughts that led Socialist Party leader Bettino Craxi (Box 5.5), when he himself was accused of corruption, to conclude that the Milan prosecutors making the accusations must have targeted him for political reasons (Varese, 2000: 12). Silvio Berlusconi, who was a close friend of Craxi and who benefited enormously from his political favours, has continued the theme in his attempts to deal with his own legal difficulties.

In denouncing investigations into allegations against him as the work of communist sympathisers who have been using the judicial system 'to eliminate political adversaries … by means of contrived allegations … and monstrous sentences' (quoted by della Porta and Vannucci, 1999b: 56), Berlusconi has found a certain popular echo. This derives not merely from his charisma or his promise to do for Italy what he has done for himself, but from widespread popular perceptions that justice not infrequently *is* delivered in ways that fall short of ensuring equality before the law, as well as from the widely adhered to norm (exemplified by Moroni's note) that law and its enforcement is to be considered as something negotiable (LaPalombara, 1987: 50). Under these circumstances, centre-left complaints that Berlusconi sought, as Prime Minister after 2001, to use legislative means to solve his legal problems could themselves be presented as evidence of the left-wing, anti-Berlusconi bias of the judiciary that made the measures necessary in the first place!

But whatever its impact on social norms, corruption remains *illegal*. Therefore, on the other side of the cultural conflict are 'those who see

Box 5.5

Bettino Craxi

Born on 24 February 1934, Bettino Craxi distinguished himself by being both the first Socialist to hold the office of Prime Minister and – since he held it continuously from 4 August 1983 to 17 April 1987 – by being Italy's longest-serving post-war prime minister to that date. During this period he was able to acquire something of a reputation for decisiveness, perhaps best symbolised by the Sigonella incident, in October 1985, when he refused an American request to extradite the hijackers of the *Achille Lauro* cruise ship, enforcing his decision through a stand-off between Italian and American troops at the Sigonella air base in Sicily (Box 10.6). His reputation for decisiveness was one he was able to cultivate partly because he was in the position, relatively unusual for Italian politics at this time, of occupying both the post of party secretary and the post of Prime Minister. This enabled him to keep a rather tight grip on the internal life of his party and to impose a relatively high degree of discipline on his followers in Parliament. In this way he hoped to be able to create political space and a distinct profile for his party, 'entrapped' as it was between the larger Communist Party to its left and the Christian Democrats to its right. And in fact, Craxi was rewarded for his efforts at the 1987 election, which saw his party's vote reach its post-war apogee of 14.2 per cent. However, the dilemmas of its position had caused Craxi's party to degenerate, gradually turning it into a party of opportunists and 'business politicians' largely deprived of any real ideological commitments (della Porta and Vannucci, 1999a: 69–92), from whence it derived a reputation as a party with a rather shaky grasp of the principles of honest government. No one was very surprised, therefore, when Craxi himself became caught up in the judicial investigators' nets at the height of the *Tangentopoli* scandal, something that forced him to resign the leadership of his party in 1993. The following year he became a fugitive from justice when, with the likelihood of his arrest becoming increasingly great, he fled to Tunisia. Here he was to remain until his death, on 19 January 2000, brought about by a heart attack.

themselves as the guardians of a civic morality embodying ideals about what an anti-Fascist, democratic republic should be like' (Newell, 2004: 259). They include the public prosecutors of the '*Mani pulite*' investigations. They include many of the politicians on the centre left. They include those involved in the so-called *girotondi*. These were a series of anti-Berlusconi demonstrations organised by a loose network of intellectuals in the early months of 2002. Finding their supporters mainly from among white-collar employees, teachers and the better educated – people more likely to vote for the centre left than the centre right (ITANES, 2001) – the *girotondi* gave expression to the fears of an 'informed middle class'. The interests of this class are in principle much threatened by the attitudes expressed by the likes of Berlusconi. And they are threatened by his apparent success in using his public position in pursuit

Box 5.6

Key terms: universalism, social closure

Universalism is the view that specific courses of action should be decided upon by reference to principles applicable to all cases equally. It is thus often contrasted with particularism, which embodies the opposite attitude and thus gives rise to decisions made, on a case-by-case basis, *without* reference to general principles. Often implicit in the distinction is the suggestion that while the first leads you to be treated in accordance with *what* you are, the second will lead you to be treated in accordance with *who* you are. Thereby, it will result in decisions of dubious legitimacy – e.g. to give priority in healthcare to an important person, even though his case is less serious than that of a lower-status person suffering from the same complaint.

   Social closure is a term used by Frank Parkin (1979) among others to refer to any process whereby a group seeks to monopolise control over resources and deny access to others. Property is thus only one form of social closure; another is 'credentialism' (limiting access to positions only to those in possession of given diplomas, degrees, licences and so forth): both strategies are rooted in rules that define ownership and formal qualifications and their concomitants.

of his private interests. For his activities conflict with the norm that laws should embody principles of impartiality and **universalism** (Box 5.6). And it is only through the inflexible application of such principles that members of this class are able to engage in the practices of '**social closure**' (Box 5.6) (Parkin, 1979) that enable them to claim for themselves larger shares of material resources than those available to people lower down the class structure. The cultural conflict we are talking about thus expresses a real, *material*, conflict between categories of people with different interests.

Italy's relative position

It is probably at least in part because of the internationally high profile of this clash that, as measured by Transparency International's (TI) 'Corruption Perceptions Index', Italy continues to be perceived as being among the European countries with greater rather than lesser problems, in terms of corruption. The TI index 'is compiled by combining the results of multiple surveys of business people, academics and financial analysts who are asked to rank countries according to how corrupt they perceive them to be. The resulting index ranges from zero to ten where the closer to ten a country's score is, the "cleaner" it is presumed to be' (Newell and Bull, 2003: 4). In 2008, Italy's score was 4.8, putting the country in twentieth place among the EU twenty-five (www.transparency.org/policy_research/surveys_indices/cpi/2008).

   One needs to be wary of drawing from these perceptions excessively precise conclusions about how the countries compare in 'objective' terms, however.

> **Box 5.7**
>
> *Corruption: the problem of definition*
> Critical theorists assert that it is not possible to offer definitions of terms such as 'corruption' or 'terrorism' that are independent of the perceptions of those using the terms. This is because, whatever other meaning one might wish to ascribe to them, they necessarily refer to infringements of rules – 'where a "rule" is a criterion of behaviour that indicates right and wrong ways of doing things; is something that can only exist in virtue of social interaction, and is something whose infringement is to some greater or lesser degree morally condemned in the group whose social existence gives rise to it. Therefore, to describe given acts as "corrupt" is to condemn them as illegitimate according to the standards of one's own group or at least the group with which one identifies. This in turn means that we cannot know what counts as corruption unless we know something about the moral codes of the group to which the person seeking to apply this label belongs' (Newell, 2008: 2). On this basis, critical theorists distinguish themselves from more 'mainstream' or 'orthodox' theorists by: (1) their rejection of the possibility that concepts such as 'terrorism' and 'corruption' can be made to refer to 'extra-discursive' objects of knowledge; thus (2) their view that the concepts must be seen exclusively as ones variously deployed by political actors themselves to advance their goals and manage power relationships, and hence (3) their insistence that the agenda for research should be not the analysis of causes and consequences (since the terms do not refer to objectively definable phenomena in the first place), but rather about exploring how the concepts are deployed discursively (by politicians, other academics, the mass media and so on), for what purposes and with what consequences.

Apart from anything else, comparison presupposes having a definition of **corruption** such that a given act can be classified in the same way regardless of the country in which it takes place (Box 5.7). Yet none of the definitions of political corruption so far advanced appear to meet this criterion, not even the one suggested by della Porta and Vannucci (see note 9), for it remains for the principal to decide what his/her interests/preferences are.

The Mafia

The Mafia is a secret organisation dating back to about the middle of the nineteenth century. With a membership of about five thousand, its unity derives from what Durkheim called 'mechanical solidarity' (Paoli and Wolfgang, 2001). That is, its approximately one hundred 'families' are structurally homologous units, each of which is recognised by all of the others as forming part of the same association in virtue of the fact that they all share common rituals and routines. The 'family' is defined on a territorial basis, usually a town, city or part thereof, within which it seeks, in opposition to the laws of the state, to acquire a monopoly in terms of the exercise of jurisdiction over economic life. That is, through the threat of violence it seeks to regulate and to 'tax' economic activity, both legal and illegal. 'This allows it to reap most of the rents from… illegal transactions without running the full cost and risk involved in the direct management of the businesses' (Fiorentini and Peltzman, 1995: 2). And it gives it a quasi rule-making or governing role through which it settles disputes and underwrites transactions.

Like corruption, Mafia activities at one and the same time both reflect low levels of social capital and are destructive of it. This is because, in the areas where the organisation is strong, it owes its influence precisely to the inability of citizens to trust public institutions or each other, while its influence reinforces such inability.

In the period following Unification, the public authorities in Sicily were unable to acquire the characteristic that defines the modern state. This is the exercise of a monopoly on the legitimate use of violence. Consequently, the state in Sicily found itself caught in a vicious circle. Public hostility undermined their ability to guarantee public security, their inability in this respect fed public hostility. This helped to fuel the demand for alternative, Mafia-provided, means of guaranteeing order and security. It also helped to fuel the supply of such means; for it reinforced popular codes of honour, including *omertà* or the 'conspiracy of silence'. Thereby, it helped to keep in being norms of behaviour of which the Mafia itself was the quintessential expression. Such norms strengthen the Mafia as an organisation; and they do so even where they are in fact much disliked because they help to enhance the Mafia's reputation. For the mere belief that the Mafia has widespread influence and that approaches to the police could therefore lead to reprisals reinforces the organisation. It gives substance to the fear and suspicion from which the Mafia draws its strength in the first place. Thus even those opposed to *omertà* are obliged, in Mafia strongholds, to come to terms with its practical consequences. Meanwhile, widespread *omertà* further diminishes the capacity of the agencies of law enforcement to provide the guarantees that citizens legitimately demand. By thus confirming empirically that citizens are correct to mistrust the capacity of public institutions to protect them, it legitimises the search for alternative, Mafia-provided, means of obtaining security. In this way, it keeps in being a vicious circle whereby growing illegality and declining social capital feed upon each other.

In the communities where the Mafia is present, the nature of its influence is such that acquiescence can shade imperceptibly into collaboration – as the testimony of ex-*mafioso* Gaspare Mutolo made clear:

> When the entrepreneur then gets in touch and pays, he sometimes benefits too: first, because a friendship develops between the person who goes to collect the monthly payment, and the entrepreneur, who is thus able to see that the local mafioso is a normal person who behaves that way for the money; and secondly because he has the guarantee that if something is stolen from him, those in Mafia circles will make it their business to see that he gets back what has been stolen – or if someone cheats

him, that there is available a whole circuit to force payment. Then again, there are business opportunities: for example, suppose that you are the owner of a firm that produces ashtrays and you sell, for example, a thousand, and I propose the setting up of a company that can sell ten thousand. You'll do your calculations and appreciate that the proposition is attractive; and then it will be up to me, through the districts of Palermo, to force shops to stock that type of ashtray. So it is not the case that the entrepreneur only loses: sometimes he gains. With the development of such a relationship, naturally, when a man or woman comes to me and says, 'Listen, my son is about to get married and needs a job', I take the matter up among these factories and I find work for him. It's not a problem: one speaks to the owner and says: 'Take on one, two, three or however many there are'. It may be that the factory owner needs a couple of weeks or a month to dismiss someone else or to create the post, but it is always possible to find a way to do it. *(CPM, 1993: 1223, my translation)*

Influence of this kind and on this scale is especially threatening to the state; for it allows the Mafia to pose as an alternative source of the legitimate exercise of force. Thereby it implicitly challenges the state's claim to a monopoly in this area, thus striking at the very heart of its public authority. But precisely because of this, the state has for much of its history found it easier to seek 'peaceful coexistence' with the Mafia rather than its complete elimination, relying on it for help in maintaining order. For example, there is considerable evidence that between 1945 and 1990, fear in ruling circles of the apparent threat posed by the PCI provided the rationale for a range of illegal activities on the part of elements of the political class and state bureaucracy, including making use of the Mafia's ability to control the votes of citizens in the areas where it is strong (Box 5.8).[10]

This in turn means that while, from one perspective, the Mafia is an organisation that is outside and against the state, from another perspective it must be seen as being within and part of the state (Santino, 1994: 127). In particular, politicians who accept Mafia-controlled votes and other illegal favours make use of a resource – the threat of violence – that is potentially turned against them and to which they are especially vulnerable; for, by putting themselves on the wrong side of the law, they deprive themselves of the law's protection. Thus, while not fully integrated into the organisation, they in effect become 'men of honour' for all practical purposes, obliged to defend the organisation's interests whenever this is demanded of them.

It is perhaps not surprising then that the extent of Mafia infiltration of the institutions of local government is such that between 1991 and May 2005, no fewer than 135 town councils (of which all but one were in the South) were dissolved because of suspected infiltration of this type (Mareso and Serpone, 2005). However, from this it would be a mistake to accept as true the widespread assumption that illegality and crime are intertwined with the history of Italy to a greater extent than other Western countries. As Paoli and Wolfgang (2001) point out, 'Statistical yearbooks do not suggest that Italy's rates of crime and illegality are especially unusual.' While mafia groups have a particularly high profile in Italy, the murder rate, at 1.61 per 100,000, was in 1997

Box 5.8

The Mafia and voting

How is the Mafia able to control votes given the secrecy of the ballot? One answer is given in the report of the Italian parliament's anti-Mafia Committee:

> The Mafia makes it known in the environment in which it operates that it is able to control the vote and it thus makes voters fear reprisals … More often, no outright intimidation is needed. Advice is sufficient. The absence of political energy and passion, the notion that a vote serves only to mark one's adherence to a clientele group and not to indicate a choice of ideas, and the levelling of political traditions among the different parties all lead [voters] almost naturally, without any forcing, to respect the 'marching orders' [given by the Mafia].
>
> *(quoted by della Porta and Vannucci, 1999a: 226)*

Another answer is that until the change of electoral law in the early 1990s, the Mafia was able to exploit the system of preference voting for parliamentary elections, which took place on the basis of the open list system of proportional representation. This allowed the voter to express up to four preferences among his or her chosen party's list of candidates.

> Preferences could be expressed by writing on the ballot paper either the names of the preferred candidates or the numbers assigned to them. By telling voters what combination of names and/or numbers to write on their ballot papers, the mafia could, if not completely destroy the secrecy of the ballot, gauge how closely voters in its districts adhered to its instructions. Third, by obtaining one blank ballot paper, the mafia is apparently able perpetrate electoral fraud. This works as follows: the *mafioso* fills in the ballot paper and gives it to a voter as s/he enters the polling station. Once inside, the voter obtains his or her ballot paper, but instead of using this paper, s/he deposits in the ballot box the paper given to him or her by the *mafioso*, giving the *mafioso* his or her own blank paper as s/he leaves the polling station. The *mafioso* then fills in that paper, giving it to the next voter – and so the process continues. *(Newell, 2006)*

considerably lower than in Spain (2.60) and in countries supposedly rich in social capital such as Finland (2.76). Meanwhile, it was over four times lower than in the United States (7.34). What the Mafia suggests is not that *contra legem* phenomena are specifically Italian or manifest themselves with a particular intensity in that country, but rather that countries differ in the intensity with which given types of *contra legem* phenomena manifest themselves.

The 'Third Italy'

The 'Third Italy' is a term that is used to distinguish the industrial districts of central and north-eastern Italy from the established industrial area of the

Figure 5.2. Scene of the murder of Giovanni Falcone, the public prosecutor blown up by the Mafia on 23 May 1992 in revenge for his role in securing the conviction of dozens of *Mafiosi* in the so-called 'Maxi trial' from the mid-1980s

North-West, and from the relatively under-industrialised South. What distinguishes the Third Italy is the dominance of small and medium-sized enterprises. Since the early 1970s, these have been able to establish 'a strong position in world markets in a number of so-called traditional products – shoes, leather handbags, knitwear, furniture, tiles, musical instruments, food processing – and also in the industries which supply machinery to these sectors' (UNIDO, 2005).

The rise of the 'Third Italy'

The Third Italy's rise was unexpected. In 1951, the area was not particularly distinct (at least as compared to the South) either in terms of the proportion of its firms that were small or in terms of the nature of its industrial products (Boschma, 1998: 7–11). Small firms were regarded as unlikely supports of industrial growth since they were seen as unable to take advantage of the economies of scale available to large firms. They were also seen as having restricted access to capital and technology. And they were seen as being often dependent on large-firm customers. Meanwhile, the industries that came to characterise the Third Italy had low rates of value added and a low intensity of technology, and their markets were largely saturated. For these reasons, the industries were thought to be especially vulnerable to competition from low-wage countries (Boschma, 1998: 7).

Not surprisingly, then, the Third Italy's rise has spawned a large literature. Though attempts to explain the area's development are not always compatible, most authors appear to concur in emphasising certain themes. These themes are necessarily addressed to two essential questions: how can we explain the *timing* of the phenomenon? How can we explain its *location*?

The timing of the Third Italy's rise

As far as the first of these questions is concerned, part of the answer is based on the observation that growing real incomes from the 1950s boosted the demand for consumer goods. Meanwhile, the growing demand, from the 1970s, for more varied and customised goods gave small firms an advantage as compared to large firms. Small firms in traditional, artisan, sectors are in a position to offer custom-made goods, manufactured on the basis of short production runs, in a way that large firms are not. This is because they have a greater capacity than large firms for flexibility and adaptation. In large firms, internal economies of scale require heavy investments of capital and therefore involve a sacrifice of flexibility.

The location of the Third Italy

One of the reasons why the Third Italy emerged in the Centre and North-East is because these areas were relatively well able to host 'industrial districts'. These are a kind of productive environment that appears to be particularly well adapted to the success of small enterprises. An industrial district is a geographically delimited productive system, characterised by a large number of enterprises. These belong to the same vertically integrated sector and thus all contribute to the production of a single type of product. That is, each firm specialises either in a different phase of production of the product (for example, sewing or weaving for the clothing industry) or provides ancillary services (such as packing or transport) for the industry. As such, an industrial district must be thought of as a unified social and economic system. Within it there are close relations between political, economic and social spheres; and the functioning of one is shaped by the functioning and organisation of each of the others (Pyke and Sengenberger, 1991: 16). In the district, each group of enterprises specialising in a given phase of the production process or in the supply of services is complementary to each of the others. Hence relations between them resemble those described by Durkheim's concept of 'organic solidarity'. This concepts refers to the awareness of all units of their dependence on each of the other units. As a consequence, thanks to co-operative purchasing arrangements, expensive machinery can be fully utilised to provide for the needs of all the members of the district. This means that the entire community of small enterprises is able to obtain those economies of scale once thought to be the preserve of large enterprises (Pyke and Sengenberger, 1991: 17).

Why were the Centre and North-East relatively well able to host industrial districts? Why were they better able to do so than the South, say? Part of the answer to these questions have to do with the fact that the success of each firm in industrial districts depends not only on its success in competing with other firms, but also on the success of firms generally in establishing co-operative relations (1) with each other, (2) with their workers and (3) with the local authorities. Let us examine each of these in turn:

(1) By establishing co-operative relations with each other, firms may establish purchase consortia – to obtain their inputs at a lower price – credit consortia – where several of them band together to guarantee each others' loans – and trade associations able to provide accountancy and bookkeeping services. The aim in such cases is to take advantage of all possible economies of scale, where these forms of co-operation sometimes represent the only ways in which small businesses are able to remain viable (Brusco, 1995: 57–8).

(2) Since success for firms in the industrial districts is highly dependent on their capacity to adapt, employers cannot control their workers by tying them to a single machine but must establish the kind of good will that will allow them to assign tasks flexibly.

(3) Competition between large numbers of firms means that opportunism and **free-riding** (Box 5.9) are ever-present threats – and yet the success of the industrial district in global markets depends on confidence in the quality of its products. This means that the firms must be willing to acquiesce in measures taken by the authorities – from the circulation of information to the establishment of quality controls – that reduce the opportunities for free-riding (Brusco, 1995: 65–6).

In short, the success of industrial districts requires large stocks of social capital; and such stocks appear to be more plentiful in the Centre and North-East than in the South. But why is this the case? And how does social capital have its effects? On these issues there is considerable disagreement among scholars.

Putnam's argument

On the one hand, there are those who take their lead from Robert Putnam (1993). For Putnam, differences in social capital between different parts of the country are to be explained in terms of civic traditions stretching back to early medieval times. In a nutshell, Putnam's argument is as follows.

In the South, the Norman monarchy ensured that civic life was regulated from the centre and from above, and hierarchy remained the dominant feature of politics and society in the subsequent centuries. In northern and central Italy, on the other hand, communal self-government ensured that political relationships were characterised less by vertical hierarchy than by horizontal collaboration. If in the South autocracy was the solution found for the

Hobbesian problem, in the Centre and North it was self-help and mutual assistance.

Though initially the two areas were equally effective in producing prosperity and efficient government, the Centre and North eventually pulled ahead since self-help and mutual assistance encouraged trust. This made possible credit, which made possible new prospects for economic development. Economic development in turn reinforced ties of collaboration and civic solidarity. In the South, on the other hand, authoritarianism and hierarchy gave rise to exploitation and dependence, along with the fomentation of mistrust and the destruction of horizontal ties of solidarity, in a strategy of 'divide and rule'. Under these circumstances, by the late nineteenth century, voluntary associations, mutual aid societies and other co-operative responses to the strains of industrialisation were much less likely to develop in the South – thus reinforcing vertical bonds of clientelism as the only alternative strategy for survival.

In short, the argument is that owing to path dependency and the self-reinforcing nature of qualities such as trust and its absence, the differing stocks of social capital can be explained by varying cultural traditions handed down over the course of several centuries. In turn, social capital makes possible the co-operation characteristic of successful industrial districts because trust and norms of reciprocity allow people to overcome problems of collective action.

The arguments of Pizzorno and Trigilia

On the other hand, there are those, such as Pizzorno (2001) and Trigilia (2001), who argue that social capital does not invariably have positive consequences, political or economic. Thus in order correctly to understand its implications, one has to explore the conditions under which it will have the kinds of consequences observed in the case of the Third Italy.

For example, we know that the Mafia, as an organisation based on **generalised reciprocity** (Box 5.9) (Paoli, 2000), embodies a great deal of social capital. We know too that, though generally it destroys the latter among those on the outside, it is also able, because of the reputation it has, to create it (Pizzorno, 2001: 28–9). One of the ways in which it does this is by underwriting cartel agreements among firms, for example in the area of public works contracts. By providing credible assurances to members of the cartel that it will take decisive action against firms who try to defect from the agreement, and by excluding outside firms unwilling to submit to the rules, it creates great co-operation among the firms. It considerably reduces the uncertainty they have to face and greatly raises the level of profits of the firms collectively.

However, we also know that such arrangements are inimical to the long-run economic growth of the community as a whole. Trigilia (2001) therefore argues that it is not the absence, in the South, of social capital that explains the area's

> ## Box 5.9
>
> *Key terms: free-riding and generalised reciprocity*
> **Free-riding** is said to take place when an actor fails to contribute his or her share of the costs of production of a resource while continuing to consume it. Free-riding is particularly likely to arise in the case of public goods precisely because no one individual can be excluded from benefiting from them if they are to be provided at all. The individual is thus driven not to contribute, hoping that others will pay for the good anyway, enabling him or her to receive the benefit at no personal expense. Free-riding is thus a problem as it may, if large numbers engage in it, lead to non-production of the good at all. It is for this reason that public goods such as defence are rarely financed by voluntary contributions – taxation and coercion being instead the main means used to ensure that the goods are supplied.
>
> **Generalised reciprocity** 'refers to a continuing relationship of exchange that is at any given time unrequited or imbalanced, but that involves mutual expectations that a benefit granted now should be repaid in the future' (Putnam, 1993: 172).

'backwardness' as compared to the Third Italy; rather, it is the different political uses that have been made of social capital understood as a resource.

In this respect, Trigilia (1995) places much emphasis on the importance of the Catholic and Communist subcultures referred to in chapter 1. Thus, in the Third Italy, the subcultures freed political leaders from particularistic demands, ensuring that, through the provision of collective goods for the whole community, social capital would be used to promote growth. In the South, where the Catholic and Communist movements were much weaker, politics remained much more tied to the pursuit of particularistic interests, so that social capital could not be used in this way.

■ Recent political developments

The themes developed in the preceding sections can help to throw light on the most significant party-political developments of the last fifteen years: the party-system crisis of the early 1990s and, intimately connected to this, the emergence and growth of the Northern League and Forza Italia.

Cultural accounts of crisis of the early 1990s

If there is a single cultural trait that runs through everything we have discussed so far, then it is the widespread presence of negative attitudes towards the state and the institutions of government. Intimately connected to such attitudes towards the state are a number of more specific attitudes. These, it has recently been suggested, can be taken as indicators of a kind of populism, one referred to using the term 'anti-politics'.

Populism is a term that scholars have had particular difficulty in defining. However, it can be said to be a political cultural element 'connected with the way a political system ought to work' (Pasquino, 2005: 6). It is an element that, in emphasising the importance of 'the people', is generally suspicious of established elites (political, economic or social). It is also intolerant of minorities – whose claims represent illegitimate obstacles in the way of the popular will. Populism is therefore intolerant of institutional limitations on the use of power by majorities; and it is intolerant of the idea of inalienable rights of citizenship. 'No matter who succeeds in "awakening" and mobilizing the people, and *pour cause*, becomes the populist leader' (Pasquino, 2005: 8), one who is perceived as being both *of* the people and *uniquely qualified to lead* the people. Albeit in a relatively mild form, Margaret Thatcher had a populist style of politics (Mastropaolo, 2000: 32).

Anti-political attitudes are ones that involve a rejection of conventional political activities, politicians and parties. Typically, it would seem, these are perceived as damaging to the interests of the people for reasons that allow no appeal: either electoral competition masks more fundamental collusion between established politicians, denying the people any real choice, or else party competition prevents the resolution of the people's problems by placing an obstacle in the way of a sense of common purpose.

Mastropaolo (2000: 34–5) argues that a distinguishing feature of the anti-political kind of populism that has appeared in a number of democracies in recent years is that its themes are exploited not only by oppositional or marginal forces but also by governing parties. This allows him to offer the following original interpretation of the party-system upheavals of the early 1990s in Italy.

- Anti-political sentiments, for long nourished by the cultural diffidence of citizens towards their institutions of government, were for many years after the war held in check by the legitimacy of the traditional mass parties and by the force of the Cold War ideological divisions they represented.
- As these ideological divisions became weaker, anti-political sentiments were allowed to resurface once more, expressing themselves in growing levels of electoral abstention and in the emergence and growth of new parties.
- The traditional parties and their representatives sought to recover ground by riding the tide of popular sentiments and embracing a number of anti-political themes, including ones developed in intellectual circles, that quite exaggerated the defects and shortcomings of Italian democracy.
- Thus, in denouncing, in their different ways, the various shortcomings of *partitocrazia* – shortcomings which, they claimed, could only be addressed by root-and-branch institutional reform (on whose terms they were, however, never able to agree) – the parties offered an image of themselves that underscored unjustifiably catastrophic interpretations of the health of party government in Italy.

173

- These interpretations eventually becoming a new orthodoxy. Thereby, they came to inform the outlooks of voters as well as politicians and gave substance to the view that only a popular movement against the political class, of the kind seen with the referendum of 1993, could offer to restore some kind of health to Italian democracy.

On this interpretation, then, the disintegration of the governing parties and the onset of regime transition in the early 1990s must be seen as the outcome of a kind of self-fulfilling prophecy, an outcome that was in some way written into long-standing cultural beliefs about the quality of democracy in Italy.

The Emergence and Growth of the Northern League and Forza Italia

If this interpretation has some force, then it allows us to see the emergence and growth of both the Northern League (LN) and Forza Italia (FI) 'not simply as a contingent reaction against the established parties, but as the reappearance of attitudes that have always characterized the Italian political culture' (Pasquino, 2005: 23); for the propaganda of both is clearly populist and anti-political in style.

From the beginning, both stressed their outright rejection of the traditional political establishment:

- Bossi developed the theme of '*Roma ladrona*' (thieving Rome). Berlusconi developed his image as a successful entrepreneur whose sense of duty drove him to use his talents to save the country from a government of the left and the disasters provoked by professional politicians unable to agree on anything (Tarchi, 2003: 164).
- Bossi sought to use linguistic codes that would mark an unbridgeable fracture with the language of the traditional political parties and allow the ordinary person to feel that 'when Bossi speaks it is as if I am speaking'. Berlusconi adopted a similar strategy. Notwithstanding his accumulated wealth, so the message runs, he retains all the qualities of 'the man next door'. In this, the message continues, he is quite unlike his adversaries, who have shown themselves incapable of being anything other than professional politicians. It is in this light that the gaffes and mockery for which he has become famous must be interpreted (Tarchi, 2003: 173–4).
- While Bossi frequently subjects the institutions of government to sarcasm and invective, Berlusconi generally adopts a more moderate tone, though he too rails against institutions that refuse to subordinate themselves to the will of the people as expressed through the majority in Parliament. For Berlusconi, the fact that he stood at the head of a popular majority itself made the corruption and other charges laid against him in recent years illegitimate. The fact that the judges are not elected by the people, is, from this viewpoint, itself evidence that their actions were politically motivated.

What is less immediately clear is why, if Putnam's thesis about civic traditions is correct, a party as exclusionary and xenophobic as the Northern League was actually able to make any headway, bearing in mind that it made its appearance in that part of the country where social capital was supposed to be especially plentiful. And if the LN was a response to the socio-economic malaise of northern small businesspeople, the question arises as to why it was able to take hold in the North-East, but not in regions like Emilia-Romagna and Tuscany.

The answer is most probably to be found in a combination of (1) the kinds of social relations that are productive of social capital and (2) the different subcultural realities of the two areas:

(1) As Pizzorno (2001: 22–37) shows, of the kinds of social relations that give rise to social capital, there is really only one type that is devoid of all considerations of self-interest whether material or symbolic. This is the kind of social relation that arises when A helps B for *no* other reason than adherence to some principle of a universalistic kind. This means that most forms of social capital are compatible with social exclusion and that they may even encourage it bearing in mind the importance of identity in their formation. That is, in order for the kinds of relations productive of social capital to be established, the participants have to recognise each other as being the kinds of person with whom that kind of relation is normally established. And in fact, the groups most productive of social capital are found among those that are most exclusive in terms of their membership.[11]

(2) The political subcultures, whose declining influence provided room for the League, left behind very different traditions. That is, both the Catholic and Communist subcultures of the North-East and Centre respectively had placed much emphasis on the obligations of solidarity. But whereas in the first case, solidarity was something preached as a moral obligation by a Church that was hierarchical and demanded conformity, in the second case solidarity had – by virtue of its importance in trade unionism, for example – implications that were much more clearly those of empowerment and inclusivity.

▮ Conclusion

In this chapter we have explored the significance of political culture for an understanding of Italian politics. Based on a broad definition of the term 'political culture', the underlying argument can be summarised in a series of four points.

(1) It is not possible to identify a single 'national culture' that can be viewed as a 'cause' of political behaviour.

(2) Cultural phenomena can, however, help us to gain understanding, where the latter term must be understood to mean 'render intelligible' rather than 'explain causally'.

(3) Exploring the origins and significance of such cultural phenomena as a weak sense of nation, varying levels of social capital and the presence of anti-political attitudes allows one to acquire insight into patterns of behaviour – including such widely discussed phenomena as clientelism, corruption and the Mafia – that contribute to the socio-political context within which governance must take place in Italy.

(4) Analysis of these patterns lends support to the overall argument of this book. That is, though often regarded as an 'anomaly', Italy is nevertheless fully comparable with other democracies. Its seemingly anomalous character is the consequence of its specific combination of institutional, cultural and historical features that are by and large common to such countries.

Political culture, we have suggested, cannot be understood apart from the political behaviour through which it manifests itself. A subtype of this behaviour is political participation. This is action undertaken with the intention of influencing who governs, or the decisions taken by governments. Such action is itself often grouped into two categories: formal and informal. The former refers to participation in the electoral arena and includes things like voting, running for office, being active in a political party. The latter refers to participation in activities outside this arena, the most significant type being pressure-group activity. Therefore, against the cultural background sketched in the preceding paragraphs, our attention in the following chapter turns to the role of pressure groups, and in chapter 7 to voting and political parties.

■ Further reading

Not surprisingly, perhaps, there is a rather more substantial English-language literature on cultural phenomena in Italy than there is on the somewhat 'drier' topic of Italian political institutions. On corruption, the author who has contributed the most significant work in this area is Donatella della Porta. See, among the pieces she has produced, alone and with others, her book with Alberto Vannucci, *Corrupt Exchanges: Actors, Resources and Mechanisms of Political Corruption* (Berlin and New York: De Gruyter, 1999). Her edited volume with Yves Mény, *Democracy and Corruption in Europe* (London: Pinter, 1997), contains a chapter on Italy along with chapters on other European countries and thus facilitates comparison with the position elsewhere. On the Mafia, the best up-to-date book currently available in English is, in the author's opinion, Letizia Paoli's *Mafia Brotherhoods: Organised Crime Italian Style* (Oxford: Oxford University Press, 2003). Indispensible for an understanding of the themes considered in this chapter are the works that have driven much of its discussion: Edward Banfield's *The Moral Basis of a Backword Society* (New York: The Free Press, 1958) and Robert Putnam's *Making Democracy Work: Civic Traditions in Modern Italy* (Princeton, NJ: Princeton University Press, 1993). The acclaimed volume *Twenty-First Century Populism: The Spectre of West European Democracy*, edited by Daniele Albertazzi and Duncan McDonnell (Basingstoke: Palgrave, 2007), contains an important chapter by Marco Tarchi on Italy. This, and the volume generally, offers further insights into the significance of populism and anti-political sentiments for the country's politics by allowing them to be seen in comparative context. Finally, the collection edited by David Forgacs and Robert Lumley, *Italian Cultural Studies: An Introduction* (Oxford: Oxford University Press, 1996), brings together a wide range of specialists to offer a lively introduction to a variety of cultural phenomena that include, but extend beyond, questions of political culture.

Notes

1. One deludes oneself if one thinks that it is possible to obtain direct access to people's desires and beliefs without having to rely on any inferences from their behaviour. Imagine asking John to confirm the correctness of one's assumptions about the desires and beliefs responsible for some particular gesture on his part. Imagine also that John replies 'yes'. In order to be able to interpret this behaviour as an answer to our question, rather than (say) an involuntary grunt, we have to assume the existence of a large number of further beliefs on the part of John. For example, we have to assume that John wants to answer our question, that he believes that emission of the grunt we interpret as signalling assent is an appropriate way to do this in the English language … and so forth. And the only way in which we could test these further assumptions would be by asking additional questions, and that is, by making further inferences from behaviour.
2. A 'reason' is different from a 'cause' in that, rather than being an outside force moving the actor, it is something that renders the actor's behaviour intelligible by showing it to be rational, appropriate, efficient, reasonable, correct and so forth, according to some criteria.
3. The danger that the meaning ascribed to reality is determined by preconceptions of it is a real one regardless of chosen method. However, the danger is particularly acute with survey methods because some prior decision has to be made about what questions to ask, where such questions are almost always of the fixed-format variety. The fact that questions are of the fixed-format variety only increases the likelihood that the picture the survey investigator comes away with is a function not of the reality under investigation but of the questions s/he has chosen to ask in the first place.
4. Having published an Italian translation of the work in 1961, il Mulino republished it in 1976, including in the same volume, abridged versions of nine of the most significant of the critical articles. In 2006 il Mulino published a new edition of the work without the critical articles but including a new preface by Arnaldo Bagnasco that might be of some interest.
5. Perhaps the one who came closest to doing so was Frank Cancian (1976) who argued that, while Banfield thought that the peasants' incapacity to act collectively for the good of the community was because they did not look beyond the immediate material interests of themselves and their own families, it was also possible that the peasants' incapacity lay in the fact that the very concepts, such

as 'community', required to make such action possible, were not comprehensible to them.

6. Thus, in the civic community, citizens are actively involved in the pursuit of public, as well as private benefits (Putnam, 1993: 87–8); in a society of amoral familists, 'no one will further the interest of the group or community except as it is to his private advantage to do so' (Banfield, 1958: 85). In the civic community, citizens are bound together 'by horizontal relations of reciprocity and cooperation, not by vertical relations of authority and dependency' (Putnam, 1993: 88); in a society of amoral familists, 'the weak will favour a regime which will maintain order with a strong hand' (Banfield, 1958: 96). In the civic community, 'citizens are helpful, respectful and trustful toward one another, even when they differ on matters of substance' (Putnam, 1993: 88–9); in a society of amoral familists, 'the claim of any person or institution to be inspired by zeal for public rather than private advantage will be regarded as fraud' (Banfield, 1958: 98). In the civic community, citizens have a 'propensity to form civil and political organizations' (Putnam, 1993: 89); in a society of amoral familists 'it will be very difficult to give life to, and keep alive, forms of organisation (that is organised activities based on explicit agreements)' (Banfield, 1976: 108–9).

7. In 2000/2, for example, while in most of the northern regions GDP per capita exceeded 125 per cent of the average for the EU twenty-five, in most of the South it was below 75 per cent. Meanwhile, in 2003, unemployment in Campania, Calabria and Sicily exceeded 20 per cent. *Regions: Statistical Yearbook 2005*, p. 43, map 3.2; p. 69, map 5.5 http://epp.eurostat.cec.eu.int/cache/ITY_OFFPUB/KS-AF-05–001/EN/KS-AF-05–001-EN.PDF.

8. The reason is that resources furnished by the national authorities to promote growth have tended to be disbursed more with an eye to providing selective benefits for isolated individuals and groups of individuals than with a real commitment to the provision of infrastructural public goods capable of attracting private external investment.

9. Della Porta and Vannucci (1997: 231–2) define political corruption as something that takes place when: (1) there is a secret violation of a contract that, implicitly or explicitly, involves a delegation of responsibility and the exercise of some discretionary power … (2) by an agent who, against the interests or preferences of the *principal* … (3) acts in favour of a *third party*, from whom he receives a reward … [where] (4) the principal is the state, or better, the citizens'.

10. Writing in 1994, Umberto Santino (1994: 131) noted that journalists' estimates had placed at 4 million the number of votes controlled in various ways by organised crime in Italy.

11. Pizzorno (2001: 28) refers to the example of religious sects whose reputations for honesty enable their members to undertake business transactions even in communities where they are not known and are unable to provide any other assurances of trustworthiness. Naturally, all this encourages such sects to be very particular about whom they admit as members.

6   Interests and interest mediation: voluntary associations and pressure groups

▨ Introduction

In chapter 4 we discussed the distribution of power and influence over policy between legislature, political executive and bureaucracy. We argued that, generally speaking, in democracies bureaucracies have a power resource in the policy-making process that is less readily available to the other two actors. This is one that derives from their interaction with interest groups whose co-operation must often be secured in the formulation and implementation of policy.

In chapter 5, we saw that a very influential strand of thinking in political science associates interest groups (and associations more generally) with social capital. On the one hand, social capital makes it possible for people to organise for their mutual benefit. On the other hand, organisation generates social capital since interaction generates norms of reciprocity. Meanwhile, co-operation builds on the self-reinforcing character of trust, making it more likely that people display the behaviour that demonstrates empirically that their fellows were correct to trust them in the first place. In turn, it is thought that the capacity of interest groups to generate social capital enhances democracy because the reciprocity, co-operation and trust such groups sustain allow self-interest to be pursued in a way that is alive to the interests of others, that is '"enlightened", rather than "myopic"' (Putnam, 1993: 88).

The concerns of the last two chapters therefore throw a spotlight on the concerns of this one, namely:

(1) What contribution do interest groups make to democracy in Italy?
(2) Do they enhance or diminish democracy in that country?

These are questions that are at one and the same time important and very difficult to answer. Their importance is captured by the title of Harold Lasswell's (1936) famous book which noted that politics is about who gets what, when and how. This being the case, one of the central concerns of a study such as the present one must be to throw light on the location of power in the political system under examination. We have explored this issue in relation to the interaction, in policy-making, of the principal institutions of government. We now need to bring interest groups into the picture; for public policy is, as LaPalombara (1994: 25, my translation) notes, 'always the product of the interaction between an ensemble of forces organised as interest groups in competition with each other'. This does not mean that parties, elections and other institutions are not important in this regard; it does, however, mean that they do not operate in a vacuum but rather under the constant influence of interest-group activity. This highlights that elections and voting are not the only, or even, perhaps, the most important, of the potential avenues available to citizens to influence public policies. This in turn suggests that the question whether interest-group activity enhances or diminishes democracy is of not insignificant practical consequence.

The questions posed above are difficult ones to answer for four reasons:

(1) One has to decide what is covered by the term 'interest group'. The standard political science distinction between an 'interest group' and a 'party' sees interest groups as bodies that seek to *influence* public policy. Parties, on the other hand, field candidates in elections with a view to being able to *make* public policy. But this begs the question of what we are to make of so-called 'interest parties'. These are groups that run candidates in elections, assuming the activities of a party but remaining focused on the quest for private benefits and/or a single issue (Thomas, 2001: 5). Or, if we define the term 'interest group' broadly, so that it becomes, say, any organisation that seeks to influence public policy, then one immediately wants to know what lies behind the term 'organisation'. How formal and permanent must organisations be? Does the definition encompass or exclude ad hoc groups of the nimby ('not in my backyard') variety, for example? Seeking 'to influence public policy' raises similar questions. All kinds of organisations, public and private, seek to do this from time to time, without it being their principal *raison d'être*, however. In short,

without being able to say clearly what does and does not belong to the category defining one's objects of analysis, one can hardly begin to study their effects.

(2) If we want to be able to say something about the impact of the activities of interest groups, then we have to have criteria enabling us to attribute outcomes and consequences to them. Observable activity and institutional relations with political actors allow us to do this; but secret activity and informal relations may escape our notice, while the absence of any activity or relations may, if we forget the **law of anticipated reactions** (Box 6.1), mislead us into thinking that there has been no influence.

(3) The task is further complicated by the two traditional perspectives on the political role of interest groups. On the one hand, proponents of the **pluralist** (Box 6.1) perspective argue that, by competing for the attention of government, groups keep the latter responsive. Meanwhile their large number ensures that most people have multiple, 'cross-cutting', memberships. This lowers the intensity of political conflict and ensures that no one interest is able to dominate any of the others. On the other hand, those with a less optimistic perspective point out that interest groups in fact often work for selfish ends. They point out, too, that the pluralist playing field is far from level, some groups being far more successful in getting a hearing than others. And they note that the role of some of the most important groups, especially capital and labour, often shows **corporatist** (Box 6.1) tendencies so that, though formally accountable to their members, they in fact impose policy on them in a top-down fashion. The problem is that, in practice, a polity is likely to display characteristics that lend support to both the optimistic and the less optimistic views, thus rendering even more problematic the search for an overall conclusion.

(4) The democratic implications of a given kind of activity are likely to vary significantly depending on the aims of the group concerned. Thus, we might argue that parliamentary lobbying by groups seeking to advance specific aims contributes to the work of the legislature; for it keeps parliamentarians in touch with public opinion, and it provides them with information. We are much less likely to reach such a conclusion in the case of powerful economic groups whose only intents are to secure the modification of legislation in such a way as to increase their profits (Garella, 1994: 88).

The student might therefore legitimately wonder whether study of the political and democratic implications of interest-group activity represents a worthwhile investment of time at all. In reply, we would deny the necessary existence of a direct, inverse correlation between the degree of difficulty of an enterprise and its value. We would suggest too that, though it may be difficult to draw conclusions about the present topic with the same degree of confidence that is possible in some other areas, this does not mean that nothing of value can be asserted. What is important is that one is explicit about

Box 6.1

Key terms: the law of anticipated reactions, pluralism, corporatism, position issues

The law of anticipated reactions 'refers to the process in which certain actors predict the probable reactions of strategically located figures to their desires and then adjust their position before openly stating it to make it more acceptable to these groups. The phenomenon, operating largely below the level of public observable behaviour, is difficult to measure, yet crucial to consider, in attempting to measure relative power' (Connolly, 2006: 41).

Pluralism is the political theory which holds that power in society is not concentrated in the hands of a small elite but rather is widely dispersed among interest groups. These groups compete with each other for the attention of policy-makers in the state, which acts as a sort of umpire mediating and adjudicating between the demands of the different groups in the field.

Corporatism 'is a relationship between the state and interest groups in which major decisions on domestic matters emerge from discussion between the government and a few leading protective groups, especially business associations and trade unions. In return for their influence, the interest groups are expected to ensure the compliance of their members' (Hague, Harrop and Breslin, 1998: 126).

Position issues are issues on which opinion among the public is divided and as such are usually contrasted with 'valence issues', that is, issues on which opinion is uniform, or 'all on one side'. Abortion is a good example of a position issue, some taking the view that it should be less freely available than at present, others taking quite the opposite view. Corruption is a good example of a valence issue: no one is in favour of more corruption. Rather, and this is true of valance issues in general, the difference of opinion comes over the best means to achieve the end that is uniformly desired (i.e. less corruption in this case).

definitions and successful in identifying significant issues that, if not exhaustive, are directly relevant to the questions we have posed.

With this in mind, we will base our analysis on a not watertight but nevertheless helpful distinction between protective, promotional and institutional groups (Hague, Harrop and Breslin, 1998: 115).

- Protective groups are ones formed to defend and advance the material interests of their members. Trade unions and employers' organisations are the prime examples.
- Promotional groups are ones formed to defend and advance specific ideas or aims in a given area of policy such as the environment, civil rights, animal welfare and so forth.
- Institutional groups are formal organisations, such as churches and universities, not formed for the purpose of exerting political pressure but which in fact do so from time to time.

Given these distinctions, in the following section we will explore the nature of the interaction that takes place between the institutions of government and the peak organisations (that is, the organisations representing interest groups in the given sector) of capital and labour: Confindustria and CGIL-CISL-UIL respectively. Capital 'votes' for specific policies whenever it makes investment decisions, and there are few policies whose success or failure is unrelated to the health of the economy. For these reasons, the acquiescence of capital and labour is indispensable, making them the most influential interests in advanced capitalist societies. Analysing how their peak associations interact with the state should say much about the contribution of these two interests to democratic governance bearing in mind the role of the associations in speaking on behalf of their members and securing their co-operation with any agreements reached with the state.

In the third section, we will ask (a) what are the most significant institutional avenues through which groups communicate with decision-makers and (b) how, through such channels, influence is typically exerted. Both elements are likely to make a difference to the nature of democratic governance. For example, according to a thesis well known to Italian politics specialists, the political parties have traditionally been a favoured channel for some of the most influential groups. Indeed, instead of aggregating demands, the parties have at times functioned as instruments of the groups, transmitting to government un-aggregated, sectional, demands and weakening the state in the process (LaPalombara, 1964: 8).

In the fourth section, we consider the opportunities for political influence available to the growing number of promotional groups. Italy, like other industrial democracies, has been subject to the process of cultural change that has been referred to as 'post-materialism' and that has seen the proliferation of groups and movements expressive of new cultural values. Such groups are more likely than others to be 'outsiders' (not normally consulted by government) and to be obliged to address government indirectly by seeking to attract the attention of the mass media through forms of political action that include protest activities. Because of the (variable) potential for conflict inherent in the activities of these groups, the extent to which a political system affords them a hearing can be taken as indicative of its democratic quality.

Finally, we will consider the political role of what is arguably the most significant of the institutional groups in Italy: the Catholic Church. This role is of lesser significance now than it was in the early post-war period when the Church regularly used its enormous influence among the population 'to ensure that individuals voted as Catholics and that they voted as a single block' (Bull and Newell, 2005: 83). However, the Church's political role continues to raise issues of considerable importance for Italian democracy; for, to a greater extent than is true of other groups, the public decisions it seeks to influence typically concern **position issues** (Box 6.1) of concern to the entire society or very large parts of it.

▤ Confindustria and the trade union confederations

Confindustria

As with so much else in Italy, the way in which Confindustria and the trade union confederations have traditionally engaged with the state has been heavily conditioned by the political parties and the party system. Unlike the unions, which were reconstituted by the parties towards the end of the war, Confindustria was unable to establish formal ties with any of the main parties aside from during the first legislature between 1948 and 1953. Its natural interlocutor would have been the Christian Democrats (DC) (given their anti-communism and permanence in government). But the party itself was a 'brokerage party' housing a range of interests not all of which were especially compatible with those of business. Under these circumstances the party sought to escape from dependence on Confindustria's money by acquiring control of, and exploiting for patronage purposes, public holding companies and other parts of the state apparatus. Unable, either, to condition the DC by means of any particular vote-mobilising capacity, Confindustria sought, instead, to advance its aims by establishing direct relations with the Ministry of Industry and Commerce.

The employers' organisation's independence has, not surprisingly, survived the 1990s transformation of the party system and the emergence of bipolarity. Identifying too closely with the centre right would limit the organisation's ability to pursue its members' interests through dialogue with the unions (whose traditional political reference points now all belong to the coalition of the centre left). Identifying too closely with either coalition would make dialogue difficult with a government staffed by the opposing coalition.

For a time after the combative Antonio D'Amato became president of Confindustria in 2000, it seemed that the overlap of his economic policy outlooks with those of the centre right under Berlusconi might bring stable, in-principle collaboration between the two. In a celebrated speech delivered to the industrialists' congress in April 2001, Berlusconi had declared that Confindustria's programme coincided with his own. 'By applauding that speech, the industrialists had in essence agreed to settle for a subordinate role in their relations with the future government, thus greatly weakening their ability to influence the executive by taking an independent stance' (Berta, 2005: 229). Moreover, collaboration with the Government led to unproductive conflict with the unions (see below). Therefore, the change of guard that in April 2004 brought Luca Cordero di Montezemolo to the presidency coincided with a robust reassertion of Confindustria's political independence.

The Unions

By contrast, the unions were from the beginning heavily dependent on the parties. Having been brought into being by them, the unitary CGIL was unable to survive the onset of the Cold War and the consequent deep divisions between the parties. It soon divided into three rival confederations – the Communist/Socialist CGIL, the Catholic CISL and the Social Democrat/ Republican UIL. The division for many years undermined the unions' power in collective bargaining. This in turn reduced their membership and increased their organisational dependence on the parties even more. This dependence was considerably reduced but not entirely eliminated by subsequent developments. When socio-economic change culminated in the 'hot autumn' of worker protest at the end of the 1960s, it brought considerably heightened membership levels. This produced greater independence of the parties and hence a greater capacity of the three confederations to act, in a united fashion, as autonomous actors in pursuit of political reforms. But though the confederations could negotiate such reforms with government, the latter's capacity then to steer Parliament was, as we saw in chapter 4, weak. And the persistence of partisan attachments within the unions meant that they were in no position to translate their market power into a vote-mobilising capacity designed to force governments to deliver. In short, the unions' capacity to engage with the authorities to good effect has to varying degrees been diminished in the post-war period by their continuing 'capacity' for disunity.

The Italian industrial relations system

Partly because of this, the Italian industrial relations system has, for most of the period, been characterised by a relatively low level of institutionalisation. This means that despite periodic efforts at 'concertation' (or 'decision-making through consensus' (Ishikawa, 2003: 3)), for most of the time it has not been possible, either in relations between unions, employers' associations and governments, or at more decentralised levels of collective bargaining, to discern much by way of established practices and accepted ways of doing things. This has made it difficult to control conflict; for uncertainty over rules has made agreements permanently vulnerable to sudden shifts in the balance of power between the so-called social partners. This in turn has contributed an additional difficulty to management of the economy.

This is not to say that 'relationships among the three major actors were completely non-existent'; on the contrary: governments frequently consulted the social partners separately before introducing major economic policy measures such as the annual budget (Regini and Regalia, 1997: 213). But 'consultation itself does not carry with it decision-making power' (Ishikawa, 2003: 3). Therefore, the consultations that did take place did not amount to tripartite policy-making.

Given this, the July 1993 *protocollo* between government, employers and unions on the cost of labour represented a radical new departure; for it set out for the first time, 'a stable architecture for incomes policies and collective bargaining' (Regini and Regalia, 1997: 214). It was a new departure that was made possible by

- perceptions of the difficulties that Italy seemed likely to have in qualifying for the single currency;
- recognition that once the currency had been adopted, it would no longer be possible to compensate for inflation by means of devaluation;
- the profile of then prime minister, Carlo Azeglio Ciampi, as a non-partisan figure (in the past, united trade union agreement to government proposals had often been precluded by their perceived partisan implications).

The 1993 protocollo

First, the *protocollo* institutionalised the distinction between national and company-level bargaining.

- National collective employment contracts for each sector were to last for two years and be tied to the so-called programmed inflation (Drexel, 2003: 18). This is an inflation rate 'concerted' between employers, unions and government and written into the *Documento di programmazione economica e finanziaria* (Economic and Financial Planning Document, Dpef), which the Government is obliged to present to Parliament in the spring of each year (see chapter 4). Differences between programmed and actual inflation rates would be compensated for in subsequent bargaining rounds.
- Company-level agreements were to last for four years, were to determine conditions of employment and were to be allowed to award pay increases beyond those established at the national level only if the increases could be justified in terms of productivity gains.

Second, two annual meetings were to take place: one to establish the programmed inflation, as well as the expected growth of Gross National Product (GNP) and rates of unemployment (Levy, 1994: 71); the other 'to verify the coherence of behaviour of the parties engaged in the autonomous exercise of their respective responsibilities' (Regini and Regalia, 1997: 214).

Third, a new uniform system of workplace representation was established to enable the company-level agreements to be reached on an orderly and predictable basis. Generally acknowledged as having made a significant contribution to improved economic performance and widely viewed as a model for other countries to follow, the *protocollo* remains the 'constitution' underlying the Italian industrial relations system.

Concertation

Industrial relations matters are not the only ones to have been subject to concertation since Economic and Monetary Union came onto the agenda of Italian politics at the beginning of the 1990s. In addition, taxation, public expenditure, labour law and pensions issues have all been subject to the process (Ishikawa, 2003: 18; De Marco, 1998: 434).

Table 6.1. Density of trade union membership, 1995

Country	1995%	Change 1985–1995%
Sweden	91.1	8.7
Iceland	83.3	6.3
Denmark	80.1	2.3
Finland	79.3	16.1
Malta	65.1	35.8
Hungary	60.0	−25.3
Italy	44.1	−7.4
Austria	41.2	−19.2
Poland	33.8	−42.5
United Kingdom	32.9	−27.7
Germany	28.9	−17.6
Netherlands	25.6	−11.0
Portugal	25.6	−50.2
Greece	24.3	−33.8
Israel	23.0	−77.0
Switzerland	22.5	−21.7
Spain	18.6	62.1
France	9.1	−37.2

Source: International Labour Organisation, 'ILO highlights global challenge to trade unions', Tuesday, 4 November 1997, www.ilo.org/public/english/bureau/inf/pr/1997/28.htm.

Pensions, in particular, have had a rather high profile in recent years owing to perceptions, shared with policy-makers in other European countries, that ageing populations require existing pension arrangements to be modified. Such perceptions can be challenged since they fail to take account of the fact that productivity is constantly increasing. Nevertheless, pensions reform has been viewed as especially urgent in Italy because increasing longevity has coincided with comparatively sharp falls in birth rates, and with low employment levels, especially among women and older age cohorts (Natali and Rhodes, 2005: 173).

In 1994, the Berlusconi government sought to test whether it could exclude the trade unions from policy-making altogether by the unilateral introduction of proposals for the abolition of seniority pensions.[1] Still relatively strong by European standards (see Table 6.1), CGIL, CISL and UIL showed, through their strike activity and successful street demonstrations, that they were too powerful to be ignored. The result was that reform had to wait until the following year when a new government, under Lamberto Dini, was able to win union agreement to a revised set of proposals (Regini and Regalia, 1997: 215–17). Although further reform, introduced by the second Berlusconi government in 2004, was also undertaken unilaterally, the Government was this time very careful to ensure that the reform process took the form of policy diplomacy and cautious consensus creation (Natali and Rhodes, 2005: 175).

Nevertheless, it remains true that the election of the Berlusconi government in 2001 represented a significant change of attitude towards concertation with the social partners. The preceding coalitions of the centre left had seen it as a fundamental component of good governance, especially so in the light of the 'national economic emergency'. By contrast, the 2001 government's *Libro bianco sul mercato del lavoro* (Labour Market White Paper), published in October that year, complained that concertation had 'performed governing functions well beyond the objectives of developing a proper relationship between the parties' (quoted by Accornero and Como, 2003: 243, my translation). The expressed desire to put an end to what was described as the 'trade union veto' was without doubt partly a reflection of the populism, and thus the intolerance of constraints on their freedom of action, of two of the governing parties (the Northern League, LN, and Forza Italia, FI). And it is without doubt this same populism that explains the willingness of the Government to engage, in 2002, in head-on confrontation with the unions over article 18 of the **Workers' Statute** despite the arguably limited practical significance of the issues at stake (Box 6.2). The matter was quietly dropped towards the end of the year. In the meantime, the Government had succeeded in dividing both the trade unions and the opposition parties on the issue. It therefore doubtless concluded that it was now better off abandoning proposals whose employment – if not symbolic – implications were entirely unclear (Baccaro and Simoni, 2004: 208–12).

In questioning the virtues of concertation, the Government was casting doubt on a role that is played by the social partners in most advanced industrial societies. That is, almost nowhere do the social partners limit themselves to communicating demands to arenas that enjoy decision-making authority. Rather, they are themselves active participants in such arenas. They themselves exercise authority in the processes whereby policies are formulated, amended, decided and implemented (Berger, 1983: 36). In a number of instances in Italy, this is given explicit legal recognition.

For example, article 99 of the Constitution establishes a body consisting of representatives of sectors of industry and commerce, the National Council for the Economy and Labour. This could almost be described as a third chamber of Parliament; for it has the right to introduce bills and may contribute to the drafting of economic and social laws. Its actual role appears to be fairly circumscribed: Furlong (1994: 69), in his study of policy-making in Italy, describes it as 'largely without influence and indeed without history'. However, its powers do include the right to provide advice to both Parliament and the Government.

Or, to take another example, the governing body of the National Social Security Institute (INPS) consists of representatives of the trade unions, industry, agriculture and commerce. INPS provides pensions and other income-support payments to almost all private-sector employees and most of the self-employed. Its governing body is responsible for setting its strategic objectives and

Box 6.2

The Workers' Statute

One of the fruits of the so-called hot autumn of worker militancy that broke out in 1969, the Workers' Statute (introduced in 1970) represents in many respects the cornerstone of Italy's system of labour law, and it brought significant improvements to conditions of employment generally. In particular, it enshrines in law a number of workplace rights, including that of re-engagement in cases where dismissal is found by the courts to have been unfair (article 18). Driving the Statute's introduction were:

- the post-war Constitution (whose initial articles describe Italy as a democratic republic founded on labour in which each citizen has the right and the duty to work);
- the dramatic economic and social changes of the initial post-war decades with their large-scale internal migrations, transforming the country from a predominantly agricultural society into one where the vast majority were either industrial workers or white-collar employees;
- pressure from the Socialist Party, in government from 1963, seeing in the introduction of the Statute a means to consolidate and expand its electoral following and bring a greater degree of order to the system of industrial relations.

The Berlusconi government of 2001 wanted to restrict the applicability of article 18. On the one hand, the restrictions proposed were partial and temporary. On the other hand, the trade unions opposed them on the grounds that they undermined a principle (automatic re-engagement) that acted as a strong deterrent against unfair dismissal.

approving its budget. It therefore gives the social partners a policy-making role in an area that is of direct and great concern to the large majority of the population.

A significant question is whether such close involvement is democratic. In a number of democracies in recent years, institutionalised policy-making by interest groups has been criticised on the grounds that, in bypassing Parliament and tying the hands of governments, it is corrosive of principles of political accountability. When it attacked concertation, it was essentially this argument that the Berlsuconi government had in mind.

◼ Channels of access

Parliament

'Interest groups follow power' (Hague, Harrop and Breslin, 1998: 117); so not surprisingly given what we said in chapter 4, the legislature's significance for interest groups (Box 6.3) has traditionally been rather greater in Italy than in many, if not most, other democracies. Indeed, the legislature is not just an arena to which groups *transmit* demands, but one in which groups have been significant and active *participants*.

One of the best examples of a group that has acted in this way is the small farmers' organisation, Coldiretti. Though it is far less significant now than it was in the initial post-war years when agriculture formed a far larger part of the economy, it remains an interesting case. Like the trade union confederations, Coldiretti was a creation of the parties – in this case the DC, with which it had extensive and intense formal and informal ties. Indeed, so close were these ties that Coldiretti representatives were members of the DC's governing bodies and were regularly elected, as DC candidates, to Parliament. Here they controlled up to 13 per cent of the party's deputies (Lanza, 1991: 89–90). On the one hand, the group had considerable 'vote-delivering prowess' (LaPalombara, 1964: 337).[2] On the other hand, it used this prowess to establish a position of power for itself within the DC. Given the DC's permanence in office and capacity to intervene in the administrative system, Coldiretti's position within the party enabled it to condition policy in both the rule-making and rule-applying spheres of the political system (Bull and Newell, 2005: 85).

If one cannot be a player in the game, then one must try to influence those who are players. Seeking to influence Italian parliamentary players is worthwhile because they have considerable influence. Symmetric bicameralism; decentralised decision-making; unlimited powers of legislative initiative; the absence of limits on the role of law in policy-making: all these place considerable resources in the hands of parliamentarians.

For example, article 70 of the Constitution gives legislative authority to the two chambers without qualification, while article 72, as we have seen, enables each chamber to give law-making powers to its committees. In combination, therefore, the two articles reduce the barriers in the way of law invading spheres that in other jurisdictions are more typically dealt with by administrative action, while giving the Italian parliament an unusually large capacity for the production of legislation.

If this makes its committees an important focus of attention of interest groups, then it also assists the latter in gaining a hearing; for, as compared to the full assembly, committee memberships are much smaller, thus making possible – in a way that (owing to its size) is *impossible* in the full assembly – *deliberation*.[3] Moreover, the committees' meetings, unlike those of the assembly, are relatively private affairs, thus reducing their members' exposure to cross-cutting pressures.

Of the resources groups can draw upon to gain the attention of committee members, one of the most important is information:

- in order to be in a position to consider and draft legislative proposals, Parliament's committees require knowledge;
- their almost unlimited powers of inquiry allow them not only to commission research but also to invite anyone to answer questions (Massai, 1992: 229–31);

- 'it is unlikely that parliamentary research bodies can provide up-to-date information about the social and economic life of the country as well as those representing the economic or social sectors in question can' (Garella, 1994: 89, my translation).

Government

Prior to the 1990s, the Government too was thought of as an institution that, comparatively, was rather permeable to the activities of interest groups – and this for reasons not dissimilar to those for which Parliament was so viewed.

- One reason was the difficulties faced by prime ministers in acting as policy-coordinators.
- Another was the insistence of coalition partners in competition for the support of societal interests that they be left with a free hand in the management of the ministries assigned to them.
- A third reason was the inadequacies, discussed in chapter 4, of the public administration. Such inadequacies meant that the administration found it difficult to provide ministers with adequate support and information services.
- Of particular importance was the role of the DC as fulcrum around which all feasible governing coalitions revolved. Under these circumstances, it was in the DC's interests that governments be open to the articulation of group demands as this allowed the party to play that role of 'ring-keeper' that was essential if it was to retain its role as fulcrum.

On the other hand, precisely this role of 'ring-keeper' meant that while permeability guaranteed a *hearing*, it did not guarantee a favourable *decision*; and, in view of the changes discussed in chapter 4 (especially those that have reinforced the role of Prime Minister), it is probable that the chances of such outcomes have since diminished. In any case, groups have rarely succeeded, in any straightforward fashion, in getting their demands inserted wholesale into the programmes of governments or ministers. In order to do so, a group must normally be successful:

(1) in the prior public-relations activities necessary in order to create a social climate favourable to the desired decision;
(2) in presenting itself as an especially authoritative source of information;
(3) in presenting its interests as coterminous with more general interests (Pasquino, 1988: 130–1; Trupia, 1989: 178–9).
Otherwise, it must
(4) 'be very powerful (especially in an economic sense), very well known and have close ties to certain parties or political groups' (Garella, 1994: 95, my translation).

Box 6.3

Pressure-group activity

As in other European countries, so too in Italy in recent years there has been a shift of focus in the types of public engagement people are willing to undertake away from political parties and towards interest groups. Thus, while party-political membership has declined quite rapidly, as the following figure shows, those involved in voluntary associations have increased with equal rapidity: as the following data, compiled by the National Statistic Institute (ISTAT) suggest, between 2002 and 2005 alone, the proportion of those active in voluntary associations rose by over 11 per cent.

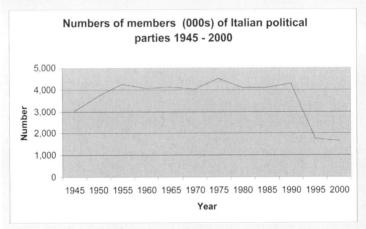

Number of members of Italian political parties, 1945–2000
Source: 'La democrazia: nuovi scenari, nuovi poteri. Spunti per un dibattito', web. tiscalinet.it/pslvr/download/feb/feltrin.ppt.

Proportion of persons aged fourteen and above who have at least once in the past twelve months undertaken unpaid work for a voluntary association.

Geographical area	Year	
	2002	2005
North-West	9.1	10.4
North-East	12.7	12.9
Centre	7.0	8.2
South	4.9	5.8
Islands	6.1	6.0
Italy	8.0	8.9

Source: ISTAT, www.istat.it.

The bureaucracy

The bureaucracy represents a third significant channel of influence. It is one that provides the basis for what LaPalombara (1964) called ties of *clientela*, that is, sets of privileged relations between a group and an administrative agency. Through these relations, the agency comes to act as the group's unofficial but acknowledged representative within the sphere of government. In exchange the group, when necessary, seeks to apply pressure on other branches of government on the agency's behalf. Ties of *clientela* are thus said to exist when the group succeeds in becoming, in the eyes of the agency, 'the natural expression and representative of a given social sector which, in turn, consti-tutes the natural target or reference point for the activity of the administrative agency' (LaPalombara, 1964: 262).

The relations that, we said, were established by Confindustria with the Ministry of Industry and Commerce in the early post-war period were ties of *clientela*. The alternative mode of access to the bureaucracy, in LaPalombara's analysis, was through ties of *parentela* – involving 'a relatively close and integral relationship ...[with] the politically dominant Christian Democratic Party' (LaPalombara, 1964: 306) – of the kind established with the latter by Coldiretti.

Precisely how significant *clientela* remains, forty years after LaPalombara's book was published, is difficult to say. As a concept, it appears to have much in common with the notion of a 'policy community'. This is a close-knit group, consisting of public officials and group leaders, that settles detailed issues in its policy area 'in a confidential and depoliticized atmosphere of trust, based on shared interests' (Hague, Harrop and Breslin, 1998: 123). Cross-nationally, 'policy communities' are thought to have become less significant with the passage of time as mass media developments and the emergence and growth of new consumer groups have obliged bureaucrats and major interests to engage in more transparent forms of interaction. This has forced 'policy communities' to give way to 'policy' or 'issue networks'. These are much looser sets of relations involving larger numbers of groups, the influence of each of which varies from issue to issue depending on its expertise (Hague, Harrop and Breslin, 1998: 124). Since Italy has not been unexposed to such international developments, the most reasonable conclusion is that in cases where administration-interest group relations resembled those of *clientela*, the resem-blance has probably faded in recent years.

The judicial system

A fourth channel through which groups can influence policy is provided by the courts. It is one that, in Italy as elsewhere, has gained in significance in the post-war decades. This growing significance has been a result of the process known as the 'judicialisation of politics'. Judicialisation is related to three trends:

(1) a growing capacity of judiciaries to constrain other branches of government, especially the legislature;

(2) a growing willingness of judges to use their 'legislative' powers and thus

(3) a growing willingness to allow themselves to be drawn into political conflict.

In Italy, the growing capacity of judiciaries to constrain other branches of government was set in motion by the setting up of the Constitutional Court in 1956. The Court cannot subject laws to examination prior to their promulgation; it cannot hear cases brought by individuals claiming violation of their constitutional rights, and it cannot itself initiate proceedings. Moreover, only a limited number of applicants have the right to initiate 'direct review' independent of any other proceedings. These are the State in the case of a challenge to regional legislation, and Regions in the case of a challenge to state legislation or the legislation of another region (Certoma 1985: 157). Nevertheless, over the years, the Court's activities have allowed the constitutional judiciary and the ordinary judiciary in dialogue with one another to acquire a significant legislative function.

This legislative function has been acquired for three reasons:

(1) The Constitutional Court and its judgements have made it possible for individual judges, during the course of proceedings, to request rulings on the compatibility of legislation with the articles of the Constitution, including those embodying the fundamental rights and liberties enshrined in Part I. Since the latter articles in particular are open to wide interpretation, the Court has acquired what amounts, in effect, to 'a massive, virtually open-ended delegation of policy-making authority' (Stone Sweet, 2000: 58). It is an authority in whose exercise ordinary judges participate; for their power to refer cases to the Court in effect requires them to assess legislation in the light of the Constitution and themselves to engage in principled constitutional reasoning (Stone Sweet, 2000: 115).

(2) An increasing proportion of the judgements issued by the Constitutional Court over the years has consisted of 'binding interpretations' (Stone Sweet, 2000: 72). These are declarations that laws are to be considered constitutional only if interpreted in the way that the Court specifies. Such declarations in effect re-write legislation and thereby give the Court real authority over Parliament. For as the corpus of policy-relevant constitutional interpretations grows, legislators are thereby increasingly obliged, in framing legislation, to anticipate the likelihood of referrals and thereby to engage, when proposing and debating legislation, in modes of reasoning similar to those employed by the Court itself.

(3) The fragmentation of Parliament makes it extremely difficult for the latter to react to Court decisions by seeking to make constitutional those acts that have been censored. For constitutional amendment requires a higher level of consensus among the parties than does ordinary

legislating (Stone Sweet, 2000: 89). In most cases, therefore, legislation impugned by the Court can only be saved by altering it in such a way as to comply with the Court's preferences.

When these developments are combined with the growing willingness of judges to use their 'legislative' powers (the second trend involved in judicialisation: for details see Newell, 2005) and thus to allow themselves to be drawn into political conflict (the third trend), it becomes clear that as an object of attention for the interests that structure system politics in Italy, the courts have gained increasing importance. And the courts are likely to acquire still greater importance thanks to two developments:

(1) Governments' attempts to pursue reforms of a decentralising kind. These reforms imply an increasingly significant role for the Constitutional Court in arbitrating between the competing claims of the different levels of government.
(2) Processes of European integration. By extending the reach of sets of supranational rules and institutions, integration has increasingly challenged the Constitutional Court's claim to be the exclusive arbiter of the legitimacy of national statutes. In so doing, it has paved the way for the *ordinary* judicial system successfully to claim authority to exercise such a power.

To these should be added the December 2007 action of the 2006 Prodi government in passing legislation to introduce, into the Italian legal system, the possibility of 'class actions'. These are a form of lawsuit, which originated in the United States and which enable large groups of people to bring claims, collectively, to court. Of particular significance to consumer groups, class actions empower individuals by overcoming the problem that the likelihood of only small recoveries in any individual case discourages solo claims against a defendant causing widespread harms but doing so minimally against each individual plaintiff. The new legislation came into force on 1 January 2009.

Evaluation

The democratic consequences of groups' attempts to exercise influence through these four channels have not, for much of the post-war period, been especially positive. Owing to the way they are structured, the arenas we have looked at are all permeable. This means that their representatives have difficulty in filtering the specific demands focused upon them, in the light of their own assessments of general needs and interests. The courts, of course, are expressly enjoined to refrain from such assessments. That is, they must exclude from consideration anything not immediately relevant to each of the specific cases examined. This has the positive effect of helping to ensure equality before the law. But in each of the three remaining channels we have looked at, an unwillingness to assess demands in the light of general needs has a number of unfortunate consequences:

(1) By allowing demands to be transmitted to the authorities in their raw, un-aggregated, form, it helps to perpetuate a view of the state less as an entity capable of making authoritative decisions in the general interest, than as a terrain of conquest. It thereby helps to perpetuate a vicious circle under-mining the standing and authority of the state among ordinary citizens.

(2) It helps to reduce the predictability of decision-making processes and their outcomes (Pasquino, 1988: 143–5). Unpredictability is a problem for interest groups as it increases the risks associated with (e.g. investment) decisions. This makes the costs of activities both higher and less easy to quantify in precise terms. The relatively high levels of unpredictability derive from the very way in which the institutions involved are structured. The constitutional and other rules defining the workings of Parliament, for example, make the times required for the enactment of given proposals 'effectively incalculable' (Pasquino, 1988: 144). There is thus a 'built-in' incentive to attempt to reduce unpredictability by means that include recourse to ones that are less than legitimate.

The nature of these means will depend on the resources groups are able to mobilise in their efforts to exercise influence. Where these resources are votes, clientelism is likely to be a feasible strategy. Though not necessarily illegal, clientelistic exchanges are by definition driven by particularistic, rather than by universalistic criteria and the application of rules to cases. This renders them of doubtful democratic legitimacy. Moreover, narrowly focused, clien-telistic, legislation is more likely than comprehensive legislation to create gaps and inconsistencies implying non-uniform treatment and requiring sub-sequent remedy.

While votes make possible clientelistic exchanges, money provides the basis for corrupt exchanges. In 1973, the oil scandal revealed the attempts of Vincenzo Cazzaniga, president of the association of oil derivatives producers, Unione Petrolifera, to 'buy', from the parties of the governing coalition, a change in energy policy priorities. This precipitated the first of a series of efforts to combat the problem in the form of laws providing for the public funding of parties and candidates (Rhodes, 1997). Decisions that are the pro-duct of corrupt exchanges are unlikely to be good ones; for corrupt exchanges are almost always hidden. This means that they undermine the assurances offered by conventional, public, decision-making processes that decisions will be at least minimally coherent and mutually consistent.

The combination of (a) institutions' permeability, (b) unpredictability and (c) the possession of conspicuous resources has made possible a number of celebrated alliances between politicians and private economic interests in post-war Italy. They include:

- the close relationship between Silvio Berlusconi and Bettino Craxi. Craxi's influence as leader of the Italian Socialist Party (PSI) and as Prime Minister in the 1980s was of fundamental importance in securing the passage of legis-lation crucial in helping Berlusconi to consolidate his growing media empire;

- the relationship between seven-times prime minister Giulio Andreotti and the Caltagirone brothers, builders and presumed financiers of Andreotti's DC faction;
- the relationship between Craxi and Salvatore Ligresti, another builder who, in the 1980s, appears to have played a key role as an intermediary between the PSI leader and celebrated financier Enrico Cuccia, in the privatisation of the merchant bank, Mediobanca.

Protest activity and promotional groups

If the Italian state is permeable to many types of interest-group activity, then there is one type of activity to which it appears – on the face of it, at least – to be anything but permeable. This is the activity of groups which resort to protest. Such groups usually lack conspicuous material resources and are unable to get a hearing through the channels of government. They therefore take actions that put pressure on the authorities either by being disruptive in some way, or because they attract the attention of the mass media, or by virtue of both of these things. Groups with influence in government circles – usually powerful protective groups – often combine direct communication with officials with use of the media. In this way, through advertising and publicity campaigns, they seek to create a climate of opinion favourable to their objectives. Groups without access to government channels – usually, but not exclusively, promotional groups – must seek to create a climate of opinion favourable to their objectives through protest, especially if they lack great financial resources. Of course protest, if not carefully managed, can also create an *un*favourable climate of opinion. However, protest will usually draw attention to the group's aims; and if no one pays any attention to it, the group can be certain that it will fail in its objectives. Frequently in the period since the war, the protest that the Italian authorities have been willing to tolerate has been rather limited.

This was especially true in the 1950s. These were years of 'preventive repression', characterised by widespread limitations on the rights and freedoms of expression guaranteed by the Constitution. Influenced by the legacy of pre-war Fascist mass movements, governments were convinced that protest represented a threat to democracy and therefore that the preservation of democracy required strict controls on the exercise of democratic rights by a left opposition that was perceived as loyal to 'the other side' in the Cold War. The usual means by which public order was thus maintained was through the use of firearms by the police against demonstrators, strikers and peasants occupying estates. Thus it was that between 1948 and 1962, ninety-five demonstrators were killed as the result of police using firearms in the process of charging demonstrations and marches (della Porta, 1996: 45).

The control of protest activity has by and large been carried out in much less repressive ways in the decades since then. Nevertheless, the period has by no means been free of less-than-tolerant attitudes on the part of the authorities. Such attitudes have been revealed by, among others,

- the so-called 'strategy of tension' in the 1970s – when parts of the secret services appeared to be willing to collaborate with right-wing extremists in fomenting disorder and may even have been complicit in acts of right-wing terrorism. This took place at a time when growing divisions within the governing majority led to early dissolutions of Parliament (in 1972 and 1976). It was a period marked by the cycle of student and worker protest that had begun in the late 1960s. All this seemed to feed frustration with the Government's apparent inability to enact measures effective in producing 'law and order'. The aim of the strategy of tension therefore appeared to be to create a climate favourable to an authoritarian 'restoration of order'.
- the response to the 'anti-globalisation' protests in July 2001 at the G8 summit in Genoa. Here, disturbances led, among other things, to a demonstrator being killed, and there was widespread criticism, both at home and abroad, of the management of protest by the police. The police, in Italy, is built on the 'king's police' rather than the 'citizens' police' model. That is, it is built primarily with public-order responsibilities in mind and with strong ties to the central government (della Porta and Reiter, 2001: 878). The latter, in its turn, felt itself under particular pressure at the G8 to demonstrate to the international community its capacity to exercise a monopoly of force within its territory. After all, such capacity is the indispensable corollary of sovereignty in international relations (della Porta and Reiter 2002: 124). Public reaction to deployment of force on this occasion provoked demonstrations in large numbers of Italian cities, and the setting up of a parliamentary committee of inquiry into the events (for details see della Porta and Reiter, 2002).

The impression remains, then, that the predominant reaction of the authorities to protest is management of a repressive rather than a tolerant type.

Why might this be? Two factors seem important:

(1) As we have said more then once hitherto, the Italian state has traditionally not been a strong state. Thus, it has not enjoyed very high levels of confidence in its capacity to provide effectively for its citizens and to do so in accordance with principles of impartiality and equality. In parts of the South, such perceptions have on occasion called into question the authorities' ability successfully to claim a monopoly on the legitimate use of force (the defining characteristic of the modern state). States whose capacity thus to guarantee public order is in doubt are, in the extreme case, ones whose own survival is in question. Repression, including, on occasion, recourse to illegality, seems to be a typical reaction of weak states, under pressure from protest activities to give proof of their ability effectively to remain sovereign within their territory.

(2) The nature and activities of the protest groups involved. The most salient manifestations of protest activity, in Italy as elsewhere in recent decades, have been the work of entities belonging to the 'left libertarian' family of social movements (Kitschelt, 1990; della Porta, 1996). A social movement is an informal network of individuals and groups with a shared identity that from time to time mobilise in the pursuit of social and/or political objectives. Left libertarian movements are ones that share a negative stance towards markets and towards public and private bureaucracies, together with a positive stance towards egalitarian redistribution and towards the economic, political and cultural autonomy of individuals and groups. On the one hand, this is an ideology that representatives of the state, and in particular the police, find it difficult to sympathise with; for it is one that involves more than a series of *practical* demands. It is expressive of *cultural* challenges to the political system as a whole. As such, it tends naturally to arouse the diffidence of police officers; for their duties enjoin suspiciousness of people and thus scepticism towards those perceived as 'different'. On the other hand, the ideology is one that, in certain contexts, has given rise to radical, sometimes illegal, forms of protest. These include occupations, unauthorised marches, 'proletarian shopping', rent strikes and so forth – and in extreme cases, violence. For example, in the 1970s, interaction with counter-movements of the extreme right drew groups such as Autonomia operaia into, sometimes daily, clashes with fractions of these movements in a rising spiral of violence (while the most spectacular examples of political violence were, of course, those perpetrated by the Red Brigades (Box 6.4)). Later, from the early 1980s – when successful dismantling of the remaining 'red' and 'black' 'terrorist' groups broke the escalation of violence – both ideology and forms of protest became more moderate. Ideologies became more pragmatic and less utopian in character. Forms of protest became more innovative but decidedly less violent. As a consequence, official attitudes towards protest have on the whole been more relaxed, although the events of Genoa, and more recently those of Val di Susa,[4] suggest that the shift is not one that can be considered irreversible.

Evaluation

While the authorities have frequently been intolerant of the *manifestations* of protest, they have not been unresponsive to many of the protestors' *demands*. Some of the most significant reforms in post-war Italy appear, on the face of it, to have been the more or less direct consequence of pressure exerted by movements belonging to the left libertarian category. For example,

- 1969 and 1970, in the immediate aftermath of the workers' and students' protests, saw
  - improvements to the pensions system,

Box 6.4

The Red Brigades

The most extreme form of protest activity a group can engage in to draw attention to its cause is the use of violence and coercion. Inspired by Marxism–Leninism, the Red Brigades are probably the most famous of the groups having recourse to these means in post-war Italy. Established by Renato Curcio, a student at the University of Trento, and others, the Red Brigades were active mainly in the 1970s. During this period, it is suggested, they were responsible for some 14,000 acts of violence (Martin, 2003). The proximate cause of their emergence was the so-called Piazza Fontana bombing, in Milan, on 12 December 1969, which killed seventeen people and wounded eighty-eight others and marked the beginning of the 'strategy of tension': the use of violence and bombings apparently as a means of creating a climate of fear that would enable the authorities to proclaim a state of emergency, the principal victims of which would be the Communists. Widely viewed by activists in the workers' and students' movements of the time as an outrage that had been perpetrated with the complicity of parts of the state, the Piazza Fontana bombing served to stimulate questioning, within the movements, about the political uses of violence. Several answers were given of which that of the Red Brigades was one: for them what was required was recourse to 'armed propaganda', that is, sensational, but not bloody, gestures (incendiary attacks, sudden kidnappings, acts of public humiliation and so forth) that would shake and arouse a revolutionary consciousness. The bloody episodes came later, from 1974, when members of the Brigades, in reflecting upon the results of their efforts to that point, decided to shift the focus of their action to an all-out attack on the institutions of the state. The event for which they became most notorious was the kidnap and murder of the DC politician and former Prime Minister, Aldo Moro, in 1978. Moro had been the principal architect of a growing understanding with the Communist Party. This understanding was designed to overcome the *conventio ad excludendum* practised against the PCI and had seen the Communists join the DC in a legislative (though not government) coalition between 1976 and 1978. The Red Brigades were for the most part successfully broken up by the authorities in the 1980s as the result of scores of arrests facilitated by the willingness of those already in custody to turn state's witness in exchange for more lenient treatment of their own cases.

- the passage of the so-called Workers' Statute (which, among other things, established the right of workers to meet and organise at their place of work),
- the introduction of divorce,
- the legislation giving effect to the constitutional provisions providing for the establishment of decentralised (i.e. regional) government and for abrogative referenda.
- In 1976, the movement for urban renewal was successful in obtaining passage of law no. 278. This increased the opportunities for popular

Figure 6.1 Photograph of Aldo Moro in captivity, issued by the Red Brigades on 20 April 1978 in order to counter assertions, contained in a false communiqué appearing two days earlier, that the senior Christian Democrat had been killed and his body dumped in Lago della Duchessa. After 54 days of captivity, the Red Brigades murdered Moro and left his body in a car parked, with apparent symbolism, half way between the Rome headquarters of the Christian Democratic party and the Communist party (see Box 6.4)

participation in local decision-making by providing for the election of decentralised, neighbourhood councils in municipalities of over 30,000 inhabitants.

- In the course of the 1980s, a large number of the social circles set up in the wake of the youth movement of 1977 gained official recognition as associations able to fill a number of the gaps in the provisions of the welfare state. A number of the circles even received public subsidies (della Porta, 1996: 47, 79, 82).
- 1986 saw the establishment of a new ministry for the environment.

What appears to have been particularly important among the factors influencing the authorities' receptiveness to the demands of the movements is the extent to which the movements have been successful in acquiring institutional and party-political allies. At times, they have been notably unsuccessful. This was true for much of the 1970s when rising spirals of violence led to isolation from the movements' natural potential ally, the Italian Communist Party (PCI). Having always been kept far from government office, the party was anxious for legitimation and was unwilling to tolerate groups to its left that it did not control. Hence, it actually became the most vociferous among the parties demanding severity in the state's dealings with the movements.

In the 1980s, on the other hand, the environmental and peace movements were able to establish important channels of access to representative institutions (most obviously through the Green Party (Verdi), established in 1980). Thereby they acquired local authority allies willing to assist by means of sponsoring conferences and cultural events, declaring 'nuclear-free' zones and so forth.

What appears to be important in influencing the movements' success in acquiring allies are, once more, (perceptions of) the nature of their protest activities and their demands. For example, both before and after Genoa, the anti-globalisation movement, a movement that once again presents an ideology embodying demands for systemic change, found it difficult to gain the support of a centre-left coalition most of which was critical, not just of the small minority willing to use violence, but even of those engaging in civil disobedience (della Porta and Reiter, 2002: 138).

▪ The Church

The position of the Catholic Church within the Italian political system has some similarities with that of the groups and movements described in the previous section:

(1) Its wide variety of organisations make it a cross between 'a territorially ramified and organisationally complex array of powerful pressure groups and a highly articulated social movement' (Donovan, 2003: 96).
(2) It cannot take support for its agenda for granted but is obliged actively to campaign to gain a hearing and acceptance of its point of view.[5]
(3) It is obliged to place considerable reliance on the mass media and direct appeals to the public as means of influencing policy. For many decades after the war, it was able to exploit privileged relations with the DC. But since that party's demise, it has had to avoid being identified with one coalition to the exclusion of the other; for Catholics distribute their voting support across the centre-left/centre-right political divide.

The Church's challenge to democracy

However, the Church has traditionally posed, and continues to pose, challenges for Italian democracy that are in many respects very much greater than those posed by most of the groups discussed in the previous section. This is because the Church

(1) has some of the characteristics of what the American sociologist Louis Coser (1974) called 'greedy institutions'. These are institutions that 'make total claims on their members and which attempt to encompass within their circle the whole personality' (Coser, 1974: 4). In other words, they demand of their members adherence to precepts concerning conduct not just in *specific* areas of their lives, but in *every* aspect of their lives.

(2) Partly because of this, the Church does not just seek to influence the content of public policy; rather, it poses an implicit challenge to state sovereignty itself. To appreciate this, we have to look back in time to the essential characteristics of the confessional states antedating the French Revolution.

The nature of the confessional state

Prior to the French Revolution, there was, throughout Europe, no distinction between Church and State. Religious precepts informed all spheres of social life. Therefore, just as individuals had religions, so did states. And if states had religions, these could only be singular, admitting no dissent on the part of either ruler or ruled; for churches claimed to be the fount of all truth, against which there existed only error. States therefore had a duty to uphold the one true faith, by persecution if necessary, denying to dissenters legal rights enjoyed by the remainder of the population. Consequently, there was no perceived distinction between religious faith and political allegiance.

This was challenged by the French Revolution with its 'Declaration of the Rights of Man and of the Citizen'. This proclaimed, among other things, that 'No one shall be disquieted on account of his opinions, including his religious views.' For the first time, rights and the enjoyment of citizenship were uncoupled from any test of religious belief. So, therefore, were Church and polity uncoupled. France for long remained the only European country to have undertaken such a radical breach, but during the course of the nineteenth century other countries followed (Rémond, 1999: chs. 2–4).

The legacy of the confessional state

Many, if not most, of the Church's stances in the period since then have reflected a desire to maintain and enhance its authority by recovering, if only partially, the kind of institutional and political status it enjoyed under the *ancien régime*:

- In 1929 Mussolini signed the Lateran Pacts and Concordat in order to end the Church–State conflict inherited from Unification. These Pacts deemed Church marriages legally sufficient, reflecting an earlier era in which responsibility for the legal registration of births, deaths and marriages lay with the Church: religious and secular formalities amounted to the same thing. The 1929 arrangements were continued into the post-war period as a result of the decision of the Constituent Assembly to give the Pacts constitutional status. The decision, while arguably offending against the liberal principle of state neutrality in religious matters, was of more than trivial importance. The significance of the legal status of church marriages was that it would ensure that they, rather than civil marriages, would continue to remain the norm. This, in turn, would reinforce the Church's influence: not in the crude sense of 'indoctrination', but in the more ephemeral, but no less real sense that to give the Church *legal* authority was thereby to give it *social* authority.
- In the 1974 referendum on the issue, the Church spoke against the legalisation of divorce. In insisting that the state use its monopoly on coercion to uphold Catholic teaching regardless of the views of a majority of Italian citizens, the Church's arguments reflected an age when politics and religion were not two separate spheres and when, therefore, there was no conception that moral rules (as defined by the Church) and legal rules, could diverge.
- In post-war elections, popes and bishops gave 'guidance' to the faithful, going as far – in the 1948 election – as to threaten the withdrawal of sacraments to anyone voting for the PCI. The assumption that there was nothing inappropriate in this was underpinned by the deep-rooted certainty that, whatever the democratic implications of such behaviour, it was justified by the Church's privileged access to the truth. It is this that makes the Church a challenge for democracy: having privileged access to the truth, there is no area, public or private, political or social, that the Church regards as beyond its remit.

We can thus identify three specific challenges posed by the Church to the sovereignty of the Italian state:

(1) Having privileged access to the truth, it expects unquestioning obedience to its teachings. It must at least potentially remain, therefore, an alternative focus for the political allegiance of Catholics, in competition with the allegiance demanded by the state.
(2) Given the Church's claim to speak with authority regarding all spheres of human existence, and given the state's need to remain free of religious tutelage as the necessary condition of its retention of sovereignty, a condition of latent tension must always underlie relations between Church and State.

(3) If, for the State, the principle of majority decision-making is paramount among the criteria lending legitimacy to public policies, this can never be so for the Church, for 'freedom of conscience' is not one that makes any sense within a paradigm of religious truth.

The Church's role today

The Church's role in Italian politics today can best be expressed in terms of four major points.

(1) The practical political significance of the above-mentioned challenges to the state has declined over the six decades since the war; for this period has been one of declining influence of the Church among the population at large. One of the most significant effects of the so-called economic miracle, from the mid-1950s on, was declining Church attendance, and falling membership for most of the Church's layper-sons' organisations. For rising incomes brought with them new leisure opportunities and growing geographical mobility. They also brought exposure to an increasingly wide variety of sources of information and (with rising levels of education) growing sophistication. They there-fore reduced the extent to which even those remaining faithful to the Church were likely to accept its political edicts unquestioningly. Such processes of secularisation have continued, more or less unabated, to the present.

(2) However, religion-related controversies have acquired an increasingly high profile in recent years and their number has grown, not dimin-ished, with time. For the Church has always claimed a responsibility for defining the Christian position in relation to moral problems public and private; and scientific progress has brought to the fore new problems on which the Church has wanted to take a position (Rémond, 1999: 36). The best examples are those related to bioethical issues. In relation to these, the Church has scored some striking successes. In 2005, for example, there was a referendum in Italy on artificial insemination. The Church urged abstention and thus success-fully defeated the four referendum proposals through lack of the required 50 per cent turnout. Its argument for retention of the restric-tive legislation passed by the Berlusconi government in 2004 appeared to have found an echo even among left libertarian voters, apparently worried by the ethical and practical implications of not subjecting to adequate democratic controls scientific research whose implications are often difficult to interpret. No longer identified with a specific political party or – with the end of the Cold War – with one side in a great ideological conflict, the Church no longer faces a public that is either prejudicially *for*, or prejudicially *against*, any of its specific mes-sages (Ceccarini, 2005: 857–8).

Table 6.2. Left–right self-placement and church attendance in Italy, 2001

	Left-right self-placement		
Frequency of church attendance:	Left	Centre	Right
At least 2 or 3 times per month	285	354	371
	26.6%	48.0%	40.5%
Less frequently	786	384	545
	73.4%	52%	59.5%
Totals	1071	738	916
	100%	100%	100%

Source: My calculations based on Italian National Election Study (ITANES) data available at http://csa.berkeley.edu:7502/cattest.html.

(3) In widening the spheres of social life in relation to which the Church feels compelled to take a public stand, continuing economic and scientific development has brought with it a seeming paradox. That is, while promoting secularisation, it has created new opportunities for Church initiatives, thus spawning new types of religious organisation and hence a larger 'presence' for the Church in political and social life generally. In particular, the Church has taken on an increasingly active role in the health, welfare and voluntary sectors, making up for the state's inability fully to fund services that the public would like (Donovan, 2003: 113). In these developments a number of commentators have discerned a vitality among Catholic organisations much greater than in the past when it 'lay more hidden between the folds of a secularised society' (*il Mulino*, 2005: 821, my translation).

(4) The Church's ability to influence voting behaviour is today nothing like it was in the immediate post-war period (McCarthy (2000: 148) suggests that it can today probably influence the votes of about 15 per cent of the electorate). But in the bipolar world of Italian party politics, what is important is to be able to influence the behaviour of the small proportion of 'swing voters'. These are the voters who make the difference between a victory for the centre left and a victory for the centre right. Located, by definition, in the centre of the political spectrum, they are more likely to be susceptible to Church admonitions than others; for they attend Church significantly more frequently than voters on the left or the right: see Table 6.2. This means that, even while maintaining a stance of formal non-alignment in Italian party politics, the Church can exercise considerable leverage over the policy positions espoused by the competing coalitions. For example, in the run-up to the 2006 election, Pope Benedict declared that it was 'a grave error to obscure the value and functions of the legitimate family founded on marriage by giving improper legal recognition … to other forms of union' (quoted by Politi, 2006: 11, my translation). In making this declaration, the Pope was

repeating the Church's very loud opposition to the centre left's proposals to extend to unmarried, including same-sex, couples the legal rights and obligations in the areas of property, inheritance and welfare currently enjoyed by married couples. The evident embarrassment of some of the centre left's spokespersons (Politi, 2006) was revealing of the power of the Church, on an issue that goes to the heart of the question of state neutrality in religious matters, to drive a major wedge between the coalition's two largest parties, one of whose traditions were rooted directly in those of Christian Democracy.

Summary and conclusion

Our objective in this chapter has been to explore how, and to what extent, interest groups are able to influence public policy in Italy and to consider what this tells us about the quality of democracy in that country. The material considered in the preceding paragraphs makes it apparent that those staffing the institutions of government formulate, enact and implement legislation under the constant pressure of interest-group demands. Policy-making is therefore an activity that in one way or another engages the entire polity. In this respect, Italy is no different from any other pluralist democracy. The distinctive traits of the policy-making process in Italy, from the perspective of interest groups' roles in it, appear to be these:

(1) The peak organisations of labour and capital do not just transmit demands to actors who make policy in other arenas. In not insignificant instances they are themselves actors in such arenas. This raises questions about political accountability and the extent to which the resulting concertation bypasses Parliament.

(2) Along with the executive, the bureaucracy and the courts, Parliament provides to interest groups channels of access to the authorities. These channels of access have traditionally been rather permeable to groups' activities. This, by diminishing the predictability of policy-making, has sometimes given rise to less legitimate forms of influence. Thus it has made a negative contribution to the authority of the country's political institutions.

(3) Lacking great reserves of authority, such institutions' representatives have traditionally not taken an especially tolerant approach to dealing with protest. However, attitudes have softened over the past two and half decades, and protest is in no sense an ineffective form of political participation in Italy.

(4) Among the institutional groups that have traditionally been among the most effective policy influencers is the Catholic Church. This is an organisation which, a bit like the monarchy in Britain, is able to play an important role in setting certain *cultural* parameters despite

secularisation. The Church's influence continues, though to a lesser degree than in the past, to raise questions about the role of state neutrality in religion-related issues in Italy.

Further reading

Joseph LaPalombara's *Interest Groups in Italian Politics* (Princeton, NJ: Princeton University Press, 1964), though forty years old, will repay careful reading: in offering an account of the place traditionally occupied by interest groups in post-war Italian politics, it is essential for an understanding of more recent developments. On the trade unions, see Gino Bedani's *Politics and Ideology in the Italian Workers' Movement: Union Development and the Changing Role of the Catholic and Communist Subcutlures in Postwar Italy* (Oxford: Berg, 1995). Phil Edwards' *More Work! Less Pay!': Rebellion and Repression in Italy, 1972–77* (Manchester: Manchester University Press, 2009) analyses the 'cycles of contention' of the 1960s and 1970s. In so doing, it provides theoretically informed and innovative material relevant for an understanding of the significance of protest activity in Italian politics. *The Power of Judges: A Comparative Study of the Courts and Democracy*, by Carlo Guarnieri and Patrizia Pederzoli (Oxford: Oxford University Press, 2002), throws further light on the significance of the judiciary for interest groups; for it argues that a polity, like that of Italy, in which power is divided and fragmented, offers wide opportunities for the judiciary to intervene in the political process. René Rémond's *Religion and Society in Modern Europe* (Oxford: Blackwell, 1999) is a fascinating exposition of the relationship between religion on the one hand, and the state and society on the other, in Europe over the last 200 years. Though not focusing specifically on Italy, the intimacy of the relationship between the Church and Italian politics, historically speaking, makes the book indispensable reading for an understanding of the contemporary place of the Church in the public life of the country and of the positions typically taken by the Church on public issues.

Notes

1. These are pensions that allow the worker to retire at any age provided s/he has accumulated thirty-five years of contributions.
2. For details of the foundations on which this prowess rested, see Bull and Newell (2005) chapter 5.
3. Deliberation is a form of communication the participants to which aim at reaching decisions by offering reasons potentially acceptable to the other participants, rather than by having recourse to arguments rooted in coercion, power or emotion.
4. In late 2005 and early 2006, protests against the building, through the Val di Susa in Piedmont, of a high-speed rail link connecting Turin and Lyon were met with sometimes heavy-handed policing that included baton charges and sometimes resulted in injuries among the police and demonstrators.

5. Thus, while about 90 per cent of Italians identify themselves as Catholics and large majorities say they trust the Church as an institution, only 27 per cent attend mass weekly (Bordignon, 2005: 18). Moreover, most say they dislike Church attempts to influence political decisions and impose on the public its moral teachings. The challenge this poses for the Church is not made smaller by immigration and growing religious pluralism in Italy.

7   Elections, voting and political parties

■ **Introduction**

Elections lie at the heart of the political process in regimes normally called 'democratic'. They do so in two senses.

- On the one hand, they provide an institutional channel for the input of ordinary citizens into the political process. Thereby they give authority to those duly elected to make binding decisions for the polity as a whole. By that token they rule out as illegitimate alternative means of bringing about political change, unless these have been sanctioned by the elected themselves. And, since parties increase their vote shares by successful appeals to electors located beyond their ideological heartlands (provided they are also successful in retaining their 'core' support), they are, in most circumstances, under strong pressures to moderate their appeals as the price of electoral success. So the institution of elections makes a significant contribution to political stability.
- On the other hand, elections do not offer citizens as *individuals* much by way of empowerment; for citizens' roles are limited to an infrequent choice between pre-packaged alternatives. However elections do ensure that citizens *collectively* have an influence on public policy: elite competition for office and the law of anticipated reactions ensure that, however

Table 7.1. Political participation in Italy, 2001

Type of activity	Percentage undertaking the activity 'in the last 4–5 years'
Participating in a political debate	25.3
Signing law proposals or referenda	24.3
Attempting to persuade somebody to vote for a party or candidate	19.9
Signing the nomination papers of a party or election candidate	13.8
Taking part in a demonstration	11.9
Writing or complaining to a public authority	9.0
Giving time to, or working for, a party	6.8
Writing to a newspaper	4.8
Donating money to a candidate, party, or party newspaper	3.9

Source: My elaboration based on Italian National Election Study (ITANES) data available at http://csa.berkeley.edu:7502/cattest.html.

vulnerable atomised voters' opinions are to elite manipulation, disharmony between majority opinion and the substance of public policy is most of the time kept within tolerable limits. In this way too do elections contribute to stability.

Moreover, the principal mechanism by which most ordinary citizens are engaged in the policy-making process is through elections. Of course, citizens are engaged in many ways besides this – as they are, for example, when they read newspapers or respond to opinion polls. But in terms of the more *proactive* forms of participation, most citizens in most liberal democracies do little beyond voting. That Italians are no exception in this respect is confirmed by the figures in Table 7.1. Therefore, if we wish to deepen our understanding of the way democracy works in Italy, we need to have some appreciation of the role of elections in determining who comes to occupy the principal public offices in that country.

Analytically, the outcome of any election can be thought of as being the product of three sets of factors:

(1) The profile of party and candidate alternatives among which voters are called upon to choose in the first place.
(2) The nature of the electoral system. The impact of the electoral system is both direct and indirect. Its direct impact is felt in terms of the way in which it translates a given distribution of votes into a given distribution of seats. Its indirect impact is felt in terms of its influence on parties' and voters' perceptions of its *likely* effects. Such perceptions in turn affect parties' decisions about the line-ups to offer, and voters' decisions about

211

the choice to make between such line-ups. In 'first-past-the post' systems, for example, voters are much more likely than in proportional systems to confine their choices to the two 'front runners'. They do this in order to avoid 'wasting' their votes.

(3)   All the 'external' social and other factors impinging upon voters' choices.

With this is mind, the remainder of the chapter is divided into the following sections:

- The next considers the parties and party coalitions. The period since the party-system upheavals of the early 1990s and the resulting change of electoral law in 1993 has seen the gradual consolidation of a bipolar system built around two electoral coalitions each competing for overall majorities of parliamentary seats. We therefore describe the most significant characteristics of the coalitions and how they have changed over time.
- The third section considers the nature of the current electoral system and the circumstances that gave rise to its adoption in December 2005.
- The fourth section considers the most important social factors influencing voters' electoral choices.
- The fifth section considers how the impact of party line-ups, electoral system and voters' choices combined to produce the outcomes of the general elections of 2006 and 2008 with their victories for centre left and centre right respectively.

▤ The two coalitions

Composition

The centre right

In chapter 1 we saw that the centre-right coalition, the House of Freedoms (CdL), that assumed the reins of government in 2001 had four principal components: Forza Italia (FI), the National Alliance (AN), the Northern League (LN) and Christian Democrat heirs, the CCD–CDU. The latter in fact consisted of two very small parties. These were the Christian Democratic Centre (CCD) and the Christian Democratic Union (CDU). At the 1996 and the 2001 elections, they fielded a joint list of candidates for the Chamber proportional arena. In this way, they had reduced the risk of failing to cross the 4 per cent threshold that had to be surmounted in order to gain entitlement to participate in the distribution of these seats (Box 7.1).

Though the CCD–CDU managed to cross the Chamber proportional threshold in 1996, in 2001, when its share of the vote was 3.2 per cent, it was unsuccessful: see Table 7.2. Consequently, at a founding conference in December 2002, its component parties merged together with a third formation, Democrazia Europea (European Democracy, DE). This was an organisation that had run independently of the two main coalitions the previous year but whose ideological roots also lay in Christian Democracy. The addition of its modest vote tally

Box 7.1

The 1993 electoral system

The 1993 electoral-law reform had provided that three-quarters of the 630 Chamber seats would be distributed according to the single-member, simple plurality system, one-quarter proportionally. In order to achieve this, it had divided the country into twenty-seven constituencies, subdividing the latter into 475 single-member colleges in each of which voters were required to make a single choice of candidate. Candidates had to be supported by at least one of the parties, or party coalitions, presenting lists at the constituency level for distribution of the remaining 155 seats. A second ballot was made available to the voter to make a choice among such lists. Once the polls closed, in each constituency an 'electoral total' was calculated for each list receiving at least 4 per cent of the national total of the valid list votes cast. The 'electoral total' was the constituency vote total minus, for each of the party's candidates elected in single-member colleges in the constituency, a sum of votes equal to the total obtained by the second-placed candidate. The sum of all qualifying lists' electoral totals was then divided by the number of proportional seats allocated to the constituency to obtain the constituency electoral quotient, each party's electoral total then being divided by the quotient to determine the number of seats to which it was entitled (Bull and Newell, 2005: 75). A substantially similar system – though with a single ballot used to decide the allocation of seats in both the plurality and the proportional arenas – was introduced by the 1993 reform to determine distribution of the 315 Senate seats.

to that of the CCD–CDU drove hopes that united, the three forces might be able to revive the tradition of Christian Democracy as a more-than-marginal force within the centre right. The new party was called the Union of Christian Democrats and Centre Democrats (Unione dei Democratici Cristiani, UDC).

A second significant change came in November 2003, when Mussolini's granddaughter, Alessandra Mussolini, announced that she was leaving AN to form her own organisation, Libertà d'Azione.[1] Though she was followed by no politicians of any significance, the long-standing criticisms of the AN leader, Gianfranco Fini, that underlay the move were shared by others. Thus it was at least possible that her new movement would be able to exercise, in future electoral contests, not insignificant blackmail power. In 1996, for example, the centre right arguably lost some four dozen seats as the result of independent candidatures by the far-right Fiamma Tricolore (Newell and Bull, 1996).[2]

The centre left

On the centre left, the picture of instability and change appears in even sharper colours. At the election of 2001, the coalition already consisted of no less than nine parties.[3] It was widely believed that the centre left had lost the 2001 election because it had been divided (and especially because it had failed

Table 7.2. The Chamber of Deputies Elections of 2001

Plurality vote			Proportional vote		
Coalition	Vote (%)	Seats (no.)	Parties and alliances	Vote (%)	Seats (no.)
			DS	16.6	31
			Margherita	14.5	27
L'Ulivo-SVP*	1.6	8	Girasole‡	2.2	0
L'Ulivo	43.7	184	PdCI	1.7	0
Total	45.3	192	Total	35.0	58
			RC	5.0	11
L'Ulivo + RC	**45.3**	192		**40.0**	69
			CCD–CDU	3.2	0
			FI	29.5	62
			AN	12.0	24
			New PSI	1.0	0
			LN	3.9	0
CdL	**45.4**	282	Total	**49.6**	86
Bonino List†	1.3	0	Bonino List	2.2	0
MSFT	0.3	0	MSFT	0.4	0
IdV	4.1	0	IdV	3.9	0
DE	3.6	0	DE	2.4	0
Others	0.0	1	Others	1.5	0
Total	100	475		100	155

Note: * SVP = South Tyrolese People's Party (Südtirolervolkspartei);
† Bonino List = Radicals;
‡ Girasole = 'Sunflower' (comprising SDI and the Greens).
Source: Bull and Newell, 2001.

to reach stand-down agreements with Antonio Di Pietro's Italy of Values (Italia dei Valori, IdV) and, in the Senate election, with Communist Refoundation (Rifondazione Comunista, RC). Thus, the months and years after the election saw a coming together of forces that was somewhat paradoxical. It was paradoxical because on the one hand, the process represented a growing unity of intents, but on the other hand each addition or merger served only to reduce cohesion by rendering the coalition ever larger and more heterogeneous. There were four stages to the process.

(1)   In March 2002, three of the centre left's nine parties – Italian Renewal (Rinnovamento Italiano, RI), the Democrats (Democratici) and the Italian People's Party (Partito Populare Italiano, PPI) – merged to form the

Margherita (or 'Daisy'). The principal ideological reference points of this party were a left-leaning version of Christian Democracy. 'Margherita' was the name chosen for the joint lists fielded in the Chamber proportional arena by RI, the Democrats, the PPI and the Union of Democrats for Europe (Unione dei Democratici per l'Europa – UDEUR) in 2001. When it became a party, it was far from representing the highest example of unity: the formation located most firmly in the centre of the left–right spectrum, the UDEUR refused to join and the Margherita was divided internally between those who saw themselves as secular, left-of-centre reformists committed to a bipolar future for Italian party politics, and those who hankered after the idea of a party able to hold power by exploiting its location in the centre of the political spectrum, much as the Christian Democrats (DC) had done for so many years.

(2) In 2004 the 'Federation' emerged. This was an agreement for closer co-operation between the Left Democrats (Democratici di Sinistra, DS), the Margherita, the Socialists (Socialisti Democratici Italiani, SDI) and the European Republicans (Repubblicani Europei). It took shape after the 2004 European Parliament elections and induced RC to seek membership of the centre-left coalition. RC probably realised that it faced a real risk of losing influence in the event that the Federation succeeded in drawing more radical forces, such as the Greens (Verdi) and the Party of Italian Communists (Partito dei Comunisti Italiani, PdCI), into its orbit. At the 2001 election, RC had been unable to agree candidacies with the remaining centre-left parties. This was partly a result of the technicalities of the electoral law (for details see Newell, 2002); but, more profoundly, it reflected the perspective of a party convinced that, from the point of view of defence of the working class and the poor, its interlocutors could be distinguished from 'Berlusconism' in terms that were at most quantitative, not qualitative. Therefore, its attitude to the coalition had always been that while it was happy to consider the possibility of joint initiatives against the centre right whenever possible, it was against the idea of committing itself to anything resembling a long-term alliance with the rest of the centre left in advance of agreement on the programmatic content of such an alliance. It was for this reason that, in 1996, its agreement with the Olive-tree Alliance (Ulivo) had been limited to a series of stand-down arrangements and it had made clear, after the elections, that it would support the government on a case-by-case basis only. Its 2004 decision to seek alliance with the centre left in advance of detailed programmatic discussions appeared to represent a softening of its traditional stance. But the party appeared to remain significantly different from the rest of the coalition in at least one important respect. That is, for most of the rest of the centre left, elections are above all about winning government power – so that policies are to be judged primarily in terms of the degree to which they make this possible. For RC, in contrast, elections have traditionally been viewed as a means, but not the only means, of

exerting political pressure to defend the poor and the vulnerable. Therefore, there have always been significant limits to the compromises RC has been prepared to make for the sake of coalition unity.

(3)   IdV sought to become part of the centre-left coalition. It was a small party led by Antonio di Pietro, the former public prosecutor who had become famous at the time of the '*Mani pulite*' investigations in the early 1990s. Like RC, it too had fielded its own, independent, candidates at the 2001 election. But its central mission was to combat illegality and less-than-impartial application of the law. This meant that its natural home was in a coalition that questioned Berlusconi's right to govern on similar grounds. Its decision was also driven by the fact that its independent stance in 2001 had resulted in failure to elect a single deputy. It was a potential source of disunity within the centre-left coalition if for no other reason than the fact that it was an additional party with its own goals and values: parties everywhere are entities for which alliance with other parties has instrumental but not intrinsic value – while unity and cohesion are public goods necessarily exposed to the collective-action problem.

(4)   In November 2005, the formation of la Rosa nel Pugno (literally, 'the Rose in the fist', RnP), bringing together the SDI and the Radicals, drew into the orbit of the Unione (as the centre left now called itself) a party – the Radicals – that had previously found it difficult to coalesce with either of the two main coalitions. For its emphasis on individual responsibility gave it an uncertain location on the left–right spectrum. On the one hand, it takes strongly libertarian stands on civil rights issues. On the other, it takes firmly liberal positions in matters economic. The Radicals' failure to achieve any parliamentary representation in 2001 provided strong arguments for a search for allies. The SDI was a willing partner because it shared with the Radicals strong opposition to the involvement of the Vatican in Italian politics, and because the alliance offered the SDI an alternative to further involvement with the Federation parties. Such involvement carried the risk of eclipse by the DS.

The causes of coalition instability

As we said in the introductory section, the changing and unstable nature of the contending alliances has had three fundamental causes. These are described under each of the following five subheadings.

The coalitions' fragmentary character

This is due to the circumstances surrounding introduction of the 1993 electoral law. This law encouraged the formation of electoral coalitions. However, it was introduced at a time when the traditional parties of government were disintegrating while new parties' positions had not yet been consolidated. This created uncertainty concerning the likely strength of the competing parties. Such uncertainty in turn added to the parties' power to blackmail each other when it came to negotiating the distribution of candidacies across the single-member colleges established by that law. Smaller parties were especially well placed to threaten to run independently if their demands for safe seats were not met. With less to lose than their larger rivals, they were aware that while independent candidacies had few prospects of victory, what was much more certain was that they could make their larger rivals lose. Moreover, if their support was territorially concentrated, they might actually expect independent candidacies to be successful, perhaps even delivering the balance of power in Parliament. This was a strategy followed (unsuccessfully as it happened) by the Northern League in 1996. Finally, the parties were aware that while the coalitions of centre left and centre right were alliances whose cohesion was required in the *electoral* arena, inside *Parliament* the party groups would not face the same imperatives.

Ideological heterogeneity: the centre left
On the centre left, ideological heterogeneity has been apparent in a range of divisions, the most important of which have been three in number.

(1) The division between the two largest parties, the DS and the Margherita. These were the heirs of parties – the Italian Communist Party (PCI) and the DC – that stood on opposite sides of the principal political divide during the 'First Republic' (Diamanti and Lello, 2005: 10). The importance of the division stemmed from the obstacles it placed in the way of the attempts to overcome coalition fragility through closer organisational ties between the two parties. The obstacles were made greater by the fact that to a large extent the two parties fished in the same pool of voters and were therefore close electoral competitors.
(2) The division represented by the presence in the coalition of RC. This is a party whose capacity for compromise for the sake of coalition unity has been limited not only by the factors we have discussed above, but also by the fact that, in the period following the centre left's 2006 election victory, it had somehow to reconcile its governing responsibilities, in unfavourable economic circumstances (see chapter 8), with defence of the interests of its working-class supporters and the maintenance of its image as a party of 'struggle and resistance'.
(3) The division represented by the presence of the Rosa nel Pugno. The ideological profile of this formation had the potential to bring it into conflict with the DS on economic issues, and the even greater potential to bring it into conflict with the Margherita on religion-related issues: on the one hand, the number and significance of religion-related issues has, as we saw in the last chapter, grown, not diminished, in recent years. On the other hand, the proportion of regular churchgoers among supporters of the Margherita was larger than among voters generally. Thus, it could

not afford to stray too far from conservative positions on issues on which the Rosa nel Pugno took diametrically opposed stances.

Finally, fragility has been made the greater by the sheer range of ideological traditions the coalition has sought to encompass – from Christian democracy (the UDEUR, the Margherita) through environmentalism (the Greens) and secular reformism (parts of the Margherita, Italia dei Valori, the Repubblicani Europei) to socialism, social democracy (the PdCI, the DS and the SDI) libertarianism (the Radicals) and left libertarianism (RC) (Box 7.2).

Ideological heterogeneity: the centre right

Ideological heterogeneity on the centre left has been mirrored to some degree on the centre right, though here, the largest three of the coalition's components – FI, AN and the LN – have been reasonably united in representing different shades of the ideological profile to which Mastropaolo (2005) refers by using the label 'new right'. In its starkest form, this is an ideology that involves an attachment to an ordered and communitarian conception of social and political life, one centred on the conventional family, Christianity (as a cultural identity rather than a set of precepts), the nation (an invented one – 'Padania' – in the case of the LN) and social and cultural conformity. Hence, the ideology is one that is violently opposed to extending the rights of married couples to gays and unmarried heterosexuals; to Islam; to multiculturalism, and to tolerance of behaviour deemed 'deviant' such as the use of hard or even

---

Box 7.2

Ideological diversity on the centre left

In many respects, the considerable difficulties that have always confronted the Italian centre left in remaining united need no more explanation than the one implicit in a brief description of the range of ideologies it has been home to:

Christian democracy is in some respects a rather eclectic political outlook in that it is 'right-leaning' with respect to 'moral' issues and 'left-leaning' with respect to labour-market and industrial issues. What unifies these two perspectives is Christian democracy's emphasis on the importance of the dignity of the human person – which leads it to adopt a conservative position in relation to issues such as abortion; a liberal position in relation to issues having to do with human rights and individual initiative, and a socialist position in relation to such issues as the welfare state and the relief of poverty.

Environmentalism advocates that the underlying principle guiding public policy-making should be the sustainable management of natural resources. That is, the Earth's resources should not be used at a rate faster than that at which they can be naturally replenished – otherwise, the environmentalist position asserts, it is not possible for the present generation to meet its needs, without compromising the ability of future generations to meet theirs.

Secularism is a political outlook that advocates a separation of Church and State and insists that policy decisions must be made without regard to religious principles of any kind. Sustaining this position is a commitment to the importance of reason in human affairs, empirical evidence as the basis of decision-making, tolerance, and a refusal to commit oneself to any one view concerning the nature of the universe and of humans' place in it.

Social democracy is a political outlook that involves a commitment to the reform of capitalism with a view to its regulation, in order thereby to remove its injustices and inefficiencies. Unlike democratic socialists, who advocate the reform of capitalism with the aim of bringing about its eventual supersession, social democrats argue that the principles of social justice and equality to which socialists are also committed require only that capitalism be appropriately regulated through welfare states, progressive taxation, social programmes and so forth.

Socialism advocates the supersession of capitalism through the creation of a society in which the means of production, distribution and exchange are collectively owned. Beyond that, there is considerable disagreement among those calling themselves 'socialists' over what common ownership should mean more specifically, and over how the socialist society should be brought about. Some socialists advocate wholesale nationalisation; others public ownership within the framework of a market economy; still others, alternatives to state ownership through workers' councils and workplace democracy. With regard to how socialism is to be achieved, the basic distinction is between reformist and revolutionary socialism. The former is rooted in the assumption that the socialist society can be achieved through winning elections and the passage of legislation taking the means of production into public ownership. Revolutionaries contend that the use of force is necessary to achieve socialism since those privileged by capitalism will always resist its supersession whatever might be the outcome of elections.

Libertarianism is a political outlook of which, in the Italian context, the Radicals are the most significant expression. In emphasising the importance of individual liberty and personal responsibility with respect to all matters, libertarians argue that the only thing that may legitimately be demanded of others is non-interference. Hence, libertarians oppose state intervention to help individuals achieve self-realisation (e.g. through welfare measures) or to protect them from themselves (e.g. through legislation against the sale and use of drugs). And on the same grounds they staunchly support private property and unregulated markets.

Left libertarianism shares libertarianism's insistence on the ontological and normative primacy of individuals as against states and other kinds of organisation, but sees private property and unregulated markets as institutions that are *themselves* potentially detrimental to individual liberty. In advocating a society without hierarchies or authoritarian institutions of any kind, left libertarianism opposes *both* the coercive power of the state *and* the private ownership of the means of production. In the Italian context, Communist Refoundation (RC) comes closest to expressing a left-libertarian attitude to politics.

soft drugs. In economic and social matters, it combines an attachment to free markets with 'welfare chauvinism' (the denial of welfare services to 'undeserving' cases), in this way succeeding both in espousing a smaller role for the state and in reassuring those who might lose as a consequence. This profile has been an advantage to the coalition; for it is one that with differing emphases has been shared by all three of the aforementioned parties. This has provided the basis for a profitable 'division of labour' between them. That is, with the most strident and crude expressions of the ideology being delegated to the LN and the other two offering more 'respectable' versions, all three parties have been able to maintain reasonably distinct profiles. The problem is that at the same time, the ideology can bring the parties into conflict. In the case of the LN, for instance, welfare chauvinism is also often directed against southerners, that is against precisely that part of the electorate in which AN finds its strongholds. These are areas 'with particularly high levels of unemployment and where the public sector plays a key role in the local economy. As a result, one finds significant demand in these areas for social protection and state intervention' (Diamanti and Lello, 2005: 16).

An additional difficulty for the centre right arises from the fact that the largest party, Forza Italia, is not one whose ideological profile actually stands out very sharply in all respects. It often uses the slogans of neo-liberalism in its political discourse (Hopkin, 2005). But far more salient features of its party image are the personality and qualities of its leader. This reflects the extraordinary degree of financial and organisational dependence of the party on the entrepreneur. As Hopkin (2005) has pointed out, FI does not even try to put on a show of internal democracy. Instead, the party's statutes are unique in their openly recognised attribution of vast powers to the leader. This means that it is difficult to imagine the party – at least in its present shape – continuing to have a meaningful existence after Berlusconi leaves the political scene. This, in turn, has reinforced the natural aspirations of allied parties to capture leadership of the coalition for themselves given that they could, perhaps, expect to capture parts of the entrepreneur's party in the process.

The absence of strong 'coalition makers': the centre left

A 'coalition maker' is a party which, by virtue of its relative size, is able to dictate the terms on which negotiations within the coalition will take place and therefore to impose a minimum of discipline on its allies.

The lack of such a party is a problem that has traditionally been especially acute on the centre left. Here, the strongest candidate for the role has hitherto been the DS – but it was never a serious candidate bearing in mind the proportion of the coalition's support it controlled. Too weak to impose on the coalition a leader of their own choosing, the DS was not, however, willing to stand by and see the choice made by others. The DS was aware of the potential electoral dividends accruing to the parties that provide their coalitions' leaders.[4] They could not therefore accept a leader provided by one of the other parties, and they always wanted to have at least as much say in matters of leadership selection as any of the other parties. As a result, leaders of the centre left have hitherto been chosen as 'independent' figures, from outside the coalition's main parties. However, lacking parties of their own, such leaders have, consequently, found it extremely difficult to wield any authority within the coalition. In other words, having (until October 2005) been *chosen* by the parties, centre-left leaders have to a greater or lesser degree always remained *hostage* to the parties. Let us examine the centre left's efforts to overcome the problem.

The centre left's primary elections, held in October 2005, were merely the latest of the attempts, after 2001, to acquire greater cohesion through stronger leadership. For the 2001 election, the parties chose the telegenic mayor of Rome, Francesco Rutelli, to run against Berlusconi. After the election Rutelli's position as leader was undermined by his role as leader of the Margherita; for this role meant that he was unable to count on the unconditional support of the DS. It thus came to be accepted that it would be necessary to find a replacement for Rutelli. It was recognised, however, that the leadership issue was inseparable from the need to give the alliance and its leader some kind of organisation that would enable the making of alliance-wide decisions free of the threat of veto by one or the other of its component parties; for only through such an organisation could a replacement for Rutelli be found by means other than simple negotiations among the party leaders.

Efforts to create such an organisation were undermined by precisely the centrifugal forces they were designed to overcome in the first place. Then, in July 2003, European Commission president and ex-Ulivo leader, Romano Prodi, launched the idea of a single coalition list to be presented at the European Parliament elections the following year. This suggestion carried considerable authority. For there was a widespread belief within the coalition that Prodi was the only leader capable of beating Berlusconi, and therefore there was a strong desire to secure Prodi's agreement to lead the coalition at the end of his term as Commission president. Thus it was that the DS, the Margherita, the SDI and the European Republicans (Repubblicani Europei) all declared not only that they would present a single, joint, list at the European elections, but that they would follow this up with the attempt to establish, within the coalition, a 'Federation'. This would initially consist of the four but would be open to the involvement of other coalition parties. Its leader would be Prodi. In this way Prodi might eventually acquire a party, while the alliance would thereby acquire the 'coalition maker' that it lacked. The agreement establishing the Federation gave it power to take apparently binding decisions in various policy areas. However, nothing was done to ensure that individuals could be members of the Federation other than by virtue of membership of the parties composing it. In the final analysis, therefore, the organisation remained nothing other than an agreement among party elites with no independent power to enforce its decisions against attempts, by the party representatives of which it was composed, to exercise a power of veto. Therefore, when Rutelli announced his opposition to the presentation of a single, Federation-wide list for the 2005 regional elections and, later, for the parliamentary elections of 2006, he effectively killed the Federation project in the short term. In doing so, he provided further confirmation, if any were needed, of the near impossibility of reducing the power of the parties by organisational means. Such means had the effect of simply shifting conflict to new fora; for the problem of coalition unity arose, not from *organisational* defects, but from the parties' *political* muscle.

It was in this context that Prodi was able to win the agreement of the parties to the idea of primary elections, to be held in October, to decide the issue of the coalition's leadership. On the one hand, this was an idea that had been discussed before but put aside in the wake of the regional elections: their positive outcome had argued against what would be a novel initiative which, depending on the turnout and support for Prodi it generated, might undermine the coalition as a credible opponent of the Government at the 2006 election. On the other hand, in the context in which it was made, the proposal was in effect an invitation by Prodi to the parties to 'back me or sack me' over the issue of the single list and the broader Federation project bound up with it: if Prodi were able to win primary elections handsomely, then he would strengthen his authority and thereby revive the Federation project, which he considered an essential part of efforts to ensure that a future centre-left government had sufficient cohesion to be able to govern effectively. The proposal for primary elections was one to which he was able to win the parties' agreement by virtue of divisions within the Margherita over the stand being taken by Rutelli: in effect, agreement to the elections was the quid pro quo for Prodi's declining to sponsor a split within the Margherita. Held on 16 October, the elections attracted the participation of 4,311,149 people of whom 3,182,686 or 73.8 per cent voted for Prodi (Box 7.3).

This was an outcome that considerably raised the leader's stature; for it demonstrated that Prodi had taken a political gamble that had paid off. Not only was his support, as compared to that of the other candidates overwhelming, but against the expectations of the vast majority of commentators (Pasquino, 2005: 8–11), participation in the primary extended far beyond the membership of the coalition's constituent parties. Therefore, it provided sorely needed ballast for the project for coalition unity that Prodi represented. Most importantly, it enabled him to persuade the DS and the Margherita to accept the idea of a joint list for the Chamber of Deputies elections, along with the creation of unified groups in the two chambers after the election, as initial steps towards the long-term goal of merger of the two in a new 'Partito Democratico'(PD).

The absence of strong 'coalition makers': the centre right

The problem of coalition leadership has been less acute for the centre right than for the centre left, but by no means irrelevant. On the one hand, Forza

Box 7.3

The October 2005 centre-left primary elections

Primary elections are a method of selecting candidates whereby the choice is entrusted to voters in a given jurisdiction rather than to party caucuses, conventions or nominating meetings. The basic distinction is between closed and open primaries. Closed primaries are said to take place when membership of the relevant party is a requirement for eligibility to vote. Open primaries, as the term suggests, are in contrast open to members and non-members alike. In between these two basic types, the further distinction between semi-closed and semi-open primaries is also often made. In a semi-closed primary, registered party members can vote only in their *own* party's primary, though the election is open to unaffiliated voters as well. In a semi-open primary, the voter, regardless of membership, must choose which party's primary to vote in, and, having made that choice, cannot *also* vote in the primary of *another* party.

In Italy, primary elections appear to have been used for the first time in 1995, when the Northern League held a closed primary to select candidates for the regional elections held in Lombardy that year (Franco, 1995). They were then used by the Unione and the DS in January and February 2005 respectively, to select a candidate for the presidency of the Puglia region and candidates for the Tuscan regional council. Both primaries were open – as was the primary resulting in Romano Prodi's election as leader of the Unione in October 2005. Indeed, this contest was even open to foreigners who had at least three years' residence, something that contributed to making it the largest event of its kind to be held in Europe to date. Persons wishing to participate were required to make a financial contribution to the Unione of at least one euro (most gave far more than this) and to sign the coalition's policy platform. Primaries were subsequently employed by the Unione to select candidates for the position of mayor of Milan (January 2006) and of Genoa and Palermo (February 2007). The centre right has never held primary elections of any significance.

The only legislation relating to the conduct of primaries in Italy is the Tuscan region's law no. 70 of December 2004 which sets out, for those parties wishing to have recourse to them, rules for the conduct of primaries for the selection of candidates to the regional council and presidency. Parties are not obliged to hold primaries or follow the procedures set out in the law (this would be unconstitutional), but they have at least some incentive to do so in that it is regional and local officials who apply the law's procedures – meaning that the primaries are in effect held at public expense.

Italia occupies a dominating position within the coalition and has been extraordinarily successful. Built by Berlusconi in the space of a few months, it is by far and away Italy's largest party. FI is fulcrum around which the centre right revolves. 'Without Berlusconi and FI it would be impossible to imagine the other parties of the Right in any kind of alliance or coalition' (Diamanti and Lello, 2005: 11–12). And the party 'has yet to poll less than 20 percent in any

Table 7.3. European Parliament elections, 2004

Electorate	49,804,087	Valid votes	32,516,246
Voters	35,717,655	Non-valid votes (including blank ballots)	3,201,256
% voting	71.72	Blank ballots	1,587,544

Lists	Votes	%	Seats
Uniti nell'Ulivo	10,105,836	31.08	25
FI	6,806,245	20.93	16
AN	3,736,606	11.49	9
RC	1,969,776	6.06	5
UDC	1,914,726	5.89	5
LN	1,613,506	4.96	4
Greens (Verdi)	803,356	2.47	2
PdCI	787,613	2.42	2
Bonino List	731,536	2.25	2
Di Pietro Occhetto	695,179	2.14	2
United Socialists (Socialisti Uniti)	664,463	2.04	2
Alleanza popolare UDEUR	419,173	1.29	1
Social Alternative (Alternativa Sociale)	400,626	1.23	1
Pensioners' Party (Partito Pensionati)	374,343	1.15	1
MSFT	237,058	0.73	1
Republicans and Sgarbi Liberals (PRI i Liberal Sgarbi)	233,144	0.72	0
Others	1,023,060	2.66	0

Source: Ministry of the Interior, http://elezionistorico.interno.it/index.php.

nationwide election' (Hopkin, 2005). On the other hand, it owes this success for the most part to the marketing of an image that is almost completely dominated by Berlusconi and his supposedly extraordinary personal qualities.

Now this was a very potent weapon at the 2001 election when FI could claim to be led by a self-made entrepreneur who would do for Italy what he had done for himself. However, it lost a great deal of its force thereafter. A message based on Berlusconi's charisma became much less convincing in the light of the Government's lacklustre economic performance. Moreover, it denied space, in FI's communications, to a clear ideological and programmatic profile. This left the party with very few means of attempting to retain voter loyalty when this loyalty was put under strain by the economic problems. Consequently, while Berlusconi was in an extraordinarily powerful position immediately after the 2001 election (which he could claim had been won largely thanks to him), his capacity to maintain coalition discipline, and with it his capacity to resist the leadership aspirations of allied parties, declined thereafter. This was especially true in the months following the 2004 European elections (Table 7.3) with their revelation that, if a government in difficulties was going to have to pay an electoral price, then, in the context of a proportional electoral law such as that used for the European Parliament, it would be paid by FI rather than its allies, and that they rather than the opposition parties would be the principal beneficiaries.[5]

Matters worsened following the 2005 regional elections. These were a disaster for the centre right. The loser in twelve of the fourteen regions where voting took place, it took 12,220,858 votes (43.9 per cent) to the centre left's 14,632,412 (52.6 per cent) and lost control of six of the eight regions it had won in 2000. It was in this context that Berlusconi launched the idea of a single party of the centre right. He was apparently driven by the belief that the single party would place his hold on the leadership beyond the immediate attacks of his allies. For their acceptance of such a proposal would then make it possible for him to insist that the matter of the leadership should be settled democratically, only *after* the new party had been constructed. The idea also seemed to offer the prospect of reinvigorating Berlusconi's image as the leader promising innovation and renewal. It thereby also held out the prospect that the centre right might actually be able to avoid having to fight the coming general election by defending its lacklustre record, allowing it, rather, to pose as innovators (Newell and Favretto, 2006). The initiative was, however, superseded by a second one: the return to proportional representation for parliamentary elections, which the governing majority forced onto the statute book in December 2005.

▪ The electoral law

The advantages offered to the centre right by the return to proportionality appeared to be at least three in number.

(1) By allowing each of the parties to compete independently, the new law considerably reduced the significance of Berlusconi's personal popularity for the prospects of his allies and those of the coalition as a whole. One of the lessons of the 2004 European elections was that if voters disillusioned with Berlusconi and FI seemed more likely to switch to an allied party than to a party of the centre left, then as a whole, the centre right might not suffer very much. And in fact, though its combined total, at 45.4 per cent, was 4.1 per cent lower than its 2001 tally, its total was a mere 0.7 per cent behind that of the centre left. However, with their in-essence plurality electoral systems, the 2005 regional elections made clear that where the parties were obliged to line up behind single candidates representing the coalition as a whole, then they might suffer badly; for in such contexts voters dissatisfied with Berlusconi and FI would have no means of giving expression to their dissatisfaction other than by action (abstention or voting for the centre left) also damaging to the entrepreneur's allies.

Box 7.4

Candidate-centred campaigning

'Candidate-centred' campaigning is a term that refers to efforts to win votes by emphasising the positive qualities of candidates rather than the images and policies of the parties they represent ('party-centred' campaigning). And in candidate-centred campaigns, there is, naturally, an attempt to draw attention to the supposed negative qualities of rival candidates and/or an effort to emphasise the supposedly superior qualities of one's own candidates. It is thought that election campaigns in democracies generally in recent years have become more candidate-centred (though in the case of parliamentary, as opposed to presidential, elections it might be more accurate to say 'leader-centred') – this as the result of a number of interlinked developments. These include declining ideological conflict – which has shifted attention from position to valence issues and thus to candidates' competence. Television and other electronic media, by allowing candidates to appeal directly to voters, have diminished the requirement for good party organisation and thus the attention to party itself in campaigns. Development of the mass media of communications has also rendered the lives of the individuals who walk on the public stage 'much more visible than they ever were in the past' (Thompson, 2000: 6). Not only have they detached publicness from co-presence and allowed distant others to be audible and visible at the moment they act, but most importantly, the electronic media have made possible a shift from rhetorical aloofness to mediated intimacy, through which politicians can present themselves not just as leaders, but as human beings – and the more politicians have sought to present themselves as 'one of us', the more their audiences have been inclined to assess them in terms of their character as individuals (Thompson, 2000: 39–41).

In Italy, candidate- or leader-centred campaigning was, in the early 1990s, catalysed as the result of two specific developments: the political debut of Silvio Berlusconi (whose charisma inevitably led to a focus, when public attention turned to the centre left, on the qualities of *its* leader) and the emergence of bipolar competition. This meant that in casting a vote for one or the other coalition, the voter was choosing an alliance whose leader was a candidate for the premiership. Hence the alliance's fortunes were to a significant extent dependent on its ability to sell itself as an entity led by a credible would-be prime minister.

(2) Therefore, the new law held out the prospect of considerably reducing the leadership issue as a source of friction and instability within the centre right. This was especially important in the run-up to 2006. Reflecting cross-national trends, election **campaigning** in Italy has been markedly more '**candidate-centred**' since the end of the 'First Republic' than it was before then (Box 7.4). That is, the focus in parties' campaigns has been much more on their candidates and their qualities than on their programmes and ideologies. This makes it seem likely that there has been a corresponding increase in the significance, in voters' electoral choices, of

their assessments of candidates. Hence, obliging the centre-right parties to line up behind a single prime-ministerial candidate whose popularity was in decline did not augur well for them. The new electoral law, unlike the one passed in 1993, makes this unnecessary. In the run-up to 2006, each party was able to present its own prime-ministerial candidate while the coalition as a whole was able to claim that in this way it was offering voters something akin to the centre left's primary elections since, in the event that the coalition was victorious, the identity of the Prime Minister would depend on the distribution of votes between its constituent parties.

(3) The results of the three previous general elections suggested that the centre right's ability to compete with the centre left was much greater in the proportional than in the plurality arena, while the two previous elections suggested that in the proportional arena its constituent parties had a collective reach that extended beyond the pool of voters prepared to support their candidates in the plurality arena.[6] This therefore provided an additional argument in favour of a return to proportionality.

The details of the law are set out in Appendix 1 at the end of this book. In essence, for elections to the Chamber of Deputies, parties present lists of candidates in each of twenty-six multi-member constituencies, voters being required to make a single choice among the lists with which they are pre-sented. Parties can either field lists independently or as part of a coalition with other parties. Seats are distributed between the parties proportionally except that to be eligible to participate in such distribution, parties must obtain at least 4 per cent of the national total of valid votes cast if they are running independently or as part of a coalition whose combined total turns out to be less than 10 per cent. If they are part of a coalition whose combined total is 10 per cent or more, then they must obtain at least 2 per cent of the national valid vote total or have the largest number of valid votes among the coalition's parties below this threshold. If an initial proportional distribution of seats results in the largest party or coalition receiving fewer than 340 seats, then it is assigned as many seats as are necessary to bring it up to that figure. This so-called *premio di maggioranza* (or 'majority premium') thus ensures, for the party or coalition concerned, an overall majority in the 630-seat Chamber. The remaining seats are distributed proportionally among the other parties and coalitions. Given the fragmentation of the Italian party system, the effect of the law is, on the one hand, to encourage parties to field their lists as coalitions rather than independently while removing the pressure upon them to unite behind candidates representing the coalition as a whole. On the other hand, the law combines, for the voters, the choice of party and coalition into a single choice, while allowing them to support a coalition without having to cast a vote for a candidate drawn from a party other than their most preferred party.

Arrangements for the Senate are essentially the same, but with the impor-tant differences that (1) seats are assigned to regions (in accordance with their populations) rather than to constituencies; (2) seat distribution (including assignment of the *premio di maggioranza*) takes place region by region (that is, seat assignment depends on parties' and coalitions' regional, not national, totals); (3) the *premio* in each region consists in the number of seats, awarded to the largest coalition or party, that is necessary to bring it up to 55 per cent of the seats assigned to the region; (4) in order to be eligible to participate in the distribution of seats, parties have to have attracted, if running independently or as part of a coalition whose combined regional vote total turns out to be less than 20 per cent, at least 8 per cent of the valid votes cast in the region concerned. If it is running as part of a coalition whose combined vote is above 20 per cent, then it must have attracted at least 3 per cent of the region's valid vote total.

Voting behaviour

In Italy, as in the other advanced democracies, economic and social change in recent decades has seen the emergence of an electorate, more likely than the voters of earlier decades, to be influenced in their choices by factors of a short-term nature. Such factors include the characteristics of candidates, and the specifics of parties' policies. In the Italian case, the 'economic miracle' from the 1950s onwards brought unprecedented rates of economic growth and with them, increased rates of geographical and social mobility, increased levels of education and greater exposure to the mass media of communications. With the process of generational turnover, that is as older people progressively died off, the electorate came increasingly to be composed of people exposed to these novel circumstances during their formative years, that is during their youth. The experiences of youth tend to be especially important for the formation of attitudes, which are decreasingly likely to change the older one gets. Therefore, as suggested by growing rates of electoral volatility from the mid-1970s on, the electorate came increasingly to be composed of relatively critical voters. More sophisticated than their forebears, these voters' choices were less likely to be influenced by factors of a longer-term nature such as those associated with geographical, class, religious and ideological divisions.

This is not to say that these divisions no longer have any significance, far from it. Moreover, they are of great significance for the political system in its entirety; for their influence ensures that most voters are stable in their voting habits, or in other words that they vote for the same parties at one election after the other. This provides political stability by ensuring that changes in the distribution of the vote at successive elections are rarely very dramatic and rarely such as to result in sudden surges in support for new and unknown parties. Let us examine each of these divisions in turn.

Geographical divisions

Conventionally in Italy, a distinction is made between four geopolitical areas whose voting profiles are still rather distinct. These are

(1) the North-East, or 'white belt', coinciding, with sufficient approximation, to the regions of Friuli-Venezia Giulia, Veneto, and Trentino-Alto Adige;
(2) the 'red belt' (Emilia Romagna, Tuscany, Marche, Umbria);
(3) the North-West (Lombardy, Liguria, Piemonte, Aosta);
(4) the South and islands (the rest of the country).

The North-East is an area where the Church has traditionally been especially influential: 'the White provinces are those where, under the Austrian Empire before unification, the local clergy led and defended Italian nationality against the foreign ruler' (Allum, 1973a: 42). In the immediate post-war period, the Church's parishes and collateral associations provided the basis for the emergence of a distinctively Catholic political subculture. Even today church attendance here is higher than in the rest of the country.[7] This made the area one of the DC's strongholds. The area's subcultural characteristics, especially their emphasis on the local mediation of interests (see chapter 5), then allowed the Northern League to replace the DC as the dominant party when the latter went into irreversible decline.

The 'red belt' is an area that formed part of the Papal States. Here, oppressive rule meant that the movement for Italian unification was driven by strongly anti-clerical sentiments. This favoured the subsequent rise of socialism, and then, in the immediate post-war years, the PCI was able to build on this to establish its own subcultural stronghold in opposition to that of the DC. As in the 'white belt', so too in the 'red belt', exposure to subculturally specific flows of communication reinforced the normal processes of intergenerational transmission of values and attitudes through the family. This ensured high and stable levels of support for the left.

The North-West was the area that was first to industrialise and is still the area having the highest concentration of large-scale industry. Traditionally, left and right have been evenly matched here.

In the South, economic and social conditions were such as to allow the DC to establish an additional stronghold on the basis of clientelism. Thus, the DC's 'successor parties' (the UDC, UDEUR and the Margherita) along with FI (whose anti-communist rhetoric has enabled it to pose as a 'functional equivalent' of the DC) have inherited most of these voters. The South is also the area where, as mentioned earlier, support for AN reaches a peak. As heir to the Italian Social Movement (MSI), AN has inherited the support of a neo-fascist party whose advocacy of a strong state, including robust welfare arrangements, enabled it to do relatively well in an area where the Fascist regime had had a relatively 'benevolent' face with fewer of the violent and murderous characteristics it had shown north of the 'Gothic line'.

Socio-economic changes since 1945 have led to a decline in the distinctiveness of the voting profiles of the four areas, and especially to a decline in the impact of the 'red' and 'white' subcultures on electoral choice. Still, the continuing influence of geography on the distribution of the vote is clearly apparent from the figures in Table 7.4 and from Figure 7.1.

Table 7.4. Vote by geographical area (Chamber proportional vote), 2001

	Area									
	North-West		White belt		Red belt		South and islands		Total	
	Col %	N	Col %	N	Col %	N	Col %	N	Col %	N
Party voted for										
AN	9.3	65	1.2	34	12.9	58	14.7	159	12.5	316
FI	35.7	252	26.9	81	25.9	117	32.7	353	31.6	803
LN	4.6	32	6.2	19	0.9	4	0.0	0	2.2	55
CCD–CDU	1.0	7	1.5	5	2.3	10	1.7	19	1.6	41
Margherita	10.8	76	15.5	47	9.1	41	9.1	98	10.3	262
DS, PdCI, RC	19.4	137	16.0	48	37.1	168	24.2	262	24.2	615
Others	7.9	56	11.9	36	5.6	25	5.4	58	6.9	175
Blank ballot/didn't vote	11.3	80	10.8	32	6.2	28	12.2	132	10.7	272
Total	100.0	705	100.0	300	100.0	453	100.0	1,081	100.0	2.539

Source: My own elaboration based on Italian National Election Study (ITANES) data available at http://csa.berkeley.edu: 7502/cattest.html.

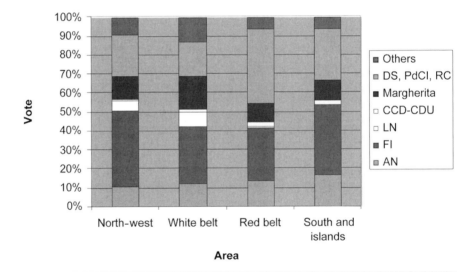

Figure 7.1. Vote by geographical area (Chamber proportional vote 2001)

Social class and occupation

Traditionally in Italy, class has been of lesser relevance for voting than in many other democracies. There are two reasons for this.

(1) The religious division – separating practising Catholics from those whose Catholicism is at most nominal or who harbour feelings of antipathy

towards the Church – has always cross-cut class divisions. This means that a worker who attends mass regularly may feel unable to support (the traditionally anti-clerical) parties of the left with the result that class solidarity in voting is reduced.

(2) The First Republic's two largest parties, the DC and the PCI, both mobilised support on a cross-class basis. This was especially so in their subcultural strongholds. Here, support for each was a function of integration in dense social networks co-ordinated by the dominant party and involving all the major social classes (whose relations were thus largely collaborative rather than conflictual).

In most other advanced democracies a number of social trends have brought about a decline in the relevance of class for voting in recent decades. Such trends include all those associated with the post-war boom, such as rising living standards, growing levels of geographical and social mobility, rising levels of education and so forth. Paradoxically, these same social trends have in Italy led to an *increase* in the relevance of class for voting. For they have brought growing secularisation and a decline in the capacity of 'subcultural belonging' to mobilise voters. Since religion and the subcultures had 'dampened' the effects of class, the result of their waning has been to increase the latter's relevance (Diamanti and Mannheimer, 2002) (Box 7.5).

Religious divisions

Religion is less relevant in structuring the distribution of the vote than it was in the initial post-war decades. There are three reasons for this.

(1) The social trends mentioned above have brought a decline in the proportion of the religiously observant: In 1992, 55 per cent of voters attended church at least two or three times per month; by 2001 this had declined to 39 per cent (Table 7.5).

(2) The same social trends have brought a decline in the political distinctiveness of those who have nevertheless continued to be observant: In 1992, a much larger proportion of the regular church goers supported the DC than was true of voters generally, and they gave very short shrift to parties standing in the communist tradition. In 2001, this basic pattern remained. That is, larger proportions of regular churchgoers than of voters generally voted for parties (FI, CCD-CDU, the Margherita) that claimed to be the DC's 'rightful heirs', and the proportions supporting parties standing in the communist tradition continued to be below average. But the pattern was less pronounced.

(3) The party-system destructuration of the 1990s led parties that were 'successors' to the DC to resurface on both sides of the main centre-left/ centre-right divide. In other words, parties that specifically appealed to

Box 7.5

The significance of class in Italian electoral politics
As Diamanti and Mannheimer (2002) have shown, the most striking class/occupational divisions in terms of voting appear to be those, within the middle class, between the self-employed and the employed, and among the latter, between those who are employed in the private sector and those who are employed in the public sector. Thus, if at the 2001 election the self-employed gave 65.7 per cent of their votes to the centre right, then they gave only 27.2 per cent to the centre left. The corresponding distribution among the employed was 40.0 and 52.1 percent for the centre right and centre left respectively. Meanwhile, among those employed in the private sector, the centre right won 50.6 per cent (to the centre left's 41.1), while among those employed in the public sector, it won only 36.5 per cent (to the centre left's 55.3) (Diamanti and Mannheimer, 2002: tables 3 and 5). Elsewhere in the system of social stratification, voting profiles are not nearly as distinct (manual workers, for example, divide their support pretty much evenly between the centre right and centre left). However, socio-economic distinctions in voting are politically important since the categories concerned are large and are ones whose demands have occupied a central place in political competition between centre right and centre left in recent years. For example, the self-employed (that is, artisans, shop-keepers, small businesspeople and self-employed professionals) constitute over one-third of the economically active population (Diamanti and Mannheimer, 2002: 140). And though the centre left continues to do well among this category in the 'red belt', elsewhere the centre right, and especially Forza Italia and the Northern League, have successfully capitalised on its demands by giving an especially high profile to issues such as reducing levels of state intervention, tax cuts and labour-market 'flexibility'.

Catholics *as* Catholics, as the DC had successfully done, were now to be found in *both* of the two main coalitions of centre left and centre right. As a result, religion has only a very weak impact on support for one or other of the two coalitions. Thus, regular churchgoers are slightly more likely than the population of voters as a whole to support parties of the centre right, and slightly less likely to support parties of the centre left. But the differences are not large: only about 5 per cent in each case.

This is not to say that religion is now *irrelevant* for electoral politics. That this is far from being the case is suggested by the row percentages in Table 7.5. These show – for example – that the proportion of regular churchgoers among supporters of FI, the CCD–CDU and the Margherita is larger than among voters generally, and that the CCD–CDU, indeed, derives almost all of its support from this category. It is not surprising, then, that of all the parties, this is the one most closely identified with the positions of the Church on such issues as bioethics, gay and lesbian rights and so forth. However, given the composition of their electorates, none of the three parties can afford to stray too far

Table 7.5. Religious observance and party support, 1992 and 2001

Column % / Row % / N of cases	Frequency of church attendance 1992				Frequency of church attendance 2001		
Party voted for 1992	Once per month or less	Two or three times per month or more	Total	*Party voted for 2001*	Once per month or less	Two or three times per month or more	Total
MSI	1.9	2.9	2.5	AN	14.4	12.1	13.5
	35.6	64.4	100.0		65.2	34.8	100.0
	5	9	14		204	109	312
LN	11.0	8.3	9.6	LN	2.5	2.2	2.4
	52.6	47.4	100.0		63.7	36.3	100.0
	28	25	53		35	20	55
DC	16.9	44.0	31.6	F1	31.0	39.7	34.4
	24.3	75.7	100.0		52.2	44.8	100.0
	42	132	175		438	355	794
				CCD–CDU	0.4	3.9	1.8
					14.5	85.5	100.0
					6	35	41
				Total centre right parties	48.3	57.9	52.1
					56.8	43.2	100.0
					683	519	1,202
				Margherita	10.1	13.3	11.3
					54.4	45.6	100.0
					142	119	261
PSI	17.5	9.7	18.4	Other centre left	3.2	19.2	26.6
	59.1	40.9	100.0		55.6	44.4	100.0
	44	29	101		45	172	613
PDS, RC	28.7	10.1	13.5	DS, PdCI, RC	31.2	4.0	3.5
	71.2	28.8	100.0		71.9	28.1	100.0
	72	30	74		441	36	81
				Total centre left parties	44.5	36.5	41.4
					65.8	34.2	100.0
					628	327	955
Others	20.5	21.3	20.9	Others	4.4	3.4	4.0
	44.6	55.4	100.0		67.3	32.7	100.0
	52	64	116		62	30	92
Spoilt or blank ballot	3.5	3.6	3.6	Spoilt or blank ballot	2.7	2.2	2.5

Table 7.5. (*cont.*)

Column % Row % N of cases	Frequency of church attendance 1992				Frequency of church attendance 2001		
	44.4	55.6	100.0		66.7	33.3	100.0
	9	11	20		39	19	58
Total	100.0	100.0	100.0	Total	100.0	100.0	100.0
	45.5	54.5	100.0		61.2	38.8	100.0
	251	301	552		1,412	896	2,308

Note: Within each cell, top figure = column per cent; middle figure = row per cent; bottom figure = no. of cases.
Source: My own elaboration based on Italian National Election Study (ITANES); data available at http://csa.berkeley.edu: 7502/cattest.html.

from more-or-less conservative positions on such issues; for, as well as winning over *new* voters, they must retain the support of *existing* voters if they are grow.

The problem for parties is that it is often extremely difficult to pursue the two goals simultaneously. Consequently, rather than facing the uncertain electoral consequences of radical innovation, parties may prefer, instead, to emphasise existing issue positions. In this way, they guard against losing the support they already have. And in doing so, they perpetuate the salience in political debate of these issues, and therefore the impact on voters' choices of the broader division – religion in this case – to which the issues are related. So although religion is now of lesser significance for understanding the behaviour of the Italian electorate than it once was, it cannot yet be considered extinct.

Ideological divisions

At least in terms of its traditional manifestations, ideology too has declined in significance without disappearing altogether. Prior to the collapse of the Berlin Wall in 1989, communism and fear of communism defined what was the most deeply felt division running through the electorate. Anti-communism was one of the three main pillars on which support for the DC rested (the other two being clientelism and Catholicism), and it went a long way towards explaining the seeming paradox that though on average Italians have a lower opinion of their politicians and institutions of government than the publics of most other European democracies, the proportions that turn out to vote are regularly among the highest (Figure 7.2). Though one may not particularly like the political party one votes for, if the alternative appears sufficiently odious or fearful, then one will be induced to support it more or

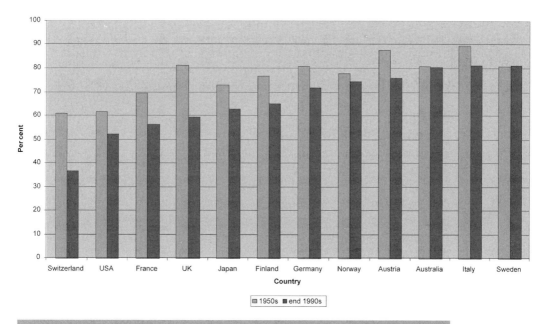

Figure 7.2 Turnout at general elections in twelve democracies
Source: 'La democrazia: nuovi scenari, nuovi poteri. Spunti per un dibattito', web.
tiscalinet.it/pslvr/download/feb/feltrin.ppt.

less regardless of its apparent shortcomings. The conservative newspaper editor, Indro Montanelli, was aware of this when, in the face of the PCI's predicted advance in 1976, he famously exhorted his readers to hold their noses and vote Christian Democrat.

One way of measuring the significance of ideological divisions in the electorate is by asking survey respondents about parties they would never consider voting for under any circumstances. In the 1980s, Mannheimer and Sani (1987: 109) found that 57 per cent of their respondents indicated that they 'would never' vote for the PCI. By 1990, this proportion had declined to 51 per cent and by 2001 to 46 per cent. In 2001, the proportions mentioning Forza Italia as a party they would never vote for were even lower – 37 per cent – and even AN is totally precluded as a possibility by less than half (46 per cent).[8] This is surprising, because AN is perceived as relatively extreme by voters: they give it an average of 8.6 when asked to score it 1 to 10 to indicate their perceptions of its location on the left–right spectrum.

An ideological – or perhaps more aptly, cultural – difference that appears to be growing in significance in Italy as in other democracies is the one separating 'materialists' on the one hand, from 'post-materialists' on the other. These two terms derive from the work of Ronald Inglehart (1971), who has claimed to discern a 'silent revolution' in the political cultures of

Western democracies. Reduced to its essentials, Inglehart's thesis is that the combination of affluence, peace and security of the post-war years as compared to the years before the war has brought a shift in the balance of value priorities among Western electorates away from concerns with personal security and material affluence towards a concern with 'quality-of-life' issues such as the environment and civil liberties. More precisely, the argument is that since political attitudes and beliefs tend to take shape during one's formative years and to become increasingly resistant to change thereafter, those whose youth was spent in the relatively lean, pre-war years will give greater priority to 'material' values than post-war generations for whom, as compared to their forebears, 'post-material' values will be of relatively greater importance. Consequently, the proportions of Western electorates for whom post-material issues have greater priority than material issues can be expected to increase with the passage of time as older cohorts gradually die off.

The directors of the 1994 edition of the Italian National Election Study included two questions specifically designed to measure material and post-material value priorities. Respondents were first asked which political goals they considered more important: fighting crime or guaranteeing freedom of speech. Then they were asked which of these goals they considered more important: fighting inflation or protecting the environment. Materialists are defined as those choosing the first options in both cases, post-materialists those choosing both of the second options.

According to the National Election Study data, these two 'pure' categories account for about one-third and one-fifth of the electorate respectively. In accordance with the Inglehart thesis, the proportion of the electorate falling into the second category appears to be growing with the passage of time: 14 per cent of those born before 1936 fall into the category; 16 per cent of those born between 1936 and 1955, and 23 per cent of those born thereafter.

If this suggests that the division is of major and growing numerical significance, then its political significance is suggested by the figures in Table 7.6. These show that the division has a statistically significant impact on voters' orientations. Post-materialists are almost twice as likely to identify with the left than with the right. Materialists are one-third more likely to identify with the right than with the left.

■ The general elections of 2006 and 2008

2006

The general election of 9 and 10 April was one of the closest fought in Italy's history. In the Chamber of Deputies, the centre-left Unione emerged ahead of the CdL by just 24,755 votes (though owing to the electoral law, the majority in terms of seats was a comfortable 66). In the Senate, the Unione won just two

Table 7.6. Value priorities and left–right self-placement, 1994

Column % Left–right self-placement	Value priorities Materialist	Mixed	Post-materialist	Total
Left	32.4	41.8	50.9	40.5
Centre	25.5	20.9	19.5	22.1
Right	42.2	37.3	29.5	37.4
Total	100.0	100.0	100.0	100.0
No. of cases	681	1,004	397	2,082

Note: Chi square $p < 0.01$.
Source: My own elaboration based on Italian National Election Study (ITANES) data
available at http://csa.berkeley.edu:%207502/cattest.html.

seats more than the CdL (and was behind by 124,273 votes). However, what was most striking about the outcome was less the sheer narrowness of the centre left's victory than the fact that what polls had suggested would be a certain triumph was instead an outcome that was uncertain until almost the last of the votes had been counted.[9]

Almost equally striking was the sharp decline in the support for 'third forces', unattached to either of the two coalitions. In 2001 support for these forces was 4 per cent (and the support climbs to over 10 per cent if one includes forces – Bonino List, IdV, Social Movement – Tricoloured Flame, (Movimento Sociale-Fiamma Tricolore, MSFT) – aligned in 2006, but which in 2001 competed against the two coalitions). But in 2006 it was barely 1 per cent: see Table 7.7. The proximate cause was a decline in third-force candidacies in the first place. This was a development that was strongly encouraged by the electoral law; for the latter stipulated higher thresholds for non-aligned than for aligned forces. And, most importantly, it provided that the votes of *all* parties – not just the votes of those eligible to receive seats – were to count in determining allocation of the majority premium.

The impact of long-term social factors on voters' choices could be seen in the figures showing the limited extent of vote switching between one coalition and the other. The vote in 2006 confirmed the stability, registered at previous general elections, of the overwhelming majority of voters. This can be seen from the figures in Table 7.8. These show that, as in 2001, very few of those who had voted for one of the two coalitions at the earlier contest switched to the other. The figures show, too, that what switches there were, were largely 'self-cancelling'.

In the effort to explain why, in contrast to the expectations generated by pre-election polls, the centre left's victory was so narrow, some commentators emphasised the impact on voters' choices of short-term factors associated with the campaign. Two in particular were emphasised.

Table 7.7. Election results, Chamber of Deputies, 2006

Lists/ coalitions	ITALY (Majority-Premium) Votes No.	%	Seats No.	%	VALLE D'AOSTA Votes No.	Seats No.	FOREIGN CONSTITUENCY Votes No.	Seats No.	TOTAL Votes No.	Seats No.
L'Ulivo	11,930,983	31.3	220	35.7					11,930,983	220
RC	2,229,464	5.8	41	6.6					2,229,464	41
RnP	990,694	2.6	18	2.9					990,694	18
PdCI	884,127	2.3	16	2.6					884,127	16
IdV	877,052	2.3	16	2.6			27,432	1	904,484	17
Greens	784,803	2.1	15	2.4					784,803	15
UDEUR	534,088	1.4	10	1.6			9,692	0	543,780	10
Pensioners' Party	333,278	0.9	0	0.0	1,135	0			334,413	0
SVP	182,704	0.5	4	0.6					182,704	4
Other Unione parties	255,405	0.7	0	0.0					255,405	0
Autonomie Liberté Democratie	–	–	–	–	34,167	1			34,167	1
L'Unione-Prodi	–	–	–	–			422,330	6	422,330	6
UNIONE (tot.)	19,002,598	49.8	340	55.1	35,302	1	459,454	7	19,497,354	348
FI	9,048,976	23.7	137	22.2			202,407	3	9,251,383	140
AN	4,707,126	12.3	71	11.5					4,707,126	71
UDC	2,580,190	6.8	39	6.3	2,282	0	65,794	0	2,648,266	39
LN-MPA*	1,747,730	4.6	26	4.2	1,566	0	20,227	0	1,769,523	26
DC-New PSI	285,474	0.7	4	0.6					285,474	4
Alternativa Sociale	255,354	0.7	0	0.0	1,587	0	7,102	0	264,043	0
MSFT	230,506	0.6	0	0.0	430	0	1,133	0	232,069	0
Other CdL parties	122,487	0.3	0	0.0					122,487	0
FI-AN	–	–	–	–	13,372	0			13,372	0
Per l'Italia nel mondo	–	–	–	–			73,289	1	73,289	1
CdL (tot.)	18,977,843	49.7	277	44.9	19,237	0	369,952	4	19,367,032	281
OTHERS (tot.)	172,902	0.5	0	0.0	24,118	0	146,008	1	343,028	1
TOTAL	38,153,343	100.0	617	100.0	78,657	1	975,414	12	39,207,414	630

Note: * MPA = Movimento per le Autonomie.
Source: Chiaramonte (2008, table 10.1).

Table 7.8. Vote flows 1996–2001 (Chamber plurality arena) and 2001–2006

Vote in 2001	Vote in 1996 Column percent				
	Centre right	Centre left	Other	Abstention / blank ballot	Too young
Centre right	84.7	9.0	40.4	29.3	34.2
Centre left	4.9	80.7	17.3	15.3	27.6
Other	1.5	1.4	28.8	1.3	4.8
Abstention blank ballot	9.0	8.8	13.5	54.1	33.4

Vote in 2006	Vote in 2001 Column percent				
	Centre right	Centre left	Other	Abstention	Too young
Centre right	77.2	7.2	32.0	26.9	34.6
Centre left	8.1	80.7	40.5	25.6	42.1
Abstention	14.4	11.8	25.4	47.3	23.3

Source: Figures for vote flows 1996–2001 based on my own elaboration of Italian National Election Study (ITANES) data available at http://csa.berkeley.edu:%207502/ cattest.html; figures for vote flows 2001–2006 taken from the results of an Swg survey published in *la Repubblica*, 13 April 2006, p.13.

(1) It was pointed out that the fiscal aspects of 'the new start' that the centre left was proposing allowed centre-right spokespersons to push it into a corner and keep it on the defensive for the last ten days of the campaign. In particular, Berlusconi was able to exploit ambiguities surrounding the centre left's proposals for the reintroduction of inheritance tax for (unquantified) 'large estates', and proposals to harmonise the tax rates on financial activities. In doing so, Berlusconi reinforced the impression of a reversal of governing and opposition roles, with the centre left, not the centre right, being forced to account for its policy choices. One of the most widely accredited hypotheses advanced to account for the unexpected narrowness of the centre left's victory is therefore that which emphasises the significance of the tax issue (Diamanti, 2006).

(2) Much was made of the presumed shortcomings of the centre left's campaign more generally. It was said, for example, that while Berlusconi 'imposed his frantic populism' in messages 'inspired by individual wealth, houses, cars, mobile phones', Prodi 'condemned the elimination of the primary surplus, a notion impossible to grasp', in a 'dull' and 'affected' campaign that emphasised his technical 'competence' (Berselli, 2006: 32–8).

There are three problems with these explanations:

(1) They are based largely on conjecture and post-hoc reasoning: had Prodi achieved the expected convincing victory, then it would no doubt have been said that he had done so because while Berlusconi's frantic populism failed to convince voters disillusioned by the absent miracle, Prodi's campaign was sober and highly effective in appealing to competence, etc.

(2) To ask 'Why did the centre left fail to do as well as expected?' is to assume that the pre-election poll results, which appear to have been at variance with reality, can instead be taken as an accurate benchmark against which to measure performance. This shifts the focus of explanation away from the technical problems associated with polling to supposed anomalies in the objective behaviour of parties and/or voters.[10]

(3) The assumption that the centre left 'failed' overlooks the fact that if we take as our benchmark not poll-based expectations but actual voting behaviour in the past, then it was not *reasonable* to anticipate a victory more comfortable than the one actually achieved.

It was not *reasonable* to anticipate a victory more comfortable than the one actually achieved because at all of the three previous elections, the centre left trailed the centre right in terms of votes,[11] while in 2006, for the first time, its Chamber vote moved from a position 3.8 per cent behind the centre right to a position 0.3 per cent ahead. We also know that at any election, by far the largest single pool of voters consists of stable supporters of one or the other of the two coalitions with very few voters ever switching between them. A modest victory is therefore all that one was entitled to expect.

The most parsimonious explanation for it is that after the experience of five years of centre-right government, voters were on balance more convinced by the offering of the centre left. It is an explanation whose plausibility is enhanced by the figures in Table 7.8. These show that the vote flows between 2001 and 2006 were of an entity similar to those between 1996 and 2001, but that they took place in the opposite direction.

2008

However it was to be explained, the centre left's victory quickly turned out to be – as Briquet and Mastropaolo (2008) have put it – 'poisoned'. As we have seen, in the circumstances of 2006, the electoral law encouraged the formation of the broadest coalitions possible. Consequently, the government that took office was staffed by no fewer than nine parties, that is, roughly from left to right: by RC, the PdCI, the Greens, the DS, the Socialists, the Radicals, the Margherita, IdV and the UDEUR. The electoral law also allowed voters to support a *coalition* without having to vote for a party other than their most *preferred* party; and it stipulated that every vote counted for the purposes of assignment of the majority premium, even those of parties below the thresholds. This undermined incentives on the parties to remain united, encouraging them, after the election, to cultivate their own electoral niches by distinguishing themselves from their allies and turning their backs on 'responsible' behaviour. The Government's instability was further enhanced by the fact that each party was indispensable for its survival in office; for this gave even the smallest an opportunity to seek to get its own way in negotiations with coalition partners by threatening to bring the executive down.

All of this nourished a vicious circle of growing instability and growing unpopularity. Each party, seeking to maximise its own support and therefore to compete for media attention, was driven to engage in provocation and confrontation. Finding it difficult, therefore, to control the political agenda to ensure its survival, the Government was, consequently, able to do little to counteract the tendency of the media, in their constant search for the newsworthy, to highlight feuds and divisions and so frame the government as 'catastrophic' (Roncarolo and Belluati, 2008). In doing so the media necessarily gave credence to the opposition's portrayal of the Government as incompetent and lacking the support of a clear majority of voters – so fuelling the downward trajectory in its poll ratings, shortly after it took office. And the more the Government was *portrayed* as litigious and unstable, the more likely it was *actually* to be so as the parties, first, argued about how to retrieve the position and then came to be driven by a logic of *si salvi chi può*.

When this situation came to be combined with objective economic difficulties, enabling the state of the country to be framed as one of irreversible decline and depression (Capriati, 2009; Campus, 2009), the climate of opinion thus created made easier the abandonment of the Government by UDEUR leader, Clemente Mastella, whose actions, in January 2008, were precipitated by attempts to reform the electoral law, which had done so much to destabilise the Government from the start (see Newell 2009). Fresh elections were called for 13 and 14 April.

The choices presented to voters at the election differed radically from those of the past and were heavily influenced by the merger of the Margherita and the DS, in 2007, in the Democratic Party (PD). Though the combination might have seemed unlikely, it was arguably facilitated by

- the thought that it would enhance the cohesion of the centre left by giving it the 'coalition maker' that it lacked;
- the groundswell of support for the project that had accumulated among centre-left supporters;[12]
- the reduction in size of the ideological obstacles in the way of merger through the ex-Communists' adherence to a rather indistinct and eclectic set of reformist values – shared on the other side by the heirs to a political outlook (that of the left of the old DC) – that already had a tradition of seeking accommodation with the Communists (Berselli, 2007: 45);
- neutralisation of the power of potential losers from the project within the two main founding parties by the October 2007 election of the leader and

241

constituent assembly. This, like the October 2005 primaries, was open to everyone. It thus gave those *without* any prior involvement with either party the opportunity to be involved in the foundation process on the same terms as those *with* such involvement.

Most important to note is that the PD's emergence was accompanied by a declaration by Walter Veltroni, elected leader in October 2007, that governments had hitherto been too heterogeneous to be able to act incisively with regard to the country's structural problems. For this reason, Veltroni continued, the PD would 'move beyond the idea that what counts is to win elections, that is, to beat the opposing line-up by fielding the broadest coalition possible regardless of its actual capacity to govern the country' (Veltroni, 2007: 20); that therefore at the next election the PD would run alone, whatever the electoral law.

When the 2008 elections were called, Veltroni had good reasons to confirm this choice:

- Fighting the elections on the basis of the coalition that had presented itself in 2006, and therefore having to defend a government that was deeply unpopular, was not a winning proposition[13] – while running alone enabled the PD to be presented as something new and Veltroni to take his distance from the Prodi government.
- An independent stance offered to give Veltroni bargaining power that Prodi never had. It enabled him to offer to the very small parties, the so-called micro-formations, an arrangement that would be confined to places on *his* lists and on *his* terms, failing which these formations might risk electoral annihilation.
- An independent stance offered the possibility of squeezing the vote of rivals on the left, whose supporters would be forced to decide between a vote for their *most* preferred choice and a *voto utile* for the formation most likely to defeat the prospect of their *least* preferred outcome.[14]
- Even if, as seemed likely, the PD failed to win, running alone had the advantage that, since the thresholds are higher for non-aligned than for aligned lists, the seats not assigned to the winning coalition would have to be shared with fewer lists (Floridia, 2008).

The only exceptions Veltroni made to his decision involved a coalition arrangement with Antonio di Pietro's IdV, and the agreement to host a small number of Radicals on the PD's lists. The agreement with IdV was designed to bring the support of those voters driven by anti-political sentiments (Vecchi, 2008: 13). The agreement with the Radicals was designed to reassure voters with left-wing sympathies that the new PD would not concede too much to those in the party whose sympathies are strongly driven by religious values.

Veltroni's decision then precipitated a sequence of actions and reactions on the part of the other main political actors that showed how the construction of the electoral offer for 2008 could be explained as a game of strategic interdependence given the framework of constraints imposed by the electoral system.

First, the emergence of the PD had provoked the breakaway, from the DS, of the Sinistra Democratica (Democratic Left, SD). Since it saw in the merger of the DS and the Margherita the simultaneous disappearance – uniquely in Europe – of Italy's main party of socialism and the left, the SD had as the fundamental objective giving life to it in the first place the unification of the parties of the Italian left in a single organisation. Its view of the significance of the PD's appearance is one that was shared by RC. Consequently, the 2008 election saw RC and the DS form, together with the PdCI and the Greens, an electoral coalition, in competition with the PD, that took the name Sinistra l'Arcobaleno (Rainbow Left, SA). As the largest of the groupings to the left of the PD – and of those groupings, alone capable of surmounting the vote thresholds – RC saw in the SA an opportunity to establish for itself a position of leadership over the Italian left as a whole. The PdCI and the Greens, which had already come together for the purposes of the 2006 election, saw in the new SA an opportunity to escape the consequences of any new electoral law that might penalise smaller groupings running independently.

On the centre right, the belief that the probable election winner would be Berlusconi immediately strengthened the entrepreneur's position as coalition leader, putting him in a similar position of power vis-à-vis his own potential allies as the one in which Veltroni found himself vis-à-vis *his* potential allies. This then enabled him to insist on the idea of a single list, the Popolo della Libertà (People of Freedom, PdL), bringing together FI and AN, and whichever of the remaining centre-right parties could be persuaded to join it:

- AN leader, Gianfranco Fini, was more than willing to embrace Berlusconi's idea given that he, of all potential contenders, would be the best placed to assume the leadership after Berlusconi.
- Northern League leader, Umberto Bossi, on the other hand, had considerable bargaining power because his electoral support was highly concentrated geographically. This enabled him to decline the invitation to renounce his party's separate identity within a single list and instead to obtain a coalition agreement.
- The micro-formations – small 'personal' parties based on the charisma of single individuals – were in no position to resist this and quickly fell into line (Buzzanca, 2008a: 2).
- The UDC and la Destra (bringing together a number of AN dissidents and groupings of the far right) were more than just 'virtual' or 'personal' parties, and unlike the latter had identities and genuine political traditions to defend. Faced with the choice between the threat of liquidation or defence of their autonomy, albeit in unfavourable circumstances, they chose the latter and decided to run alone (Di Caro, 2008: 2).

Berlusconi and the centre right won a decisive victory (Table 7.9). But from the point of view of voting behaviour, the 2008 election held relatively few surprises. Voters were clearly not static: analyses of how voters changed their choices between 2006 and 2008 (Buzzanca, 2008b; Consortium, 2008) showed

Table 7.9. Chamber of Deputies election results, 2006 and 2008

2006 election				2008 election				
Parties and alliances	Vote (%)	Vote (%)*	Seats (no.)	Parties and alliances	Vote (no.)	Vote (%)	Vote (%)*	Seats (no.)
Unione				*Walter Veltroni*				
L'Ulivo	31.3	30.4	220	PD	12,092,998	33.2	32.4	211
IdV	2.3	2.2	16	IdV	1,593,675	4.4	4.3	28
RC	5.8	5.7	41	SA	1,124,418	3.1	3.0	0
PdCI	2.3	2.3	16					
Greens	2.0	2.0	15					
RnP	2.6	2.5	18	Partito Socialista	355,581	1.0	1.0	0
Udeur	1.4	1.4	10					
Other Unione parties	2.1	2.0	4					
Total	49.8		340					
Overseas constituency				*Overseas constituency*				
Unione		1.1	6	PD	331,567		0.9	6
IdV		0.1	1	IdV	41,589		0.1	1
				SA	28,353		0.1	
Udeur		0.0		Partito Socialista	31,774		0.1	
Total (National + overseas)		**49.7**	347					
CdL				*Silvio Berlusconi*				
FI	23.7	23.1	137	PdL	13,628,865	37.4	36.5	272
AN	12.3	12.0	71					
LN	4.6	4.5	26	LN	3,024,522	8.3	8.1	60
				MPA	410,487	1.1	1.1	8
UDC	6.8	6.6	39	UDC	2,050,319	5.6	5.5	36
DC-New PSI	0.7	0.7	4					
MSFT	0.6	0.6	0	La Destra	885,229	2.4	2.4	0
Other CdL parties	1.0	1.0	0					
Total	49.7		277					
Overseas constituency				*Overseas constituency*				
FI		0.5	3	PdL	314,357		0.8	4
Per l'Italia nel mondo – Tremaglia		0.2	1					
UDC		0.2		UDC	81,450		0.2	
LN		0.0						
Other CdL parties		0.0		La Destra	14,609		0.0	
Total (National + overseas)		**49.4**	281					

Table 7.9. (*cont.*)

2006 election				2008 election				
Parties and alliances	Vote (%)	Vote (%)*	Seats (no.)	Parties and alliances	Vote (no.)	Vote (%)	Vote (%)*	Seats (no.)
Others				*Others*				
Autonomie Liberté Democratie (Valle d'Aosta)†	0.1	0.1	1	Autonomie Liberté Democratie (Valle d'Aosta)	23,311	0.1	0.1	1
Others	0.5	0.5		Others	1,161,267	3.4	3.1	2
Others (overseas const.)		0.4	1	Others (overseas const.)	169,387		0.4	1
National total	100.1	97.6	618	National total	36,350,672	100.0	97.5	618
Overseas const. total		2.5	12	Overseas const. total	1,013,086		2.6	12
Overall total		100.1	630	Overall total	37,363,758		100.1	630

Notes: * The percentages in this column are based on the overall total of votes cast, i.e. including the overseas constituency.
† Autonomie Liberté Democratie was associated with the Unione. Votes cast in the single-member Valle d'Aosta constituency are not included in the totals used to determine allocation of the majority premium.
Sources: www.repubblica.it/speciale/2006/elezioni/camera/index.html (2006 figures); www.repubblica.it/speciale/2008/elezioni/camera/index.html (2008 figures).

that the UDC lost votes to its right in the name of a *voto utile*, as did the SA, for the same reason. A significant proportion of former supporters of the SA parties abstained. The PD's gains from the parties to its left were to a degree offset by losses to the UDC. The LN and IdV made dramatic gains. But as at previous elections, once again, shifts overwhelmingly took place within the centre left and centre right rather than across them (Natale, 2008). Thus, the change in the distribution of voting preferences between the two main coalitions was much less dramatic than underlying shifts between the parties within them.

By contrast, the party-system consequences were considerable. The decline in support for the SA parties meant that the list failed to cross the vote thresholds thus ensuring that, for the first time since 1948, Parliament would have no socialist or communist representatives of any hue whatsoever. In fact, leaving aside the linguistic minority parties and one independent candidate in the overseas constituency, the UDC was the only third force to achieve parliamentary representation at all.[15] As a consequence, there was a dramatic reduction in party-system fragmentation. The actual number of groups in the Chamber of Deputies declined from the fourteen in existence at the end of the previous legislature, to six: the PdL and the LN on the governing side; the PD and IdV on the centre left; the UDC and the residual 'mixed' group (Table 7.10). The main parties of government and opposition, the PdL and the PD, now shared a proportion of seats (78 per cent) that was higher than ever previously achieved in the history of the Republic.

Table 7.10. Composition of the parliamentary groups, Chamber of Deputies and Senate, 2008

Group	Chamber No.	Chamber %	Senate No.	Senate %
IdV	28	4.4	14	4.3
Lega Nord Padania	60	9.5	26	8.1
PD	218	34.6	119	37.0
PdL	273	43.3	146	45.3
UDC	35	5.6	11	3.4
Groupo Misto	16	2.5	6	1.9
Total	630	99.9	322	100.0

The reduction in party-system fragmentation meant that the government that took office did so with prospects of lasting the entire legislature that were better than those of any other since the war: the small number of its parties and the narrowness of the ideological space they covered freed it from the blackmail to which the previous government had been exposed; the power of the incoming Prime Minister was symbolised by the fact that he is said to have gone in to the customary post-election meeting with the President with the list of ministers already prepared.

A governing majority staffed by just two groups and the emergence of a 'shadow cabinet' – a relative novelty in the Italian context – drawn from the largest of the non-governing parties made it seem reasonable to anticipate that the capacity of the executive to subordinate the legislature to its will would increase. It also seemed likely that the legislature would be marked by rather more straightforward patterns of interaction between more cohesive majority and minority coalitions than had been true of the past. Politics since the war had of course always been based on the assumption that at any given moment certain parties were part of the governing coalition and the remainder part of the 'opposition'. However, the legislative behaviour of the parliamentary groups had often belied such simple conceptualisations. As we saw in chapter 4, most proposals that made it on to the statute book did so thanks to ample majorities drawn from across the governing/opposition divide. Moreover, there was no formal recognition in Parliament's standing orders of *an* official opposition.

As Russo and Verzichelli (2009) point out, if in some respects, initial evidence points in the direction of a 'strong' legislature in terms of decisiveness and government steering capabilities, the evidence for the emergence of an 'adversarial' pattern of interaction between two cohesive bodies, the majority and the opposition, is so far mixed. Therefore, the extent to which the XVI legislature will see the emergence of a new relationship between it and the executive remains uncertain, with much depending on changes in the policy agenda and what this does for intra-coalition tensions on both the governing and opposition sides.

Conclusion

The 2006 general election brought about a further consolidation of the bipolar characteristic of Italy's party system, though it was a bipolarity based on a party system that remained highly fragmented. The 2008 election outcome changed that. In addition, for the third time in post-war Italy a contest was won by a single, pre-constituted, coalition aiming at an overall majority of seats, so that the composition of the Government that took office after the election was the unmediated reflection of the choices of voters. That this was the case was undoubtedly facilitated by the new electoral system which ensured that with *one and the same* vote, the voter was able to make a choice *both* of party (to which seats are allotted in proportion to its vote) *and* of coalition (where the coalition with most votes wins an automatic majority of seats, at least in the Chamber).

The election also brought to office a government whose composition – with a clear cabinet majority for Berlusconi's own party – reflected the power, within it, of his position as Prime Minister. The days of the 'mediator prime minister', a figure without any of the leverage over the conduct of ministers that goes with the power to hire and fire, appeared finally to come to an end with the 2001 election – without, however, fully giving way to an alternative model of prime ministers as authoritative leaders: Berlusconi had still been obliged to manage a range of centrifugal tendencies within his coalition (Bull and Newell, 2005). As his coalition is seemingly less fragmented and ideologically diverse now even than his 2001 coalition was, Berlusconi's position within it must be adjudged as stronger. This could only be of benefit to the Government as it sought to tackle Italy's long-standing economic problems, the topic to which we turn our attention in the next chapter.

Further reading

For an analysis of the significance of the latest general election for the evolution of Italy's party system, see the chapters brought together in my edited volume *The Italian General Election of 2008: Berlusconi Strikes Back* (Basingstoke: Palgrave, 2009). Also very useful in this respect will be many of the articles in the 2008 edition of *Italian Politics* (New York and Oxford: Berghahn, 2009). Readers wishing to deepen their understanding of the evolution of the party system from a somewhat longer time perspective will find the annual *Italian Politics* volumes helpful generally. They might also wish to consult my edited volumes devoted to the two elections preceding the latest one, the elections of 2001 and 2006: *The Italian General Election of 2001: Berlusconi's Victory* (Manchester: Manchester University Press, 2002); *The Italian General Election of 2006: Romano Prodi's Victory* (Manchester: Manchester University Press, 2008). From an even longer time perspective, a very influential study of the evolution of the Italian party system from the immediate post-war period up to the 1970s is Paolo Farnetti's *The Italian Party System* (London: Pinter, 1985). An up-to-date overview of the most salient characteristics of voting behaviour in Italy can be found in chapter 3 of Maurizio Cotta and Luca Verzichelli's *Political Institutions in Italy* (Oxford: Oxford University Press, 2007). See also, Luciano Bardi, 'Electoral change and its impact on the party system in Italy', *West European Politics*, vol. 30, no. 4, September 2007, pp. 711–32).

▪ Notes

1. The precipitating factor was statements made by party leader Gianfranco Fini, during to an official visit to Israel a few days earlier, concerning the crimes of Fascism. The statements appear to have led Mussolini to feel that her continued membership of the party was made impossible bearing in mind her personal relationship to the dictator and the significance of 'nostalgia' within the party.
2. Though we cannot be absolutely certain of this as we do not know how many of the voters that in fact supported the centre right would have refused to support a coalition that also included a party as extreme as the Fiamma.
3. The DS, the PPI, RI, the Democrats, the UDEUR, the Greens, the SDI, the PdCI, the European Republicans.
4. In 2001, the Margherita, whose leader, Francesco Rutelli, was at that time also the leader of the coalition, took 14.5 per cent of the proportional vote in the election for the Chamber of Deputies, a result that represented a considerable increase on the combined result (8.9 per cent) obtained by the Margherita's constituent parties at the European elections of 1999.
5. FI's vote declined from the 29.5 per cent it had won in 2001 to 21.0 per cent, while both the UDC and the LN saw their vote shares rise (to 5.0 and 5.9 per cent respectively). Meanwhile, the parties of the centre left made only modest gains, passing from a combined share of 44.5 per cent in 2001 to 46.1 per cent in 2004.
6. That is, in 1996, the centre right won 40.3 per cent of the vote in the plurality arena, but 42.1 per cent in the proportional arena – while in 2001, when it took 45.4 per cent in the plurality arena and 49.6 per cent in the proportional arena, the difference was even larger.
7. In 2001, 43.6 per cent said they attended church at least two or three times per month as compared with 38.4 per cent of those in the rest of the country (Italian National Election Study (ITANES) data available at http://csa.berkeley.edu:7502/cattest.html).
8. Figures calculated from Italian National Election Study survey data for 1990 and 2001 available at http://csa.berkeley.edu:7502/cattest.html.
9. Recent narrow victories include the Israeli Knesset contest of 1981 (which saw the Likud party beat Labour by just 10,405 votes); the US presidential contest of 2000 (decided by just 537 votes in the state of Florida); the German federal election in 2005 (when the CDU/CSU emerged ahead of the SPD by just 1 per cent of the vote).
10. That there has long been reason to be doubtful of the polling evidence is suggested by the fact that the discrepancy between the coalitions' poll ratings and their actual performance was not something new but long-standing. For example, with just one exception, the opinion poll reports on the site 'Il

termometro politico', at http://brunik.altervista.org/index.html, had put the centre left ahead by some 5 per cent throughout the year 2004. The one exception was the report giving the actual results of the European Parliament election, where the distribution of the vote between the centre left and the centre right (46.1 per cent to 45.4 per cent) was similar to and every bit as close as the result for the 2006 election. It is for this reason (as well as the fact that opinion polls and exit polls told the same story) that the hypothesis according to which some centre-right supporters are unable or unwilling to reveal their true sympathies (Natale, 2006) is persuasive. Less persuasive is the hypothesis according to which the poll results were largely accurate and that there was a significant shift of support in favour of the centre right in the final stages of the campaign that was not publicly registered because of the ban on publishing poll findings after 24 March (Jampaglia, 2006).

11. It won in terms of seats in 1996 only because the centre right's vote was split.

12. This was demonstrated by the overwhelming endorsement given to Romano Prodi in the 2005 primaries and by the 2006 elections when the combined Ulivo list, presented for the Chamber by the DS and the Margherita, had a clear advantage (at 31.3 per cent) over the lists of its constituent parties (at 27.7 per cent) for the Senate.

13. As opinion polls confirmed. See, for example, Gualerzi (2008).

14. At least in the Chamber. For the Senate contest, the situation would vary, depending on the region of residence of the voter concerned.

15. Despite its independent stance, it was only slightly squeezed by the 'rational vote' argument (obtaining 5.6 per cent as compared to 6.8 per cent in 2006). Indeed, it was able to benefit, on the centre right, from perceptions that without it, Berlsuconi's coalition was skewed too far to the right, and on the centre left from voters disappointed with the outgoing government but unwilling to express such disappointment by going as far as to vote for the opposing coalition (Carbone and Newell, 2008).

IV

Policies and performances

8   Economic policy

▪ Introduction

In this and the next three chapters our attention shifts from the structures and processes of government to Italian governments' policy objectives. The nature of such objectives and how successfully they are pursued are important objects of study because of their impact on political behaviour and therefore, ultimately, on political stability. Governments' policy objectives and their success in achieving them are also, of course, of importance to ordinary citizens. Indeed, for most citizens they are essentially the only aspect of politics that really matters to them. Politics is not a central life interest as far as most people are concerned. Thus, they are unlikely to get excited about matters relating to political structures and processes – such as whether or not voting in Parliament should be secret, whether or not the President should be directly elected, as so on. About such policy matters as the crime rate, the cost of living, immigration, drugs and so forth, they do get excited, however.

   In this chapter the focus is on economic policy. By this I mean the predispositions of governments with regard to decisions whose purpose is to influence the production of commodities. We begin with economic policy because what governments are able to do in other policy areas is very heavily dependent on their policy in this area. Most other policy decisions require economic resources (taxation or borrowing) in order to fund them. This, in turn, requires measures to maintain and enhance society's capacity to produce the goods and services from which these resources can be derived. But that is not all. Since the early years of the twentieth century, expectations of what governments ought to accept responsibility for providing have expanded enormously. This means that the achievement of economic growth has become of increasing importance to governments. With growth, they are under much less pressure than they are without growth, from difficult allocation choices obliging them to reward one group at the expense of another (Calvert, 2002: 125). It is no exaggeration, then, to say that economic policy lies at the heart of governments' capacities to acquire, to use and to retain political power.

More so in the area of the economy than in most other policy areas, governments can will the means to desired outcomes but find it much more difficult to will the outcomes themselves. That is, they have the power to take measures they hope will *influence* outcomes, but not the power to *control* those outcomes. The achievement of these depends also on the behaviour of a range of non-state forces and actors whose collective power, in most instances, considerably exceeds that of individual governments.

This, in turn, highlights what can be termed the 'structural dependence' of states on the economic environment in which they operate and to whose characteristics they are, consequently, obliged to adapt themselves. In particular, in a globalised world, geography is of decreasing significance for what goes on in any one part of it, and this places major restrictions on governments' room for manoeuvre in economic matters. For example, they can levy taxes on businesses, but if the taxes are deemed too high, it is possible or likely that the businesses will just go elsewhere. When money can flow in and out of countries within minutes, changes in interest rates in the world's largest economy, the United States, have immediate implications, especially in terms of exchange rates, for the economic parameters facing governments elsewhere. Finally, in Italy's case, its decision to relinquish powers in the areas of interest and exchange rates, inherent in its decision to adopt the euro, constitutes an additional constraint with which governments must come to terms in matters economic.

In the light of these considerations, it will help understanding of the nature of Italian economic policy to begin with a description of the most important parameters of the economic context governments must work with.

■ The economic context

From a comparative point of view, Italy's economy is huge. In 2004, its Gross Domestic Product (GDP) at over 1.67 trillion dollars ($1,672,302,000,000) was the sixth highest in the world and amounted to over 5 per cent of the combined GDP of the 'high income' countries as defined by the World Bank.[1] Inevitably, given the existence of smaller economies but with wealthy inhabitants, Italy falls to a lower ranking when the comparison is in terms of GDP per head of population. Nevertheless, according to the Central Intelligence Agency's 'World Fact Book', with a GDP per head of $28,500, in 2005 the country retained a ranking that put it in thirtieth place out of 232 countries.[2]

There is a very sharp difference in terms of economic wellbeing between the northern and southern regions of the country. This difference is revealed by all the usual economic indicators. The eight regions of the South (Abruzzo, Molise, Puglia, Basilicata, Campania, Calabria, Sicily and Sardinia) account for approximately 36 per cent of the Italian population but only 24 per cent of its GDP. GDP per head amounts to 57 per cent of that of the central and northern regions (Signorini and Visco, 2002: 97). In 2003 unemployment in the southern regions was about double the average for the EU twenty-five, while in the North it was about half.[3] The southern question is thus among the most salient of the country's economic problems. The others are widely thought to be ones associated with the nature of the state, and its activities, on the one hand, and with the functioning of markets in Italy on the other.

Together, these three broad classes of factor are viewed as being linked to what have been much slower rates of growth since 1990 as compared both to earlier decades and to other countries. Whereas the average rate of growth for the 1970s was 3.9 per cent and for the 1980s 2.4 per cent, in the 1990s it went down to 1.4 per cent and in the six years between 2000 and 2005, it fell even further – to 1.1 per cent.[4] Whereas until 1990 growth rates generally speaking equalled and exceeded those of the other large European countries and the United States, since then they have been below the growth rates of these countries (Rossi, 2004, table 1) (Figure 8.1).

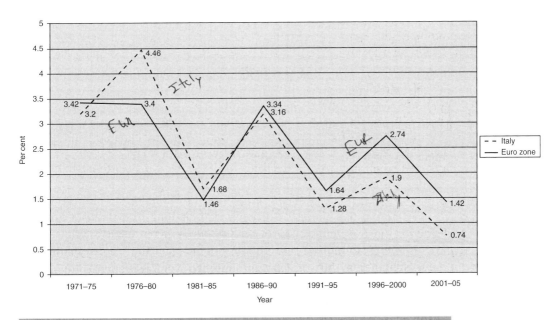

Figure 8.1. Growth of GDP in Italy as compared to growth rates of principal competitors
Source: adapted from OECD.Stat Extracts, http://stats.oecd.org/WBOS/index.aspx.

▪ The 'decline' thesis

These figures have given rise to a debate among scholars about whether they can be taken as evidence of a decline of the Italian economy and if so, what should be done about it.

The arguments in favour

Those convinced by the 'decline' thesis draw, with varying emphasis, on five arguments to support their case.

(1) Declining growth rates are above all a reflection of the continuing gap between North and South.
(2) The period from 1970 saw a number of important economic and social changes that initiated a long-term upward trend in the level of public debt.
(3) Compared to the other industrialised countries, Italy suffers from a number of shortcomings in terms of public services and regulation.
(4) The structure of Italian industry is problematic.
(5) The country's industrial structure has left Italy unusually exposed to the growth of competition from the newly industrialising countries (NICs).

Let us examine each of these in turn.

Continuing disparities between North and South

Supporters of the thesis of economic decline argue that had southern growth rates been higher, then it is likely that there would have been no overall decline. Instead, the early 1990s saw a growing divergence between the two areas. This was due, among other things, to labour-market rigidity, with national-level collective bargaining (see chapter 6) preventing wages from varying to reflect lower levels of productivity in the South. The divergence in terms of growth became smaller after 1996, but this, it is argued, was due less to a process of autonomous southern growth than to increases in rates of migration from south to north (Faini, 2003: 1079).

Supporters of the decline thesis are pessimistic about the prospects for an improvement in the economic position of the South:

(1) Past government efforts, throughout their long history, have failed to bring about economic convergence between North and South.
(2) There is an important vicious circle standing in the way of the South's relative improvement. This is the vicious circle that arises from the fact that an area that has an initial disadvantage is likely to remain disadvantaged because firms will prefer to locate in richer areas with their more promising markets. Among other things, firms' decisions to locate in such areas enable the provision of better infrastructural facilities than in poorer areas – this influencing the location decisions of subsequent firms, and so on.

The growth in public debt

The period from 1970, it is suggested, saw a number of important economic and social changes that initiated a long-term upward trend in the level of public debt. On the one hand, higher levels of public expenditure were induced by reforms such as the institution in 1970 of regional government (bringing a decentralisation of spending but not of taxation decisions), and the establishment in 1978 of a national health service. On the other hand, the growing significance for the Italian economy of small and medium-sized enterprises, especially in the 'Third Italy' (see chapter 5), ensured that tax receipts failed to match the growth in expenditure: in the first place, small enterprises bring with them opportunities for tax evasion unavailable to more visible larger enterprises (Trento, 2003: 1101–2); in the second place, Christian Democrat (DC)-led governments were unwilling to take measures that would reduce tax evasion but would damage the interests of a significant part of their electoral base.

Consequently, Italy experienced a growing level of public debt which reached a peak of almost 125 per cent of GDP in 1994. Efforts to reduce it since then have required significant increases in the burden of taxation (thus limiting the resources available for investment), while its sheer size (which remained at 106 per cent in 2003) has severely limited the scope for using public expenditure as a tool of macroeconomic management.

Relative shortcomings in public services and regulation

In policing and the system of justice, it is argued, frequent delays raise firms' transaction costs. Meanwhile, shortcomings in the system of public education, it is suggested, have resulted in a relatively uneducated, and thus a relatively immobile, inflexible, labour force. Being much more marked in the South than in the North, these problems highlight once again the significant role of 'southern backwardness' in depressing economic growth.

There have been reforms introduced under pressure from the EU's single-market requirements, and significant progress has been made since 1990 in the area of administrative reform and *delegificazione* (see chapter 4). Nevertheless, economic activity is still said to be handicapped by inefficiency in the public administration and by regulations whose effect is to restrict competition in a number of markets. These range from the markets for professional services to those for retail sales, tourist services and the distribution of news.

Since none of these factors, nor those mentioned in the two previous sections, is new, supporters of the 'decline' thesis are obliged to explain why they made their impact on growth felt only from 1990 and not before. Here they have recourse to the 'catching up' argument. This is the argument that growth in the earlier period took place despite the economy's structural weaknesses, because the latter were offset by the fact that the country was starting from a lower base as compared to its principal competitors. Growth

Table 8.1. Value added of manufacturing sectors (as percentage of total) for various countries, 1999

	Italy	Germany	France	UK	Japan	US
Food, drink and tobacco	10.6	9.0	14.6	13.2	11.9	9.8
Textiles, leather, shoes	13.3	2.6	5.0	5.2	3.1	3.9
Wood and wood products	2.8	2.0	1.6	1.3	0.9	3.1
Paper, printing and publishing	7.2	7.8	8.3	12.3	8.2	10.6
Chemicals, rubber, plastics	13.9	15.9	17.6	16.9	14.4	17.0
Non-metallic minerals	6.3	4.0	4.5	3.3	3.3	2.9
Metals and metal products	13.9	13.2	13.4	10.9	12.1	11.1
Machinery and equipment	20.8	28.0	19.7	22.2	30.1	26.6
Transport vehicles	5.9	14.6	11.5	10.6	10.2	11.5
Recycling, other manufacturing sectors	5.3	5.3	3.8	4.1	5.8	3.6

Notes: The data for the United States relate to 1998.
Source: Bianco, 2003: 68, table 3.

was easier to obtain in such circumstances than it is now as it could be had by imitating the success of others; now that catch-up has taken place, it is more likely to require more difficult original innovations.

The structure of Italian industry

Traditionally, Italian industry has been characterised by the import of raw materials and energy resources (in relatively short supply domestically). These have then been transformed into finished products in 'traditional' sectors – especially textiles, fashion, knitwear, footwear and furniture – and in mechanical engineering sectors – especially machinery, machine tools and household appliances – requiring relatively small quantities of capital, technology and highly qualified labour (Table 8.1).

Meanwhile, in almost all sectors, Italy has a larger proportion of small firms (Table 8.2), of a smaller average size than in other industrialised countries. Thus, firms with fewer than ten employees each, represent 95 per cent of the total; the average number of employees per firm is 3.9; 68.6 per cent of manufacturing employees work for firms employing fewer than a hundred people (Trento, 2003: 1095).

Specialisation and size appear to be related; while the link between the two has made it more difficult for Italy than for other countries to engage in the kind of industrial restructuring necessary to meet the shift that has taken place in world demand in the direction of high-tech products. That is, concentrating on traditional products in small-scale enterprises using employees with relatively low levels of human capital makes it difficult for firms to engage in the research and development required to move into the high-tech sectors and to grow in size (Trento, 2003; Onida, 2004). Unable to grow, firms have been obliged to remain focused on the traditional sectors where, as we saw in chapter 5, small scale is an advantage.

Therefore, while in the last decade other industrialised countries have been diversifying, Italy has reduced the number of sectors in which it specialises, focusing even more heavily on the traditional sectors, and suffering a declining share of world trade in the process. Thus, in 1995, Italy's share of world exports was 4.5 per cent. By 2003, that had dropped to 3.3 per cent.

The growth of competition from the NICs

This factor is directly related to the last one; for to a greater degree than is true of the other advanced countries, Italy's industrial structure mirrors that of the NICs. In other words, these countries are characterised by a concentration on precisely those sectors – such as clothing, textiles, footwear, furniture and wood products – in which Italy specialises, thus leaving Italy unusually exposed to competition from these countries.

This would not necessarily be a problem were it not for the fact that the sectors in question are labour intensive and that labour is precisely the factor of production that is most abundantly available in the NICs. Because it is abundantly available, it is also cheap and this means that, from the point of view of cost, the NICs' products are particularly competitive (those of China having caused particular alarm). Moreover, with advent of the euro, Italy is no longer able to maintain its competitive advantage by having recourse, as it once could and did, to devaluation of its currency.

As a consequence, the loss of market shares in the traditional sectors has been significant in recent years. Thus, between 1990 and 2002, Italy's share of the market in the EU fifteen declined from 21.6 to 12.3 per cent in lighting equipment; from 20.5 to 14.8 per cent in furniture and kitchens; from 30.2 to 15.2 per cent in sofas and chairs; from 24.1 to 10.5 per cent in metal household goods; from 16.4 to 12.9 per cent in ironware, furniture hinges, handles and locks; from 50.2 to 34.8 in ornamental stonework (Fortis and Curzio 2003: 1110–12).

The Arguments against

Those sceptical of the decline thesis make four points.

Overall growth rates, or growth rates per head?

First, they argue that growth rates can be misleading if viewed in isolation from information about population changes. What is important, they say, is the rate of growth *per head of population*. All other things being equal, the overall rate of growth must decline if the size of the economically active population is also declining. Largely because of falling birth rates (the rate of fertility declined continuously from 2.67 children per woman in 1965 to 1.44 in 1985), and notwithstanding growing immigration from the mid-1980s, the size of the labour force declined from 24,257,000 in 1992 to 23,598,000 in

Table 8.2. Economic decline? Key indicators 1971–2005

Indicators	Years						
	1971–5	1976–80	1981–5	1986–90	1991–5	1996–2000	2001–5
Av. public debt as % of GDP	50.1	59.9	70.5	92.7	114.9	116.9	106.7
Employment in manufacturing enterprises employing < 20 as % employed in manufacturing	n.a.	n.a	n.a	n.a	n.a	29.3	30.2
Productivity: annual % growth in GDP per hour worked	3.9	4.1	1.2	2.3	2.1	0.9	0.0
Unemployed as % of civilian labour force	n.a.	n.a	7.1	9.4	9.8	11.0	8.4

Source: Figures for public debt: Bull and Newell, 2005, ch. 2, 2004–5, Ministero dell'Economia e delle Finanze, www.dt.tesoro.it/Aree-Docum/Debito-Pub/DebitoPIL.htm_cvt.htm; remaining data drawn from OECD.Stat Extracts, http://stats.oecd.org/WBOS/index.aspx.

Table 8.3. Rates of population growth, fertility, and GDP per capita, 1971–2005

Indicators	Years						
	1971–5	1976–80	1981–5	1986–90	1991–5	1996–2000	2001–5
Av. annual rate of growth of population	0.59	0.35	0.06	0.04	0.04	0.04	0.57
Fertility: no. of children born to women aged 15–49	2.33	1.87	1.51	1.34	1.25	1.22	1.29
GDP per capita ($US, current prices and PPP)	4,443.98	7,433.25	11,518.12	15,571.56	19,655.42	23,586.35	27,257.89

Source: Adapted from OECD.Stat Extracts, http://stats.oecd.org/WBOS/index.aspx.

2000. Faini (2003) argues that the declining rates of growth can be explained in terms of factors such as these and that when growth is measured in per capita terms, the differences with the rest of Europe and the United States disappear altogether (Tables 8.3 and 8.4).

Reform of public services and regulations

Second, sceptics point out that it is true that the Italian economy suffers from structural problems such as inefficiencies in the provision of some public services and regulations that restrict competition. But, they argue, the 1990s witnessed a number of measures to correct these problems. They included

Table 8.4. Italy compared with major competitors on a range of economic indicators, 2006

Indicators (2006)	Italy	France	Germany	Countries UK	US	EU15	OECD
GDP per capita*	28,866	31,048	31,950	32,990	43,801	31,364	31,469
Growth in GDP per capita 1970–2006	2.1	2.0	2.0	2.1	2.0	2.1	2.1
Gross fixed capital formation as % of GDP	20.8	20.4	18.0	17.9	19.3	20.7	21.0
Labour compensation per hour**	21.3	28.4	26.7	n.a	n.a	n.a	n.a
Average hours actually worked***	1,800	1,564	1,436	1,669	1,797	1,625	1,777

Notes: * $US, current prices and PPP.
** Total economy, $US calculated using PPP, figures are for 2005.
*** Hours per year per person in employment.
Source: Adapted from OECD.Stat Extracts, http://stats.oecd.org/WBOS/index.aspx.

- the setting up, in 1990, of the Italian Competition Authority. This, as we saw in chapter 4 (Table 4.4) acts to ensure free competition and the avoidance of restrictive practices, the abuse of monopoly power and unfair and misleading advertising;
- liberalisation of the capital and credit, telecommunications, air transport and energy markets;
- the administrative reforms we discussed in chapter 4.

Therefore, while the effects of these measures in terms of growth have yet to be felt, and more remains to be done, the bases have been laid for future economic resurgence.

Competition of the NICs

Third, though Italy may be exposed to competition from the NICs in terms of cost, the latter is only one of the bases on which competition may take place. The other is quality. Therefore, some scholars argue that Italy's model of specialisation is not really at risk since competitive pressure from the NICs is attenuated by the inferior quality of the latters' products. In other words, the similarity of the industrial structures of Italy and the NICs is only apparent – meaning that they are not, in effect, competing in entirely the same markets. Others argue that Italy has an additional advantage as compared to the NICs in that its specialisation in traditional sectors has allowed it to acquire a comparative advantage, 'upstream', in production of the machinery and equipment required by its specialist sectors (Bianco, 2003: 72).

The capacity to adapt to change

Fourth, 'decline' implies incapacity to adapt an old model of production to changes in the surrounding world. But, it is argued, this is far from being the case with regard to Italy's present economic difficulties. Disappointing economic results since 1990 have at least in part been due to the efforts required to reduce inflation and budget deficits in order to qualify for membership of the single currency. And, while the Italian economy does have certain structural deficiencies, its capacity to adapt to change, with a future resurgence of growth, is assisted by a number of structural assets. These include:

- high levels of income per head, levels that in the North are among the highest in Europe;
- levels of labour productivity among the highest in the world;
- rates of return on invested capital that are at least as high as the European average;
- levels of remuneration of labour that are among the lowest in Europe;
- rates of growth that, notwithstanding 'the southern question', have in the last fifteen years been higher in some areas of the South than in the North (Toniolo, 2004: 15–16).

◼ Institutional and political influences and constraints on policy-making

Regardless of whether they are optimists or pessimists with regard to the thesis of Italy's economic decline, scholars have drawn attention to a range of economic policy issues that have been officially recognised as ones that need addressing if the country's overall economic performance is to be improved. Such issues include

- the excessively high levels of public debt,
- the relatively low levels of human capital possessed by the labour force and
- the small average size of enterprises (Table 8.5).

The ways in which governments have responded to these issues are discussed in the next section. In the meantime, in order fully to understand why their responses have taken the form that they have, it is necessary to appreciate the nature of the institutional and political factors that influence and constrain the economic policy choices governments can make.

The nature of the available economic policy instruments

In the first place, in pursuit of their objectives, Western governments typically draw on a number of economic policy instruments which, for convenience, can be divided into two categories: macroeconomic and microeconomic:

Table 8.5. Government debt, education and size of enterprises: Italy compared with major competitors

Indicators	Countries						
	Italy	France	Germany	UK	US	Eurozone	OECD
General government gross financial liabilities as % of GDP (2006)	118.7	70.9	69.3	46.6	61.9	74.8	77.1
Tertiary attainment for age group 25–64 (2005 or latest available year)*	12.2	24.8	24.6	29.6	39.0	n.a.	26.0
Employment in manufacturing in enterprises with less than 20 employees (2005 or latest available year)**	30.7	17.0	14.1	14.8	11.1	n.a.	n.a

Notes: * Percentage of population in that age group.
** As percentage of total number of employees in manufacturing.
Source: Adapted from OECD.Stat Extracts, http://stats.oecd.org/WBOS/index.aspx.

- The macroeconomic category includes: budgetary policy (covering aggregate taxation and spending decisions); monetary and exchange-rate policy (covering decisions about interest rates and the money supply); incomes policy (covering decisions about wages and salaries). Together the instruments are designed to influence movements in prices, incomes and unemployment with the aim of stabilising the economy as a whole.
- The instruments of microeconomic policy, on the other hand, include a wide range of types of public intervention, each of which seeks to influence the functioning of markets or individual parts of the economic system. Such influence is wielded by affecting the relevant actors directly – either through the passage of laws regulating behaviour or through the passage of laws whose effect is to reallocate or redistribute resources among actors.

European integration

In the second place, since the early 1990s, Italian governments' choices in the area of macroeconomic policy have been heavily constrained by processes of European integration, especially **Economic and Monetary Union** (Box 8.1).

Constraints in the period prior to European Monetary Union (EMU)

Prior to the launch of the single currency, the constraints came from two sources.

Box 8.1

Key terms: single market, economic and monetary union

A single market is a customs union within which capital and labour, goods and services can move freely. A customs union is an agreement between participant countries providing for free trade between them (that is, they levy no tariffs on goods and services traded between them) combined with a common external tariff. Single markets go beyond customs unions in that they remove a range of non-tariff barriers to trade – for example, physical, technical and fiscal barriers – between the participating countries. In the case of the European Union, the abolition of internal tariff barriers was achieved by 1968. Then, in 1986, the Single European Act set 1992 as a deadline by which, through a range of detailed measures, remaining obstacles to free movement would be removed.

   Economic and monetary union, like a single market, can be seen as a stage in a process of economic integration. In that respect, it goes beyond a single market in creating a single currency, which its participant countries share, along with the pooling or co-ordination of economic policy. In a sense, economic and monetary union is a logical extension of a single market in so far as it stems from the recognition that, among the barriers to trade that a single market attempts to remove, there have to be counted those stemming from the uncertainties associated with currency fluctuations, the ability of states to favour their own goods and services through competitive devaluations of their currencies and so forth.

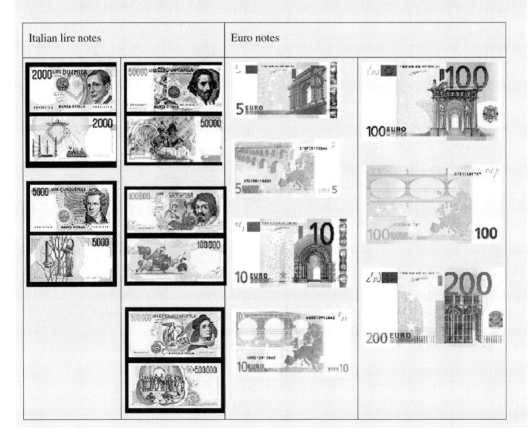

Italian lire notes	Euro notes

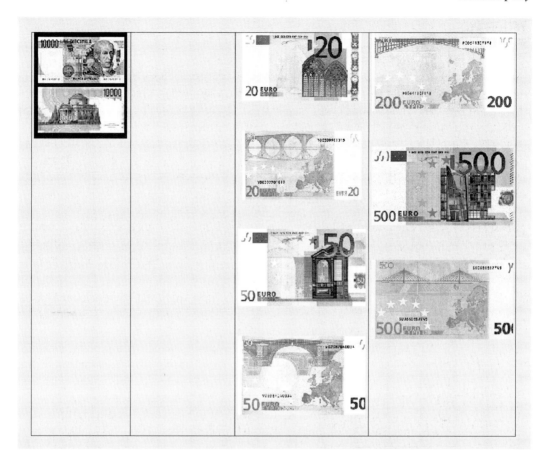

(1) The 'convergence criteria' set out in the Maastricht Treaty signed on 7 February 1992 by Italy and the other eleven members of the European Community. The criteria stipulated that a country wishing to be part of the euro at its launch on 1 January 1999 had to fulfil five conditions. These conditions concerned (a) the size of the country's budget deficit, (b) the level of its public debt, (c) its rate of inflation, (d) interest rates and (e) variations in the rate of exchange of its currency. Italy met none of the criteria before May 1996 and had to overcome not insignificant opposition in certain European quarters to its request to be part of the currency at its outset. Therefore, the government's macroeconomic decisions, aimed as they were at meeting the criteria, were, in more than a metaphorical sense, made for it.

(2) The Government's strong desire to be part of the currency in the first place.

This desire was ultimately rooted in the circumstances of the currency's origins and these arguably date back to two events:

(1) the 1969 Hague summit – when the six members of the then European Economic Community set themselves the objective of creating an Economic and Monetary Union;

(2) US President Nixon's 1971 decision to suspend the convertibility of dollars to gold (which, by putting an end to the Bretton Woods system of fixed exchange rates led to the first attempt, in the form of the European currency 'snake', to regulate currency fluctuations at European level).

More profoundly, however, the single currency can be said to have been inherent in the European project from the beginning; for the project has been subject to constant processes of 'spillover'. This term refers to the realisation on the part of policy-makers that European integration in one area of policy, if it is to be successful, requires integration in another area and so forth. Consequently, integration in one area (for example, energy production) creates pressure for integration in another (for example, transport) in a cumulative manner. According to this view, completion of the **single market** (Box 8.1) project created pressure for monetary integration by creating the risk that, as one of the few remaining barriers to trade, national currencies might be used as the basis for competitive devaluations among countries (Rossi, 2000: 199–120; Sadeh, 2002: 10).

An example of the protectionist pressures to which competitive devaluations can lead was the Italian–French quarrel arising from devaluation of the lira in 1992 (Rossi, 2000: 120), and this provided Italian policy-makers with one argument for seeking membership of the euro. Another argument they were able to draw upon was that membership of the currency would eliminate the risks, uncertainties and other transaction costs that arise when international trade requires currency conversions. This was a very powerful argument bearing in mind that Italy's largest trading partners were, and are, all in the EU. A third argument was that EMU would bring low interest rates and fiscal discipline. Finally, European integration in general was widely viewed, by policy-makers and public alike, as a panacea – the answer to a wide range of real and imagined institutional and political problems. Thus, at least until 2001, when 'eurosceptic' voices began to be heard in some quarters on the centre right, overwhelming majorities viewed membership of the single currency, more or less uncritically, as a necessary and unqualified good.

Constraints in the period since EMU

As in the period prior to the currency's launch (Box 8.2), so in the period since, restrictions on Italian governments' room for manoeuvre in the macroeconomic sphere has come from two sources.

(1) As we have already mentioned, control of monetary policy has been relinquished to Europe where primary responsibility in this field lies with the 'Eurosystem'. This consists of the central banks of the countries that have adopted the euro, and the European Central Bank (ECB).[5] In

depriving member governments of much of their former powers with respect to monetary policy, the euro means that exchange rates can no longer be used as a means of rapid adjustment to cyclical disequilibria or economic shocks of a localised nature. It means, too, that Italy is subject to interest-rate decisions made by the ECB in the light of inflationary pressures in the eurozone as a whole, even though such pressures may not be uniformly distributed. If, for example, inflation is lower in Italy than elsewhere, then a decision to raise interest rates, through its effect in depressing economic activity, means, in effect, that Italy pays the costs of adjusting to disequilibria arising in other countries.

(2)   A series of limitations in the area of budgetary policy, stemming from the Stability and Growth Pact (SGP).

The Stability and Growth Pact

The Stability and Growth Pact (SGP) was concluded by the European Council at the Dublin summit in December 1996. Building on the 'convergence criteria', the pact obliges the eurozone countries to ensure that their budget deficits do not exceed 3 per cent of their GDP in any one year and that they do not allow total public debt to exceed 60 per cent of GDP. The rationale for the SGP is that under conditions of monetary union the incentives on governments to pursue 'responsible' budgetary policies are fewer than they are when the governments have their own, national, currencies. When governments have their own currencies, the possibilities for 'excessive' budget deficits are limited by their effects on interest and exchange rates and therefore on countries' capacities to export. In a monetary union, member countries are not subject to such constraints. Moreover, if a number of them run excessive deficits, they may create inflationary pressures obliging the central bank to raise interest rates with the result of depressing economic activity even in countries without, or with lower, deficits (Bini Smaghi, 2001: 46). So ultimately, the rationale for the SGP has to do with perceptions of equity between members of the eurozone.

EU member states are obliged to report to the Commission details of government finances by 1 March and 1 September each year. If a country is found to have breached the terms of the pact, then it is subject to the Excessive Deficit Procedure. This involves the Council making recommendations to the country concerned and establishing a deadline for corrective action to be taken. If the country fails to comply with the Council's decisions, then the Council can impose sanctions. These initially take the form of non-interest-bearing deposits with the Commission and may escalate, in the event of continuing breaches, to the imposition of fines. Importantly, a country is not deemed to be in breach of the pact if, despite having a budget deficit above the limit, the latter results from an unusual event outside the country's control or results from a severe economic downturn (that is, if there is an annual fall of GDP of over 2 per cent).[6]

Box 8.2

Introduction of the euro

When the euro replaced the lira as Italy's currency, it did so first as an accounting currency in 1999: only later (on 1 January 2002) did the euro coins and banknotes come into circulation. The rate of exchange was fixed at 1936.27 lire to the euro. Curiously, adoption of the euro was not the first occasion on which Italy had been involved in a monetary union, but the third! The first occasion came about as the result of the process of Italian unification itself when the Sardinian lira in effect became the national currency, replacing, among others, the Lombardy-Venetia florin, the Tuscan fiorino and the Parma lira. The second came with the Latin Monetary Union established in 1865 when France, Belgium, Italy and Switzerland agreed to peg the exchange rate of one unit of their respective currencies at 4.5 grams of silver and to make them freely interchangeable. The Union was broken by the First World War and came to a formal end in 1927.

Italian lire notes and Euro notes

An additional important feature of the SGP is that it commits its signatories to achieve balanced budgets over the medium term. The aim here is to allow budgets to continue to act as 'automatic stabilisers' in the face of fluctuations in demand and employment. That is, when demand and employment fall, the budget serves to weaken the forces pushing in the direction of economic downturn. This is because falling demand and employment result in lower tax receipts and higher levels of public (social security) expenditure. Budgets have the opposite effect in the event of the economy 'overheating'. In the case of Italy, it is estimated that these automatic stabilisers bring about an increase in the budget deficit of 0.5 per cent of GDP for every 1 per cent decline in the rate of growth (Bini Smaghi, 2001: 45). Clearly, if at the moment of an economic downturn budgets are already heavily in deficit, then, by virtue of the 3 per cent limit and the sanctions that can be imposed for exceeding it, there may be little or no room for using tax and spending to counter possible recession. From this point of view, it may be said that Italy has not been very well placed in recent years in so far as its budget deficit was 2.6 in 2001, 2.3 in 2002,[7] and 3.2 in 2003 and 2004.[8] The situation was particularly serious in 2005 when the deficit reached 4.3 per cent of GDP. At that time, the Government was forced to cut its growth forecast for the year to 0 per cent and the European Commission decided to recommend application of the Excessive Deficit Procedure, giving Italy until 2007 to bring its deficit below the 3 per cent ceiling (EurActive, 2005b).

The Commission's recommendation (subsequently endorsed by the Council of Ministers) was based partly on the view that Italy's level of public debt, still well above the debt-to-GDP ratio of 60 per cent established by the SGP, 'ha[d] not declined at a satisfactory pace over recent years, nor w[ould] do so in the near future on account of the present level of the primary surplus' (European Commission, 2005). The term 'primary surplus' draws attention to the fact that net of interest payments, Italian budgets have featured an excess of income over expenditure since the early 1990s, this feature having been a requirement in order to stop the level of debt rising as a result of the accumulation of interest. This has acted as an additional obstacle in the way of using budgetary policy as an effective tool of macroeconomic management.

The obstacle has a formal as well as a practical dimension. The formal dimension derives from the requirement on eurozone countries, under the SGP, to submit to the Commission, on an annual basis, 'stability programmes'. These oblige the countries to describe the budgetary and other measures they are taking or propose to take to meet their economic policy objectives given their SGP obligations. In the case of Italy, this means an obligation to show what measures it is taking to ensure that its public debt is '"approaching the reference value at a satisfactory pace"… taking into account macroeconomic conditions and debt dynamics, including the pursuit of appropriate levels of primary surpluses' (Ecofin Council, 2005: 7).

■ The policy response

In light of these rather severe constraints on governments' room for 'creativity' in terms of macroeconomic policy, we now consider how they have responded to some of the major issues raised by awareness of the economic difficulties discussed in the third section. We begin with the debt problem and then consider the most significant recent measures in the area of microeconomic policy. The attention governments give to microeconomic, relative to the attention they give to macroeconomic policy, has necessarily increased given the restrictions imposed by the euro.

The public debt

When the centre-right government elected in 2001 presented its first stability programme in November of that year, it forecast that the debt-to-GDP ratio would fall from 110.5 per cent in 2000 to 98.0 per cent in 2004. According to the programme it presented in December 2005, the ratio had fallen to only 106.5 per cent. Why was the government unsuccessful in meeting its targets? The divergence between forecast and outcome can in part be explained in terms of lower-than-expected rates of GDP growth (forecast to average 2.6 per cent between 2000 and 2004 but in fact only 1.3 per cent): as a consequence, total government receipts were lower than hoped for, while total expenditure was higher (by some 2 per cent of GDP).

To some extent, the lower-than-expected growth could in turn be attributed to the downturn in the world economy from 2001 and the political and economic uncertainties provoked by the Twin Towers attack in September that year. However, in its initial stability programme document, the Government had said that it would take a series of measures, including 'privatisations and liberalisation', with a view to achieving 'a significant increase in the economy's potential growth rate'.[9] So a more complete understanding of the Government's handling of the debt issue requires some insight into what actually transpired in these areas.

Privatisation

Privatisation was especially important because its impact on debt-reduction could be expected to be direct. Moreover, the Government expected its impact to be significant, helping to bring the debt-to-GDP ratio down to 94 per cent by 2006. In the privatisation plan set out as an annex to the 2001 stability programme, the Government envisaged generating privatisation proceeds of about €60 billion between 2002 and 2006. However, the Ministry of the Economy and Finance's privatisation report, presented to Parliament in May 2005, suggested that the Government was very unlikely to meet that figure. Net proceeds of sales carried out by the Ministry between January 2002 and the end of 2004 amounted to only €25.65 billion, that is, less than half the aforementioned figure. The 2002 stability programme indicated that the Government decided to delay its privatisation plans because of poor stock-market performance, and in fact prior to December 2004, the Ministry had disposed of assets worth only €3.77 billion (Ministero dell'Economia e delle Finanze, 2005: 17, table 1).

Taxation and spending

An additional possible approach to the debt problem – in principle at least – was to act on spending and taxation directly. Significantly, while the Government's initial stability document talked in general terms about 'tax and welfare reform' (p. 5), it said little that could be interpreted as implying a specific commitment. In the area of expenditure, for example, the closest it got to mentioning containment (let alone cuts) in any specific area was when it mentioned (p. 15) 'a new stability pact with the regional governments, for stricter control of health spending'. This should not surprise. Beyond the obvious point that cuts in expenditure carry political risks, there is a considerable degree of inertia built into existing patterns and levels of spending. As Calvert (2002: 136) notes, budgets in any country are typically compiled from bids originating in a large number of government departments all of which start from the assumption that existing operations need to be maintained at the current level. Therefore, none take account of the overall amounts of money likely to be available, and they inflate their bids knowing that, in the process whereby the latter are reconciled, they are likely to be trimmed. Ex-Treasury Minister Vincenzo Visco (2005: 701–2) provides a graphic description of the sheer pressures to which Italian Treasury ministers are subjected by cabinet colleagues all fighting their own spending corners in the annual budget round. And he points out that the opposition parties are able to exert additional spending pressure, during the process of parliamentary consideration of the budget, by exploiting potential and actual divisions within the governing coalition.

Once budgets have been agreed, spending departments have little incentive to economise, knowing that under-spending will weaken the cases they are able to make for significant resources the following year. In addition, Visco (2005) argues that a further obstacle in the way of effective control of spending in the Italian case is a shortage of reliable data on public-spending patterns. For example, 'the stipulation, included in the 2001 Finance Law, providing for general practitioners to be linked via the Internet with the aim of controlling prescribing – and whose implementation would have allowed the explosion of pharmaceutical expenditure consequent upon the abolition of prescription charges to be avoided – [was ignored by the Berlusconi government]' (Visco, 2005: 699–700, my translation). Leaving aside whatever bias there might or might not be in the words of an opposition politician commenting on the actions of the Government, Visco (2005: 700) is surely right to point out that 'it is obvious that without adequate information, no complex system can be governed and managed and no long-term planning is possible'. In light of this and the inertia mentioned in the previous paragraph, it is perhaps not

Table 8.6. Components of public expenditure, 2001–2005

Expenditure components	2001 (a)	2001 (b)	2002 (a)	2002 (b)	2003 (a)	2003 (b)	2004 (a)	2004 (b)	2005 (a)	2005 (b)
Consumption of goods and services	7.3	15.5	6.8	14.1	7.2	14.9	7.2	14.8	7.3	14.8
Transfer payments	27.2	57.6	28.9	60.0	29.1	60.2	29.7	61.2	29.9	60.6
Interest	6.2	13.1	6.0	12.4	5.3	11.0	5.3	10.9	4.9	9.9
Subsidies	1.1	2.3	1.1	2.3	1.0	2.1	1.1	2.3	1.1	2.2
Gross fixed capital formation	2.5	5.3	2.1	4.4	2.6	5.4	2.3	4.7	2.7	5.5
Other	2.9	6.1	3.3	6.8	3.1	6.4	2.9	6.0	3.4	6.9
Total	47.3	99.9	48.2	100.0	48.3	100.0	48.5	99.9	49.3	99.9

Notes: (a) = as proportion of GDP; (b) = as proportion of total expenditure.
Source: 'Italy's Stability Programme' 2001/2 – 2005/6: available at: http://europa.eu.int%20/comm/economy_finance/about/activities/sgp/scplist_en.htm.

surprising that the last stability programme document submitted by the Government before the 2006 election suggested that levels and patterns of public expenditure in 2005 differed rather little from what they had been when the Government took office (Table 8.6).

Election promises

A third factor involved in the government's difficulties in meeting its debt-to-GDP ratio targets is probably the fact that it had won the 2001 election promising *increases* in expenditure in a number of specific areas (such as welfare and law and order) as well as income-tax cuts – in effect counting on growth to remove the conflict between the two. The cuts were in the end modest: record low levels of growth in 2002 and 2003 meant that in the autumn of 2004, Berlusconi had, in effect, to threaten to destroy the government to secure agreement to a modest version of the tax reductions on which he had staked his personal political fortunes, and the reductions were for the most part quietly compensated for by tax increases elsewhere. However, in making these promises, the Government had created an additional, directly electoral, fetter on its freedom of action. And it was a fetter that was a particularly strong one; for citizens strongly desire to have both high spending levels and low taxes, and they are often unable (or unwilling), generally speaking, clearly to perceive the links between spending and tax decisions (Guerra, 2004: 490).

Microeconomic policy: education and training

Policy-makers see the importance of education and training as a policy issue as stemming from at least four factors.

Box 8.3

The new economy
This is a term that has gained currency as a result of US economic expansion in the 1990s. This was 'new' in the sense that the growth of production was accompanied by strong growth in the rate of employment without the inflationary pressures that had been characteristic of similar phases of expansion in the past. This led observers to suggest that the expansion had been generated by a substantial and enduring increase in productivity, in its turn attributable to the large-scale diffusion of the new information and communications technologies. Given that the United States has seen rates of productivity growth far higher than those of the other industrialised countries, Italian policy-makers, along with their counterparts elsewhere in Europe, are concerned to explore the potential for using the new ICTs to raise productivity in their own countries, and they are aware of the studies that suggest that this potential will not be realised unless enterprises can call upon a suitably qualified workforce (Bianco, 2003, ch. 5).

(1) Levels of education and training are related to the productivity of labour. The educational endowments of Italy's labour force are rather lower than those of most of her competitors: for example, 'the proportion of working-age males with a secondary education or higher is the fifth lowest in the OECD area after Portugal, Turkey, Spain and Mexico' (Bianco, 2003: 121, my translation).
(2) Improved levels of educational achievement are seen as crucial to enabling the country to meet the challenge posed by the '**new economy**' (Box 8.3).
(3) Improvements in education and training can help to reduce regional employment disparities (the highest in the EU).
(4) They can also help to increase employment rates (currently among the lowest in the EU).[10] In turn, increasing employment rates are seen as important for the contribution they can make to the future financial sustainability of the pensions system in view of Italy's ageing population (Table 8.7).

The 'Moratti reform'

In seeking to meet these challenges, the Government introduced a major reform of the education system, the 'Moratti reform', in March 2003. The law empowered the Government to give effect to its provisions through the adoption of a series of legislative decrees within twenty-four months of its passage (later extended by six months). Through its provisions, it sought to reorganise the system of education below university level by establishing what were two 'cycles'.

(1) The first cycle, from age six to fourteen was to consist of five years of primary education and three years of secondary education where the primary phase was to include the provision of teaching in at least one foreign language, the

Table 8.7. Proportion of population over 65, and employment rates: Italy compared with major competitors

Indicators	Countries						
	Italy	France	Germany	UK	US	EU15	OECD
Ratio of inactive population 65 and over to total labour force (%) (2000)	42.7	36.2	34.5	30.8	23.5	n.a.	n.a.
Employment rates: male (2006)*	70.5	67.5	72.9	78.4	78.1	73.5	75.6
Employment rates: female (2006) *	46.3	57.7	61.5	66.8	66.1	58.5	56.8
Employment rates: total (2006)*	58.9	62.3	67.2	72.5	72.0	66.0	66.1

Notes: * Figures show percentage of persons of working age (15–64) in employment.
Source: Adapted from OECD.Stat Extracts, http://stats.oecd.org/WBOS/index.aspx.

secondary phase to include the study of information technology and a second foreign language. Success in the public examination at the end of the eight-year period would then give access to the second cycle.

(2) The second cycle was to offer two alternative pathways.

    i One would provide lyceum education for five years with a final-year examination, success in which would give access to university education.

    ii A second would provide four years of vocational training with the option, at the end of the four years, to undertake an additional year. Success in the examination at the end of this year would give access to university. In addition, from age fifteen, pupils were to be given the option of combining education with periods of work experience or of undertaking apprenticeship training.

(3) There was to be a gradual raising of the leaving age: through adoption of the relevant legislative decrees, pupils would eventually be required to remain within the education system, on one or other of the two pathways of the second cycle, until they had obtained the relevant leaving qualification, otherwise until age eighteen.

(4) Pupils were to be tested annually.

(5) There was to be a new Istituto Nazionale per la Valutazione del Sistema di Istruzione (National Institute for Evaluation of the Education System, INVALSI) whose responsibilities were to include the periodic evaluation of teaching quality.

(6) The new law made a number of provisions for the improvement of teacher training.

Implementation and impact of the Moratti reform

The relevant legislative decrees were adopted during the course of 2004 and 2005. Of these, the most significant were the one enabling pupils to combine education and work experience and the one raising the leaving age. This provided for an initial increase, encompassing the first two years of the second cycle, starting in academic year 2005/6. The decrees were, however, also the ones most difficult to enact from a technical point of view and were not finally approved until March 2005. It is therefore too early to pronounce definitively on the new law, though some initial points can be made.

First, the reform has clearly been driven by an overriding intention of gearing the education system much more closely to the needs of the country's productive system than has hitherto been the case. This is apparent from what it says about (1) teaching and assessment, (2) the training of teachers and (3) the responsibilities of schools in terms of the links they are required to establish with industry.

(1) Teaching and assessment: The law places heavy emphasis on information technology, singling out training in the new technologies as one of the principal goals of provision in both the first and second cycles. Together with its associated decrees, it places institutions offering education as part of the second cycle under an obligation to impart work-related and transferable skills and to accredit pupils' acquisition of such skills.

(2) The training of teachers: The law establishes specific teacher–training requirements, at university level, for all teachers. It thus moves decisively away from the traditional system in which teacher training had been required only of teachers below the secondary level, who did not, however, require a degree (Dei, 1998: 101).

(3) The responsibilities of schools: The decree enabling pupils to combine education with work experience places the responsibility for initiating, developing and implementing work-placement opportunities on the schools. These are under a specific obligation to establish relations with employers for this purpose.

The European Commission was very enthusiastic about the reform;[11] but most of the opposition parties and the trade-union confederations were considerably less enthusiastic. They saw in the two pathways to be made available as part of the second cycle, a revival under a new guise of educational arrangements that had been in place until 1962 (Iucci, 2003). The arrangement had been based on a system of selection that divided pupils, at age eleven, into vocational and academic streams. They had been abolished in part because only the latter stream gave access to further and higher education. The arrangements were therefore seen as a considerable obstacle in the way of equality of opportunity and opportunities for upward social mobility (Dei, 1998: 52–8).

Third, aside from the issue of the numbers with given *credentials*, in terms of the *knowledge* they actually acquire, Italian pupils, at least at the primary level and the initial years of the secondary level tend to come very near the top in international league tables (Dei, 1998: 104). Arguably, the real problems lie higher up the education system and especially at the university level. Here, drop-out rates have traditionally been high, and the proportions of the population with education to degree standard low, as compared with universities in other industrialised countries. As Capano (2000) shows, much of this has to do with the traditional characteristics of higher education in Italy: until 1990, essentially the only higher education qualification available was the *laurea* (degree). Its purpose was the education to a high standard of excellence of a restricted elite. Its requirements were therefore such that it was more similar to what in Anglo-Saxon countries are known as 'masters degrees' than to what are referred to as 'bachelors degrees'.

The reform of universities

In Italy, as elsewhere, higher education is a source of social mobility but, given the characteristics mentioned in the previous paragraph, access to it has always been strongly correlated with class membership. A society in which access to higher education credentials is more strongly influenced by class than by ability in effect wastes its resources. If its higher education system can adapt its offering such as to widen access to these credentials, then it uses its resources more effectively. There has therefore in recent years been a need to raise the productivity of universities, and to attune their offerings more closely to the economy and the needs of a system of mass education (the number of university students rose from 310,000 in 1960 to 1,700,000 in 2001 (Bianchi, 2004)). In 1999, therefore, there was a reform of the structure of degree programmes.

In essence, the old, four- to six-year, degree programme was replaced with a new, two-tier structure offering a three-year *diploma di laurea*, possession of which would then offer access to the second tier, consisting of a two-year *laurea specialistica*. The intention was that from academic year 2000/1, the *diploma di laurea* would offer an education enabling access to the labour market for most of the activities for which the old *laurea* had once been required, while the new *laurea specialistica* would offer the advanced training necessary for the successful exercise of certain specific activities.

On the face of it, the reform seems to have had some success. The 2005 annual report of the Comitato Nazionale per la Valutazione del Sistema Universitario (National Committee for the Evaluation of the University System) suggests that between 2000 and 2003 the number of degrees awarded rose by some 47 per cent (from 159,438 to 234,672). Meanwhile, the same report shows a modest increase in indicators of retention together with a significant increase (from 5 per cent to 44 per cent) between the old and the new systems in the proportions of students managing to complete their degrees within the number of years prescribed for their programmes.[12]

Microeconomic policy: the size of enterprises

This is an issue that is directly related to the last. If policies to improve the quality of human capital are successful, then governments will have to address the issue of the relatively small size of enterprises: better-educated workers, with expectations concerning decision-making autonomy and the exploitation and enhancement of their skills, are more difficult to insert into smaller enterprises, with their more rudimentary organisational structures, than into larger organisations. Smaller enterprises also have the disadvantage that they limit the possibilities for technological and organisational innovations that can reduce costs and raise productivity. For example, the advantages, in terms of the reduction of co-ordination costs, to be had by deployment of the new information and computer technologies (ICTs) are much greater in large organisations, with their formal organisational structures, than in small, informal ones. Moreover, large scale implies that the adoption of ICT innovations is easier and more rapid, as it makes possible the imposition of decisions from the top, whereas with large numbers of small firms adoption can only be the outcome of large numbers of autonomous, unco-ordinated, decisions.

To be sure, small size is not always a drawback. For example, a system of small firms would appear to have as much to gain from the co-ordination possibilities opened up by a development such as the Internet (with its 'open' character and low access costs) as a system of large firms. Therefore, the problem faced by Italy's productive system has to do, less with disadvantages of small size *as such*, than with something else. This is the fact that it has been difficult to benefit from the advantages of large size, owing to certain obstacles that have traditionally impeded the growth of firms. These obstacles are related to (1) the ownership and control structures typical of Italian firms, (2) the availability of enterprise finance and (3) certain aspects of company law.

Ownership and control structures

Ownership in Italian firms tends to be very heavily concentrated in single individuals and families. In 2000, the average size of the largest shareholding in unlisted manufacturing companies was 65.2 per cent (Bianco, 2003: 99; Onida, 2004: 131). The understandably strong desire of proprietors to be kept fully informed of how their enterprises are being managed necessarily translates into the exercise of more or less close control of managers – unless proprietors are able to combine the desire to be informed with the contrasting desire to delegate. In turn, the difficulty experienced by proprietors in fully relinquishing control to teams of professional managers makes it difficult for the firm to grasp opportunities and to innovate in the kinds of ways that will allow it to grow. There are three reasons for this.

(1) Proprietors are understandably relatively 'risk averse' – concerned, above all, to protect their already-existing capital.
(2) Managers may lack the degree of decision-making autonomy they require to exploit opportunities effectively.
(3) The correlation between the possession of managerial skills and the ownership of enterprises must be assumed to be less than perfect. Therefore, when a successful proprietor passes control of a firm to the next generation, the probability that success will continue is less than 1.0, and less than it is when intergenerational transfer of *ownership* takes place alongside continuity of *control* in the hands of a professional manager.

The availability of enterprise finance

In turn, the preponderance of family ownership limits the sources of external finance available for growth. On the one hand, firms are reluctant to have recourse to the stock market (the number of listed firms in Italy is 265 as compared with 715 in Germany, 737 in France and 2,045 in the UK (Onida, 2004: 137)) because of what this implies in terms of a reduction in control: even if the family retains a majority shareholding, a degree of control has to be sacrificed to rules of transparency and other stock-market requirements and to the need to retain the confidence of outside shareholders. These, if they withdraw their capital, may bring about a fall in the value of the firm's stock.

On the other hand, the heavy concentration of ownership has served to increase the risks associated with investing in such firms – thereby reducing the supply of outside capital in the first place. For example, it is common in Italy for family-dominated companies to have recourse to pyramid holdings as a means both of controlling large numbers of subsidiaries with relatively small amounts of capital, and of limiting their responsibility. A pyramid means that if a company, A, owns 60 per cent of subsidiary B, which in its turn owns 60 per cent of subsidiary C, A is able fully to control C though possessing only 36 per cent of its capital. Since the subsidiaries belonging to the pyramid are legally separate entities, in the event of their failure, the liability of the company at the apex extends not to its entire capital but only to its share of the capital of the firm concerned. Meanwhile, if the majority shareholder at the apex is free of controls on his actions by virtue of the fact that his capital is concentrated, other shareholders are deprived of power by virtue of the fact that their capital is dispersed among the firms making up the pyramid.

Given these circumstances, firms tend to rely to a comparatively large degree on bank loans, usually of a short-term nature, to finance their expansion. Such loans are, however, relatively inefficient as a means of financing investments because of the debt-servicing costs they bring with them. This in turn brings the perpetuation of the vicious circle, criticised in 2002 by the then Governor of the Bank of Italy, Antonio Fazio, between the small size of enterprises and the low level of demand for financial services: 'Growth of the stock market is limited, the availability of long-term investment capital is reduced; firms fail to grasp opportunities for investment and growth' (quoted by Onida, 2004: 127, my translation). If part of the problem arises from the risks faced by outside investors, then the vicious circle might be less compelling in the presence of legislation protecting more effectively the interests of minority shareholders.

Company law

Bianco (2003: 112) argues that until recently, the quality of such legislation placed Italy behind such countries as Britain and the United States. In these countries there are

- incisive fiduciary obligations on the part of majority shareholders and administrators towards all shareholders;
- prohibitions on transactions involving conflicts of interest;
- mechanisms allowing minority shareholders to participate actively in company deliberations (such as quorum requirements for the convocation of shareholders' meetings, arrangements for proxy voting, representation on supervisory boards).

Italian legislation, on the other hand, was thought to be wanting, especially in the sphere of rules allowing minority shareholders to intervene effectively in company decision-making and rules preventing pyramids from being used in ways damaging to minority shareholder interests.

Recently, two sets of changes to company law have sought to improve the position.

(1) The 'Draghi Law' of 1998. This applies to listed companies and among other things:
  i considerably reduces the minimum proportion of shareholders whose support is required to give effect to requests for the calling of shareholders' meetings and to trigger investigations by a company's college of auditors;
  ii introduces new safeguards preventing abuse of arrangements for proxy voting;
  iii makes obligatory the inclusion, in companies' colleges of auditors, of members elected by the minority shareholders;
  iv excludes from membership of a company's college of auditors the relatives of directors and the relatives of the directors of firms controlling or controlled by the company (Cottino, 1999).
(2) Law no. 366 of 2001. This empowers the Government to adopt legislative decrees aiming, among other things, to extend to minority shareholders in non-listed companies the kinds of safeguards offered by the Draghi Law to minority shareholders in listed companies.

As before, it is not possible, so soon after the legislation has come into force, to pass a categorical judgement on its effectiveness, but nevertheless, some useful points can be made.

(1) Some have argued (Cottino, 1999; Bianco, 2003) that the changes represent very significant improvements in the quality of protection offered to minority shareholders.
(2) If the effects, in terms of enterprise size, concentration of ownership and the number of listed firms, appear so far to be rather limited (Bianco, 2003: 106), then this may be because more time is required for the changes to have a real impact (some of the legislative decrees pursuant to the 2001 changes, for example, did not come into force until 2004). Alternatively, it could be because the changes are insufficient to bring about the kinds of effect desired. For example, Onida (2004: 174–5) points

to the fact that certain differences in the treatment of non-listed as opposed to listed companies remain despite the law of 2001 – with the result that firms are likely to continue to face disincentives to launching themselves on the stock market.

(3) Bianco (2003: 107) points out that 'take-up' of most of the legal instruments made available by Draghi to minority shareholders seeking to assert their rights has so far been rather limited and presumes that this has to do with the costs of using them, including the high average length of time required for judicial proceedings in Italy. The judicial system and its procedures is a topic we shall focus on in some detail in the following chapter.

■ Summary and conclusions

We began by noting that economic policy lies at the heart of the ways in which political power is won, retained and lost in a democracy. This is because success in virtually every other area of policy (and therefore success in retaining an electoral following) are very heavily influenced by economic-policy outcomes. Because of all this, the 'bottom line' for Western governments is the achievement of economic growth – but to a far greater degree than is the case with other policy objectives, governments can will the means but can be much less certain of success in achieving the ends. The preceding section analysed the responses of Italian governments to three of the most important policy issues thrown up by the debate about whether or not Italy is in economic decline: the public debt; education and training; the size of enterprises. The analysis shows that the difficulties of achieving desired outcomes extend far beyond growth. As we have seen, the difficulties arise in part because of the relative powerlessness of any government seeking to manage, as part of a supra-national system of the kind discussed in the fourth section, the national effects of global economic trends. In part the difficulties arise from the political and public-opinion constraints on governments' room for manoeuvre – constraints that are especially strong in the area of taxation and public expenditure. Such constraints are equally as strong with regard to matters of welfare and civil liberties – the areas of policy to which we turn our attention in the next chapter.

■ Further reading

A discussion of the challenges of economic adjustment and development, and of how Italy's elites have responded to these challenges since the 1970s, is to be found in Marcello De Cecco's 'Italy's dysfunctional political economy', *West European Politics*, vol. 30, no. 4, September 2007, pp. 763–83. *Business, the State and Economic Policy: the Case of Italy* (Routledge, 2004), by Grant Amyot, explores the relationship between the state and capital as well as some of the major directions taken in macroeconomic policy. Richard M. Locke's *Remaking the*

Italian Economy (Ithaca, NY: Cornell University Press, 1997) addresses the seeming contradiction between the apparent 'backwardness' and 'corruption' of the Italian politico-economic context and the country's success, at times, in outperforming some neighbouring states considered more efficient and stable. Finally, *Government and Economies in the Post-War World* (edited by By Andrew Graham and Anthony Seldon and published by Routledge, 1991) contains a chapter on Italy and allows the reader to view Italian economic policy-making from a comparative perspective, considering, as it does, the main objectives and instruments of economic policy, the institutional frameworks, and the political structures of the countries analysed, as they took shape in the period following the Second World War.

▓ Notes

1. World Bank data taken from http://siteresources.worldbank.org/DATASTATISTICS/Resources/GDP.pdf.
2. Data taken from: www.cia.gov/cia/publications/factbook/rankorder/2004rank.html.
3. *Regions: Statistical Yearbook 2005*, p. 69, map 5.5 http://epp.eurostat.cec.eu.int/cache/ITY_OFFPUB/KS-AF-05-001/EN/KS-AF-05-001-EN.PDF.
4. Data for 1970s, 1980s and 1990s taken from Bull and Newell (2005: ch. 2); data for 2000–2005 taken from the World Bank at http://devdata.worldbank.org/external/CPProfile.asp?PTYPE=CP&CCODE=ITA and from the 'CIA World Fact Book', at www.odci.gov/cia/publications/factbook/geos/it.html.
5. This is directed by an Executive Board consisting of a president, vice-president and four other members appointed by common agreement of the eurozone countries. The Executive Board is responsible for implementing monetary policy as defined by the ECB's Governing Council (consisting of the Executive Board and the governors of the twelve central banks of the eurozone).
6. In March 2005, a reform of the Pact abolished the stipulation that GDP had to fall by 2 per cent for a country to avoid the excessive deficit procedure under the 'severe economic downturn' criterion. Since the reform, it has been sufficient for a country to experience negative growth of any entity in order to avoid the procedure. In addition, the reform extended the range of 'relevant factors' to which a country could refer to avoid the procedure. It also extended from one to two years the deadline by which countries had to correct deficits in the event of the procedure being invoked (EurActiv, 2005a).
7. Data taken from *The Economist*, 'country briefing' at www.economist.com/countries/Italy/profile.cfm? folder=Profile%2DEconomic%20Data.
8. Data taken from *International Business and Finance Daily*, 'Italy's budget deficits breached SGP rules in 2003, 2004, EC says', 27 September 2005, http://subscript.bna.com/SAMPLES/ibd.nsf/125731d8816a84d385256297005f336a/86b0cc0633f26de4852570880080be91?OpenDocument.
9. 'Italy's stability programme: November 2001 update', p. 1, available at http://europa.eu.int/comm/economy_finance/about/activities/sgp/country/countryfiles/it/it20012002_en.pdf.

10. Note that as conventionally defined, there is no direct inverse relation between the rate of employment and the rate of unemployment. The first refers to the proportion of persons of working age that is employed. The second refers to the proportion of the economically active population that is without employment, where the 'economically active population' consists of the working-age population that is employed or seeking employment.

11. In January 2006, it singled out 'measures aimed at improving educational performance' as one of the specific strengths of Italy's 'National Reform Programme for Growth and Jobs': http://europa.eu.int/rapid/pressReleases Action.do?reference=MEMO/06/38&format=HTML&aged=0&language=EN&gui Language=en.

12. Comitato nazionale per la valutazione del sistema universitario, 'Sesto Rapporto sullo stato del Sistema Universitario', available at www.cnvsu. it/_library/downloadfile.asp?id=11294.

9   Welfare and rights

◼ Introduction

In the last chapter we saw that the Italian state has lost autonomy in economic policy-making in recent years. According to some scholars, the same can be said of policy-making in relation to welfare. The reason for this, it is argued, is that in common with the governments of many other advanced industrialised countries, the Italian authorities are facing changes, outside their sphere of control, in the international economy and in the age structure of the population:

- On the one hand, it is said, growing world trade, along with increases in international capital flows, have placed governments under pressure to embark on a 'race to the bottom' in welfare by cutting taxes and spending – this being the price they must pay to remain internationally competitive.
- On the other hand, with the OECD population over sixty-five having nearly doubled in the past four decades and set significantly to increase in the future, governments are also facing the opposite pressure on welfare budgets. The political difficulties this exposes them to are revealed by the protests that took place in France, Austria and Sweden in 2003 against proposals to reduce the generosity of existing old-age pensions schemes (Castles, 2004: 5).

The actual dimensions of these pressures in the Italian case, and how governments have responded to them, are matters we consider below. For now we need to define terms.

'Welfare policy' here means the predispositions of governments with regard to decisions concerning the provision of social services to individual citizens. These services are designed to provide protection against the consequences of hazards and accidents (such as ill health) and against potential causes of poverty (such as old age, dependent children, unemployment and so forth). In principle, the services

- may be provided by public or private agencies;
- may take the form of cash or services in kind (such as medical care or subsidised housing), and
- may or may not be conditional, in terms of their provision, upon the fulfilment of given criteria.

These criteria most commonly take the form of:

- prior contributions (meaning that the services are provided as part of what amounts to an insurance scheme);
- the demonstration of need (as in the case of means-tested and discretionary benefits);
- membership of given categories (such as veterans of armed forces or people with disabilities).

The provision of any given service may embody a combination of these criteria (as with means-tested benefits available to defined categories).

'Rights' policy is here understood in a way that relates it quite closely to welfare policy in so far as it is used to refer to the predispositions of governments with regard to decisions concerning safeguards given to citizens in matters of personal liberty. Rights policies are all ones that in one way or another help to define the realm within which one may act unobstructed by others. The category therefore includes

- policies concerning protection from the arbitrary exercise of power by other individuals or groups, including the state, as well as
- policies concerning the conditions under which given types of behaviour are to be permitted and their free exercise guaranteed.

If the focus of welfare policy is the restrictions imposed on citizens by incapacity, then the focus of rights policy is the restrictions that may and may not be legitimately imposed upon them by fellow-citizens and the authorities.

Political scientists are interested in welfare and rights policies because they go to the heart of what the modern state is all about. To cite Max Weber's famous definition, the state is 'a human community that (successfully) claims the monopoly of the legitimate use of physical force within a given territory'. Both cause and consequence of success in making the claim is that the state defines and enforces rules establishing the extent and the limits of citizens' rights. But to make such rules is to hold that a state has certain responsibilities towards its citizens. From this point of view, welfare provisions represent an extension of the realms to which states' responsibilities for their citizens are thought to extend; and like policies concerning rights, they too are intimately connected to matters of political stability and the maintenance of state authority. One of the earliest welfare-state developments makes this clear: famously, Bismarck introduced in Germany in 1889 the first state-run social insurance programme paying retirement benefits, with the explicit hope of stemming the rising tide of socialism.

Obviously, the two policy categories we have defined embrace a potentially vast number of more specific policy issues, coverage of which would be impossible within a single chapter. We are therefore forced to be selective.

- Under the heading of welfare, we will focus mainly on policy in relation to unemployment, sickness and old age as these three are among the largest single categories of public expenditure, together accounting for about two-fifths of the total (Table 9.1).
- Under the heading of policies concerning rights, we will focus on what are commonly referred to as 'civil rights', that is, the safeguards offered to citizens against abuse of power by the authorities. Even this is a potentially very large category, so we shall focus our attention on one specific area, namely, the civil rights associated with judicial policy.

As in the previous chapter, we shall in each case begin with an analysis of the main issues thrown up by the 'policy context' before examining recent government responses to these issues.

■ The welfare policy context

There are five challenges facing welfare coverage in Italy:

(1) imbalances between types of programme;
(2) the risks covered;
(3) the challenge of ensuring legality;
(4) the challenge of ensuring efficiency;
(5) the challenge of funding.

Let us examine each of these in turn.

Imbalances between types of programme

As in other West European countries, so in Italy the principal pillar of welfare coverage against the risks of unemployment and poverty in old age is provided by social insurance. 'Compulsory social insurance was introduced between 1898 (work injuries) and 1919 (old age, invalidity and unemployment) for all employees' (Ferrera, 2005: 14). A national health service has been in place since 1978. The weakest pillar in Italian welfare coverage is the system of **social assistance** (Box 9.1) in so far as (a) resources are concentrated on social insurance measures (implying the greater protection of some categories to the detriment of others) and (b) there is no **national minimum income scheme** (Box 9.1).

Table 9.1. Public expenditure in Italy, 2006

COFOG* level 1	Expenditure (€ millions)	COFOG level 2	Expenditure (€ millions)	Expenditure as % of total
General public services	130,696			17.5
Defence	21,222			2.8
Public order and safety	28,982			3.9
Economic affairs	94,060			12.6
Environmental protection	7,630			1.0
Housing and community amenities	12,302			1.7
Health	104,167			14.0
Recreation culture and religion	11,949			1.6
Education	65,746			8.8
Social protection	268,804			36.1
		Sickness and disability	25,497	
		Old age	180,104	
		Survivors	38,764	
		Family and children	15,191	
		Unemployment	7,949	
		Housing	268	
		Social exclusion n.e.c.	568	
		R&D Social protection	0	
		Social protection n.e.c.	463	
TOTAL	745,558		268,804	100.0

Notes: * COFOG stands for Classification of the Functions of Government. It is a framework that defines public-expenditure distributions in terms of the primary ends pursued by governments and is used by international bodies such as the UN and the OECD to facilitate comparisons of public expenditure distributions across countries.

Source: Adapted from Istituto Nazionale di Statistica (ISTAT), 'Spesa delle Amministrazioni pubbliche per funzione. Anni 2000–2006. Classificazione per gruppi COFOG', www.istat.it/dati/dataset/20080226_00/notaPA.pdf.

The relatively low profile of the social assistance pillar in Italian welfare can be attributed to three constraints that Italy shares with the other three countries of southern Europe. As Maurizio Ferrera (2005: 8–11) explains, these constraints are (1) the role of the family, (2) the presence of an 'underground' economy and (3) administrative difficulties:

(1) The role of the family: as Ferrera points out, demand for public social assistance has been kept down by the persistence of the extended household and the intensity of the solidaristic ties among its members. This has enabled the family to continue providing welfare services in a range of

Box 9.1

Key terms: social assistance, national minimum income scheme, relative and absolute poverty

'Social assistance' is here used to mean benefits of a non-insurance nature. They are therefore potentially available to everyone regardless of contributions history, and they are 'aimed at guaranteeing a modicum of resources to those who are in a manifest situation of need' (Sacchi and Bastagli, 2005: 131). As such, these benefits are means-tested and may have categorical elements (that is, involve the requirement that recipients belong to a given category (such as lone parents). Their importance arises from the fact that social insurance, by its vary nature, inevitably leaves welfare gaps. For example, it is unable to cover those seeking first-time employment, those unable to work because of permanent disability, the elderly with incomplete contributions records and so forth.

'National minimum income scheme' is here used to mean non-categorical, means-tested benefits, designed to ensure that no-one, whatever their circumstances, falls below a given level of income.

'Relative poverty' refers to the proportion of the population that is below some proportion of the average income or expenditure for that population. **'Absolute poverty'**, on the other hand, refers to the proportion of the population below a given level of income or expenditure defined in absolute terms and regarded as being necessary in order to satisfy some definition of 'basic needs'. In the present case, relative and absolute poverty are defined and calculated in such a way that they imply consumption expenditure of less than €823.50 per month (relative poverty) and less than €573.60 per month (absolute poverty) for a family of two. For details see Sacchi and Bastagli (2005: 94–8).

fields, from child care to unemployment assistance and care of the elderly and disabled. Most of the services provided in this way are delivered by unpaid female labour. However, the syndrome also means that the poor remain more firmly integrated into the social fabric than they are in northern Europe.

(2) The underground economy: the presence of a large 'underground', undeclared, economy (accounting for between 15 and 30 per cent of GDP) offers employment and therefore income to groups, such as women and young people, with restricted access to the social insurance benefits. This too weakens the political demand for publicly provided social assistance.

(3) Administrative difficulties: administrative competencies have been slow to develop in southern Europe and this has restricted the availability of publicly provided social assistance by operating on the supply side. Traditionally, the pragmatic and relational skills needed to manage means-tested benefits effectively have been in short supply among public

Table 9.2. Relative poverty by geographic area, 2006–2007 (000s and percentages)

	North		Centre		South		Italy	
	2006	2007	2006	2007	2006	2007	2006	2007
000s								
Families in poverty	595	631	315	297	1,713	1,725	2,623	2,653
Resident families	11,378	11,532	4,598	4,670	7,591	7,679	23,567	23,881
Persons in poverty	1,447	1,563	889	827	5,201	5,152	7,537	7,542
Resident persons	26,458	26,648	11,244	11,421	20,669	20,688	58,371	58,757
Percentages								
Families in poverty	22.7	23.8	12.0	11.2	65.3	65.0	100.0	100.0
Resident families	48.3	48.3	19.5	19.6	32.2	32.2	100.0	100.0
Persons in poverty	19.2	20.7	11.8	11.0	69.0	68.3	100.0	100.0
Resident persons	45.3	45.4	19.3	19.4	35.4	35.2	100.0	100.0
Incidence of poverty (%)								
Families	5.2	5.5	6.9	6.4	22.6	22.5	11.1	11.1
Persons	5.5	5.9	7.9	7.2	25.2	24.9	12.9	12.8

Source: ISTAT, 'La povertà relativa in Italia nel 2007', table 1, www.istat.it/salastampa/comunicati/non_calendario/20081104_00/testointegrale20081104.pdf.

administrators; and authorities have also been dissuaded from a whole-hearted embrace of social assistance by the realisation that large informal economies and tax evasion make it objectively very difficult for administrators to assess 'real' need and eligibility.

The risks covered

Resources are disproportionately concentrated on providing protection against poverty arising from old age and from short-term unemployment. By contrast, there is little protection available against poverty arising from large families or from long-term unemployment.[1]

The resulting gaps in the system of welfare coverage show through in the statistics relating to the incidence of poverty. In 2002, 11.0 per cent of households were living in **relative poverty**, 4.2 per cent in **absolute poverty** (Box 9.1). Poverty is more widespread in the South than in the North (Table 9.2 and Figure 9.1). It is also more widespread among households with three or more children than it is among couples where the head of household is over sixty-five (Sacchi and Bastagli, 2005: 94–8). These outcomes are what one would expect given the distribution of expenditure between functions described in the previous paragraph. From a comparative perspective, Italy ranks among the eight EU countries (along with Estonia, the UK, Portugal, Spain, Greece, Ireland and Slovakia) with the greatest incidence of poverty: Figure 9.2.

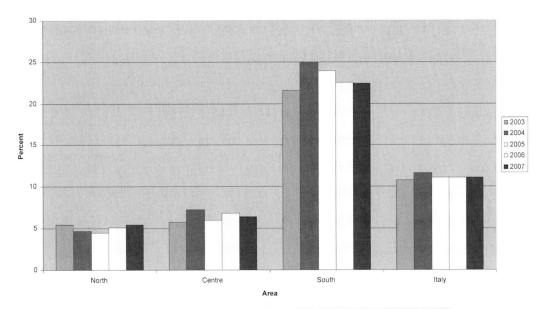

Figure 9.1. Percentage of families in relative poverty by geographical area, 2003–2007
Source: ISTAT 'La povertà relativa in Italia nel 2007', Figure 1, http://www.istat.it/ salastampa/comunicati/non_calendario/20081104_00/testointegrale20081104.pdf.

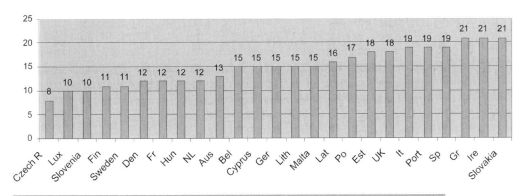

Figure 9.2. At-risk-of-poverty rate after social transfers EU-25 2003
Notes: Figures show the share of persons with an equivalised disposable income below the risk-of-poverty threshold, which is set at 60 % of the national median equivalised disposable income (after social transfers). Figures for Italy and Sweden refer to 2004; figures for Malta refer to 2000.
Source: Eurostat, Structural Indicators, http://www.europa.ue.int/comm/eurostat.

Box 9.2

Unemployment protection in Italy
In Italy, unemployment protection takes four forms. First, there is unemployment benefit (*indennità di disoccupazione*), which pays 40 per cent of a worker's wages for six months. To be eligible for it, the worker must have been insured for at least two years and have at least fifty-two weeks of contributions. Second, there is the Ordinary Wage Supplementation Fund (*Cassa integrazione guadagni ordinaria*, CIG). This provides 80 per cent of wages for a period of up to two years where the firm in question is obliged to suspend or reduce the scale of its activities for a temporary period. In such cases it is the firm that requests the service, not the workers – who are deemed to be still employed. The Special Wage Supplementation Fund (*Cassa integrazione guadagni straordinaria*, CIGS) also provides 80 per cent of wages, but for a period of up to four years, and its services are requested when the firm is facing significant restructuring difficulties. Finally, mobility allowance (*indennità di mobilità*) is available to workers made redundant by firms eligible for CIGS. The worker must have been on the payroll for at least twelve months and have actually worked for at least six. Paying 80 per cent of wages in the first year and 64 per cent in subsequent years, the mobility allowance is available for up to four years depending on age and area of residence (Mancini, 2000: 42–5; Felletti, 2002).

The challenge of legality

Italy is by no means the only country in which legality in connection with welfare is a challenge,[2] but it is possibly one where the challenge arises from circumstances that are more or less specific to it. Traditionally, these have included:

(1) The welfare gaps we have already discussed. For example, one of the effects of a large underground economy is to prevent those employed in it from gaining access to adequate protection against the risks of unemployment. By its very nature, an underground economy prevents employees from building up the contributions records that would entitle them to protection in the first place (Box 9.2). In such circumstances, 'functional equivalents' have to be found. Particularly in the South, where the underground economy is most deeply rooted, invalidity pensions have often served this purpose, as well as providing a basis for clientelistic exchanges between politicians and beneficiaries.
(2) The political parties' funding needs. Thus, one of the forms of corruption that came to light in the period of the *Tangentopoli* scandal in the early 1990s concerned the bribes paid by pharmaceutical companies via the ministerial and inter-ministerial committees responsible for approving new drugs and setting prices. 'The Court of Accounts has estimated that the kickbacks … paid to politicians by pharmaceutical companies between 1983 and 1993 … added, on average, 3,000 milliard a year (*c*. 0.3 percentage points) to the public finance bill (due to artificially higher prices)' (Ferrera, 1996: 455).

The challenge of efficiency

The example of the health service can also be drawn on to illustrate the challenge of efficiency. During the 'First Republic' healthcare was used by the political parties as a resource for obtaining support – with the result that the rationality of funding and administrative arrangements was inevitably trumped by political considerations. For example, in the 1950s and 1960s, doctors with large emoluments and social guarantees sometimes acted as 'electoral advisers' to patients, and the clientelistic ties between doctors and parties tended to undermine professional standards. Later, when the National Health Service was established, places on the boards of local health units (*unità sanitarie locali*, USL) were in the gift of the political parties. This meant that board members sometimes lacked technical competence. The priority given to parties' distributive concerns over requisites of good management generated waste and inefficiency. This in turn ensured that when, with the establishment of the health service, the former health insurance funds were dissolved, the latter had accumulated debts amounting to 3.2 per cent of GDP. This had to be written off by transferring them to the public debt (Ferrera, 1996: 450).

The challenge of funding

As with legality and efficiency, funding is a challenge, not just for Italy, but for welfare systems everywhere. This is because funding is an issue that often involves politically difficult distributive decisions. The principal components of the challenge, some specific to Italy, others shared to a greater or lesser degree with other countries, are of two kinds:

(1)   Those that place upward pressure on spending. These include the separa-tion of tax and spending decisions in healthcare, the growing demand for health services, the changing age structure of the population.
(2)   Those that restrict the resources available to meet acknowledged needs. These include debt problems, political blocks on tax increases, interna-tional pressures.

Both of these two categories are explained below.

Upward pressures on spending

The separation of tax and spending decisions in healthcare
To understand this issue, we have first to appreciate that law no. 833 of 1978, establishing the National Health Service, created a three-tier structure:

(1)   At the top, the state had responsibility for establishing the broad param-eters of health policy and allocating resources.
(2)   The regions were given responsibility for passing, in accordance with the parameters laid down centrally, laws governing the provision of health services in their regions, and responsibility for financing the USL.

(3)   Within each region the USL had responsibility for the administration of service delivery, including the management of hospitals, within their areas.

The overall sums of money to be allocated to the system were determined by means of three-year national health plans (modifiable by the annual finance laws) and then divided among the regions according to allocative formulae which tended to change periodically but which sought to fulfil various criteria of geographical equity. Once they had received their funding allocations, regions and the USL were expected to keep their spending within the limits set by such allocations and were forbidden from running deficits (Mapelli, 1999: 81). The reality, in the years following the reform, was different.

Since regional-level politicians were aware that they could take spending decisions without having to take any corresponding, possibly unpopular, tax decisions – which were taken at the centre – they had little interest in keeping spending down. Thus it was that the regions soon became involved in a tug of war with governments. These would set ceilings as part of the autumn budget; adjust the budget in the spring to meet the previous year's deficit; face alarm in the summer as insufficiency in the funds allocated prevented the USL from paying their suppliers; agree in the autumn to make further emergency allocations, while lowering the ceiling in the subsequent budget – and so on. The upshot was that the gap between *ex-ante* and *ex-post* expenditure rose from 4.5 per cent of the former in 1983 to 20.3 per cent in 1990 (Ferrera, 1996: 453).

The growing demand for health services

This has in turn come from three sources: (1) economic growth, (2) scientific and technological change, and (3) the fact that services are free at the point of delivery:

(1)   Economic growth: for over a century, in all the industrialised countries, continued economic development has been accompanied by considerable increases in life expectancy, largely owing to a significant decline in infant mortality rates. This, together with declining fertility rates in many of these countries since the mid-1960s, has led to an increase in the proportion of the population represented by the elderly, who on average make greater demands on health resources than the rest of the population (Table 9.3). At the same time, economic development has in recent decades brought an increase in the incidence of illnesses associated with affluence. These include illnesses arising from food ingredients, environmental pollution and consumption styles. It is well known, therefore, that there is a close correlation between health spending and economic output, both between countries and within single countries over time. Between 1960 and 1995 health spending in Italy grew at a rate of 4.5 per cent per year in real terms (Mapelli, 1999: 95).

(2)   Scientific and technological progress has added to the pressure by making it increasingly possible to diagnose and treat diseases previously

Table 9.3. The changing age structure of the Italian population

Year	1955	1960	1970	1980	1990	2000	2005	2010	2020	2030	2040	2050
Population over 65 as % of total pop.						17.7	19.3	20.4	23.2	27.1	32.1	33.7
Life expectancy: men						76.6	77.6					
Life expectancy: women						82.5	83.2					
Life expectancy: total	66.0	68.5	71.0	73.6	76.2	78.2	78.7					82.5
Infant mortality (per 1,000 live births)		44.0	30.0	15.0	9.0	4.5	4.7					

Sources: OECD.Stat Extracts, http://stats.oecd.org/WBOS/index.aspx Globalis, http://globalis.gvu.unu.edu/.

untreatable (Dirindin, 2005: 84). Thus, not only has the real volume of resources devoted to health increased year on year, but it has also increased faster than the growth in GDP: between 1960 and 1995 spending as a percentage of GDP rose from 3.6 to 7.4 in Italy (Mapelli, 1999: 94).

(3) Finally, these pressures have been made the greater by the fact that services are largely provided free of charge; for the absence of payment means the absence of a mechanism for bringing demand into line with the available supply. The most visible of Italian governments' efforts to deal with this problem have traditionally taken the form of various types and levels of prescription charging (accompanied by legislation on exemptions) as well as charges for certain other services. That all these problems are ones that are not unique to Italy is suggested by the fact that as a proportion of GDP, its health expenditures are fully in line with those of other EU countries (Eurostat, 2005).

The changing age structure of the population

While in 1960 average life expectancy for men was sixty-seven and for women seventy-two, at the beginning of the new century it was seventy-seven and eighty-three for men and women respectively (ISTAT, 2005: 47). Meanwhile, fertility rates declined from 2.4 to 1.3 children per woman (ISTAT, 2005: 50). The consequence has been a rise in the proportion of the population over sixty-five from 9.2 to 18 per cent, and it is estimated that the proportion will grow to 33 per cent in 2050 (Castles, 2004: 123; Cesari, 2000: 18).

Pensions in Italy have since 1945 been financed essentially according to the method of apportionment (that is they are paid by the contributions of those currently in employment) rather than by the method of capitalisation (where the worker's contributions are invested to create capital which s/he then uses,

Table 9.4. Total tax revenue as a percentage of GDP, 1955–2005

Year:	1955	1960	1965	1970	1975	1980	1985	1990	1995	2000	2005
Italy	30.5	34.4	25.5	25.7	25.4	29.7	33.6	37.8	40.1	42.3	41.0
France	n.a.	n.a.	34.1	34.1	35.4	40.1	42.8	42.0	42.9	44.4	44.1
Germany	30.8	31.3	31.6	31.5	34.3	36.4	36.1	34.8	37.2	37.2	34.8
UK	29.7	28.5	30.4	37.0	35.3	35.2	37.6	36.3	34.7	37.3	36.5
US	23.6	26.5	24.7	27.0	25.6	26.4	25.6	27.3	27.9	29.9	27.3
EU15	26.0	26.0	27.6	29.5	32.1	34.8	37.4	38.0	38.8	40.4	39.7
OECD	24.0	24.6	25.5	27.6	29.5	31.2	32.7	33.9	34.9	36.2	36.2

Source: OECD.Stat Extracts, http://stats.oecd.org/WBOS/index.aspx.

either directly, or to provide a life annuity, at retirement). (Baranes, nd: 6). The result has been a growing deficit between contributions and pension outlays (Cesari, 2000: 22; Ferrera, 1997: 234).

Downward pressures on spending

Debt problems

High levels of public debt reduce the resources available for investment.[3] They also oblige governments to run continuous primary surpluses. They *must* do this if they are to prevent the debt spiralling out of control and provoking financial crisis (Musu, 1998: 47–56). But the effects tend to be regressive, distributing income and wealth away from wage-earners without investments, to those in possession of state bonds (and who tend to be among the wealthier).

Political blocks on tax increases

Unfortunately, however, attempting to bring down the debt simply by raising taxes and contributions, without attacking welfare spending is not easy. Between 1980 and 1990, social contributions paid by employers and employees rose by 48 per cent while, as a proportion of GDP, the total tax take of general government rose from 30.2 to 40 per cent (Ferrera, 1997: 239). Although since then these aggregates have remained more or less steady – social contributions went from 14.6 to 12.9 per cent of GDP between 1994 and 2004, general government revenues from 44.0 to 45.3 per cent (Table 9.4)[4] – this is only after a significant decline in the degree of public consensus on tax and welfare matters. In 2001, 46.4 per cent agreed that taxes should be reduced even if this meant cuts in public services, while 48.4 per cent disagreed.[5] Prior to the 1990s, recourse to deficit spending meant that voters were relatively unaware of the real costs of welfare measures and had little real interest in curbing them. Since then, the need for retrenchment associated with things like European Monetary Union (EMU) have made the relationship between welfare and taxation much more explicit as well as giving rise to a new territorial cleavage on the issue symbolised by the emergence and growth of the Northern League (Ferrera, 1997: 243–7). It is an issue that is destined to remain salient for voters as a result of the new, permanent constraints on deficit financing that have come with adoption of the euro.

International pressures

Finally, the international pressures tending to restrict governments' freedom in welfare spending are of two kinds: political and economic:

(1) The political pressures have in recent years come mainly from the EU, especially from its greater involvement in the area of poverty stemming from the Lisbon European Council of March 2000. This launched an EU-wide strategy against social exclusion, based on the open method of co-ordination (OMC),[6] which obliged member states, every two years, to produce action plans for social inclusion. Such plans were to translate EU objectives into national policies and to be analysed and assessed by the Commission and the Social Protection Committee. Their conclusions were to be embodied in a report comparing and contrasting member states' approaches and giving recommendations. Italy's first plan was 'rather … non-committal' (Sacchi and Bastagli, 2005: 90)[7] and the second one possibly even less committal (Ferrera and Sacchi 2004: 18). But it can be argued that the EU's strategy places potential restrictions on spending by raising the prospect of the application of pressures that oblige governments to channel welfare efforts in some directions rather than others.

(2) External economic pressures arise from globalisation and the increasing significance of international trade[8] (though it has to be said that Castles (2004) casts some doubt on the *strength* of these pressures).[9] They are directly related to the Lisbon strategy; for the latter has been driven, at least in part, by fears that economic integration would give rise to 'social dumping' and the above-mentioned 'race to the bottom' in welfare (Pochet, 2005).

■ Welfare: the policy response

The challenges we have discussed in the previous section together constitute the backdrop to a series of structural reforms of the welfare system introduced by governments in recent years. The most important of these have been the two sets of reforms of the pensions system (between 1992 and 1997 and in 2004), the two sets of reforms in the health service (in 1992/3 and in 1999) and a 1998 reform in the area of unemployment.

The pensions reforms

The pensions system prior to the 1990s

Prior to the reforms of the 1990s, the pensions system for most of the employed and of the self-employed was managed by the National Social

Security Institute (Istituto Nazionale della Previdenza Sociale, INPS) whose funds derived partly from general taxation and partly from compulsory social security contributions paid by the worker and the employer. In essence, INPS paid two kinds of old-age pension: (a) a non-contributory 'social pension' available to all citizens of limited means at age sixty-five; (b) an 'old-age pension', available from age fifty-five for females and age sixty for males with a minimum contribution period of ten years. It paid a maximum of 80 per cent (2 per cent per year for a maximum of forty years) of the average salary achieved during the last five years in employment. In addition, however, it was also possible to retire at any age if one had thirty-five years of contributions – in which case one received what was known as a 'seniority pension' paying 70 per cent of former salary. As we have seen, the system was one in which pension payments were: (1) calculated on the basis of the worker's earnings, not on the basis of the value of the contributions paid while in employment; (2) financed on the basis of apportionment rather than capitalisation. The 1990s reforms changed both of these elements.

The 1990s reforms: from an earnings to a contributions basis

Law no. 335 of 1995 introduced the contributions-based system for the calculation of pensions. In essence, this means that the annual pension payments due to the worker are calculated by taking his/her (notional or actual) annual contributions, compounding them by a rate of interest (in this case the average rate of growth of GDP in the last five years) and then dividing the total by the average life expectancy at the age of retirement. This system was applied to all workers joining the labour market from 1996. Workers who, at the end of 1995 had fewer than eighteen years of contributions were to have their pensions calculated on the basis of a mixture of the earnings-based scheme (with regard to years of employment until then) and the contributions-based scheme (with regard to subsequent years of employment). Those with more than eighteen years of contributions at the end of 1995 were to continue to have their pensions calculated according to the old scheme (although law no. 421 of 1992 had already introduced a gradual extension of the reference period for pensionable earnings, a period extended to encompass the entire period of employment for new entrants to the labour market).

The 1990s reforms: from apportionment to capitalisation

The reforms also initiated a gradual shift towards a capitalisation-based method of financing pensions. Thus legislative decree no. 124 of 1993 introduced, alongside the public pension, a 'second pillar'. That is, it established the legal framework necessary for supplementary pensions to be paid through occupational pension funds. Essentially, with the changes to the first pillar it was anticipated that the 'rate of replacement' – that is, pension payments expressed as a proportion of final salary – would decline rapidly after 2010.[10] Besides the ones described, the changes to the first pillar also included increases in contributions and in the retirement ages for men and women respectively to sixty-five and sixty. So, the new pension funds are designed to ensure adequate future pensions in the face of these downward pressures on the rate of replacement. The funds are of two types: closed and open funds.

(1) Closed funds are essentially those established by means of collective agreements between workers and employers, or between groups of the self-employed, and are closed in the sense of being reserved for those working in some particular sector (e.g. chemicals or mechanical engineering).
(2) Open funds are those initiated by financial institutions, legally empowered to manage such funds, and are available to all potential contributors who wish to join.

There is also a distinction to be made between funds based on fixed contributions (where pension payments depend on the performance of the fund's investments) and funds based on fixed pensions (where pension payments are defined at the outset and contributions revised periodically to achieve the pre-defined levels). Only free professionals and the self-employed may establish funds of the latter type.

The legislative decree of 1993 also established a third pillar, one constituted by the so-called individual supplementary pension. This offers, on an entirely individual basis, a channel for additional voluntary pension contributions. It is like the second pillar in that it involves contributing to an investment fund with the aim of securing pension payments financed according to the capitalisation method; and like the second pillar it also offers tax relief on contributions (as well as various other tax incentives). The pension plans offered by the third pillar are strongly linked to already existing financial products, such as life insurance policies, the objective being to encourage people to use medium- and long-term savings for pensions provision.

The 2004 reform

The 2004 pensions reform introduced a number of measures designed to increase employment rates among older age cohorts and to increase pension-system revenues:

- From 2008 the minimum age of fifty-seven (introduced in 1995) for seniority pensions was to be increased in stages to sixty-two and sixty-three for employees and the self-employed respectively. (As a first step from 1 January 2008, the age was to be increased to sixty in the private and public sectors, and to 61 for those registered with the INPS as being self-employed. In the event, the Prodi government elected in 2006 replaced this provision with a gradual, sustainable increase in the retirement age, which took into consideration the peculiarities of unusually demanding jobs[11] (Capriati, 2009).)
- Seniority pensions will be obtainable after forty years of contributions regardless of age.

- Women will retain the possibility of retiring at fifty-seven (with thirty-five years of contributions), but their pensions will be calculated entirely according to their contributions rather than their earnings.
- Prior to 2008, workers reaching the requisite age for seniority pensions but choosing to postpone retirement were to receive tax relief designed to ensure that, when they did retire, their contributions would provide higher pensions benefits than they would otherwise have received. Alternatively, they were to be able to discontinue contributions, taking them instead in the form of a tax-free bonus equal to 32.7 per cent of gross pay.
- For all workers the reform provides for the automatic transfer of severance pay to the closed occupational funds (where available) unless, within six months of starting employment, the worker explicitly indicates a desire to receive the pay upon retirement. Prior to the reform, severance pay was only transferred in the event that the worker actually decided to participate in the fund.

The reforms can be evaluated in terms of their financial impact and their impact in terms of equity.

Assessing the pensions reforms: their financial impact

From the financial point of view, the reforms can be seen as a success. Four points can be made.

(1) In 1998, while social insurance payments were about 132 per cent of contributions, the gap between the two was already beginning to close; for contributions were growing at 5.8 per cent, payments at only 3.2 (Cesari, 2000: 37). The gap can be expected eventually to close altogether since the switch to contributions rather than earnings as the basis for calculating public pensions effectively neutralises the impact of demographic variables on the pensions system. It ensures that a growth in the number of pensioners as a proportion of the employed population automatically results in a diminution in the size of pension payments.

(2) The increasing shift towards the capitalisation method of funding pensions can be expected to assist the development of the stock market (see chapter 8) as well as increasing the volume of resources available for productive investment.

(3) EU estimates suggest that as a consequence of the reforms of the 1990s, pensions spending as a proportion of GDP will grow to about 15.7 per cent in 2030 (from 13.8 percent in 2000) to fall back, in 2050, to about the 2000 level.

(4) This means that Italy – having acted sooner than most other EU countries – can be expected to have to devote proportions of its GDP to pension payments well in line with EU averages and much below those of countries such as Austria and Greece (see Baranes, nd: 11) (Table 9.5).

Table 9.5. Public spending on pensions as a proportion of GDP in the EU15, estimates 2000–2050

Year:	2000	2010	2020	2030	2040	2050
Belgium	10.0	9.9	11.4	13.3	13.7	13.3
Denmark	10.5	12.5	13.8	14.5	14.0	13.3
Germany	11.8	11.2	12.6	15.5	16.6	16.9
Greece	12.6	12.6	15.4	19.6	23.8	24.8
Spain	9.4	8.9	9.9	12.6	16.0	17.3
France	12.1	13.1	15.0	16.0	15.8	
Ireland*	4.6	5.0	6.7	7.6	8.3	9.0
Italy	13.8	13.9	14.8	15.7	15.7	14.1
Luxembourg	7.4	7.5	8.2	9.2	9.5	9.3
Netherlands	7.9	9.1	11.1	13.1	14.1	13.6
Austria	14.5	14.9	16.0	18.1	18.3	17.0
Portugal	9.8	11.8	13.1	13.6	13.8	13.2
Finland	11.3	11.6	12.9	14.9	16.0	15.9
Sweden	9.0	9.6	10.7	11.4	11.4	10.7
UK	5.5	5.1	4.9	5.2	5.0	4.4
EU	10.4	10.4	11.5	13.0	13.6	13.3

Note: * Figures for Ireland are percentages of GNP not of GDP.
Source: Baranes, (nd), 'La riforma del system previdenziale: cause e conseguenze dell'introduzione dei fondi pensione', www.italia.attac.org/spip/IMG/pdf/Riforma_previdenziale.pdf, Table 2, p.11; Economic Policy Committee (2001).

Assessing the pensions reforms: equity

From the point of view of equity, on the other hand, the reforms are much more questionable.

(1) Overall, the new regime means that those currently in employment are having to pay twice: once to finance, through apportionment, the earnings-based pensions of those who have retired; a second time in order to build, through capitalisation, their own pensions, without, however, any guarantee as to the size of the pensions.
(2) Even worse, there is a considerable element of randomness associated with their retirement benefits since the size of these will be subject to the state of financial markets on the day of their retirement – meaning that A, retiring after a sudden fall in markets, may have a pension much lower than B's, in spite of having perhaps worked for the same number of years, paid the same contributions and received the same salary.
(3) It is doubtful whether, in public discussion of the reforms, the relative weight of the forces driving them has been accurately reflected in the amount of publicity each has been given. For example, much has been

made of the ageing population – but there are other ways of addressing the implications of this phenomenon besides attacking pensions. They include:

i   measures to increase the rate of employment (which by international standards is very low in Italy);

ii   allowing greater immigration;

iii   measures to end the pressures on women to leave work when they give birth – which could be expected to have the double effect of increasing both the rate of employment and the rate of fertility.

By contrast, very little has been said about the undoubted advantage to governments of what is, in effect, the privatisation of pensions provision. The advantage to governments is that the measures free them from the political responsibilities and constraints associated with the pensions issue. Hitherto governments have often used the pensions system as a means of redistributing resources between different categories of the population. But the choices involved in such decisions are, in a privately managed, capitalisation-based system, no longer ones that citizens can call upon governments to make.

The health-service reforms

Like many of the administrative, economic and welfare reforms of the past decade and a half, those concerning the health service are intimately connected to the early 1990s economic and political crises, arising from the process of European integration, and to the party-system upheavals of the time. Especially in the case of the 1992/3 reforms, the crises allowed the implementation of proposals that had been made in the 1980s but that had never been realised because (1) the existing system satisfied parties' distributive concerns, and (2) each party was a 'veto player' with power to obstruct attempted moves away from the status quo. Given the health system's incapacity to contain spending or to meet the above-mentioned challenge of efficiency, the twin crises created strong endogenous pressures for change, weakened the parties' capacities to act as veto players and increased the policy-making capacity of the political system through the growing autonomy of executive from legislature that we discussed in chapter 4.

The second reform of the health service

Thus it was that legislative decree no. 502 of 1992, commonly known as the 'second reform' of the health service (the first being the 1978 reform), was introduced pursuant to measures contained in law of delegation no. 421. This, in the immediate aftermath of the lira's September 1992 exit from the European Monetary System, gave the then Government under Giuliano Amato delegated powers to take drastic measures of public expenditure, health-service and administrative reform.

As modified the following year by legislative decree no. 517, the reform introduced three major changes.

(1) It began to shift the distribution of responsibility for the tax decisions arising from health-spending decisions away from the state towards the regions. In other words, it retained the pre-existing bi-partite funding system (whereby the service's resources came both from employers' and workers' social insurance contributions, and from general taxation); but it also provided that the social insurance contributions would go directly to the regions in which they had been generated. The funds to be made available from the taxation category would be determined on the basis of a definition of uniform levels of service to be provided throughout the country, and distributed among the regions on a per capita basis. Regions wanting to offer services of a higher quality than that provided for by this mechanism, and regions facing deficits, would be obliged to make up the shortfall by asking their residents for additional contributions (Maino, 2001a: 89). A further step along this road was taken when, in 1997, the health contributions were replaced by the Regional Tax on Enterprises (*Imposta regionale sulle attività produttive*, IRAP) and the regions given powers to raise the latter by up to 1 per cent (Mapelli, 1998: 84).

(2) The reform considerably enhanced the regions' powers and responsibilities in the areas of planning, organisation and control. The intention was to give the regions an additional – organisational – mechanism enabling them to deviate from national standards without having to draw on additional resources from the outside.

(3) The reform renamed the USL, *Aziende sanitarie locali* (Local Health Companies, ASL). It considerably reduced their number (and thus increased the size of the territory for which each was responsible). The party-nominated management boards were replaced by directors-general who were given unlimited administrative powers and were appointed for five-year renewable terms on the basis of private-law contracts.

In addition, the reform sought a more efficient deployment of resources by initiating a move, taken forward by more detailed follow-up legislation, towards heightened levels of administrative competition within the service:

(1) The ASLs were given freedom to supply health services either through their own structures, or by purchasing the services from public or private institutions. These would receive fixed tariffs, established by the region, for the services (rather than receiving, as they had done before, payments whose entity varied depending on, for example, the number of days the patient spent in hospital).

(2) Hospitals were allowed to become organisationally and financially autonomous entities among which patients were free to choose.

(3) Since tariffs were set by reference to average costs, health service providers had an incentive to maximise efficiency as the way to maximise profits.

Moreover, the tariffs were understood as maximum amounts the ASL could pay. They thus allowed the ASLs to negotiate prices, with providers, on the basis of the quantity and quality of the services to be provided.

The third reform of the health service

The reform of 1999, the so-called third reform of the health service, sought to complete the process of health-service reorganisation begun in 1992/3 and did so by:

- refining the system whereby health-service providers were accredited and the quality of their services monitored;
- giving the local authorities a more significant role in the planning and evaluation of health services;
- obliging doctors to choose between private practice, or else working for the health service (within whose structures they were, however, to be allowed to carry on intramural activities).

These features have led Maino (2001b: 154) to argue that though in other respects the reform moved in a direction different from that of its predecessor, it represented the logical continuation of the latter; for it sought to set out, for each institutional actor and for each occupational category within the service, the precise boundaries of its autonomy as well as its corresponding levels of responsibility.

Assessing the health-service reforms

What are we to make of these reforms? From a political point of view they appear to have been successful:

(1) At the time of the 1999 reform, the World Health Organization rated Italy second only to France for the overall performance of its health service (Maino, 2001b: 162).
(2) The most salient feature of the reforms has been a process of region-alisation of health-service provision, organisation and finance.[12] From this point of view, Italy appears to mirror trends common to a number of European countries where governments have sought to free themselves from the onerous responsibilities of a high-profile policy area, one fraught with political dangers. In this respect the health-service reforms have apparently been driven by political factors very similar to the ones driving the pensions measures.

From an economic point of view, however, the reforms appear to have been somewhat less successful. If the aim was to contain expenditure by increasing the fiscal responsibilities of sub-national levels of government, then the fact that only three regions had balanced budgets in 2001, despite the further shift of fiscal responsibilities to the regions contained in legislative decree no. 56 of 2000 (see note 11), had to be seen as a cause for concern.

The unemployment reform

As we have seen, 'the missing building block of the Italian welfare state edifice' (Sacchi and Bastagli, 2005: 84) is a national minimum income scheme. Thus, owing to the inability of some groups to access categorical, contributory benefits, rates of poverty are quite high by EU standards. Meanwhile, poverty and social exclusion have come to occupy a higher place on the EU's policy-making agenda in recent years. It was in this context that, in 1997, the then Prodi government appointed the Onofri Commission, giving it the task of producing proposals for structural reform of the entire welfare state. Its recommendations included the introduction of what, the following year, took the name of *Reddito minimo di inserimento* (or Minimum Insertion Income, RMI). The latter was envisaged less as a measure of income maintenance specifically for the unemployed than as a measure of last resort for households generally. Nevertheless, new entrants to the labour market, the long-term unemployed and underground workers are effectively excluded from Italy's other employment protection measures (see Box 9.2). Not surprisingly, therefore, the vast majority of RMI beneficiaries were in fact either unemployed or outside the labour force (Sacchi and Bastagli, 2005: 119).

RMI was introduced on an experimental basis. The 1998 Finance Law thus made provision for the scheme to be piloted by thirty-nine local authorities. These were selected according to a variety of criteria including poverty levels and the willingness of the authorities to participate. The scheme was to run for two years in the first instance and to be evaluated in a report to be presented by the Government, to Parliament, by mid-2001. It provided the difference between a threshold income (€258 in 1999) and a recipient's actual monthly income. It made entitlement to the money conditional upon participation in 'reinsertion' programmes tailored to the specific circumstances responsible for the recipient's social exclusion. The 2001 Finance Law, passed in December 2000, extended the life of the scheme for a further two years and increased the number of participating municipalities to 306. In the meantime, the evaluation report was compiled and the 2001 election produced the Berlusconi government. This government's negative assessment of the scheme led it, in the 2004 Finance Law, to provide for RMI's replacement by a *Reddito di ultima istanza* (Income of Last Resort, RUI). This was to be financed in part by means of contributions from the centre; but it was provided for by means of legislation to be passed by each region. The phrasing of the law was such that it was unclear whether introduction of the scheme would be voluntary or obligatory for the regions. In any case, it had not been implemented by the time Parliament was dissolved in February 2006. The centre left's electoral programme promised to revive RMI in the event that the coalition won the 2006 election (a promise that was kept by means of the Finance Law for 2007. This extended the life of the scheme until June of that year when a further report evaluating the impact of the scheme was presented to Parliament by the Government).

From the point of view of an evaluation of RMI, then, three points can be made.

(1) If one of the purposes of a minimum income scheme is to reduce or eliminate the inequities inherent in the gaps left by insurance-based schemes, RMI was partially, but only partially, successful. Though the law establishing the scheme established criteria for ascertaining house-holds' disposable incomes, municipalities felt themselves entitled to depart from the criteria when necessary in order to take local circum-stances into account. The problem was that such departures did not take place in a uniform way and seem to have depended, to some degree, on available resources (while the centre provided 90 per cent of the cost of the cash transfers, up to 10 per cent of the costs of the transfers, as well as the remaining costs of the scheme, had to come from the municipalities themselves).

(2) If it was to be successful, the scheme required well-developed adminis-trative capacities on the part of those managing it. Such capacities would be required in order accurately to assess claimants' eligibility and to manage the reinsertion programmes. The problem was that these capaci-ties were (and are) most lacking in precisely that area (the South) where, with its large underground and depressed economy, they are most required. Not only does such an economy pose formidable obstacles in the way of assessing eligibility, but the opportunities (or lack thereof) it offers detract from the incentives to offer well-designed reinsertion programmes.

(3) Ninety-three per cent of the RMI beneficiaries were concentrated in the South (Sacchi and Bastagli, 2005: 118). This suggested that Italy's vast regional disparities had conspired to open a gap between the scheme's *intended* function (helping marginal groups wherever located) and its *actual* function (alleviating a wide range of the social problems of a given area), with the risk of exacerbating North–South political cleavages.

■ Judicial policy and civil rights: the context

In chapter 6 we argued that as a result of the setting up of the Constitutional Court in 1956, the judicial system had acquired an increasingly significant policy-making role and had therefore become an increasing object of attention for interest groups. In our introduction to this chapter we implied that the judicial system had an important role to play in achieving public compliance with policy decisions. This is because the function of judges is to resolve grievances between citizens, between citizens and the state, and between different branches of the state, and because judges carry out this function by reference to law. If this helps to give judges' decisions themselves authority, such authority is unlikely to be assured unless the choice of judge and the procedure by which s/he arrives at her/his decisions embody rights guaranteeing the parties in dispute against an arbitrary exercise of power. Guarantees against abuse of power are necessary to ensure consent to all state decisions affecting the ordinary citizen, but they are particularly important in judicial decisions given that the function of the latter is to secure 'justice', in the sense of securing to each what is due to her/him. Questions of rights, and civil rights, therefore lie at the very heart of judicial policy and the way judicial systems are structured and function.

The Italian judicial system: structure and functioning

The structure and functioning of the Italian judicial system can be briefly described as follows. Justice, both civil and criminal, is administered by *magistrati ordinari* (ordinary magistrates) recruited from among law graduates on the basis of open competition.[13] Depending on their degree of seriousness, both civil and criminal cases are in the first instance dealt with by the *giudice di pace* (justice of the peace) or the *tribunale* (the *corte d'assise* in the case of the most serious criminal matters) whose territorial jurisdiction is defined by a series of *circondari* each of which, in turn, belongs to one or the other of twenty-nine *distretti giudiziari* (judicial districts). Each judicial district has an appeal court to which the sentences of the courts of first instance can of right be appealed.[14] At the apex of the system, in Rome, stands the Corte di Cassazione (Court of Cassation), the function of which is to ensure uniform application of the law, and to which the sentences of lower courts may be appealed – but only on grounds of legal interpretation, not interpretations of the facts.

Alongside each court sits the corresponding office of the *pubblico ministero* (public prosecutor)[15] whose function, in criminal matters, is to initiate and carry on, with the assistance of the judicial police, investigations into allegations that come to his/her attention. At the termination of these investigations, the prosecutor applies to a judge – the so-called *giudice dell'udienza preliminare* (literally, 'judge of the preliminary hearing', GUP) – either to have the case dismissed, or, if the evidence appears to warrant it, to proceed to trial.[16] In the latter case, the GUP examines the application in the presence of the prosecutor, the defendant and the defendant's legal representative. At the trial, representatives of the prosecution and (where applicable) the victim, on the one hand, and of the defence on the other each make an introductory statement of their case following which the evidence is considered by means of cross-examination. The judge may also question witnesses and the accused. Finally, the prosecution, and lastly the defence representatives each make a closing statement after which the presiding judge delivers a verdict and a sentence.

Alongside the ordinary system of justice sit the systems of administrative and military justice, and there is a fourth system for matters concerning public accounting. The system of administrative justice protects the legitimate interests of the citizen in his/her dealings with the public administration where the court of first instance (one for each region) is the Regional Administrative Court.[17] Sentences are appealed to the Council of State, which, besides its judicial functions, also provides legal advice to the Government. The system of military justice is, in times of peace, relevant only for crimes committed by members of the armed forces. The final system has jurisdiction in cases of administrative officials' management of public funds where sentences handed down by courts of first instance are appealed to the Corte dei Conti or Public Audit Office. This, as its name suggests, has a range of auditing as well as judicial functions. Disputes in matters of jurisdiction between the various systems are settled by the Court of Cassation.

Three further structures contribute in a major way to the administration of justice in Italy.

(1) The Constitutional Court discussed in chapter 6.
(2) The Ministry of Justice. In deference to the separation-of-powers principle, its role (once much more significant) is now essentially limited to the provision of support services to the judicial system, though the minister retains the authority to initiate (but not to conduct) disciplinary proceedings and to require to be consulted (but not to decide) in matters of judicial appointments.
(3) All these are tasks entrusted by the Constitution, to the Consiglio superiore della magistratura (High Council of the Judiciary, CSM), a freestanding body two-thirds of whose components are elected by ordinary magistrates from among their own members. The remaining third is elected by Parliament from among law professors and lawyers of at least fifteen years standing. The intention behind the two-thirds/one-third division is to provide for judicial independence while avoiding the emergence of a judicial 'corporation'. Presided over by the President of the Republic, the CSM is responsible for recruitment, appointments, transfers, promotions and disciplinary proceedings as regards judicial personnel.

The Italian judicial system, and rights

The civil rights which the Italian judicial system, like those of other democracies, seeks to protect are numerous. They include the right to be presumed not guilty before sentence is passed, the right to a defence, the right to a fair trial and the right to be tried by a 'natural judge' (that is, one nominated before the event to try all cases of the kind in question, not one appointed ad hoc, to try the specific case in question). These rights in turn each imply or strongly suggest a number of more specific rights. For example, the right to be presumed not guilty implies a whole series of rights surrounding the circumstances in which defendants can be remanded in custody and if so, the conditions of such custody; the right to a defence is unlikely to be plausibly guaranteed unless there is a right to cross-examination, a right to be heard by the judge before s/he makes any decision, a right to be tried in public, a right to adequate time to prepare one's defence, a right to participate in the gathering of evidence, a right to silence and so forth (Salerno, 2002: 84). All of these rights are arguably specific expressions of a general, overarching right, namely the right to have one's case dealt with by judicial personnel who are independent (that is, free of outside influences irrelevant to a judgement of the merits of the case) and impartial (that is, free of any predisposition to favour one or the other of the parties in dispute).

The nature of the Italian judicial system

The Italian judicial system seeks to assure this right in ways that identify it as clearly belonging to a different category than the one to which the system of England and Wales and those like it belong. In fact, whereas the latter are said to be based on the adversarial model, the Italian, along with other continental European systems, are said to embody the inquisitorial model.

In adversarial systems, the role of the judge is to act as a referee between the parties, while conclusions about the truth of the case rely on the skill of each side in presenting its position and arguing over the admissibility of evidence. The adversarial model tends to be found in common-law systems. These are systems in which previous cases, and therefore precedents, are the primary source of law and where statutes are thus always subject to interpretation in the light of them. Because of the heavy emphasis on case law in such systems, judges are usually recruited from long-standing and reputable advocates, together with whom they form a corporation of jurists; and it is in part by virtue of this corporation being itself a source of law that the judicial system's independence of other branches of the state is secured.

In inquisitorial systems, judges play a much more active role in ascertaining the truth, themselves being involved in the gathering of evidence and the questioning of witnesses. This does *not* mean that the roles of prosecutor and judge are necessarily conflated since judges are enjoined to look for *both* incriminating *and* exculpating evidence and investigating judges do not preside at subsequent trials. Here, separate trial judges hear both the prosecution and the defence put their cases. The inquisitorial model is usually found in civil-law systems, that is, systems in which statutes are the primary source of law. In such systems the separation-of-powers principle is interpreted to mean that the judge's role is merely to apply the law as decided by the popularly elected legislature. Under these circumstances, judges look for guidance in interpreting the law not to case law or precedent but, in the Italian case, where possible to the accumulation of rulings given by the Court of Cassation – which thus provides a functional equivalent to case law. Lacking the relative autonomy of statutes of their common-law counterparts, civil-law judges tend to be recruited separately from advocates and to be part of a bureaucratic apparatus not very different from the rest of the public administration. Under these circumstances, judicial independence relies on a more-or-less formal and elaborate series of legal and constitutional provisions. In the Italian case, these include provisions providing for the irremovability of magistrates, provisions concerning the powers and functions of the CSM – and so forth. Finally, the

Table 9.6. Average duration of civil proceedings, in days, in courts of first instance and in appeal courts

Year	First instance	Appeal
1991	804	868
1992	900	1,004
1993	850	963
1994	859	1,004
1995	833	1,074
1996	864	1,031
1997	802	986
1998	815	997
1999	789	940
2000	839	950

Source: ISTAT, *Rapporto Annuale 2001*, Rome: Poligrafico dello Stato, 2002: 250, table 5.3.

fact that judges in inquisitorial systems not only make rulings of law but also findings of fact (a role normally performed by juries in adversarial systems), combined with their 'subordination' to legislation, tends to mean that judicial impartiality is also underpinned by a series of explicit guarantees. In the Italian case, these include the constitutional provisions requiring all judicial decisions to be accompanied by a formal statement of the reasons for them, and those guaranteeing defendants' rights of appeal (rights that tend to be much more restricted in common-law systems).

The capacity of the Italian judicial system to ensure that the right to an independent and impartial administration of justice is observed in all cases has been questioned with regard to the following four considerations in recent years.

(1) The suggestion that the roles of judge and prosecutor are imperfectly separated.
(2) The obligations on public prosecutors to initiate criminal proceedings.
(3) The treatment of prisoners on remand.
(4) The amount of time typically required by civil and criminal proceedings (Table 9.6).

The first three, in particular, have occupied a position high on the agenda of public debate owing to the emergence, from the early 1980s, of a climate of growing diffidence and hostility between sectors of the 'political class', on the one hand, and members of the judiciary on the other. This has in turn been related to two interconnected trends:

(1) the growing 'judicialisation of politics' discussed in chapter 6;
(2) the growing willingness of members of the judiciary to investigate the behaviour of individual politicians and groups of politicians in matters

such as corruption and illegal party funding – a trend that reached a climax with the explosion of the early 1990s *Tangentopoli* scandal (Guarnieri, 1997; Newell, 2000; Guarnieri, 2001; Bull and Newell, 2005).

This growing climate of hostility was the background cause of each of the judicial reforms considered below. For now let us consider each of the four questions that have been raised concerning the Italian judicial system's capacity to ensure an independent and impartial administration of justice.

The suggestion that the roles of judge and prosecutor are imperfectly separated

Claims that the roles of judge and prosecutor are imperfectly separated in the Italian system arise essentially from the argument

(1) that the main body of evidence on which courts reach their decisions is the written evidence emerging from the pre-trial 'preliminary investigations' (and thus that they are unlikely to be able to assess what weight to give to the interpretative and filtering processes of the author of that evidence); and
(2) that the investigating judges responsible for the evidence, and trial judges, both belong to the same profession, 'usually work in neighbouring offices' (di Federico, 1989: 31) and frequently switch between the two roles.

This set of circumstances, it is argued, brings with it the risk that trials represent little more than the 'formal confirmation' (Certoma, 1985: 243) of conclusions reached by the *pubblico ministero* during the pre-trial phase. This risk was, perhaps, symbolised by the fact that until 1988 (see below) the *pubblico ministero* sat beside the judge in court, both facing the defendant and his/her advocate (Grilli, 2005: 52).

The obligations on public prosecutors to initiate criminal proceedings

Second, it is argued that assurances of judicial impartiality are further corroded by the practical operation of the constitutional principle making criminal action obligatory. The reference here is to article 112 of the Constitution which states that 'The public prosecutor has the duty to initiate criminal proceedings.' In the formal terms of the Italian code of criminal procedure, this means that whenever convinced of the guilt of a person s/he has been investigating, the prosecutor may not fail to apply to the GUP for the case to be sent for trial. If not so convinced, s/he must still apply to the GUP, in which case s/he must apply for the case to be dismissed.

The provision was originally intended to ensure the equality of all citizens before the law by removing from the *pubblico ministero* any discretion over whether or not to initiate proceedings in a case. It thus eliminates any role for considerations of whether proceedings are *opportune*. However, the principle is ambiguous in terms of its concrete implications.

Its presence as part of the Constitution is superfluous without procedures to ensure its observance, so various powers are available to the GUP to check that the investigations on which applications are based are full and complete, and so forth. This has led some observers to the conclusion that the principle implies that prosecutors must initiate investigations into all alleged or suspected crimes that are reported to them. In that case, however, discretion on the part of the prosecutor is impossible to eliminate simply because of the sheer number of alleged incidents reported every day. This means that there is a need for decisions about which of the reports are to be taken seriously, the ones to be given priority and so forth. Moreover, there are various safeguards preventing prosecutors from using their investigatory powers with a persecutory intent. These include the one limiting their powers of independent initiative in relation to evidence that comes to their attention outside the course of their official duties (Pizzorusso, 1990: 169). However, article 330 of the code of criminal procedure enables prosecutors to acquire knowledge of facts constituting evidence of a crime, not just through the reports of others, but also 'on their own initiative' (Grilli, 2005: 185). Finally, when applying for a case to be sent for trial, a prosecutor has to formulate a specific charge. This means that s/he has to specify what was done and what law was broken. This implies that s/he must make a decision about which of a large number of laws, with varying penal implications, the charges are to be brought under.

The treatment of prisoners on remand

When it is necessary to ensure public safety and/or the integrity of preliminary, pre-trial, investigations, the judiciary has the power to remand defendants in custody. Doubts have been raised about the robustness of safeguards designed to prevent abuse of this precautionary measure. At the time of *Tangentopoli*, it was suggested in some quarters that investigating magistrates' use of preventive custody powers had been decisive in securing the confessions. This provoked accusations that custody had been used to acquire evidence by placing defendants under illegitimate pressure – rather than for its proper purpose of preventing the risk of defendants (1) tampering with evidence, (2) escaping, or (3) posing a danger to the public.

Proper safeguards are essential to ensure that precautionary measures cannot be used as a form of punishment before guilt has been established. Thus the code of criminal procedure stipulates that no precautionary measure may be taken unless

(1) there is strong evidence of guilt;
(2) one of the aforementioned three risks exist, and
(3) the crime for which the person is being investigated carries a penalty of at least three years.

It provides also:

(1) that the specific measure applied must be adequate for prevention of the risk involved, proportionate to the gravity of the offence of which the person is suspected, and informed by their specific circumstances (for example, mental infirmity);

(2) that measures cannot be applied by prosecutors on their own authority but must be authorised by a judge through the issue of an injunction;

(3) that copies of the injunction, setting out the reasons for it, must be made available to the defence;

(4) that the defence has a right of appeal.

What appears to trouble critics is that decisions about injunctions are made entirely on the basis of evidence supplied by the prosecutor, and the defence has no opportunity to contest the injunction before it becomes effective.[18]

The amount of time typically required by civil and criminal proceedings

Finally, observers of the Italian judicial system frequently complain about the length of proceedings, arguing that justice delayed is justice denied. Certainly, the available evidence suggests that legal actions in Italy are lengthy by international standards. For example, according to Guarnieri (2001: 76) civil proceedings in a court of first instance typically require between 26 and 46 months, as against 4.6–6.5 in Germany, 7.4 in France and 19 in the United Kingdom.

There are various reasons why such a situation might be deemed unsatisfactory:

(1) Being subject to prosecution implies being subject to all kinds of pressures, psychological if nothing else (so that there is a right, recognised by the European Convention (article 6), 'to a fair and public hearing within a reasonable time').

(2) Delays place obstacles in the way of the system's ability to produce decisions that are substantively 'just'. For example, delays sometimes allow the guilty to avoid punishment (because proceedings come to be barred by the statute of limitations), or else they oblige judges to hand down unjustifiably lenient sentences.[19]

(3) A slow and inefficient system of justice seems likely to be itself a factor in criminality and to undermine public confidence in it.

In seeking to account for slowness, observers have pointed fingers in several directions. Some point to the obligatory nature of criminal action, arguing that it increases the number of cases under examination at any one time beyond that which the system can deal with expeditiously. Others blame the existence of two layers of appeal which defendants make use of habitually. Still others attack the complexity of the rules of criminal procedure arguing that it induces defendants to seek to delay proceedings in order to have their cases dismissed under the statute of limitations (McNess, 2003).

◼ **Justice and rights: the policy response**

Policy-makers in recent years have attempted to address the four aforementioned issues in a large number of reforms of varying entity; of these, three are worthy of special attention.

The 1988 reform of the code of criminal procedure

In 1988, a reform of the code of criminal procedure sought to give criminal proceedings, especially at the trial phase, a more adversarial, less inquisitorial, character. By that means, the reform sought to address the complaint that the roles of judge and prosecutor were imperfectly separated and trials excessively influenced by the prosecution. The most fundamental changes were those embodying the principle that, for the purposes of establishing culpability, the only evidence that was to count was that adduced at the trial phase. Here, the task of establishing the truth was essentially to be removed from the judge and delegated to the prosecution and defence through their activities of public debate and cross-examination. Only in exceptional circumstances explicitly established by law was evidence acquired by the court, independently of a request by one or the other of the parties in dispute, to have validity.

Many of the specific changes failed to survive examination by the Constitutional Court, however, falling foul, as they did, of the fundamental presuppositions of an inquisitorial system. In such a system, the 'primary and inescapable' purpose (Constitutional Court, sentence 255/1992) of a criminal trial is to enable the judge to make a decision about the facts (as well as the law) of the case. Therefore, reasoned the Court, while the new code had deemed means such as oral cross-examination to be those 'best adapted to the need to establish the truth', 'such a choice of method … could not ignore that … rules of procedure which irrationally obstruct the process of ascertaining the facts necessary to arrive at a just decision are not consistent with a system based on the rule of law' (Constitutional Court, sentence 111/1993).

It is therefore understandable that in 1992 the Court should have declared illegitimate article 500, and in 1998 article 513. Both these articles limited the admissibility as evidence of statements made to the *pubblico ministero* during the course of his investigations, but which the person was unwilling to confirm when cross-examined at the trial. This was a particularly delicate issue because of its implications for the status of the evidence of informers in proceedings against organised crime and thus for the likely outcome of such proceedings.

Article 111

The 1988 code of criminal procedure, then, was inspired by principles that contrasted radically with assumptions deeply entrenched in the Italian legal profession. Not surprisingly, therefore, the years following the code's introduction saw a large number of referrals, from ordinary courts, to the

Constitutional Court. The latter's decisions gave rise to a lively, and still on-going, debate among jurists and policy-makers regarding the new code's detailed legal implications. The referrals and decisions can be seen as classic manifestations of that policy-making role which, as we saw in chapter 6, has been acquired by the Italian judicial system in common with those of other democracies.

Most of the time this is a role that has seen Constitutional Court and Parliament work peaceably together with the Court preferring binding inter-pretations rather than outright declarations of unconstitutionality where possible, and with Parliament amending legislation declared illegitimate rather than attempting to save legislation by changing the Constitution. The Court's judgements in relation to the new code of criminal procedure were an exception to this. Therefore, 1999 saw Parliament take steps to save the adversary principles it had sought to introduce and to do so by amending article 111 of the Constitution.

Directly inspired by article 6 of the European Convention on Human Rights, the amended article stipulates that:

- all trials must be 'based on equal confrontation of the parties before an independent and impartial judge';
- defendants 'have the right to interrogate or have interrogated, before the judge, those who testify against them; to summon and examine, under the same conditions as those granted to the prosecution, those who may testify in their favour; to have all evidence in their favour acknowledged';
- 'in criminal trials, evidence may only be established according to the principle of confrontation between the parties';
- 'no defendant may be found guilty on the basis of testimony given by witnesses who have freely and deliberately avoided cross-examination by the defence'.

Law no. 150/2005

Paradoxically, the reform of article 111 may turn out to undermine rather than to strengthen the citizen's right to an independent and impartial system of justice. Implicitly, it restrictively defines the role of *pubblico ministero* as that of prosecution. In this it contrasts with the legal imperatives requiring these officials to give as much consideration to evidence in favour of the accused as to evidence against. It has thus strengthened calls for a separation of their careers from those of trial judges.

A degree of separation was provided for by law no. 150 of 2005. This gave the Government delegated powers to make it all but impossible for investigating judges to take on the roles of trial judges and vice versa (Pederzoli, 2005). The question is what happens to the independence of investigating judges in the event that the further step is taken to make them *institutionally* separate from trial judges? As things stand, the impartiality of investigating judges is arguably assured by the fact that, with trial judges, they are part of a body of magistrates institutionally separate from other branches of the state. Detached from this body and located elsewhere, the risk is that they become organisationally dependent on the executive or legislative powers and therefore subject to questionable degrees of political influence (Salazar, 2002: 17).

■ Conclusion

This points to the dilemma at the heart of judicial matters. On the one hand, the citizen's civil rights can only be effectively guaranteed if the judiciary is independent, that is, if it can resist the interference of actors representing other branches of the state. On the other hand, excessive independence – that is, the lack of externally imposed restrictions on the behaviour of judicial actors – also carries the risk that rights are denied by abuses of power. Italian policy-makers are well aware of such dilemmas. We have seen them attempt to grapple with them in relation to the reform of criminal procedure. This must ensure that defendants have all the rights and protections necessary to enable them effectively to defend themselves against charges levelled at them. But it must also ensure that there are effective means of establishing the truth. Finding the appropriate balance between these two imperatives is by no means easy.

Much the same may be said of the dilemmas arising in the field of welfare policy. Here we have seen Italian policy-makers attempting to reconcile the conflict between real needs and demands on resources on the one hand and the macro-political and economic pressures pushing in the direction of containment on the other. In the fields of pensions and healthcare, politicians have sought to manage the resulting stresses by attempting, through privatisation and regionalisation, to shift responsibilities elsewhere. In this, as in other respects, their approaches have reflected similar strategies adopted in the face of similar problems by politicians in other countries.

A theme we have emphasised throughout this book so far is the comparability of Italy's political system and its problems with those of other democracies: true, the polity has its own particular mix of characteristics and this gives it its distinctiveness; but the thesis that it is an anomaly, inexplicable in terms of the categories used to explain the characteristics and behaviour of other democracies, appears difficult to sustain. This is also the case in relation to the final area we shall consider – foreign policy – to which we turn our attention in the chapter that follows.

■ Further reading

The Italian Legal System (London: Butterworths, 1985) by G. Leroy Certoma needs updating but still provides a good introduction to the principles underlying the workings of Italy's judicial system. See also Patrizia Pederzoli, 'The reform of the judiciary', in Carlo Guarnieri and James L. Newell (eds.), *Italian Politics: Quo Vadis?* (New York: Berghahn, 2005). *Rescued by Europe* (Amsterdam: Amsterdam University Press, 2004), by Maurizio Ferrera and Elizabetta Gualmini, examines the welfare-state reforms Italy underwent as a consequence of the 'Maastricht process', showing how the reforms have been driven by the constraints and opportunities linked to European integration. See also Ferrera's edited volume, *Welfare State Reform in Southern Europe* (London: Routledge, 2005), which analyses policies against poverty and social exclusion, focusing specifically on minimum-income schemes. With a comparative introduction, a chapter on Italy and a common framework for each of the chapters, the book provides for easy comparison of the Italian case with the other countries of southern Europe. The 2004 pension reform is discussed by David Natali and Martin Rhodes in 'The Berlusconi pension reform and the emerging "double cleavage" in distributive politics', to be found in Carlo Guarnieri and James L. Newell (eds.), *Italian Politics: Quo Vadis?* (New York Berghahn, 2005).

■ Notes

1. Of course an assertion of this kind implies a benchmark against which the distribution of expenditure is being compared. The one being used in this case is the distribution of expenditure in other EU states taking account of possible variations between Italy and the other countries in the proportions of the population actually exposed to the risks in question: see Sacchi and Bastagli (2005: 92–4).

2. Newspaper reports suggest that it may be a significant problem in the UK, for example: on 25 May 2004, the *Guardian* revealed that '[t]he parliamentary ombudsman [had] expressed deep disappointment at the failure of John Reid, the health secretary, to comply with her rulings on freedom of information' (www.guardian.co.uk/uk_news/story/0,3604,1223959,00.html) – pointing out that '[f]or two years John Reid's department has refused to give information about the award of a £32m contract, without normal competitive tendering, to Powderject for smallpox vaccine shortly after Powderject's owner donated £100,000 to Labour' (www.ex.ac.uk/~RDavies/arian/scandals/ political.html).

3. This is not the case if the spending underlying the debt represents spending on public investments; however, though it is in line with the EU average, general government fixed capital formation is but a small proportion of government spending, representing approximately 2.5 per cent of GDP.

4. Eurostat long-term national accounts data available at http://epp.eurostat.cec.eu. int/portal/page?_pageid=1090,30070682,1090_33076576&_dad=portal&_schema= PORTAL (accessed 16 March 2006).

5. Figures taken from the 2001 Italian National Election Study data available at www.istcattaneo.org/default.asp.

6. OMC is a method of EU governance resting on obligations that are not legally enforceable but whose 'compelling' quality arises from the fact that, since they rely on guidelines, indicators, benchmarking and the sharing of best practice,

they create a form of peer pressure obliging states to take certain courses of action in order to avoid being seen as the worst in the given policy area. 'Open method of coordination', *Wikipedia*, http://en.wikipedia.org/wiki/Open_Method_of_Coordination.

7. Though in that respect, it appears to have had much in common with other member states' plans (Ferrera and Sacchi, 2004: 15).

8. As well as offering another example of spillover: see chapter 5.

9. His cross-national empirical analysis shows that exposure to the international economy has little impact on spending trajectories once a variety of other factors widely theorised as important are controlled for.

10. Baranes (nd: 5) cites an EU study suggesting that for the employed with thirty-five years of contributions, the rate of replacement will decline from 67.1 to 48.1 per cent between 2010 and 2050, while for the self-employed with the same number of years of contributions, it will decline from 64.4 to 29.2 per cent.

11. Shift workers; workers who carry out repetitive tasks; drivers of heavy public-transport vehicles.

12. The process has since been taken further by legislative decree no. 56 of 2000, which has abolished earmarked transfers from the centre altogether, replacing them with a series of regional revenues not tied to any particular spending categories (Maino, 2003: 104).

13. But justices of the peace are non-career judges appointed by the Consiglio Superiore della Magistratura (High Council of the Judiciary, CSM) for four-years terms that can be renewed once.

14. Decisions of justices of the peace are appealed to the *tribunale*. Sentences handed down by the *corte d'assise* are appealed to the *corte d'assise d'appello*.

15. The *Procura della Repubblica* in the case of the *Tribunale*; the *Procura Generale della Repubblica* in the case of the Appeal Court; the *Procura Generale presso la Corte di Cassazione* in the case of the Court of Cassation.

16. In the interests of increasing the rate of judicial throughput, recent years have seen the introduction of a number of alternative, simplified procedures designed to allow a decision to be reached at the preliminary hearing stage and in such cases to eliminate the need for full trial proceedings. For example, defendants willing to forgo a trial and have their cases decided by the GUP benefit from a reduction in sentence of one-third in the event that they are found guilty. Other procedures, designed to serve the same purpose, allow the preliminary hearing to be dispensed with. For example, where the defendant has been caught in the act or has confessed, the prosecutor can apply to the *giudice delle indagini preliminari*, or 'judge for the preliminary investigations' (i.e. a different judge, not to be confused with the GUP) for a decision that the case be sent for trial directly.

17. The Constitution also gives the system of administrative justice jurisdiction, where the law specifies, in matters of subjective rights. Subjective rights exist where the law recognises the claims of their bearers, directly and immediately, to condition the behaviour of others. Legitimate interests, on the other hand, are said to exist when protection of an *individual's* interests requires the

protection of some specific *public* interest. For example, participants in a public competition are said to have a legitimate interest in ensuring the list of winners excludes those who have failed to fulfil the criteria for participation in the first place (Barbera and Fusaro, 2004: 120).

18. Although it could, perhaps, hardly be otherwise: suspects in danger of escaping can hardly be notified beforehand of moves to arrest them. Moreover, prosecutors are obliged to include in their applications for injunctions all the information available to them that will speak in the defendant's favour.

19. For example, the defendant in a given case may have previous convictions from courts of first or second instance. Since, however, such convictions cannot be considered final until the defendant has exhausted all rights of appeal, they cannot be taken into account by the judge in deciding sentence in the given case (Guarnieri, 2001: 76).

10   Foreign policy

■ Introduction

We began this book by placing the Italian polity in its temporal context; we finish by placing it in its spatial context, looking at foreign policy. The reason for doing this is simply that the Italian state, like any other, is not a self-contained, isolated, entity. Rather, along with other states, it is embedded in a system of social relations – the international state system – with profound implications for what goes on internally. As Jackson and Sørensen (2003: 1–9) point out, there are a series of values that the citizens of most states expect their governments to uphold, at least to some minimal degree. They include security, freedom, order, justice and welfare. States' success in upholding these values presupposes their membership of the international community of states: when cut off from that community, states' populations usually suffer as a consequence (Jackson and Sørensen, 2003: 1). It presupposes, too, states' success in managing the pressures and responsibilities that arise from membership of the international community: peace, and therefore the orderly conduct of international relations, is a prerequisite for the achievement of most if not all of the values.

An understanding of a country's position in the international state system and of the foreign-policy issues this gives rise to are therefore indispensable for an understanding of its politics and of how its governing institutions retain their authority. This is something that most people become aware of only when some international event threatens the values they expect their states to uphold – for example, when the possibility of invasion threatens personal freedom. Most of the time, it is something they take for granted. 'On those learning occasions people wake up to the larger circumstances of their lives which in normal times are a silent or invisible background' (Jackson and Sørensen, 2003: 6).

With this in mind, we seek, in the remainder of the chapter to throw light on four questions:

(1) What are the most important characteristics of the international state system within which the Italian polity is embedded?
(2) What position does Italy occupy within this system?
(3) What is the nature of Italian foreign-policy objectives?
(4) How successful have Italian governments been in achieving these objectives in recent years?

▩ The international state system

The basic units of the global political environment of which the Italian polity is a part are (1) other states, and (2) international organisations, governmental and non-governmental. Let us look at each of these in turn.

Other states

Other states come in various sizes and degrees of influence. There are currently 192 independent states whose GDPs in 2005 ranged from $12,410 billion (in the case of the United States) to $60 million in the case of Nauru, the world's smallest state. They all have in common their occupation of distinctive territories over which they claim sovereignty. These territories have, over the past four centuries expanded from those of Western Europe (where, in the sixteenth century, the state system found its origins) to encompass the entire globe.

Not everywhere, however, are states equally successful in asserting their authority. On the contrary, in the world's poorest countries, the limited presence of manufacturing and infrastructural facilities often locks states into a vicious circle. That is, predatory behaviour perpetuates lawlessness and insecurity which, by discouraging inward investment, act as brakes on economic development. The resulting poverty sustains predatory behaviour – and so on. In such circumstances, states have considerable difficulty providing a stable framework for the conduct of political activity within their territories. In the worst cases, they are incapable of wielding authority of any kind. Resulting humanitarian crises then often give rise to UN intervention. In so doing, they raise questions in international political debate about the extent to which states do and should exercise unqualified sovereignty over their territories.

International organisations

Most international organisations are of more recent origin: the most important, such as the UN, NATO, the EU, the OECD, the IMF and the WTO, are all twentieth-century creations and their numbers have expanded some fourfold since 1960. But they are of profound significance for the conduct of states' relations with other states – so much so that their activities are such as to render rather fluid the distinction between domestic and foreign policy.

When in the EU, for example, issues are settled at sectoral level, with the relevant national ministers defending the EU's position against the objections of their own government colleagues, it becomes clear that 'the time when "foreign policy" concerned only foreign ministries has gone for good. Most state institutions now attempt to conduct an external policy of their own' (Dehousse, 1997: 40, quoted by Hague, Harrop and Breslin, 1998: 41). International organisations such as NATO and the EU have thus, as Luca Ratti (2002: 5) has pointed out, 'permeated the political and economic structures of their member states, locking them into sets of implicit or explicit principles, norms and rules, which have created formidable constraints on state action' and made it 'very difficult for the participating states to revert to courses of action harmful to the interests of other members'.

This is not to say that international organisations leave no room for the pursuit of national self-interest or that their impact on states is everywhere the same, quite the contrary. On the one hand, developed Western states cannot ignore international economic and political pressures – but they also have enough clout to be able to *influence* them. On the other hand, the poorest countries can merely *adapt* to them. Often entirely dependent on the export of single commodities for which prices are volatile, these countries frequently require financial aid, but precisely because of their economic vulnerability are unable to bargain over its terms. In such circumstances, international organisations such as the IMF and the World Bank can impose conditions on aid that amount, in all but name, to the enforcement of externally decided domestic policies.

The development of the international state system

From an historical perspective, the international state system can be thought of as having passed through three distinct stages: (1) the modern era from 1500 to 1945; (2) the period of Cold War and decolonisation from 1945 to 1989; (3) the post-Cold War period since 1990 (Buzan and Wæver, 2003: 14).

The modern era

During the first period, sovereign territorial states came into being in Western Europe. These states, while observant of international rules and diplomatic practices among themselves, reached out to create large empires by which

Box 10.1

Italy and the major international organisations

United Nations (UN) The most all-encompassing of the international organisations in that only two states are *not* members: Taiwan and the Vatican City. Established on 25 April 1945, its aims are to maintain peace and international security; to facilitate co-operation in international law, and to promote economic development, social progress and respect for human rights. Italy joined in 1956 and is the sixth largest contributor to the organisation's budget.

North Atlantic Treaty Organisation (NATO) Brought into being by the signing of the North Atlantic Treaty on 4 April 1949, NATO was created with an armed attack by the Soviet Union against Western Europe in mind. Hence, its original twelve members were all from Western Europe with the exception of the United States and Canada and the key section of the treaty was article V which committed each signatory to regard an attack on any one member as an attack on all of them. Later additions have brought the number of NATO members to twenty-six. Italy has been a member from the start. NATO was responsible for setting up Gladio – clandestine 'stay behind' organisations in Italy and elsewhere – which would engage in sabotage and guerrilla warfare behind enemy lines in the event of a Warsaw Pact occupation of Western Europe. Gladio paramilitary groups, many of whose members belonged to neo-fascist organisations, have been accused of having been involved in the 'strategy of tension' and the terrorist attacks associated with it in an effort to impede the 'historic compromise' between the DC and the PCI in the 1970s.

European Union (EU) Established by the Treaty of Maastricht in 1993, the EU's principal precursor was the European Economic Community of which Italy was a founder member (along with the Benelux countries, France and Germany) in 1957. Italy contributes about 13 per cent of the EU's budget – in line with its shares (12 and 12.3 per cent respectively) of the EU's population and GDP. Under the Qualified Majority Voting system used in the Council of Ministers, Italy (along with Germany, France and the UK) has 29 votes (the largest number for an individual state) out of a total of 345. To pass, proposals must achieve majorities of 74 per cent of the votes and be supported by a majority of states (50 or 67 per cent) having at least 62 per cent of the EU population. This gives Italy considerable influence, since it means that Italian representatives can block proposals by acting in concert with just three of the twenty-seven other states, provided they are large enough.

Organisation for Economic Co-operation and Development (OECD) The OEDC originated in 1960 as a development of the Organisation for European Economic Co-operation (founded in 1948 to administer the Marshall Plan for the reconstruction of Europe). Numbering thirty members, of which twenty-seven are high-income countries as defined by the World Bank, its objectives are to provide a forum for the discussion and co-ordination of domestic and international policy as it relates to economic, environmental and social issues. Italy has been a member from the start and contributes 5.5 per cent of its budget (making it the sixth largest contributor after the UK, France, Germany, Japan and the United States).

International Monetary Fund (IMF) The IMF was established at Bretton Woods in 1944 with the objective of stabilising exchange rates and reconstructing the international payments system. Numbering 185 member states, it monitors the macroeconomic policies of its members as a means of overseeing the global financial system. It offers technical assistance to its members and also acts as an international lender of last resort. It performs this function by virtue of the fact that member states contribute to a pool that can be borrowed from, on a temporary basis, by countries experiencing payments imbalances. Member states are given a quota, which determines the sizes of their subscriptions, their voting weights and their access to IMF finance. Italy's quota in 2007 was 3.25 per cent of the total, placing it among the top twenty-one countries in terms of voting power. (By way of comparison, the United States had a quota amounting to 17.09 per cent of the total.)

World Trade Organization (WTO) Founded in 1995 as a successor to the 1948 General Agreement on Tariffs and Trade (GATT), the WTO's purpose is to supervise and liberalise international trade. It does this by negotiating trade agreements and policing member states' adherence to them. It is able to do so by virtue of the fact that it has 153 members accounting for 95 per cent of world trade and by virtue of their agreement not to settle trade disputes by means of unilateral action but by recourse to the WTO's multilateral machinery for dispute settlement. Although each member state has one vote, in practice decisions are arrived at through informal negotiations between small groups of states whose relative market shares constitute the largest single influence on the outcomes they are able to achieve. Italy has been a member since the outset, its contribution to the budget (currently 160 million Swiss francs) calculated on the basis of its share of the total trade conducted by WTO members.

they controlled the political communities of the rest of the world. Italy was a relative latecomer to the scramble for territory and its empire, consequently, was of relatively modest dimensions. At its height, in 1940, it included Eritrea (from 1889), Italian Somaliland (from 1889/90), Tientsin, China (from 1901), Libya (from 1911), the Dodecanese islands (from 1911/12), Abyssinia (from 1935/6), Albania (from 1939): Map 3.

These empires were important for the imperial power's economic development. Consequently, they ensured that the European states' rivalries were projected throughout the world, in terms of competition for control of desirable territories. Some of the latter were controlled by settler populations, which themselves eventually acquired statehood. This process, beginning with the American Revolution, 'launched the transition from a European state system to a Western state system' (Jackson and Sørensen, 2003: 6).

Cold War and decolonisation
During the second period, 'decolonisation completed the remaking of the global political system into the European ('Westphalian') form of sovereign territorial states that had begun with the revolutions in the Americas' (Buzan

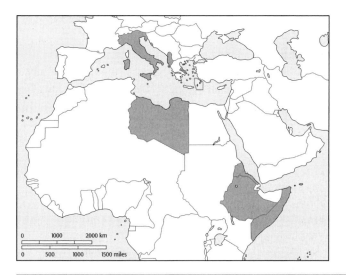

Map 3. The Italian empire in 1940
Source: http://en.wikipedia.org/wiki/Image:Italian_empire_1940.PNG

and Wæver, 2003: 19). The Cold War was a significant influence on this process: war-shattered European states, economically and militarily dependent on America, were obliged to adapt to the latter's view of the new world order. This was inspired by notions of national self-determination, first expounded by Woodrow Wilson in the aftermath of the First World War. It was also inspired by a desire to open empire territories to free trade. US policymakers viewed this as essential both to their own country's economic prospects, and to the prospects of lasting peace in the aftermath of the Second World War. In essence, they reasoned that trade barriers and imperial preference systems had contributed to the war both directly and indirectly by virtue of their contribution to the Great Depression.

Thus it was that, as a defeated power at the end of the war, Italy lost all its colonies in the Treaty of Paris. Despite the contribution of the Resistance to the struggle against the Nazis, and the country's status as co-belligerent from 1943, the treaty was imposed on Italy by the Allies in February 1947. Partial revision of the treaty was secured in 1950, but it meant only that Italian Somaliland was for ten years to become a United Nations Trust Territory under Italian administration (Saiu, 2005: 124).

Some of the independent states that came into being through decolonisation were sovereign in little more than the token sense of being legally recognised as such by the UN. This was especially the case where boundaries bore little resemblance to indigenous patterns of culture and history. Paradoxically, however, the Cold War gave states everywhere a certain degree of leverage when it came to dealing with the Western powers; for the conflict between the United States and the Soviet Union meant that these two superpowers needed 'client states'.

Box 10.2

The Treaty of Paris
Signed on 10 February 1947, the treaty covered three main sets of issues: territory, political matters and the military. Under the first heading, besides the loss of all colonies, Italy was obliged to accept a series of minor adjustments to the border with France and to cede more significant chunks of territory (notably Fiume and Istria) to Yugoslavia. Under the second heading, there was a clause designed to protect military personnel and civilians who had chosen to collaborate with the Allies since the start of the war. Thus Italy was obliged (by article 16) not to 'prosecute or molest Italian nationals, including members of the armed forces, solely on the ground that during the period from 10 June 1940 to the coming into force of the … Treaty, they expressed sympathy with or took action in support of the cause of the Allied and Associated Powers'. By article 17, Italy was obliged not to 'permit the resurgence on Italian territory of such organisations, whether political, military or semi-military, whose purpose it is to deprive the people of their democratic rights'. Under the third heading, military installations and fortifications along the borders with France and Yugoslavia were to be dismantled; Italy was banned from possessing, constructing or experimenting with atomic weapons and a series of limitations were placed on the size of the army, navy and air force.

The post-Cold War period

This changed with the end of the Cold War after 1989. In areas such as sub-Saharan Africa, the Soviet Union had been a significant geopolitical player prior to 1989. The removal of the 'Soviet threat' thus meant that these areas became less important for the Western powers. As a consequence the powers were able to acquire greater dominance than they had had before. The ending of the Cold War also left greater room for regional-level security dynamics, where the latter were fuelled by an increasingly wide range of security concerns going beyond sheer military issues. This has led Buzan and Wæver (2003) to argue that the post-Cold War order is one that can best be understood in terms of what they call 'regional security complexes' (or RSCs).

An RSC is a geographical cluster of states and other units among which security interaction is especially intense, the borders between regions being zones of weaker interaction. The reason why, in Buzan and Wæver's view, international politics are best understood in terms of such RSCs is that most threats travel more easily over shorter than over longer distances. Therefore actors are primarily concerned with the intentions and capabilities of their neighbours. Therefore patterns of interaction tend to be geographically clustered. Outside powers may penetrate such security complexes, but the end of the Cold War has given their internal dynamics greater autonomy from patterns set by global powers. The issues that sustain and drive interaction within security complexes are ones 'posited (by a securitising actor) as a threat to the survival of some referent object (nation, state, the liberal international economic order, the rain forests), which is claimed to have a right to survive' (Buzan and Wæver, 2003: 71). It is because such issues tend to be interpreted in the light of each other and therefore get tied together that the world can be divided into a definite number of exclusive, non-overlapping RSCs.

Buzan and Wæver identify nine RSCs, one of which is EU-Europe. Their approach provides useful suggestions for describing the place of Italy within the international political system.

Italy's place in the global order

From a comparative perspective, Italy's place is relatively unusual; for the RSC of which the country is a member is a security community that can in some respects be seen as a great power in its own right (Buzan and Wæver, 2003: 56). A 'security community' is here understood as a group of actors whose integration has led to the development of a sense of community such that they have come to agree that their disagreements can be resolved without recourse to violence (Deutsch, Burrell and Khan, 1957; Jackson and Sørensen, 2003: 6). It is a quality which, in the case of Europe, derives essentially from the uniquely dense network of institutions making up the EU and its associated organisations. It means that the member-state governments do not see relations among themselves as matters of *security* as such. Car drivers now have a very vivid symbol of this when, for example, they travel from Italy to France via Ventimiglia and find that the border is marked by absolutely nothing more than a road sign bearing the EU flag and the word 'France'. Threats to survival are perceived, instead, as deriving from other sources. These, in so far as they are states, are states *outside* the EU. Moreover, many of the perceived threats (for example, globalisation and terrorism) are viewed as collective problems affecting EU members more or less equally. All of this implies that to understand the place of Italy in the world, we have to have a grasp of the standing of Europe in the world and of Italy's standing in Europe.

In such matters as trade, monetary and environmental concerns, Europe has considerable actor quality in global affairs. In other words, it is for the most part able to speak with a single voice. But from the perspective of traditional security – military and defence – issues, it has relatively little actor quality. In such matters, it much more closely resembles an intergovernmental organisation than a unit with a single policy.

The EU and traditional security issues

This situation is a legacy of the early post-Second World War period. At that time, the key issues were the takeover of power by communist governments in much of Eastern Europe, and the German question. The former was decisive in the creation, in 1949, of NATO. This locked the United States into defence of

Europe against the Soviet Union by virtue of article 5 of the North Atlantic Treaty – which stipulated that an attack against any one of its members would be considered an attack against all. For this reason, NATO became the principal West European security structure eight years before the signing of the Treaty of Rome gave birth to the EU's precursor, the European Economic Community (EEC). Italy has been a member of NATO since the outset, though thirty years had to pass before membership was accepted by the Communist opposition. Its stance provided an additional reason for the special attention paid to Italy by the United States throughout the Cold War period. This attention took the form of both funding for the Christian Democrats and the planning of covert operations to be undertaken in the event that the Italian Communist Party (PCI) came to power (Bull and Newell, 2005: 99–100).

The German question arose from two things: (1) the search, on the part of 'still nervous neighbours' (Gummett, 1997: 209), for ways to contain the country's resurgence, and (2) Germany's search for a way back into international polite society. The solution that was found was the setting up of collective decision-making structures including the European Defence Community (EDC), the Western European Union (WEU), the European Coal and Steel Community, Euratom, the EEC. Such structures would contain a Germany growing in strength while allowing that growing strength to contribute to the strength of Europe against the USSR. Italy, as the other defeated power, was in a position very similar to that of Germany and therefore an equally keen integrationist.

However, while integration worked well in some areas, it worked less well in others. The failure of the EDC in particular suggested that defence and other matters of 'high politics' were not suitable areas for greater co-operation. The EDC initiative had envisaged the formation of a European army within the framework of a common budget, arms and supra-national institutions. Italy had been expected to ratify it but it foundered in 1954 before Parliament could do so, seemingly on the rock of concerns about national interests (Box 10.3). Thus it was that the most influential theories guiding integrationists came to be ones that stressed the need to avoid areas having significant sovereignty implications and to concentrate instead on areas of 'low politics'. Integration in these areas (for example, agriculture) would be easier to achieve because their sovereignty implications were much less significant. And they could be expected, through processes of technical and functional spillover, to bring integration in adjacent areas (such as food standards) in a cumulative process (Cram, Dinan and Nugent, 1999: 8–10).

The immediate post-war legacy is thus that while the EU is integrated in other areas, in the area of defence it carries out only some of the functions that were envisaged for the EDC. Moreover, it does so without the degree of supra-national control that was envisaged for the latter, and it operates alongside NATO and the **WEU** (Box 10.3). These are overlapping but distinct structures having defence functions. In the case of NATO, the United States is also a key player. Therefore, the EU cannot be regarded as a global-level actor in all

Box 10.3

Post-war European institutions

European Defence Community (EDC)   Agreed to in 1952 by France, Italy, West Germany and the Benelux countries, the EDC never went into force because of a failure to achieve ratification by the French Parliament. It was a response to American calls for West German rearmament and would have created a pan-European military contingent, a common budget and centralised arms procurement with the German component reporting not to its government but to the EDC. It failed to achieve ratification by France partly because of Gaullist opposition to a text that appeared to undermine national sovereignty, partly because of Communist fears about the extent to which it would tie the country to the United States, and partly because Britain would not join. Britain, in turn, approved the plan in principle but refused to join unless its supra-national features were attenuated.

Western European Union (WEU)   The WEU evolved from the Brussels Treaty Organisation formed by Britain, France and the Benelux countries in March 1948 with the purpose of affording mutual assistance in resisting outside aggression. It took the name Western European Union when Germany and Italy joined in 1954. As it has very little of the supra-national character that had been been envisaged for the EDC, and as the EU has its own Common Foreign and Defence Policy, the WEU has since the late 1990s been subject to a range of moves designed increasingly to incorporate its structures and functions within those of the EU itself.

European Coal and Steel Community (ECSC)   The ECSC was created in 1951 by the Treaty of Paris signed by France, Italy, West Germany and the Benelux countries. In setting up a common market for coal and steel, it laid the groundwork for the later formation of the EEC, and it was Europe's first set of institutions to be based on principles of supra-nationalism. It had a High Authority, a Common Assembly, a Special Council of Ministers and a Court of Justice whose powers and functions were analogous to those of the similarly named institutions of the later EU. The ECSC chose Washington as the site of its first external presence. Significantly, the Washington office's first *Bulletin* was headlined, 'Towards a Federal Government of Europe'.

European Atomic Energy Community (Euratom)   This was a second community set up by the Treaty of Rome in 1957 to sit alongside the ECSC and the EEC. Like the EEC, though a separate legal entity, it shared the Common Assembly and the European Court of Justice with the ECSC – while from 1965, its Commission and Council (along with the ECSC's High Authority and Council) were merged with those of the EEC. The purposes of Euratom are to develop a specialist market for nuclear power, distribute it throughout the Community, establish common safety standards and monitor the peaceful use of nuclear material.

European Economic Community (EEC)   The EEC was a third community, established, like Euratom, by the Treaty of Rome. Its purpose was to bring about the economic integration of its members: the six that had brought the ECSC into being. Under the Maastricht Treaty which came into force in 1993, its institutions became

> those of the European Union (EU), while its procedures and its policies became those of the European Community – the first of the EU's three so-called pillars. The second and third pillars cover the Common Foreign and Security Policy (CFSP) and Police and Judicial Co-operation in Criminal Matters, and what distinguishes the three is that in matters covered by the first of them, supra-nationalism has the largest role. In matters covered by the second two, the Commission, the European Parliament and the Court of Justice have little or no role at all, and the lead is taken by the Council of Ministers.

respects: in so far as it concerns security in the traditional sense, interaction in Europe continues to be heavily influenced by the United States 'and certain types of action – tough diplomacy and military action – materialise only when it so decides' (Buzan and Wæver, 2003: 373).

There are several reasons for this.

(1) The Common Foreign and Security Policy (CFSP) established as the second of the three pillars of the EU by the Maastricht Treaty is strictly intergovernmental in nature and sees NATO as responsible for the territorial defence of Europe and for 'peacemaking'.

(2) NATO itself is intergovernmental in nature but is dominated by the United States: its military forces are under the command of the Supreme Allied Commander Europe, a US general; the United States alone bears one-fifth of the cost of NATO's civil budget and one-third of its military budget; US defence expenditure amounts to some two-thirds of the total for NATO countries collectively.[1]

(3) Though the 1990s saw the development of structures for institutionalised dialogue between the United States and the EU as a unitary entity (such as the New Transatlantic Agenda structures of 1995), these are not always preferred to dialogue with individual EU member states (Peterson, 2001: 5–9).

(4) Notwithstanding the elaborate consultation machinery set up under the CFSP, the member states frequently have great difficulty in finding a unity of intents. Good examples of this difficulty were the crises in Bosnia (March 1992 – November 1995), Albania (1997) and Kosovo (1998–1999).

The difficult search for EU unity: the crisis in Bosnia

In the first case, it was arguably the determination of Germany, against the initial resistance of other EU member states, to recognise the independence of Slovenia and Croatia in 1991 that touched off the crisis (by encouraging the 1992 referendum on independence from Yugoslavia opposed by the Bosnian Serbs). The subsequent Dayton Agreement putting an end to the war was the work, not of the CFSP, but of the so-called Contact Group (consisting of the United States, Russia, Germany, France and the UK): 'a cabal that left other EU states isolated' (Peterson, 2001: 8). Given that the country's geographical location left it particularly exposed to the military and social consequences of the conflict, Italy was understandably keen to be a part of the Contact Group (and later joined), but participation was opposed by Britain and France (Bellucci, 1997).

The difficult search for EU unity: the crisis in Albania

The second case, which arose when the collapse of financial pyramid schemes caused severe social unrest, 'would have lent itself *par excellence* to a so-called "Petersberg mission" of the EU' (Blockmans, 2004: 297); but it was left to a 'coalition of the willing', under Italian leadership, to deal with the chaos and anarchy in Albania. As Albania's principal trading partner and largest investor, as well as the country most exposed to potential outflows of refugees, Italy had a special interest in the peace-keeping operation. Arguably other EU states would have been better suited to the task: in the interests of impartiality and neutrality, '[t]he UN has traditionally been reluctant to use forces from neighboring powers or from states with special interests for its peacekeeping operations' (Favretto, 1997). But unwillingness to abide by the principle that security in Europe is indivisible[2] was made clear when in March 1997, EU foreign ministers rejected Albania's call for intervention.

The difficult search for EU unity: the crisis in Kosovo

Finally, in the third case, the lead in seeking a solution to the armed conflict between Serbia and the Kosovo Liberation Army was taken not by the EU, but once again by the Contact Group; and while the UK (along with the United States) favoured a harsh military reaction, Italy and France (along with Russia) were very much opposed. Italy was especially 'loath to undertake actions that would hurt Italian companies with extensive trade and production contracts in the FRY [Former Republic of Yugoslavia]' (BASIC, nd.). In the end, Italy agreed to participate in NATO air-strikes against Serbia at least in part because then Prime Minister, Massimo D'Alema, felt that as an ex-Communist he had no alternative, in the face of US pressure in the crisis and more generally, but to give proof of his reliability as an 'Atlantic partner' (Croci, 2000: 118–19).

The EU and foreign policy

In terms of force and the threat of force, then, EU member states, including Italy, often find it difficult to speak with a single voice. However, once we go beyond the 'narrow' realm of military and defence matters to focus on foreign policy more broadly conceived, we find an EU taking on a much more clearly defined international persona (Holland, 1999). It would be surprising if this were not the case: as a fully integrated single market, with a common external tariff, some of whose members operate a single currency, the EU necessarily

Box 10.4

Italy and the Common Agricultural Policy

The Common Agricultural Policy came into force in 1962, its general objectives having been set out in the 1957 Treaty of Rome. The EEC member states intervened extensively in their agricultural sectors – but on the basis of different rules, which thus constituted an obstacle to the development of a common market in agriculture. It was hence realised that if member states wanted – as some did – to continue to provide support to their farming communities, then it would have to be provided in a co-ordinated manner at EEC level. Consequently, the CAP has functioned alongside the elimination of tariffs among the member states and efforts to eliminate non-tariff barriers to trade, to do three things:

- Impose common external tariffs and quotas on products coming into the EU;
- Set internal intervention prices. If internal market prices fall below these intervention levels, then the EU buys up produce to raise prices once more;
- Provide direct subsidies to farmers. Originally intended to direct efforts towards the production of specific crops, the subsidies led to overproduction of some foods. Consequently, since 2005 flat-rate payments based only on the area of land under cultivation have begun to replace specific subsidies. 'Set-aside' payments and production quotas have also featured as part of efforts to tackle overproduction.

1984 saw the introduction of milk quotas along with fines (set at 25 per cent above the price of milk) levied on anything produced above the quota. Farmers have been able to increase their quotas by buying or leasing quotas from others. In October 2008, for the fifth year running, Italy faced significant fines for overproduction. In 2003, after Italian protests, a deal was struck whereby farmers were allowed to pay fines in instalments, interest free, over a period of fourteen years. On the one hand, the Commission had been concerned that this might amount to a disguised form of state aid detrimental to single-market principles; on the other hand, the issue had been holding up agreement among EU finance ministers to plans to tax cross-border income from savings – which required unanimity in order to pass.

has a unified foreign policy in relevant areas. A good example of this is the EU's Common Agricultural Policy (CAP) – of which Italy is the fourth largest beneficiary (after France, Spain and Germany). In subsidising production and maintaining the prices of agricultural products sold within the EU, the CAP necessarily effects producers outside the Union. In particular, import tariffs and farming subsidies make it more difficult for outsiders to compete with EU producers. This is often said to contribute to poverty in the developing world. As much is also said of the EU's policy of purchasing products whose prices fall below CAP-established 'intervention prices'; for such products are then often 'dumped' on world markets.

The domestic and international pressures to which such situations give rise oblige the EU member states to come up with collective responses. One such response was the Lomé Convention. This came into force in 1976 and allowed developing African, Caribbean and Pacific (ACP) states to export most agricultural products and minerals to the EU without tariffs. It also established quotas for the import of products such as sugar and beef of which the EU is a large producer. In 2000, Lomé was replaced with the Cotonou Agreement which provides for a series of Economic Partnership Agreements. These will continue to provide access to the EU for ACP products – but in return for action on a range of development, human rights and governance issues.

Nor can it be said that foreign-policy measures, when they materialise, are *merely* the consequence of external pressures sufficiently strong to overcome the limits of intergovernmentalism. Rather, some owe as much to the EU's supra-national characteristics. Practically speaking, these remove from the individual member states control of the relevant foreign-policy instrument. Trade and most other economic sanctions are a good example of this. Legally, external trade is an exclusive EU competence. But leaving this aside, the single market means that bilateral sanctions would be ineffective in any event since the market guarantees the free movement of goods, services, labour and capital between the member states. This is of special relevance to Italy in relation to the apparent growth of counterfeit clothing products from China. This has recently led to calls, in more extreme quarters, for trade sanctions against the latter. It has also contributed to the emergence of a more Euro-sceptic, less pro-integrationist mood among some sections of the Italian public.

Italian foreign-policy objectives

Objectives during the Cold War

Prior to the 1980s, Italy's foreign policy tended to be rather passive (Santoro, 1994: 634) – with the result that the country has often been described using expressions such as 'economic giant but political pygmy' (Codispoti, 2001: 81). There were three interrelated sets of reasons for this state of affairs.

(1) The Communist/anti-Communist divide running through Italian politics.
(2) Awareness that security could be obtained simply by sheltering under the US nuclear umbrella.
(3) American domination.

Let us examine the three in turn.

The Communist/anti-Communist divide

This fundamental domestic division meant that for most of the period prior to 1989, there was an insufficient degree of bipartisan consensus on a conception of the 'national interest' to make possible a robust pursuit of it. In general, the more 'flamboyant' foreign-policy initiatives are less likely to succeed the less they are backed by a solid internal consensus.

The US nuclear umbrella

Italy's economic and political elites were aware that, given the internal and external Communist/anti-Communist division, and given Italy's geographical location, security could be obtained without playing any very assertive role in NATO or other international organisations. In other words, there was an awareness that, at a time when there were few issues without implications for the Cold War conflict, the United States could definitely be relied on to provide protection. It could hardly be otherwise given the electoral strength of the PCI and its international leanings; given the country's Mediterranean location; given its location on the border between East and West. In this context, Italy's elites were prepared, some with greater, others with less reluctance, to trade security for sovereignty, internal and external. They thus for the most part accepted, as proof that the United States could be relied on, the latter's interventions and vetoes in matters of domestic politics.

Interventions and vetoes were exercised through three channels: military, diplomatic and domestic.

(1) Military channels: these enabled US contingency planning from the early 1950s to include the possibility of military intervention in the event that a PCI electoral victory threatened to deliver the country to the enemy geo-political camp (Del Pero, 2003: 543). The channels existed in virtue of a series of bilateral agreements between the US and Italian governments from 1950 on. These made possible the construction of American army, air and naval bases in Italy, including the presence of nuclear missile installations.[3] Many of the agreements were secret and not presented to Parliament for ratification. This was a practice that was first defended in 1959 by Foreign Minister Giuseppe Pella. He argued that parliamentary approval of the installation of Jupiter nuclear missiles was not necessary because it merely gave effect to agreements entered into under the Atlantic Treaty, which had already been approved by legislation. Others argued that the agreements were unconstitutional – either because of their secrecy or because their 'political' character made them subject to the Constitution's article 80, which explicitly requires parliamentary ratification. Still others argued that the agreements were in any case at variance with principles of transparency one would naturally expect in a democratic polity (Gallo, 1989: 79–86).

(2) Diplomatic channels were the ones used by the United States to prod Italian governments into taking measures that would directly or indirectly counter threats of a 'drift to the left' (Gualtieri, 2004) in Italian politics. Initially, the means used were mainly positive. As Del Pero (2003: 535) points out, in the immediate post-war period, US officials understood Italian Communism as

'the degenerate product of legitimate economic and social grievances, which could be tackled only through an extensive programme of reforms and economic growth'. When, however, it became clear that initiatives under the Marshall Plan had failed to reduce the PCI to the size considered proper for anti-system parties in 'any civil and democratic country' (Del Pero, 2003: 535), more negative means were resorted to. Thus it was that in the early 1950s the Italian government was urged to remove Communist organisations from public buildings, to reduce the presence of Communists in the labour movement by discriminating against firms employing Communist labour and so forth. Whether for reasons of expedience or principle, many Christian Democrat (DC) politicians sought to resist such pressures. Meeting Henry Kissinger and US President Ford in August 1975, for instance, Aldo Moro tried to explain that most of those who voted PCI were 'also in favour of freedom and liberty' and that 'with *détente* the people "ask why [...] we keep these rigid barriers when you can see that the American President is talking to the Soviet leaders"' (Gualtieri, 2004: 439). Others, however, were less resistant to American projects: in 1954, for instance, Prime Minister Mario Scelba 'approved a package of measures against the Communist party and trade unions that was largely modelled on US plans for Italy' (Del Pero, 2003: 541). This, together with the resistance of those less willing to embrace measures of doubtful democratic legitimacy, provided the basis for interventions through the third, domestic, channel, namely, covert operations.

(3) The common denominator in these operations appears to have been a series of links and secret arrangements between the Italian and American intelligence communities. These enabled the development within the communities of 'anomalous chains of command' (Flamigni, 1991: II) – that is, ones that escaped the control of normal accountability mechanisms. They thus provided the basis for a series of illegal operations ranging from the Piano Solo coup plot of 1964, through the Piazza Fontana bombing in 1969 and the Aldo Moro kidnapping in 1978. What united these episodes and the others like them was that they appeared to be inspired by what came to be called a 'strategy of tension', that is the creation of a climate of fear and disorder that would provoke calls for an authoritarian restoration of order. Part of such restoration would involve the organisational dismantling of the left. Links were established with far-right organisations whose activities, like those of the Red Brigades and other groups of the extreme left in the 1970s, were useful in maintaining a state of political instability, even if they were not always easy to control. The exact nature and extent of American involvement in the murkier episodes therefore remains unclear. Clearer is that the resulting tension and instability suited the Americans for reasons that went beyond the East–West conflict: by keeping Italy in a state of internal weakness, the United States could hope to thwart Italian ambitions to become a more active player in the Mediterranean (see below). In the late 1960s and early

Box 10.5

Protagonists of post-war Italian foreign policy
Italy's foreign policy in the period prior to the collapse of the Berlin wall is tradi-tionally regarded as having been unassertive – for the reasons explained in the text. Yet the period was not without its moments of drama and tension: when they felt that the country had significant interests at stake, Italian leaders were ready to take firm action and often did so in no uncertain terms. Some of the most significant protagonists of these moments were:

Mario Scelba (1901–1991)
Often referred to as the 'iron Sicilian', Scelba was four times Interior Minister between 1947 and 1962, and Prime Minister between 1954 and 1955. He fully shared US fears of 'Communist disorder' and the possibility that this might draw Italy into the Soviet sphere of influence. Consequently, he is best known for his harsh stances towards left-wing protest and workers' demonstrations. These stan-ces not infrequently resulted in deaths and woundings. They were made possible by his reconstruction of the police force, which was equipped with armoured vehicles and organised into riot squads known as *reparti celeri*. A few days before the 1948 election, a Rome parade of Carabinieri and army units appeared to make clear what would be the consequences of a Communist victory, while *Time* mag-azine (12 April 1948) reported Scelba as announcing that 'the government had 330,000 men under arms, including a special shock force of 150,000 ready to take on the Communists if they tried to make trouble on election day'.

Giuseppe Pella (1902–1981)
The 1947 Paris treaty established the area surrounding the gulf of Trieste as the Free Territory of Trieste, which, however, was divided into two zones – a northern zone, Zone A, including the city of Trieste, to be administered by the British and the Americans; a southern zone, Zone B, to be administered by the Yugoslavs – until the UN Security Council could make permanent arrangements for the state. In 1953, in the face of Yugoslav threats to annex Zone B, Italy's Prime Minister, Giuseppe Pella, warned that if Yugoslavia followed through on its threats, then Italy would occupy Zone A. To back up his affirmations, he moved war ships to the Adriatic and troops to the north-eastern frontier. In 1954, a memorandum of understanding signed in London gave provisional civil administration of Zone A to Italy, and of Zone B to Yugoslavia, until in 1975 the Treaty of Osimo assigned the areas definitively to the two countries.

Enrico Mattei (1906–1962)
His oil-exploration agreement with Iran provoked the ire of the 'seven sisters' oil cartel because it undercut them. It provided that Agip and the Iranian National Oil Company (Nioc) would give life to a third company, the Société Irano-Italienne des Pétroles (Sirip), whose capital would be owned by Agip and Nioc in equal shares. Agip would bear Sirip's exploration costs with the option of withdrawing after four years if the results proved unsatisfactory. If, on the other hand, exploitable reserves

were found, Agip would have its costs reimbursed while 50 per cent of net profits would go to the Iranian state, the remaining 50 per cent being divided between Agip and Nioc. Since Nioc was state-owned, the royalties accruing to the producer country amounted to 75 per cent (Buccianti, 2005: 40–1) – in contrast to the 50 per cent share allowed in such cases by the seven sisters.

Aldo Moro (1916–1978)

Twice Prime Minister between 1963 and 1976, Aldo Moro was obliged to stand up to considerable American hostility to his efforts to bring about an accommodation between the DC and PCI in the wake of the latter's gains at the election of 1976. His wife later recounted a meeting with Henry Kissinger at which the American is alleged to have warned Moro to desist from his strategy, telling him, 'You will pay dearly for it' – as indeed he did, being murdered by the Red Brigades on 9 May 1978 after fifty-five days of captivity. In a book entitled *Abbiamo Ucciso Aldo Moro* (We Killed Aldo Moro), US envoy Steve Pieczenik claims that he was part of a crisis committee chaired by the then Interior Minister, Francesco Cossiga. According to Pieczenik, before Moro was actually killed, the committee issued a false statement, attributed to the Red Brigades, saying that Moro was dead. The aim was to prepare Italian public opinion for the worst and to indicate to the Red Brigades that there would be no negotiations for Moro's release (Moore, 2008).

Bettino Craxi (1934–2000)

For details of the Achille Lauro affair, and its consequences, see Piason (1986). The affair arose from the hijacking of the Italian cruise ship, the *Achille Lauro*, by Palestinians on 7 October 1985. Two days later, after negotiations with the hijackers, ship and passengers were released, but not before one of the passengers, an American, had been killed. On 10 October an Egyptian airliner with the four hijackers aboard was forced, by American air force planes, to land at NATO's Sigonella military base in Sicily. Here, Italian troops who had surrounded the airliner on landing were in their turn surrounded by American troops determined to capture the Palestinians. Faced with the refusal of the Italians to give way – on the grounds that it was up to the judicial authorities to prosecute the Palestinians for alleged crimes committed aboard the Italian vessel – the Americans were forced to desist and to accept that their attempts to arrest the hijackers would instead have to proceed through the normal channels provided for by the Italian–American extradition treaty.

1970s, such ambitions looked as though they might threaten the interests in that zone of the United States and some of the latter's other European allies (Bull and Newell, 2005: 103).

American domination

The third reason for Italy's relative foreign-policy inactivity, then, is that American domination simply did not allow a more active posture. The 1947

Paris treaty had imposed on Italy the demilitarisation of its frontiers, and it was able to obtain the removal of these and other punitive clauses by agreeing to join NATO in 1949. This decision was therefore for the Italian government 'a decisive step towards … reassuming its sovereignty after the defeat of the Second World War' (Del Pero, 2003: 536). However, regaining sovereignty in this way meant at the same time to surrender a part of that sovereignty, and thus the possibility of an autonomous foreign policy, since NATO was dominated by the United States. Formally, NATO policy is made by the North Atlantic Council, bringing together the organisation's members at the level of ambassadors, ministers or heads of government. But as far as military and strategic decisions are concerned, the Council has in practice for long been confined to approving or ratifying the recommendations of the organisation's Military Committee. The latter is in turn considerably influenced by the recommendations and opinions of the Supreme Allied Commander Europe, who, as a US Army general, is directly subordinate to the US President (Gallo, 1989: 77–78).

Under these circumstances, Italian governments during the Cold War tended to concentrate on domestic politics: foreign affairs did not feature highly in political debate and what bold foreign initiatives there were – such as the Pella government's move in relation to Trieste in 1953 or Bettino Craxi's stance in the *Achille Lauro* affair in 1985 – were ones taken with at least one eye on domestic considerations and in any case not central to the East–West conflict (Croci, 2002: 1–2) (Box 10.5).

Foreign-policy objectives since the end of the Cold War

Since 1989, Italy has been seeking to conduct a more assertive foreign policy having been obliged, as a result of the end of the Cold War, to rethink its security arrangements. As Croci (2002: 1–3) has pointed out, there are at least three reasons for this.

(1) If membership of NATO was an effective means of obtaining security against the Soviet Union (having been conceived with that purpose in mind), then it was not at all clear that it would be equally effective in dealing with post-Cold War threats.

(2) The collapse of the external enemy raised the possibility that disagreements between NATO allies concerning threats might become more frequent. It thus also threw a question mark over the continued appropriateness of the lack of autonomy in the use of force and diplomacy inherent in Italy's previous arrangements.

(3) Italy was aware that in the event of a disagreement between its European allies and the United States, the former lacked the institutional structures, political ability and military capacity to act alone: this too spoke against the wisdom of the former foreign-policy inactivity.

The more pro-active foreign policy can be seen in a number of different arenas – in each of which Italy has sought to acquire a more audible, visible and influential role.

Arenas of foreign-policy activity: the United Nations

Italy has been an active participant in debates surrounding reform of the United Nations Security Council whose composition still reflects the international distribution of power that emerged from the war rather than its current distribution, or states' actual contributions to the organisation. For example, though it is the sixth largest contributor to the UN budget, Italy has no permanent Security Council seat. Reform aimed at reflecting early twenty-first-century realities is widely considered necessary if the UN is not to fade as 'the primary forum for determining the will of the international community' (Peterson, 2006: 58). Germany, Japan, Brazil, and India have all demanded permanent seats and have threatened to reduce their contributions to the UN if they are not satisfied.

In March 2004, the Secretary-General's High-Level Panel on Threats, Challenges and Change 'proposed two models for enlargement, which both suggest expanding the Council to 24 members. Model A proposes adding six new permanent seats, with no veto, and three new two-year term elected seats. Model B creates a new category of eight seats, renewable every four years, and one new two-year non-renewable seat' (Global Policy Forum, 2006). In February 2005, Italy, together with Argentina, Colombia, Mexico, Kenya, Algeria, Spain, Pakistan and the Republic of Korea, circulated a position document entitled 'United for Consensus', which argued that 'model B, with appropriate improvements, represent[ed] the best option for reaching the broadest possible consensus among Member States'. In April 2005, the 'United for Consensus' countries proposed adding to the Security Council ten new, regionally distributed seats, each of whose occupants would be elected from among the countries of the region concerned. The United Nations examined the matter at its World Summit held in September 2005, but notwithstanding the fact that the issue had been debated for a decade, a decision once again eluded it.

If a permanent seat were given to Germany, then the Security Council would come to constitute an additional policy-making forum bringing together the EU's three largest members to Italy's potential disadvantage. Together, France, the UK and Germany account for over half the GDP of the entire EU-25, and under the EU's qualified majority voting (QMV) procedures, the three are able to block any proposal in the Council of Ministers with the support of just one additional country. As the EU's fourth largest country, both economically and in terms of population, Italy has always opposed the emergence of any informal Franco-British-German *directoire* within the EU, and it is therefore understandable that Italy opposes Germany's bid for a permanent UN Security Council seat. Moreover, Italy and Germany are competitors in

Table 10.1. Italy's trading partners: principal trading partners in 2006 (in millions of euros)

Country	Exports	Imports	Balance
Germany	43,936	59,104	−15,167
France	39,121	32,739	6,382
United States	24,541	10,710	13,831
United Kingdom	20,171	12,633	7,538
Spain	24,471	15,010	9,461
Switzerland	12,623	10,330	2,293
Belgium	9,558	14,863	−5,305
Netherlands	7,986	19,729	−11,744
China	5,686	17,911	−12,225
Japan	4,483	5,441	−957

Source: ISTAT, *Commercio estero e attività internazionali delle imprese,* Annuario 2007, Rome: Istituto Nazionale di Statistica, www.istat.it/dati/catalogo/20080716_00/annuario_ice_istat07_08_vol1.pdf.

areas such as Italy's near neighbour, the Balkans, where they are the region's two largest trading partners (Table 10.1).

Arenas of foreign-policy activity: the European Union

In the EU arena, Italy has sought to maintain and increase its influence by its continuing support for the further development of a more clearly defined European defence and security identity (Figure 10.1) while insisting that this must not involve any decoupling of European defence from NATO. For Italy, the continuing centrality of NATO tends to divide Britain from France (traditionally far more in favour of an autonomous European defence policy than the former); to reduce the likely emergence of the aforementioned *directoire* in defence matters, and thus to provide a guarantee that Italy 'will continue to be at the table when decisions in as crucial a field as European security and defence are taken' (Croci, 2002: 14). Thus it was that when, in the mid-1990s, the French government proposed that command of AFSOUTH (one of the three main subdivisions of NATO command of military forces) be given to a European, Italy refused to go along with a plan that would have loosened American ties without offering any concrete gain in terms of the defence of Europe's southern flank (Croci, 2002: 14–15).

Greater assertiveness in the European arena was a particular feature of the 2001 Berlusconi government whose outspokenness in dealings with Brussels and its European partners were symbolised by two episodes early in the Government's life: its unexpected decision, in October 2001, to withdraw from the European consortium involved in constructing the A400M military transport aircraft, and its opposition, in November 2001, to the proposal to introduce a European arrest warrant. Since these episodes coincided with a significant change of tone and style in the public pronouncements of government spokespersons – once invariably and uncritically pro-European in every respect; now considerably less warm, and even 'Eurosceptic' – they were interpreted as evidence of a major shift of Italian foreign policy away from support for further integration in favour of strengthening bilateral relations with the United States.

A shift in Italian foreign policy?

In fact the change was more one of style than of substance. True, the Government's pronouncements were more abrasive, its positions less accommodating than observers had become accustomed to. But this did not mean that underlying objectives had changed. The change in rhetorical and negotiating style suited the Government in its efforts to distinguish itself from its predecessors. It also formed part of its populist claims; for it enabled the Government to pose as the true representatives of the people against the 'stifling restrictions' of established institutions (many of which, after all, are associated with Europe and European integration). This was the mirror reflection of the tendency of previous governments to present Europe as the source of salvation for all kinds of woes thereby obtaining support for domestic policies otherwise difficult to implement (Croci, 2005: 71). But beneath the propaganda, while the Government certainly sought to maximise Italy's influence in Europe, it cannot reasonably be described as having been 'Euro-sceptic' or 'anti-European'. Thus it was that Berlusconi explained that he had taken the aircraft decision on business grounds and would have agreed to the project had Italy's participation been necessary to its realisation. Italy agreed to the arrest warrant once its pragmatic objections had been addressed (Croci, 2005: 63–4). It supported measures of further integration in the European convention charged with drawing up, from February 2002, a draft treaty establishing a Constitution for Europe. It was a strong supporter of measures to harmonise immigration and asylum policies and of the idea of common policing of 'the most vulnerable borders' (Boniver, 2002) – as one might expect given its geography.

The policy of seeking to combine a strong European focus with the maintenance and strengthening of Atlantic ties was shown very clearly by the Government's stance in the events leading up to the Iraq war. In the first instance it sought to avoid the rift that took place between the United States on one side and France and Germany on the other in the months prior to the initiation of hostilities; for it was apparently convinced that united opposition to Saddam Hussein made it more, rather than less, likely that armed conflict could be avoided. It was also aware that it was in everyone's interests that, if force was to be used it was used with, rather than without, the explicit authorisation of the UN. Once France and Germany had defected from this position,

Table 10.2. The use of force to resolve international problems: Italian public opinion compared to opinion in other European countries (2002 Worldviews survey)

	Germany	France	Britain	Italy	Netherlands	Poland	Europe
Using force in Iraq:							
The US should not invade Iraq	28	27	20	33	18	26	26
The US should only invade with UN approval and the support of allies	56	63	69	54	70	53	60
The US should invade Iraq even if they have to do it alone	12	6	10	10	11	10	10
Percentages favouring the following measures to combat international terrorism:							
Helping poor countries develop their economies	84	93	91	97	92	92	91
Attacks by ground troops against terrorist training camps and other facilities	58	80	78	61	77	75	69
Air strikes against terrorist training camps and other facilities	58	75	76	60	73	75	68
Assassination of individual terrorist leaders	40	50	56	48	62	72	51
Percentages who approve of the use of troops in the following situations:							
To assist a population struck by famine	83	89	90	91	93	92	88
To uphold international law	68	84	84	83	86	84	80
Percentages who feel defence spending should be cut back, kept about the same or expanded:							
Cut back	45	23	21	52	38	14	33
Kept about the same	38	47	53	33	53	36	42
Expanded	14	28	24	12	6	45	22

Source: Chicago Council on Foreign Relations, Worldviews 2002 survey, www.worldviews.org/.

the Government sought to avoid two opposing dangers. On the one hand, to have been part of the 'Operation Iraqi Freedom' forces undertaking the March 2003 invasion would have been to fly in the face of the opinions of a large majority of the Italian public. This has always had a far more cautious attitude to the use of force to resolve international disputes than many if not most other West European publics (Table 10.2).[4] Italian forces were thus not sent to Iraq until its capitulation, and then supposedly for 'humanitarian peace-keeping purposes'. On the other hand, to have sided with France and Germany would, by isolating Britain, have widened the Atlantic rift still further. This in turn would have reduced the possibilities for further European defence integration. Moreover, by linking Italy with a country – France – favourable to the development of European defences independently of America, it would once again have raised the spectre of Italian subordination to a Franco-German *directoire* (Croci, 2005: 66–9). Thus it was that the

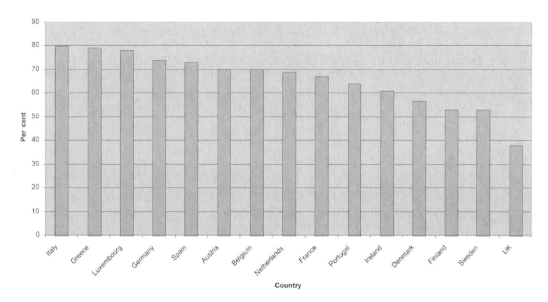

Figure 10.1. Per cent 'for' 'One common foreign policy among the member states of the European Union'
Source: Eurobarometer 58, December 2002, http://ec.europa.eu/public_opinion/archives/eb_arch_en.htm

Government spent considerable energies in the ultimately impossible task of seeking, in relation to Iraq, to re-establish a common European policy, to maintain transatlantic solidarity and to work for a resolution of the crisis within the UN framework (Croci, 2004: 140).

Italian objectives in the Mediterranean and the Arab world

This description of Italian foreign policy would not be complete without mention of two additional arenas to which Italy's geostrategic interests have traditionally led it to pay special attention: the Mediterranean and the Arab world. At least five factors have encouraged involvement in these areas in the period since the war.

(1) In contrast to Italy's Atlantic ties, friendship with the states concerned was, from the start, an objective that could unite parties across the political spectrum. The far right was drawn towards the countries by virtue of the interest shown in fascist ideologies by Arab and Islamic opponents of British and French colonial rule immediately prior to the war (Miller, 1992: 75; Piacentini, 2003: 222–3). The Catholic centre had a religiously inspired as well as an electoral interest in popular foreign humanitarian aid programmes (Miller, 1992: 77) while also being the political force most exposed to Vatican influence. The latter had opposed

341

the Zionist movement since the beginning of the twentieth century and in the Arab–Israeli conflict was discretely supportive of the Arabs among which it counted 4 million followers (Romano, 2002: 142). The left was drawn to the area and to support for bodies such as the Palestine Liberation Organisation (PLO) out of anti-colonialist sympathies.

(2) This domestic consensus then made it easier for governments to pursue their economic interests in the regions, in particular those arising from Italy's lack of domestic energy sources and thus its need to ensure secure supplies of oil and gas.

(3) Given these two conditions, the newly independent, highly nationalistic but underdeveloped states of the regions (Miller, 1992: 76) were drawn to an Italy which (a) had itself only recently become developed; (b) had a colonial past that (unlike those of Britain and France) had been brief and insignificant; (c) whose development programmes offered the prospects of internal stability, a bridge to the West and perhaps even the possibility of not having to choose alignment with either the US- or Soviet-led geo-political blocks.

(4) Italy was interested in ensuring the regions' political stability. Commercial links tend to be denser with nearer than with more distant neighbours. Therefore, states do not, in general, like to be surrounded by others unable to guarantee the security of their trade and investments.

(5) Prior to 1989, involvement in the regions offered Italy a means of mitigating, if not overcoming, its subordination to the United States and the restrictions this imposed on its capacity to conduct an autonomous foreign policy.

The most significant attempts to conduct this policy in the regions came from the late 1950s on. By this time the main issues arising from the war (the colonies and the return of Trieste) had been resolved, and the decisions most significantly defining Italy's place in the international order (membership of NATO and the EEC) had been taken. Most famous of the initiatives were those of charismatic head of the state-holding company ENI, Enrico Mattei, who conducted a sort of unofficial foreign policy aimed at freeing Italy from dependence for petroleum supplies on the Anglo-American oil cartel consisting of the so-called 'seven sisters'.

The 'foreign policy' of Enrico Mattei

Besides the strong backing of the US government, these companies (Esso, Shell, BP, Gulf, Mobil, Chevron and Texaco) had a monopoly on oil production in the Middle East. This region accounted for over 50 per cent of Europe's imports (Buccianti, 2005: 28) and two-thirds those of Italy (Miller, 1992: 41). During the war, 90 per cent of the Allies' oil supplies had come from the United States, which now wanted to conserve supplies in the interests of its own long-term security. It therefore sought, at war's end, to guarantee conditions of security and monopoly for its oil companies in the Middle East, which had accounted for only 5 per cent of world oil production at the outset of the war but where significant discoveries had been made in the meantime (Pizzigallo, 2003: 141–4). In this way, Middle East oil would be used to contribute to the reconstruction of Europe in the shadow of the Marshall Plan, strengthening it against the Soviet Union, while allowing the United States to conserve its own supplies.

As 'an oil producer without oil' (Pizzigallo, 1950: 150), Mattei was faced with the difficulty of finding new sources in a world in which two thirds of the known reserves outside the United States and the Soviet Union were controlled by the 'seven sisters'. These, together with the US government, were able easily to control the governments of producing countries by virtue of the fact that these regimes could rarely rely for their power on any kind of explicit popular support.

Mattei was significantly helped in his efforts to overcome his difficulty by two factors, one being the political backing, and therefore the backing of the foreign ministry, he was able to mobilise within Italy. This backing in turn owed much to inarticulate feelings of nationalism fed both by the punishment meted out at the end of the war by Allied powers whose own motives were clearly imperialistic in nature, and by the popular movement to free the country from the Mussolini dictatorship and consequent German occupation. It was, therefore, a nationalism that was at once anti-fascist and that had considerable sympathy with anti-colonial movements in the developing world. Famously, therefore, Mattei (who had himself had a distinguished career in the Resistance Movement) was able to use his considerable communication skills to bring pressure to bear on politicians to back him by disguised appeals to such sentiments. The most famous of these came with the discovery of natural gas and a small quantity of oil near Cortemaggiore in the Po valley. This allowed Mattei to develop the legend of *Supercortemaggiore*, the potent Italian petrol sold by the ENI subsidiary, Agip, whose symbol was a dog with six legs.

Besides this, Mattei, though incorruptible himself, was not above using straightforward bribery to secure the political backing he needed. Thus, when in April 1957, the US Ambassador to Rome, James David Zellerbach, sought to pressurise the Italian government into withdrawing from an important oil-exploration agreement signed by Mattei and the Shah of Iran the previous month, he was informed by the minister for state holdings, Giuseppe Togni, that Mattei's influence was such that it was necessary to treat him with 'considerable diplomacy' (Buccianti, 2005: 47) (Box 10.5).

The second factor Mattei was able to use to his advantage was thus one having a considerable echo in Italy and with which he personally had much sympathy. This was the tide of Arab nationalism that began to sweep the Middle East especially after the rise to power, in Egypt, of Gamal Abdel Nasser. This was a man who had overthrown a government weakened by an inability to resist British imperialist pressures and then gone on to humiliate the British and the French in the Suez crisis of 1956. There seems little doubt that anti-imperial sentiments played a central role in a large number of the deals Mattei was able to conclude. Thus, in agreeing to the above-mentioned exploration agreement, the Iranian Shah was almost certainly moved to favour Mattei over the seven sisters not only by the more generous royalties the former offered, but also by a desire for the enormous popularity his oil policy procured for him. At the end of 1957, the Algerian nationalist leader, Ferhat Abbas, pointedly announced that the Italian *Risorgimento* had much in common with the Algerian independence struggle. He continued by saying that if France failed to recognise independence, then the country would grant the right to participate in exploitation of its resources to more worthy nations (Buccianti, 2005: 65). In the spring of 1958, Mattei reached agreement for the construction of an oil refinery with a young King Hussein of Jordon, anxious to demonstrate that he would not be dictated to by the large foreign oil-producers. Winning the contract by offering a much lower price than his Anglo-American competitors, Mattei was aware that by demonstrating that he was as concerned for producer countries as for his own profits, the agreement would win him contracts in other Arab countries (Buccianti, 2005: 90).

By late 1960, Mattei's strength was such that he was even able to conclude an agreement with Moscow for the supply of low-cost oil in exchange for the supply of welded tubes. In this way he achieved the double aim of obtaining both oil at prices lower than those imposed by the Anglo-American companies and a secure outlet for Italian manufactures. The agreement added to the accusations regularly made against Mattei that he was attempting to undermine US foreign policy. It is thus not surprising that when in October 1962 he died in a mysterious plane crash, hypotheses advanced to account for the event included not only the suggestions that he had been killed by the Mafia on behalf of the American oil companies, by the French secret services for his sympathy with the Algerian National Liberation Front, or by the Israelis for his Arab sympathies, but also the suggestion that he may have been killed by the American secret services.

The post-Mattei period

In the years that followed Mattei's death, Italy was obliged to tread a narrow path in relation to the Arab world. On the one hand, there was the need to avoid, as far as possible, a foreign policy that clashed with that of the United States in the region. And, since Arab nationalism tended to seek protection from Moscow against American 'imperialism', the United States came to consider the state of Israel their best ally in the region (Romano, 2002: 138). But the stronger ties became with Israel, the greater the conflict became with Arab nationalism. On the other hand, Italian policy-makers could reasonably argue that the latter was less likely to be driven into the arms of Moscow the more the West showed understanding of its aspirations, and that Italy itself was likely to be the stronger in the Mediterranean area the more it was able to convince the Arabs of its anti-colonialism. It was this that explained the Italian government's relations with the PLO and the meeting between the president of the Republic and Yasser Arafat in 1982. Moreover, as if to overturn one of the axioms of international relations theory – according to which a country's strength is positively related to its wealth (Romano, 2002: 185) – the country's need to import energy made it more vulnerable than ever. This was especially so with the economic miracle from the 1950s on. It was for this reason that Italy adopted a conciliatory posture, despite provocation,[5] towards Colonel Qaddafi following his seizure of power in 1969. It thereby hoped to continue along the path charted by Mattei of recouping its energy costs through the sale, to the producer country, of industrial plant, machine tools and consumer goods.

In summary, then, Italian foreign policy has throughout the period since the war, been guided by

(1) an awareness of the heavy restrictions placed on its capacity for autonomous action combined with
(2) aspirations to bring the consideration paid to it in international politics closer to that to which its economic and industrial strength would otherwise entitle it.

Prior to 1989, it was frequently prevented from meeting its aspirations by a combination of US pressures and internal political tensions preventing the adoption of robust foreign-policy stances. For example, Sergio Romano (2002: 182–5) argues that if economic considerations left the country somewhat vulnerable to the threats of Colonel Qaddafi, just discussed, then the possibility of an energetic response was undermined by two things: (1) the fragility of executives; (2) the emergence and growth, from the 1960s, of libertarian, radical and ecology movements. These made politically difficult the development of alternative, nuclear-based, energy programmes. As we have seen, the end of the Cold War led to renewed efforts to meet the aspiration of ensuring that Italy's weight was properly felt in the international arena. The extent to which the makers of Italian foreign policy have been successful in this endeavour is the issue we consider in the final section.

◼ The degree of success of Italian foreign policy

The period to 2001

Sergio Romano and Maurizio Molinari argue that the election of the Ulivo coalition under Romano Prodi in 1996 marked the beginning of a new phase. This was one in which 'Italy was successful in conducting a respectable European policy' (Romano, 2002: 255) and, thanks to 'more effective and credible diplomatic activity', was successful in acquiring a stronger 'international profile' than in the past (Molinari, 2000: xi).

Box 10.6

The American presence in Italy

The United States has over 100 military installations in Italy, the most significant being:

- Aviano Air Base in Friuli-Venezia Giulia, home to the 31st Fighter Wing (a branch of the US Air Force) whose mission includes conducting air and space combat support operations in Europe's Southern region.
- Camp Ederle, a US Army post located in Vicenza. Plans to extend the base to the disused civilian Dal Molin airport nearby (which caused considerable unrest in the 1996 Prodi coalition) will bring the number of troops stationed there to 5,000.
- Naval Air Station Signonella near Catania in Sicily. Owing to its location near the centre of the Mediterranean, it supports the operations of United States Naval Forces Europe and acts as a stop for US airlifters en route from the United States to South-West Asia and the Indian Ocean.
- Camp Darby near Pisa and Livorno. Dating back to 1951, it hosts a 2,000-acre ammunitions storage facility providing strategic ammunition reserves to US Army and Air Force units in Europe. Its location enables the US military to move ammunition both by sea (from Livorno) and by air (from Pisa military airport).

The argument is one that rests on a particular view of what Italian foreign policy has traditionally been like. Though a view that is perhaps inappropriately disparaging, it is one that is often asserted. It is that Italy's foreign policy has traditionally been guided first and foremost by '*presenzialismo*'. This is a term that can be roughly translated as 'showing one's face everywhere' and which, applied to Italian foreign policy, carries a double implication: that while a constant of the country's policy has been a desire to be a part of, and to count in, significant areas of international diplomacy, this has frequently not been matched by the capacity or the willingness to take on more than token responsibilities in the areas concerned. And, lacking especially heavy responsibilities, the country has, it is alleged, frequently sought to 'do its own thing', sometimes to the detriment of the global alliances of which it has been part. During the Cold War, for example, it was sometimes argued that Italy had delegated its defence to the United States by allowing its territory to be heavily occupied by American bases – while contributing relatively little to NATO in terms of defence spending, and seeking on its own to court Moscow and the Arab states (for example in the energy field). Therefore, the argument concludes, it has often been perceived by its partners as an unreliable ally, with the result that these partners have tended to exclude it from consultations, thus preventing it from punching according to its economic and industrial weight.

The argument of authors such as Molinari and Romano is thus that since 1996, Italy has taken on more responsibilities in international affairs, has been viewed with greater confidence by its allies and thus has been able to wield a greater degree of influence. What has enabled this greater assumption of responsibilities has been the emergence of a greater, if still by no means perfect, degree of 'bipartisan' consensus on foreign policy than was typical prior to 1989.

How are we to assess this argument? Certainly, there is much evidence one could draw on to sustain a view that the country has shifted from being a 'security-consuming' to a 'security-producing' country:[6] it has played a much larger role in UN and multinational peace-keeping operations than it did before 1990 (Croci, 2002: 5). It took the lead in *Operazione Alba*[7] in 1997. Its participation in NATO bombing of Serbia in 1999 was managed by a prime minister: whose party had traditionally stood four square behind the peace movement; whose policy relied on the active support of the opposition; who, apparently convinced that Italy's international political weight depended on it, denied Parliament a role in the decision to grant NATO access to its military bases for the bombing. It agreed, in August 2006, to lead the international mission in the Lebanon, following the month-long conflict between Israel and Hezbollah. In doing so, it offered to send 3,000 troops: more than any other country (Fois, 2009: 65). But whether it is sensible to see in such evidence signs of a shift from a foreign policy once supposedly indicative of 'unreliability' and an 'unwillingness to accept responsibility', etc., is unclear. 'Reliability', 'responsibility' and so forth are normative terms expressing value judgements on the part of those who use them. But if we want to understand and *make sense* of Italy's foreign-policy actions, then it is almost certainly more illuminating to adopt an alternative approach. This is an approach that interprets Italian foreign affairs, both past and present, as the result of the best efforts of policy-makers to advance the country's interests as they perceive them, in light of the circumstances in which they find themselves.

The period since 2001

In relation to the main issue of whether Italy has been successful in acquiring a more influential role on the international scene, the available evidence suggests that if advances were made after 1996, then from 2001 there was some retrocession from such positions. Three episodes in particular point in this direction:

(1)   international reaction to the election of Silvio Berlusconi in 2001;
(2)   the subsequent personalisation of Italian foreign policy and its concentration in the hands of the Prime Minister (Andreatta and Brighi, 2003: 264);
(3)   the Italian presidency of the EU from 1 July 2003.

International reaction to the election of Berlusconi

Two weeks before polling day in 2001, the *Economist* magazine published a lengthy article explaining why, in its view, Berlusconi was 'unfit to lead Italy'. In doing so it echoed fears expressed more widely in the international community and reflected what appeared to be a new trend that had started with Jörg Haider two years before. The fears arose from the several criminal allegations Berlusconi then faced, from his apparent conflict of interests and from the political complexion of his coalition. This included an ex-fascist party and a regional autonomy party seemingly at least as extreme. When Haider's Freedom Party had entered government in 1999, Austria had been subject to symbolic but humiliating sanctions. The episode appeared to suggest the start of a new era in which, far from refraining from comment on the internal affairs of other countries, European policy-makers felt that integration had reached the point where the most intimate affairs of any one country were properly the concern of all of the others.

The personalisation of Italian foreign policy

Under these circumstances, the most pressing foreign-policy objective in the immediate aftermath of the election became the accrediting of the new government, and of Berlusconi personally, as a statesman on a par with any other. Unfortunately, the concentration of foreign policy in the hands of the Prime Minister and the high profile he sought to occupy worked against this. Initially, Berlusconi had sought to achieve the desired international legitimacy by bowing to pressure from the President of the Republic, among others, to appoint as foreign minister the well-respected diplomat and ex-WTO president, Renato Ruggiero. But Ruggiero resigned in January 2002 apparently in part because of Berlusconi's unwillingness to consult his minister properly or to back him in representing Italy by insisting that in Europe the various other ministers all 'sing from the same hymn sheet'.

When, following this, Berlusconi himself took over the portfolio, apparently as a means of imposing greater government cohesion, foreign policy came under the direct control of a charismatic leader. It was thereby exposed to a threefold danger. This was the danger: (1) that foreign policy would be ephemeral (since charismatic leadership means that policies can rarely survive their promoters); (2) that it would become hostage to internal politics and to Berlusconi's personal agenda (Andreatta and Brighi, 2003: 264–5), and (3) that it would be directly damaged by Berlusconi's propensity to make gaffes. These have become legendary. They include (1) the suggestion, in September 2001, that Islamic civilisation failed to protect human, political and religious rights and was therefore inferior to the civilisation of the West; (2) the suggestion, in July 2003, that German Euro-parliamentarian, Martin Scultz, could be likened to a Nazi concentration camp kapo; (3) the suggestion, in November 2003, that reports of the lack of respect for human rights by Russia in Chechnya, condemned by several governments and international organisations, were media distortions (Morata, 2004: 152).

Italian presidency of the EU

Finally, the Italian presidency of the EU in the second half of 2003 appears to have been a wasted opportunity. As Morata (2004: 147) points out, the EU presidency has traditionally been perceived by governments as a good opportunity for acquiring greater prestige both domestically and in the eyes of other governments. Success in this requires skills of mediation and leadership. Mediation is fundamental for the building of consensus where many decisions are still subject to QMV or unanimity. Leadership gives the capacity to work with the Commission president to maintain and enhance the image of the EU overall. The problem was that Berlusconi is a man who is intolerant of institutional restrictions and is used to giving orders. He therefore lacked the necessary diplomatic abilities. Thus, we may note the following:

(1) He was unable to draw any advantage from the fact that the Commission presidency was occupied by a compatriot. Instead, he was unable to resist attacking Prodi to appeal to domestic audiences.
(2) As his declaration on Chechnya showed, he was unable to put aside the bilateral relations he had established with Vladimir Putin and defend, as EU president, collectively agreed positions.
(3) Incidents such as these combined with substantive disappointments – such as the inability to secure adoption of the new European Constitution before the presidency expired – to feed a widespread perception that the presidency itself had been an 'enormous failure' (Morata, 2004: 163).

Many of the presidency's difficulties were due precisely to that personalisation of foreign policy that was mentioned above. As Andreatta and Brighi (2003: 277–8) point out, such an approach is bound to produce paradoxical results because whatever successes it might bring are bound to be temporary, evaporating once its protagonist leaves the scene. This also means, however, that the negative consequences of personalistic management will likewise be transitory – in turn suggesting that the less-than-positive effects of the period after 2001 are unlikely to prejudice Italy's international influence in the longer term.

Some evidence to support this view came with the election of the Prodi government in 2006. This government sought to emphasise the idea of discontinuity with the preceding Berlusconi government in foreign affairs through a sharp break with the personalistic management of Berlusconi, involving a reversion to the traditional multilateralism characteristic of Italian policy, against the bilateralism of the previous government. In this way, Prime Minister Romano Prodi sought greater cohesiveness for his coalition:

- Emphasising the foreign-policy disagreements with the previous government enabled him to present the continuation of his executive as the only viable alternative to a return of Silvio Berlusconi, and thus, to a degree, to ride the waves of the significant foreign-policy disagreements within his own government.
- The bilateralism of the previous government, centre-left spokespersons claimed, always worked in uncritical agreement with the Bush administration. Drawing back from the strongly pro-American policy of the previous government in favour of a more balanced approach helped cohesion by appealing to the Government's radical-left members. For these, the stances to be taken towards the United States and its international initiatives were among the issues with the most critical bearing on their capacity to remain loyal to the executive.

For these reasons, despite its instability and litigiousness, this government, is widely viewed as not having been without foreign-policy successes (see Croci, 2008; Fois, 2009; Walston, 2008).

■ Summary and conclusions

The Cold War and domestic politics were the main factors shaping the nature of Italian foreign policy in the period after the Second World War. Together they ensured that the main pillars of that policy would be Atlanticism and Europeanism. On the one hand, the lack of internal consensus and the presence of a strong communist party made it impossible for Italian policy-makers to stand aside from the main geopolitical conflict – as countries such as Sweden and Switzerland were able to do (Romano, 2002: 59). They also undermined the capacity of governments to exercise a strong, autonomous influence within the NATO alliance. Thus was Italy condemned to the role of a predominantly 'security-consuming' country. On the other hand, this, by weakening their capacity to resist American pressures, left Italian policy-makers potentially exposed to the opposition of a broad coalition of nationalists, Catholic pacifists and Communists. Europeanism offered them a means of meeting this challenge. For nationalists, the project of European integration placed Second World War victors and vanquished on an equal footing and held out the prospect of a larger European nation; for Catholics it offered the prospect of peace, justice and international solidarity; for Communists, once they had broken with Moscow, Europe was no longer a 'capitalist club' and instead offered a means of resisting US pressures.

The end of the Cold War has presented Italy with both the opportunity and the need to conduct a more assertive foreign policy. This led its diplomats to seek, across a range of fronts, the kind of higher-profile role that, prior to 1989, they were largely limited to seeking in the Mediterranean. In doing so, they reveal their overriding desire to ensure that Italy counts, is consulted and above all avoids relegation by others to 'serie B'. They thereby reveal ambitions that are surely universal: countries everywhere wish to maximise their capacities for autonomous influence. In this way do Italian diplomats reveal that what they are doing is contributing to the governance of a normal country.

■ Further reading

For an understanding of Italy's relationship with the United States during the Cold War period, see Mario Del Pero's 'Containing containment: rethinking Italy's experience during the Cold War' (in the *Journal of Modern Italian Studies*, vol. 8, no. 4, 2003, pp. 532–5). See also, in the same journal (vol. 9, no. 4, 2004, pp. 428–49), Roberto Gualtieri's 'The Italian political system and *détente* (1963–1981)'. The changes in Italian foreign policy that have come about as a result of the end of the Cold War have been discussed in a wide range of articles among which Osvaldo Croci, 'Italian security policy after the Cold War' (*Journal of Modern Italian Studies*, vol. 8, no. 2, June 2003, pp. 266–83). Trends in Italian foreign policy generally can be followed by consulting the chapters devoted to it that regularly appear in the annual editions of *Italian Politics* published by Berghahn. The most recent of these is the chapter by James Walston in the 2007 edition edited by Mark Donovan and Paolo Onofri.

■ Notes

1. See tables 1 and 3 at www.nato.int/docu/handbook/2001/index.htm#CH9.
2. This was the principle, enunciated at the 1990 Paris summit of the Organization for Security and Co-operation in Europe, that the security of each member state was inextricably linked to the security of all of them.
3. Space does not permit giving a description of the American military presence in Italy, but details of the situation in 1999 can be had by reading CSM (1999).
4. Perhaps not surprisingly, then, Italians are more likely than the citizens of other EU member states to welcome the idea of ceding sovereignty in foreign-affairs matters to the EU through development of the CFSP (Figure 10.1).
5. After taking power, Qaddafi confiscated Italian property in Libya and demanded reparations for Italy's colonial past apparently as a means of shoring up his own internal popularity.
6. The phrases were used by Defence Minister Salvo Andò when commenting on Italy's decision to participate in the UN mission to Somalia in 1992–3 and are quoted by Croci (2002: 4–5).
7. This was the code-name given to the mission to restore order in Albania following the collapse of the financial pyramid schemes mentioned above.

Appendix: The electoral system for the Chamber of Deputies and the Senate

Law no. 270, of 21 December 2005, introduced a series of amendents to the laws governing elections to the Chamber of Deputies and the Senate of the Republic. The nature of these amendments were such as to alter substantially the basis on which seats in the two chambers of Parliament had been distributed since the electoral-law reform of 1993. As a consequence, the details of the electoral system for each branch are now as follows.

The Chamber of Deputies

- The country is divided into twenty-six constituencies among which 617 of the 630 seats are assigned according to the population of each constituency.
- Parties field a list of candidates for each constituency, voters making a single choice among these lists. That is, the voter chooses a list but cannot choose between the candidates making up the chosen list.
- In presenting their lists, parties may either declare themselves to be independent entities or, with the consent of the parties concerned, declare themselves to be allied with others as part of a coalition.
- There are a series of vote thresholds that must be overcome. That is, in order to be entitled to participate in the distribution of seats, a party must, if running independently or if running as part of a coalition whose parties' combined national valid vote amounts to less than 10 per cent of the total, (a) have attracted at least 4 per cent of the national total of valid votes cast or (b) be a party representing one of the linguistic minorities and in that case to have fielded, in one of the 'special statute' regions providing special protection for the linguistic minorities, a list in just one constituency and to have obtained at least 20 per cent of the valid vote in that constituency. If part of a coalition whose parties' combined national valid vote amounts to at least ten per cent of the total, then it must (a) have attracted at least 2 per cent of the national total of valid votes cast or (b) have the largest number of valid votes among the coalition's parties below this threshold or (c) be a party representing one of the linguistic minorities and have attracted (as above) at least 20 per cent of the valid votes cast in the relevant constituency.

- Once votes have been cast, the national electoral office distributes seats among coalitions, parties and candidates through a series of calculations that proceed as follows.

  (1) It identifies (a) the coalitions whose national valid vote totals amount to at least 10 per cent and that have at least one party with 2 per cent or at least one linguistic minority party with at least 20 per cent in the relevant constituency; (b) (i) independent parties with at least 4 per cent, (ii) independent linguistic minority parties with at least 20 per cent in the relevant constituency, (iii) parties belonging to coalitions with less than 10 per cent but that themselves have 4 per cent, (iv) linguistic minority parties belonging to coalitions with less than 10 per cent but that themselves have at least 20 per cent in the relevant constituency.

  (2) It then distributes seats among the coalitions and parties identified in the previous paragraph by (a) dividing their combined national valid vote total by the number of seats to be distributed to obtain the national electoral quotient; (b) dividing the national valid vote obtained by each of the aforementioned coalitions or individual parties by the national electoral quotient, to obtain the number of seats to which each is entitled, ignoring any fractions. Any seats remaining unassigned after this process go to the coalitions and independent parties having the highest remainders.

  (3) It then establishes whether the coalition or individual party with the largest number of valid votes has at least 340 seats.

  (4) It then identifies, within each of the coalitions referred to at (1a): (i) the parties with at least 2 per cent; (ii) linguistic minority parties with at least 20 per cent in the relevant constituency; (iii) the largest party among those with less than 2 per cent.

  (5) If there is a coalition or individual party with at least 340 seats, then, for each coalition, the national electoral office divides the *sum* of the national valid votes obtained by the parties referred to at (4) by the number of seats already assigned to that coalition. It then divides the national valid vote obtained by *each* of the parties referred to at (4) by the latter figure to obtain the number of seats due to each. Each of the parties identified at (1b) obtains the number of seats already assigned to it on the basis of the calculation described at (2).

  (6) Within each constituency, the distribution of seats is carried out by dividing, for each of the coalitions referred to at (1a), the sum of the valid votes obtained by the coalition's component parties in that constituency by the national electoral quotient. The valid votes obtained in the constuency by each of the parties referred to at (1b) are likewise divided by the national electoral quotient. Each of the resulting figures, x, is then multiplied by the number of seats assigned to the constituency, the product being divided by the sum of x to

obtain the number of seats to be assigned, in the constituency, to each coalition or party referred to at (1).

(7) The number of seats, within each constituency, to be assigned to each of the parties making up each coalition is determined by dividing the combined total of the valid votes obtained, in that constituency, by the parties referred to at (4) by the number of seats assigned to the coalition as a result of the calculations described at (6) to obtain the constituency quotient. Each party's constituency vote total is then divided by the constituency quotient to obtain the number of seats due to it.

(8) If, as a result of the calculations described at (2), there is no coalition or individual party with at least 340 seats, then the coalition or party with the largest number of national valid votes is assigned as many additional seats as are necessary to bring its total up to 340. The national electoral office then divides the coalition's or the party's national valid vote total by 340 to obtain the majority national electoral quotient.

(9) The remaining 277 seats are assigned to the other coalitions and parties referred to at (1), the sum of their national valid vote totals being divided by 277 to obtain the minority national electoral quotient. Each coalition's and each party's national valid vote total is then divided by the minority national electoral quotient to obtain the number of seats due to it.

(10) The operations described at (4) and (5) are then carried out.

(11) For the purposes of distributing seats within each constituency, the national electoral office performs the calculations described at (6) and (7) except that, in place of the national electoral quotient, it uses the majority national electoral quotient for the coalition or party that has obtained the largest number of valid votes and the minority national electoral quotient for the remaining coalitions or parties.

(12) Seats are assigned to individual candidates in accordance with the order in which their names appear in the lists presented by the parties to which they belong.

• One seat is assigned to the region of Valle d'Aosta. Twelve seats are assigned to an additional, overseas, constituency consisting of Italians living abroad.

• Valle d'Aosta constitutes a single-member constituency within which the candidate obtaining the largest number of votes is declared elected.

• The twelve deputies representing the overseas constituency continue to be elected in accordance with the provisions of law no. 459 of 2001 and that is:

(1) The constituency is divided into four areas (Europe; South America; North America; Africa, Asia, Oceania and the Antarctic), to each of which is assigned one seat, the remaining seats being distributed between the four areas in accordance with the number of Italian citizens resident in each.

(2) For each of the four areas, the parties present lists of candidates among which the voter makes a choice. The voter also has the option of casting two preference votes if resident in an area to which two or

more seats have been assigned, and one preference vote if resident in one of the remaining areas.

(3) Once the votes have been cast, seats are distributed among candidates by:

    (a) determining the total valid votes obtained by each list in each area;

    (b) determining the total valid preference votes obtained by each candidate;

    (c) dividing the sum of valid votes cast in the area by the number of seats assigned to the area to obtain the electoral quotient, disregarding fractions;

    (d) dividing each list's vote total by the electoral quotient to obtain the number of seats due to it;

    (e) assigning any seats unallotted at the end of the process to the lists with the highest remainders;

    (f) assigning seats to individual candidates in accordance with the number of preference votes they have received and, where two or more candidates have the same number of preference votes, in accordance with the order in which they are listed.

The Senate

- Of the 315 seats, 301 are distributed among eighteen of the twenty regions (that is, with the exception of Valle d'Aosta and Trentino-Alto Adige) according to their populations.
- Parties field a list of candidates in each region, voters making a single choice among these lists. That is, the voter chooses a list but cannot choose between the candidates making up the chosen list.
- In presenting their lists, parties may either declare themselves to be independent entities or, with the consent of the parties concerned, declare themselves to be allied with others as part of a coalition.
- In contrast to the Chamber of Deputies, the distribution of seats takes place, region by region; that is, the distribution among parties and coalitions in each region takes account only of their regional vote totals, not their national totals.
- In order to be eligible to participate in the distribution of the seats assigned to a region, a party must, if running independently, or if running as part of a coalition whose parties' combined regional valid vote amounts to less than 20 per cent of the total, have attracted at least 8 per cent of the regional total of valid votes cast. If part of a coalition whose parties' combined regional valid vote amounts to at least 20 per cent of the total, then it must have attracted at least 3 per cent of the regional total of valid votes cast.
- Once votes have been cast, the regional electoral office distributes seats among coalitions, parties and candidates through a series of calculations that proceed as follows.

(1) It identifies (a) the coalitions whose regional valid vote totals amount to at least 20 per cent and that have at least one party with 3 per cent; (b) (i) independent parties with at least 8 per cent, (ii) parties belonging to coalitions with less than 20 per cent but that themselves have 8 per cent.

(2) It (a) divides the sum of the valid vote totals obtained by the coalitions and parties referred to in the previous paragraph by the number of seats assigned to the region, thus obtaining the constituency electoral quotient; (b) divides the regional valid vote obtained by each of the aforementioned coalitions or individual parties by the constituency electoral quotient to obtain the number of seats to which each is entitled, ignoring any fractions. Any seats remaining unassigned after this process go to the coalitions and independent parties having the highest remainders.

(3) It then establishes whether the coalition or individual party with the largest number of valid votes has at least 55 per cent of the seats assigned to the region.

(4) It then identifies, within each of the coaltions referred to at (1a) the parties with at least 3 per cent.

(5) If there is a coalition or individual party with at least 55 per cent of the seats, then, for each coalition, the regional electoral office divides the *sum* of the regional valid votes obtained by the parties referred to at (4) by the number of seats already assigned to that coalition to obtain the coalition electoral quotient. It then divides the regional valid vote obtained by *each* of the parties referred to at (4) by the coalition electoral quotient to obtain the number of seats due to each. Each of the parties identified at (1b) obtains the number of seats already assigned to it on the basis of the calculation described at (2).

(6) If, as a result of the calculations described at (2), there is no coalition or individual party with at least 55 per cent of the seats, then the coalition or party with the largest number of regional valid votes is assigned as many additional seats as are necessary to bring its total up to 55 per cent.

(7) The remaining seats are distributed among the other parties and coalitions by (a) dividing by the number of remaining seats the *sum* of the regional valid votes obtained by these parties and coalitions; (b) dividing by the figure resulting from the latter operation the regional valid vote obtained by *each* of these parties and coalitions.

(8) For each coalition entitled to seats in accordance with the operations described at (6) and (7), seats are distributed *between* its eligible component parties by (a) dividing the *sum* of the regional valid votes obtained by the parties referred to at (4) by the number of seats already assigned to that coalition to obtain the coalition electoral quotient; (b) dividing the regional valid vote obtained by *each* of the parties

referred to at (4) by the coalition electoral quotient to obtain the number of seats due to each.

(9) Seats are assigned to individual candidates in accordance with the order in which their names appear in the lists presented by the parties to which they belong.

- One seat is assigned to Valle d'Aosta; seven to Trentino-Alto Adige and six to the overseas constituency consisting of Italians living abroad.
- Valle d'Aosta constitutes a single-member constituency within which the candidate obtaining the largest number of votes is declared elected.
- Trentino-Alto Adige is divided into six single-member constituencies in each of which the candidate obtaining the largest number of votes is declared elected. Remaining seats assigned to Trentino-Alto Adige are distributed by

  (1) calculating, for each party, the sum of votes obtained by its candidates in the single-member constituencies minus the sum of votes obtained by those of its candidates already elected in such constituencies to obtain the party's 'electoral total';

  (2) multiplying by 100 the votes obtained by each unsuccessful candidate and dividing the product by the total of the valid votes cast in the constituency concerned to obtain each candidate's 'electoral total';

  (3) dividing each party's 'electoral total' successively, by one, two and so forth in accordance with the number of seats to be distributed, and choosing each time, among the figures thus obtained, the largest ones – the figures so chosen being equal in number to the number of seats to be distributed. Seats are assigned to the parties in accordance with the size of these figures.

  (4) allotting seats – in accordance with the number assigned to each party – to each of the party's not already successful candidates in accordance with the size of their electoral totals.

- Election of the six senators representing the overseas constituency takes place in accordance with exactly the same articles of law no. 459 of 2001 as the ones governing the election of deputies representing the overseas constituency.

References

Accornero, Aris and Eliana Como (2003), 'La (mancata) riforma dell'articolo 18',
    pp. 239–62, in Jean Blondel and Paolo Segatti (eds.), *Politica in Italia: i fatti
    dell'anno e le interpretazioni*, Bologna: il Mulino.
Albertazzi, Daniele and Duncan McDonnell (2007), *Twenty-First Century Populism: The
    Spectre of Western European Democracy*, New York and London: Palgrave Macmillan.
Allum, Felia and James L. Newell (2003), 'Aspects of the Italian transition', *Journal of
    Modern Italian Studies*, vol. 8, no. 2, pp. 182–96.
Allum, Percy (1973a), *Italy: Republic without Government*, London: Wiedenfeld and
    Nicolson.
Allum, Percy (1973b), *Politics and Society in Post-War Naples*, Cambridge: Cambridge
    University Press.
Almond, Gabriel A. and G. Bingham Powell, Jr, *et al.* (1992), *Comparative Politics Today:
    A World View*, New York: Harper Collins.
Almond, Gabriel A. and Sidney Verba (1963), *The Civic Culture: Political Attitudes and
    Democracy in Five Nations*, Princeton: Princeton University Press.
Andreatta, Filippo and Elisabetta Brighi (2003), 'La politica estera del governo
    Berlusconi: i primi 18 mesi', pp. 263–81, in Jean Blondel and Paolo Segatti (eds.),
    Politica in Italia, Bologna: il Mulino.
Andrews, Geoff (2005), *Not a Normal Country: Italy after Berlusconi*, London: Pluto Press.
Baccaro, Lucio and Marco Simoni (2004), 'Il referendum sull'articolo 18 e gli interventi
    di flessibilizzazione del mercato del lavoro', pp. 207–28, in Vincent della Sala and
    Sergio Fabbrini (eds.), *Politica in Italia: i fatti dell'anno e le interpretazioni*, Bologna: il
    Mulino.
Baldini, Gianfranco (2002a), 'The direct election of mayors: an assessment of the
    institutional reform following the Italian municipal elections of 2001', *Journal of
    Modern Italian Studies*, vol. 7, no. 3, pp. 364–79.
Baldini, Gianfranco, (2002b), 'Eleggere I sindaci diece anni dopo', *il Mulino*, no. 402,
    pp. 658–67.
Banfield, Edward C. (1958), *The Moral Basis of a Backward Society*, New York: The Free Press.
Baranes, Andrea (nd), 'La riforma del system previdenziale: cause e conseguenze
    dell'introduzione dei fondi pensione', www.italia.attac.org/spip/IMG/pdf/
    Riforma_previdenziale.pdf.
Barbera, Augusto and Carlo Fusaro (2004), *Corso di diritto pubblico*, 3rd edn, Bologna: il
    Mulino.
Barrett, Chris (1996), 'Globalization: implications for democracy', *Case Studies for Politics*,
    no. 34, Department of Politics, University of York.

BASIC [British American Security Information Council] (nd), 'Kosovo: the long road to war A Chronology 1999', www.basicint.org/europe/confprev/Kosovo/timeline3.htm.

Bellucci, Paolo (1997), 'L'intervento italiano in Bosnia e la (lenta) ridefinizione della politica di difesa', pp. 241–63, in Roberto D'Alimonte and David Nelken (eds.), *Politica in Italia*, Bologna: il Mulino.

Berger, Suzanne (1983), 'Introduzione', pp. 9–43, in Suzanne Berger (ed.), *L'organizzazione degli interessi nell'Europa occidentale*, Bologna: il Mulino.

Berselli, E. (2007), 'Destra e sinistra: con chi e come fondersi', *la Repubblica*, 10 April, p. 45.

Berta, Giuseppe (2005), 'Confindustria under Montezemolo', pp. 223–41, in Carlo Guarnieri and James L. Newell (eds.), *Italian Politics: Quo Vadis?*, New York and Oxford: Berghahn.

Bianchi, Patrizio (2004), 'Università: verso il blocco totale?', *il Mulino*, no. 2, pp. 211–20.

Bianco, Magda (2003), *L'industria italiana*, Bologna: il Mulino.

Bini Smaghi, Lorenzo (2001), *L'euro*, Bologna: il Mulino.

Blockmans, Steven (2004), 'EU conflict prevention in the Western Balkans', pp. 293–321, in Vincent Kronenberger and Jan Wouters (eds.), *The European Union and Conflict Prevention: Policy and Legal Aspects*, The Hague: T. M. C. Asser Press.

Boniver, Margherita (2002), 'Fronte europeo per fermare i clandestini', *il Giornale*, 27 March, www.grtv.it/www/2002/marzo2002/27marzo2002/rassegna8.htm.

Bordignon, Fabio (2005), 'Fiducia nella Chiesa, ma niente ingerenze. Quattro italiani su dieci: il Vaticano non faccia politica. "Scegliamo da soli"', *la Repubblica*, 18 December, pp. 18–19.

Boschma, Ron A. (1998), 'The industrial rise of the Third Italy: open window of locational opportunity?', paper prepared for presentation to the 38th congress of the European Regional Science Association, Vienna, 28 August – 1 September, www.ersa.org/ersaconfs /ersa98/papers/91.pdf.

Briquet, Jean-Louis and Alfio Mastropaolo (2008), *Italian Politics: The Center-Left's Poisoned Victory*, New York and Oxford: Berghahn.

Brusco, Giovanni (1995), 'Local productive systems and the new industrial policy in Italy', pp. 51–68, in Arnaldo Bagnasco and Charles Sabel (eds.), *Small and Medium-Size Enterprises*, London: Pinter.

Buccianti, Giovanni (2005), *Enrico Mattei: assalto al potere petrolifero mondiale*, Milan: Giuffrè editore.

Bull, Martin J. and James L. Newell (1995), 'Italy changes course? The 1994 elections and the victory of the Right', *Parliamentary Affairs*, vol. 48, no. 1, January, pp. 72–99.

(2001), 'The Italian general election of May 2001', Keele European Parties Research Unit (KEPRU), Working Paper 4, University of Keele.

(2005), *Italian Politics: Adjustment under Duress*, Cambridge: Polity Press.

Buzan, Barry and Ole Wæver (2003), *Regions and Powers: The Structure of International Security*, Cambridge: Cambridge University Press.

Buzzanca, Silvio (2008a) 'Berlusconi-Fini, via al Pdl ultimatum a Casini: dentro o fuori', *la Repubblica*, 9 February, p. 2.

(2008b), 'Sinistra Arcobaleno, un voto su due al Pd', *la Repubblica*, 17 April, p. 13.

Calvert, Peter (2002), *Comparative Politics: An Introduction*, Harlow: Pearson Education.

Cammelli, Marco (2003), 'Un grande caos chiamato *devolution*', *il Mulino*, 1/2003, vol. 52 no. 405, pp. 87–99.

Campus, Donatella (2009), 'Campaign issues and themes', pp. 137–49, in James L. Newell (ed.), *The Italian General Election of 2008: Berlusconi Strikes Back*, Basingstoke: Palgrave.

359

Campus, Donatella and Gianfranco Pasquino, (2006), 'Leadership in Italy: the changing role of leaders in elections and in government', *Journal of Contemporary European Studies*, vol. 14, no. 1, pp. 25–40.

Cancian, Frank (1976), 'Il contadino meridionale: visione del mondo e comportamento politico', pp. 207–13, in Edward C. Banfield, *Le basi morali di una società arretrata* (new edition, Una comunità del Mezzogiorno, with commentaries by F. Cancian, G. A. Marselli, A. J. Wichers, A. Pizzorno, S. F. Silverman, N. S. Peabody, J. Davis, J. Galtung, A. Colombis. Edited by Domenico De Masi), Bologna: il Mulino.

Capano, Giliberto (2000a), 'Le politiche amministrative: dall'improbabile riforma alla riforma permanente?', pp. 153–98, in Giuseppe di Palma, Sergio Fabbrini and Giorgio Freddi (eds.), *Condannata al successo? L'Italia nell'Europea integrata*, Bologna: il Mulino.

(2000b), *L'Università in Italia*, Bologna: il Mulino.

(2003), 'The long hard struggle to change a resilient institution: the case of Italian Parliament viewed from a diachronic perspective', paper presented to the workshop, 'Institutional Theory: Issues of Measurement and Change' of the Joint Sessions of Workshops of the ECPR, University of Edinburgh, 28 March – 2 April 2003.

Capano, Giliberto and Marco Giuliani (2001), 'Governing without surviving? An Italian paradox: law-making in Italy 1987–2001', *Journal of Legislative Studies*, no. 4, pp. 13–36.

(2003), 'The Italian Parliament: in Search of a new role?', *Journal of Legislative Studies*, vol. 9, no. 2, pp. 8–34.

Capriati, Michele (2009), 'The economic context', pp. 43–61, in James L. Newell (ed.), *The Italian General Election of 2008: Berlusconi Strikes Back*, Basingstoke: Palgrave.

Cartocci, Roberto and Domenico Piscitelli (2003), 'La Repubblica e i suoi riti', pp. 117–37, in Gaspare Nevola (ed.), *Una patria per gli Italiani: la questione nazionale oggi tra storia, cultura e politica*, Roma: Carocci editore.

Cassese, Sabino (1984), 'The higher civil service in Italy', pp. 35–71, in Ezra N. Suleiman (ed.), *Bureaucrats and Policy Making: A Comparative Overview*, New York and London: Holmes and Meier.

Castles, Francis G. (2004), *The Future of the Welfare State: Crisis Myths and Crisis Realities*, Oxford: Oxford University Press.

Ceccarini, Luigi (2005), 'Fedeli, secolarizzati, iregolari: I cattolici italiani', *il Mulino*, no. 5, pp. 852–62.

Cento Bull Anna, (2002), 'Towards a federal state? Competing proposals for reforming Italy's centre-periphery relations', paper presented at the 52nd Annual Conference of the UK Political Studies Association, University of Aberdeen, 5–7 April.

Certoma, G. Leroy (1985), *The Italian Legal System*, London: Butterworths.

Cesari, Riccardo (2000), *I fondi pensione*, Bologna: il Mulino.

Cheli, Enzo (2000), *La riforma mancata: tradizione e innovazione nella Costituzione italiana*, Bologna: il Mulino.

Chiaramonte, A. (2008), 'How Prodi's Unione won by a handful of votes' pp. 203–22, in James L. Newell (ed.), *The Italian General Election of 2006: Romano Prodi's Victory*, Manchester: Manchester University Press.

Chiarini, Rosalba (2003), 'Esecutiva e burocrazia: ridefinita la relazione tra amministratori e politici', pp. 179–226, in Cristina Barbieri and Luca Verzichelli (eds.), *Il governo e i suoi apparati: l'evoluzione del caso italiano in prospettiva comparata*, Genoa: Name.

Clark, Martin (1996), *Modern Italy 1871–1995*, 2nd edition, London and New York: Longman.

Codispoti, Joseph M. (2001), 'Fallen eagle: an examination of Italy's contemporary role and relations with Albania', *Mediterranean Quarterly*, vol. 12, no. 1, Winter, pp. 81–99.

Colaprico, Piero (1996), *Capire Tangentopoli*, Milano: il Saggiatore.

Colombo, Alessandro (1994), 'Nuovi scenari nella NATO e nella CEE', pp. 636–8, in Paul Ginsborg (ed.), *Stato dell'Italia*, Milan: il Saggiatore.

Connolly, William E. (2006), *Political Science and Ideology*, Edison, NJ: Aldine Transaction.

Consortium (2008), 'Elezioni del 13–14 aprile 2008: analisi dei flussi elettorali riguardanti i 5 maggiori partiti', *Istituto Piepoli SpA*, www.istitutopiepoli.it/images/Articoli/ANALISI_FLUSSI_ELETTORALI.pdf.

Coser, Louis A. (1974), *Greedy Institutions: Patterns of Undivided Commitment*, New York: the Free Press.

Cotta, Maurizio (1996), 'La crisi del governo di partito all'italiana', pp. 11–52, in Maurizio Cotta and Pierangelo Isernia (eds.), *Il gigante dai piedi d'argilla: la crisi del regime partitocratico in Italia*, Bologna: il Mulino.

Cottino, Gastone (1999), *La legge Draghi e le società quotate in Borsa*, Turin: UTET.

CPM [Commissione parlamentare d'inchiesta sul fenomeno della mafia e sulle altre associazioni similari] (1993), *Audizione del collaboratore di giustizia Gaspare Mutolo*, XI legislature, 9 February, www.liberliber.it/biblioteca/i/italia/verbali_della_commissione_parlamentare_antimafia/html/violante01/25_00.htm.

Cram, Laura, Desmond Dinan, and Neill Nugent (1999), 'Reconciling theory and practice', pp. 3–19, in Laura Cram, Desmond Dinan and Neill Nugent (eds.), *Developments in the European Union*, London: Macmillan.

Criscitiello, Annarita (1993), 'Majority summits: decision-making inside the Cabinet and out: Italy, 1970–1990', *West European Politics*, vol. 16, no. 4 (October), pp. 581–94.

(2003), 'Le strutture di supporto al Presidente del Consiglio: come cambia Palazzo Chigi', pp. 153–78, in Cristina Barbieri and Luca Verzichelli (eds.), *Il governo e i suoi apparati: l'evoluzione del caso italiano in prospettiva comparata*, Genova: Name.

Croci, Osvaldo (2000), 'Dovere, umanitarismo e interesse nazionale. L'Italia e l'intervento della Nato in Kosovo', pp. 109–30, in Mark Gilbert and Gianfranco Pasquino (eds.), *Politica in Italia*, Bologna: il Mulino.

(2002), 'Italian security policy in the 1990s', paper presented to the 52nd Annual Conference of the UK Political Studies Association, University of Aberdeen, 5–7 April.

(2004), 'La fine del consenso *bipartisan*? La politica estera Italiana e la guerra in Iraq', pp. 125–44, in Vincent della Sala and Sergio Fabbrini (eds.), *Politica in Italia*, Bologna: il Mulino.

(2005), 'Much Ado about Little: The foreign policy of the second Berlusconi government', *Modern Italy*, vol. 10, no. 1, pp. 59–74.

(2008), 'The second Prodi government and Italian foreign policy: new and improved or the same wrapped up differently?', *Modern Italy*, vol. 13, no. 3, pp. 291–303.

CSM (1999), 'La presenza militare americana in Italia: mappe di guerra', *Umanità Nova*, no. 12, 4 April, www.ecn.org/uenne/archivio/archivio1999/un12/art475.html

De Marco, Eugenio (1998), '"Gruppi di pressione", procedimento legislativo e "realizzabilità" delle leggi', pp. 427–47 in Università degli Studi di Roma "Tor Vergata", *Scritti in Onore di Serio Galeotti*, vol. I, Milan: Giuffrè editore.

De Masi, Domenico (1976), 'Arretratezza del Mezzogiorno e analisi sociologica', pp. 7–31, in Edward C. Banfield, *Le basi morali di una società arretrata* (new edition, Una comunità del Mezzogiorno, with commentaries by F. Cancian, G. A. Marselli, A. J. Wichers, A. Pizzorno, S. F. Silverman, N. S. Peabody, J. Davis, J. Galtung, A. Colombis. Edited by Domenico De Masi), Bologna: il Mulino.

De Micheli, Chiara and Luca Verzichelli (2004), *Il Parlamento*, Bologna: il Mulino.

Dehousse, R. (1997), 'European integration and the nation-state', pp. 37–56, in Martin Rhodes, Paul Heywood and Vincent Wright (eds.), *Developments in West European Politics*, London: Macmillan.

Dei, Marcello (1998), *La scuola in Italia*, Bologna: il Mulino.

Del Pero, Mario (2003), 'Containing Containment: rethinking Italy's experience during the Cold War', *Journal of Modern Italian Studies*, vol. 8, no. 4, pp. 532–55.

della Porta, Donatella (1996), *Movimenti collettivi e sistema politico in Italia 1960–1995*, Rome and Bari: Laterza.

della Porta, Donatella and Herbet Reiter (1998), 'The policing of protest in Western democracies', pp. 1–32, in Donatella della Porta and Herbet Reiter (eds.), *Policing Protest: The Control of Mass Demonstrations in Western Democracies*, Minneapolis and London: University of Minnesota Press.

(2001), 'Protesta noglobal e ordine pubblico', *il Mulino*, no. 5, pp. 871–82.

(2002), '"Voi G8, noi 6.000.000.000", Le manifestazioni di Genova', pp. 119–40, in Paolo Bellucci and Martin Bull (eds.), *Politica in Italia*, Bologna: il Mulino.

(2003), *Polizia e protesta: l'ordine pubblico dalla Liberazione ai "no global"'*, Bologna: il Mulino.

della Porta, Donatella and Alberto Vannucci (1997), 'The resources of corruption: reflections from the Italian case', *Crime Law and Social Change*, vol. 27, nos. 3–4, pp. 231–54.

(1999a), *Corrupt Exchanges: Actors, Resources and Mechanisms of Political Corruption*, Berlin and New York: de Gruyter.

(1999b), *Un paese annormale: come la classe politica ha perso l'occasione di Mani Pultie*, Rome and Bari: Laterza.

Della Sala Vincent, (1997), 'Hollowing out and hardening the state: European integration and the Italian economy', pp. 14–33, in Martin J. Bull and Martin Rhodes (eds.), *Crisis and Transition in Italian Politics*, London: Frank Cass.

(1998), 'The Italian Parliament: chambers in the crumbling house?', pp. 73–96, in Philip Norton (ed.), *Parliaments and Governments in Western Europe*, London and Portland, OR: Frank Cass.

Dente, Bruno (1985), 'Centre-local relations in Italy: the impact of the legal and political structures', in Yves Mény and Vincent Wright (eds.), *Centre-Periphery Relations in Western Europe*, London: George Allen and Unwin.

Deutsch, Karl W., Sidney A. Burrell and Robert A. Khan (1957), *Political Community and the North Atlantic Area: International Organization in the Light of Historical Experience*, Princeton, NJ: Princeton University Press.

Di Caro, P. (2008) 'Berlusconi: FI e AN unite: e dà l'ultimatum all'Udc', *Corriere della Sera*, 9 February.

di Federico, Giuseppe (1989), 'The crisis of the justice system and the referendum on the judiciary', pp. 25–49, in Robert Leonardi and Piergiorgio Corbetta (eds.), *Italian Politics: A Review*, vol. III, London and New York: Pinter.

Di Palma, Giuseppe (1977), *Governing without Surviving: The Italian Parties in Parliament*, Berkeley, CA: University of California Press.

Diamanti, Ilvo (2005), 'Confusi e infelici: dal partito dell'Ulivo all'Unione dei partiti', *il Mulino*, no. 5, pp. 863–71.

Diamanti, Ilvo (2006), 'Il falso mito del Nord', *la Repubblica*, 16 April, pp. 1, 28.

Diamanti, Ilvo and Elisa Lello (2005), 'The Casa delle Libertà: a house of cards', *Modern Italy*, vol. 10, no. 1, pp. 9–35.

Diamanti, Ilvo and Renato Mannheimer (2002), 'Le basi sociali del voto: la frattura che attraversa i ceti medi', pp. 139–63, in Mario Caciagli and Piergiorgio Corbetta (eds.), *Le ragioni dell'elettore: perché ha vinto il centro-destra nelle elezioni italiane del 2001*.

Dilmore, Norberto (2005), 'Fragili e stabili: le alleanze nel sistema politico italiano', *il Mulino*, no. 2, pp. 239–49.

Dirindin, Nerina (2005), 'Tutela della salute', pp. 81–100, in Carlo Altini and Michelina Borsari (eds.), *Welfare state: il modello europeo dei diritti sociali*, Modena: Fondazione Collegio San Carlo.

Dogan, Mattei and Dominique Pelassy (1990), *How to Compare Nations: Strategies in Comparative Politics*, 2nd edition, Chatham, NJ: Chatham House.

Donovan, Mark (2000), 'La fine dell'anomalia referendaria in Italia?', pp. 69–87, in Mark Gilbert and Gianfranco Pasquino (eds.), *Politica in Italia: i fatti dell'anno e le interpretazioni*, Bologna: il Mulino.

Donovan, Mark (2003), 'The Italian State: No Longer Catholic, no Longer Christian', *West European Politics*, vol. 26, no. 1, pp. 95–116.

Drexel, Ingrid (2003), 'Two lectures: the concept of competence – an instrument of social and political change; centrally coordinated decentralization – no problem? Lessons from the Italian case', Stein Rokkan Centre for Social Studies, Unifob AS, Working Paper 26, www.ub.uib.no/elpub/rokkan/N/N26-03.pdf.

Ecofin Council (2005), 'Specifications on the Stability and Growth Pact and Guidelines on the format and content of Stability and Convergence Programmes', http://europa.eu.int /comm/economy_finance/about/activities/sgp/codeofconduct_en.pdf.

EurActiv (2005a), 'Stability and Growth Pact reform', www.euractiv.com/Article?tcmuri = tcm:29-133199-16&type=LinksDossier.

(2005b), 'Italy given until 2007 to correct its excessive deficit', www.euractiv.com/Article?tcmuri=tcm:29-141688-16&type=News

European Commission (2005), 'Commission recommends further steps under the excessive deficit procedure for Italy', Brussels, 20 June, IP/05/809, http://europa.eu.int/rapid/pressReleasesAction.do?reference=IP/05/809&format=HTML&aged=0&language=EN&guiLanguage=en.

Eurostat (2005), *Health in Europe*, Luxembourg: Office for Official Publications of the European Communities, http://epp.eurostat.cec.eu.int/cache/ITY_OFFPUB/KS-71-05-182/EN/KS-71-05-182-EN.PDF.

Fabbrini, Sergio and Salvatore Vassallo (1999), *Il governo: gli esecutivi nelle democrazie contemporanee*, Rome and Bari: Laterza.

Faini, Riccardo (2003), 'Fu vero declino? L'Italia degli anni Novanta', *il Mulino*, no. 6, pp. 1072–83.

Favretto, Marcella (1997), 'Anarchy in Albania: collapse of European collective security?', Occasional Papers on International Security Policy, no. 21, June 1997, www.basicint. org/pubs/Papers/BP21.htm.

Felletti, Duilio (2002), 'La riforma degli ammortizzatori sociali: una sintesi degli ammortizzatori oggi esistenti e dei disegni di cambiamento per il futuro', www.ecn.org /reds/lavoro/lavoro0206ammortizzatori.html.

Ferraresi, Franco (1992), 'Una struttura segreta denominata Gladio', pp. 87–110, in Stephen Hellman and Gianfranco Pasquino (eds.), *Politica in Italia: i fatti dell'anno e le interpretazioni*, Bologna: il Mulino.

Ferrera, Maurizio (1996), 'The partitocracy of health: towards a new welfare politics in Italy', *Res Publica*, 38, pp. 447–59.

    (1997), 'The uncertain future of the Italian welfare states', pp. 231–49, in Martin Bull and Martin Rhodes (eds.), *Crisis and Transition in Italian Politics*, London and Portland, OR: Frank Cass.

    (2005), 'Welfare states and social safety nets in southern Europe: an introduction', pp. 1–32, in Maurizio Ferrera (ed.), *Welfare State Reform in Southern Europe: Fighting Poverty and Social Exclusion in Italy, Spain, Portugal and Greece*, Milton Park: Routledge.

Ferrera, Maurizio and Stefano Sacchi (2004), 'The open method of coordination and national institutional capabilities: the Italian experience', URGE [Unità di Ricerca sulla Governance Europea] Working Paper 2/2004, www.urge.it/files/papers/1_wp_2_2004.pdf.

Fiorentini, Gianluca and Sam Peltzman (1995), 'Introduction', pp. 1–30, in Gianluca Fiorentini and Sam Peltzman (eds.), *The Economics of Organised Crime*, Cambridge: Cambridge University Press.

Fiori, (1995), *Il venditore: storia di Silvio Berlusconi e della Fininvest*, Milan: Garzanti.

Flamini, Sergio (1991), 'Presentazione', pp. i–xiii, in Antonio Cipriani and Gianni Cipriani, *Sovranità limitata: storia dell'eversione atlantica in Italia*, Rome: Edizioni Associate.

Floridia, Antonio (2008) 'Gulliver unbound?: possible electoral reforms and the 2008 Italian election: toward an end to 'fragmented bipolarity?'', *Modern Italy* vol. 13, no. 3, pp. 317–32.

Fois, Giovanna Antonia (2009), 'The EU and international contexts', pp. 62–81, in James L. Newell (ed.), *The Italian General Election of 2008: Berlusconi Strikes Back*, Basingstoke: Palgrave.

Follini, Marco (1997), 'Il sincretismo costituzionale: se le regole non hanno un'idea, *il Mulino*, 372, July-August, pp. 675–84.

Fortis, Marco and Alberto Quadrio Curzio (2003), 'Alle prese con la concorrenza asiatica', *il Mulino*, no. 6, pp. 1103–13.

Franco, Cattaneo (1995), 'Un paese, 2 partiti lumbard', *Corriere della Sera*, 4 March, http://archiviostorico.corriere.it/1995/marzo/04/paese_partiti_lumbard_co_0_9503049703.shtml.

Fraschini, Angela (1993), 'Financing Communal Government in Italy', pp. 79–93, in John Gibson and Richard Batley (eds.), *Financing European Local Governments*, London: Frank Cass.

Furlong, Paul (1994), *Modern Italy: Representation and Reform*, London and New York: Routledge.

Fusaro, Carlo (2003), *Il presidente della Repubblica*, Bologna: il Mulino.

Gallo, Domenico (1989), 'Italia – USA – NATO: sovranità limitata, democrazia bloccata', pp. 69–101, in Luigi Cortesi (ed.), *Democrazia, rischio nucleare, movimenti per la pace*, Naples: Liguori Editore.

Garella, Fabio (1994), 'I gruppi di pressione nel parlamento italiano', *Associazione per gli studi e le richerche parlamentari*, quaderno no. 4, seminario 1993, Milano: Giuffrè editore, pp. 85–103.

Gilbert, Mark (2000), 'The Bassanini Laws: a half-way house in local government reform', pp. 139–55, in David Hine and Salvatore Vassallo (eds.), *Italian Politics: The Return of Politics*, New York and Oxford: Berghahn.

Ginsborg, Paul (1990), *A History of Contemporary Italy: Society and Politics 1943–1988*, Harmondsworth: Penguin.

Giraudi, Giorgio (2003), 'Le autorità indipendenti: governare senza gli esecutivi nazionali?', pp. 227–67, in Cristina Barbieri and Luca Verzichelli (eds.), *Il governo e i suoi apparati: l'evoluzione del caso italiano in prospettiva comparata*, Genoa: Name.

Giuliano, Marco and Giliberto Capano (2001), 'I labirinti del legislativo', pp. 13–54, in Giliberto Capano and Marco Giuliani (eds.), *Parlamento e processo legislativo in Italia: continuità e mutamento*, Bologna: il Mulino.

Global Policy Forum (2006), 'Security Council Reform', www.globalpolicy.org/security/reform/cluster1index.htm#2006.

Gooch, John (1989), *The Unification of Italy*, London: Routledge.

Graziano, Luigi, Fiorenzo Girotti and Luciano Bonet (1984), 'Coalition politics at the regional level and centre-periphery relationships', *International Political Science Review*, vol. 5, no. 4, pp. 429–41.

Grilli, Luigi (2005), *Corso di procedura penale*, Padua: CEDAM.

Gualerzi, V. (2008), 'Pd, sondaggio promuove Veltroni sconfitta contenuta se corre da solo', *la Repubblica*, 29 January, www.repubblica.it/2008/01/sezioni/politica/sondaggi-2008/primo-dopocrisi/primo-dopo-crisi.html.

Gualtieri, Roberto (2004), 'The Italian political system and *détente* (1963–1981)', *Journal of Modern Italian Studies*, vol. 9, no. 4, pp. 428–49.

Guarnieri, Carlo (1997), 'The judiciary in the Italian political crisis', pp. 157–75, in Martin Bull and Martin Rhodes (eds.), *Crisis and Transition in Italian Politics*, London and Portland, OR: Frank Cass.

(2001), *La giustizia in Italia*, Bologna: il Mulino.

Guerra, Maria Cecilia (2004), 'Bisogna proprio ridurre le tasse?', *il Mulino*, no. 3, pp. 489–500.

Gummett, Philip (1997), 'Foreign, defence and security policy', pp. 207–25, in Martin Rhodes, Paul Heywood and Vincent Wright (eds.), *Developments in West European Politics*, London: Macmillan.

Hague, Rod, Harrop, Martin and Shaun Breslin (1998), *Comparative Government and Politics: An Introduction*, 4th edition, Basingstoke: Macmillan.

Hine, David (1993), *Governing Italy: The Politics of Bargained Pluralism*, Oxford: Clarendon Press.

Hine, David and Renato Finocchi (1991), 'The Italian Prime Minister', *West European Politics*, vol. 14, no. 2, pp. 79–96.

Holland, Martin (1999), 'The Common Foreign and Security Policy', pp. 230–46, in Laura Cram, Desmond Dinan and Neill Nugent (eds.), *Developments in the European Union*, London: Macmillan.

Hopkin, Jonathan (2005), 'Forza Italia after ten years', pp. 83–99, in Carlo Guarnieri and James L. Newell (eds.), *Italian Politics: Quo Vadis?*, New York: Berghahn.

Ignazi, Piero and Richard Katz (1995), 'Introduzione: ascesa e caduta del governo Berlusconi', pp. 27–48, in Piero Ignazi and Richard S. Katz (eds.), *Politica in Italia: i fatti dell'anno e le interpretazioni*, Bologna: il Mulino.

il Mulino (2005), 'Cattolici in un Paese smarrito', *il Mulino*, no. 5, pp. 821–2.

Inglehart, Ronald (1971), 'The silent revolution in Europe: intergenerational change in post-industrial societies', *American Political Science Review*, vol. 65, pp. 991–1017.

Ishikawa, Junko (2003), *Key Features of National Social Dialogue: A Social Dialogue Resource Book*, Geneva: International Labour Office.

ISTAT [Istituto Nazionale di Statistica] (2005), *Annuario statistico italiano*, Roma: Istituto Nazionale di Statistica.

ITANES [Italian National Election Study] (2001), *Perché ha vinto il centro-destra*, Bologna: il Mulino.

Iucci, Stefano (2003), 'La legge punto per punto', www.rassegna.it/2003/speciali/scuola/moratti.htm.

Jackson, Robert and Georg Sørensenn (2003), *Introduction to International Relations: Theories and Approaches*, Oxford and New York: Oxford University Press.

Jampaglia, Claudio (2006), 'Intervista al più affidabile tra i maghi dei numeri della politica, prof di metodologia della ricerca sociologica', *Liberazione*, 14 April, http://brunik.altervista.org/20060415121751.html.

Jarvis, Chris (2005), 'Business Open Learning Archive', www.bola.biz/systems/bureau.html.

Jönsson, Christer (2007), 'Organization, Institution and Process: Three Approaches to the Study of International Organization', paper prepared for ACUNS 20th Annual Meeting, New York, 6–8 June, www.igloo.org/acunsnet/download-nocache/Programs%20and%20Events/ACUNS%20Annual%20Meetings/annualme/am2007pa/christer.

Kitschelt, Herbert (1990), 'New social movements and the decline of party organisation', pp. 179–208, in Russell J. Dalton and Manfred Kuechler (eds.), *Challenging the Political Order: New Social Movements in Western Democracies*, Cambridge: Polity Press.

Laasko M. and R. Taagepera (1979), '"Effective" number of parties: a measure with application to West Europe', *Comparative Political Studies*, vol. 12, no. 1, pp. 3–27.

Lanza, Orazio (1991), 'L'agricoltura, la Coldiretti e la DC', pp. 41–117, in Leonardo Morlino (ed.), *Costruire la democrazia: gruppi e partiti in Italia*, Bologna: il Mulino.

LaPalombara, Joseph (1964), *Interest Groups in Italian Politics*, Princeton, NJ: Princeton University Press.

  (1987), *Democracy Italian Style*, New Haven, CT, and London: Yale University Press.

  (1994), '"Clientela e parentela" rivisitato', pp. 23–43, in M. Caciagli, F. Cazzola, L. Morlino and S. Passigli (eds.), *L'Italia fra crisi e transizione*, Rome and Bari: Laterza.

Lasswell, H. D. (1936), *Politics: Who Gets What, When, How*, New York: McGraw Hill.

Levy, Carl (1994), 'Italian trade unionism in the 1990s: the persistence of corporatism?', *Journal of Area Studies*, vol. 5, pp. 63–79.

Lijphart, Arend (1984), *Democracies: Patterns of Majoritarian and Consensus Government in Twenty-One Countries*, New Haven, CT and London: Yale University Press.

Lippolis, Vincenzo (1993), 'Maggioranza, opposizione e governo nei regolamenti e nelle prassi parlamentari dell'età repubblicana', pp. 613–53, in Luciano Violante (ed.), *Il parlamento italiano*, Torino: Einaudi.

Lipsky, Michael (1970), 'Introduction', pp. 1–7, in Michael Lipskey (ed.), *Law and Order: Police Encounters*, New York: Aldine Publishing Company.

Luciani, Massimo (2002), 'Federalismo, pp. 141–52, in Francesco Tuccari (ed.), *Il governo Berlusconi: le parole, i fatti, i rischi*, Rome and Bari: Laterza.

Maino, Franca (2001a), *La politica sanitaria*, Bologna: il Mulino.

  (2001b), 'La ristrutturazione del Servizio sanitario nazionale: la riforma Bindi e il federalismo fiscale', pp. 148–66, in Mario Caciagli and Alan Zucherman (eds.), *Politica in Italia: i fatti dell'anno e le interpretazioni*, Bologna: il Mulino.

(2003), 'La sanità fra Stato e regioni', *il Mulino*, no. 1 (January–February), pp. 100–7.

Mancini, Massimo (2000) 'I sistemi di protezione del reddito dei disoccupati in Italia tra politica sociale e strategia per l'occupazione. Analisi e confronti internazionali', Istituto per lo sviluppo della formazione professionale dei lavoratori, Monografie sul Mercato del lavoro e le politiche per l'impiego no. 4/2000, http://spinn.welfare. gov.it/SPINN/DocPrg/cd/Cd10/documenti/03_ita/B_studi/mdl_monog00_4.pdf.

Mannheimer, Renato and Giacomo Sani (1987), *Il mercato elettorale: identikit dell'elettore italiano*, Bologna: il Mulino.

Mapelli, Vittorio (1999), *Il sistema sanitario italiano*, Bologna: il Mulino.

Mareso, Manuela and Luana Serpone (2005), 'Democrazia sospesa, per mafia', www. libera.it/ public/File/17.%20comuni%20commissariati.doc.

Martin, Clarence Augustus (2003), *Understanding Terrorism*, Thousand Oaks, CA: Sage Publications Inc.

Massai, Alessandro (1992), *Dentro il Parlamento: come funzionano le camere*, Milan: il Sole 24 Ore.

Massari, Oreste (2005), 'La crisi di governo e il bipolarismo difettoso', *Il Mulino*, no. 3, pp. 442–50.

Mastropaolo, Alfio (2000), *Antipolitica: all'origine della crisi italiana*, Naples: Ancora.

(2005), *La mucca pazza della democrazia: nuove destre, populismo, antipolitica*, Turin: Bollati Boringhieri.

(2006), 'Vita, glorie, passione, morte (e difficile resurrezione) del centrismo in Italia', paper presented to the panel, 'Back to the future? The return of "the centre" in Italian politics', held at the 56th Annual Conference of the UK Political Studies Association, University of Reading, 4–6 April.

Mauro, Ezio (2006), 'Il Paese riparte più unito anche l'economia tornerà a vincere', *la Repubblica*, 12 July, www.repubblica.it/2006/07/sezioni/politica/intervista-romano-prodi /intervista-romano-prodi /intervista-romano-prodi.html.

Mazzoni Honorati, Maria Luisa (2001), *Diritto parlamentare*, Turin: G. Giappichelli Editore.

McCarthy, Patrick (2000), 'The Church in post-war Italy', pp. 133–52 in Patrick McCarthy (ed.), *Italy since 1945*, Oxford: Oxford University Press.

McNess, Anne (2003), 'The Italian Judicial System and its Reform', unpublished paper, Foreign and Commonwealth Office.

Melis, Guido (2003), *La burocrazia–da monsù Travet alla riforma del Titolo V: vizi e virtù della burocrazia italiana*, Bologna: il Mulino.

Mény, Yves (1990), *Government and Politics in Western Europe: Britain, France, Italy, West Germany*, Oxford: Oxford University Press.

Miller, James Edward (1992), *La politica estera di una media potenza: il caso italiano da De Gasperi a Craxi*, Mandria, Bari and Rome: Piero Lacaita Editore.

Ministero dell'Economia e delle Finanze (2005), 'La relazione sulle privatizzazioni: relazione al Parlamento sulle operazioni di cessione delle partecipazioni in società controllate direttamente o indirettamente dallo Stato', May 2005, www.dt.tesoro.it/ Aree-Docum/Partecipaz/Relazione-/Imp__-01_24_-.pdf.

Molinari, Maurizio (2000), *L'interesse nazionale: dieci storie dell'Italia nel mondo*, Rome and Bari: Laterza.

Moore, Malcolm (2008), 'US envoy admits role in Aldo Moro killing', *Daily Telegraph*, 16 March, www.telegraph.co.uk/news/worldnews/1581425/US-envoy-admits-role-in-Aldo-Moro-killing.html.

Morata, Francesco (2004), 'La presidenza italiana dell'Unione europea: un semester "anomalo"', pp. 145–66, in Vincent della Sala and Sergio Fabbrini (eds.), *Politica in Italia*, Bologna: Il Mulino.

Musu, Ignazio (1998), *Il debito pubblico*, Bologna: il Mulino.

Natale, Paolo (2006), 'Sondaggi, dall'altare alla polvere e vice versa', *Europa*, 12 April, http://brunik.altervista.org/20060415123805.html.

— (2008), 'Sempre fedeli: il voto che ristagna', pp. 91–101, in R. Mannheimer and P. Natale (eds.), *Senza più sinistra*, Milan: il Sole 24 Ope.

Natali, David and Martin Rhodes (2005), 'The Berlusconi pension reform and the emerging "double cleavage" in Italian politics', pp. 172–89, in Carlo Guarnieri and James L. Newell (eds.), *Italian Politics: Quo Vadis?*, Oxford and New York: Berghahn.

Nelken, David (1996), 'The judges and political corruption in Italy', *Journal of Law and Society*, vol. 23, no. 1, March, pp. 95–112.

Neppi Modona, Guido (ed.) (1998), *Stato della Costituzione*, Milan: il Saggiatore.

Nevola, Gaspare (2003), 'Quale patria per gli italiani? Dalla "repubblica dei partiti" alla pedagogia civico-nazionale di Ciampi', pp. 139–91, in Gaspare Nevola (ed.), *Una patria per gli Italiani: la questione nazionale oggi tra storia, cultura e politica*, Roma: Carocci Editore.

Newell, James L. (2000), *Parties and Democracy in Italy*, Aldershot: Ashgate.

— (2002), 'Introduction', pp. 1–8, in James L. Newell (ed.), *The Italian General Election of 2001: Berlusconi's Victory*, Manchester: Manchester University Press.

— (2003), 'Political corruption in Italy', pp. 191–215, in Petrus C. van Duyne, Klaus von Lampe and James L. Newell (eds.), *Criminal Finances and Organising Crime in Europe*, Nijmegen: Wolf Legal Publishers.

— (2004), 'Interpretive approaches and the study of Italian politics', *Modern Italy*, vol. 9, no. 2 (November), pp. 247–61.

— (2005), 'Judicialisation and the Americanisation of Italian politics', *Journal of Modern Italian Studies*, vol. 10. no. 1, pp. 27–42.

— (2006), 'Organised crime and corruption: the case of the Sicilian mafia', pp. 147–75, in Petrus C. Van Duyne, Almir Maljevic, Maarten van Dijk, Klaus Von Lampe and James L. Newell (eds.), *The Organisation of Crime for Profit: Conduct, Law and Measurement*, Nijmegan: Wolf Legal Publishers.

— (2007), '"The mayoralty in Italy', pp. 157–72, in John Garrard (ed.), *Heads of the Local State*, Aldershot: Ashgate.

— (2008), 'Corruption and Democracy in Western Europe: Introduction', *Perspectives on European Politics and Society*, vol. 9, no. 1, April, pp. 1–7.

— (ed.) (2009), *The Italian General Election of 2008: Berlusconi Strikes Back*, Basingstoke: Palgrave.

Newell, James L. and Martin J. Bull (1996), 'The April 1996 Italian general election: the left on top or on tap?', *Parliamentary Affairs*, vol. 49, no. 4, October pp. 616–47.

— (2003), 'Introduction', pp. 1–6, in M. J. Bull and J. L. Newell (eds.), *Corruption in Contemporary Politics*, Basingstoke: Palgrave Macmillan.

Newell, James L. and Ilaria Favretto (2006), 'Editorial', *Journal of Contemporary European Studies*, vol. 14, no. 1, pp. 1–9.

Newell, James L. and Hilary Partridge (2002), 'Conclusion', in James L. Newell (ed.), *The Italian General Election of 2001: Berlusconi's Victory*, Manchester: Manchester University Press.

Newton, Ken and Jan W. Van Deth (2005), *Foundations of Comparative Politics*, Cambridge: Cambridge University Press.

Norton, Alan (1994), *International Handbook of Local and Regional Government: A Comparative Analysis of Advanced Democracies*, Cheltenham: Edward Elgar.

Onida, Fabrizio (2004), *Se il piccolo non cresce: piccole e medie imprese italiane in affanno*, Bologna: il Mulino.

Onida, Valerio (2004), *La Costituzione*, Bologna: il Mulino.

Pajno, Alessandro (2000), 'La presidenza del consiglio dei ministri dal vecchio al nuovo ordinamento', pp. 35–106, in Alessandro Pajno and Luisa Torchia (eds.), *La riforma del governo: commento ai decreti legislativi n. 300 e n. 303 del 1999 sulla riorganizzazione della presidenza del consiglio e dei ministri*, Bologna: il Mulino.

Pajno, Alessandro and Luisa Torchia (2000), 'Governo e amministrazione: la modernizzazione del sistema italiano', pp. 11–31, in Alessandro Pajno and Luisa Torchia (eds.), *La riforma del governo: commento ai decreti legislativi n. 300 e n. 303 del 1999 sulla riorganizzazione della presidenza del consiglio e dei ministri*, Bologna: il Mulino.

Paoli, Letizia (2000), *Fratelli di mafia: Cosa Nostra e'Ndrangheta*, Bologna: il Mulino.

Paoli, Letizia and Marvin E. Wolfgang (2001), 'Crime, Italian style', *Daedalus*, www.findarticles.com/p/articles/mi_qa3671/is_200107/ai_n8963559.

Paoloni, Mauro and Francesca Maria Cesaroni (1998), 'L'evoluzione della finanza locale ed i nuovi strumenti finanziari degli Enti locali', pp. 213–33, in Luciano Marchi and Mauro Paoloni (eds.), *Il processo di trasformazione contabile e finanza dei comuni e delle province: analisi applicative ed indicazioni prospettiche*, Rimini: Maggioli Editore.

Papp, Daniel S. (1991), *Contemporary International Relations: Frameworks for Understanding*, New York: Macmillan.

Parker, Simon and Duncan McDonnell (2003), 'Devolution or Neo-centralism? Centre-left cities in centre-right regions: the cases of Genoa and Venice', paper presented to the panel, 'Italian politics I: Party politics at the national and sub-national levels', held at the 53rd Annual Conference of the UK Political Studies Association, University of Leicester, 15–17 April.

Parkin, Frank (1979), *Marxism and Class Theory: A Bourgeois Critique*, London: Tavistock Publications.

Pasquino, Gianfranco (1988), *Istituzioni, partiti, lobbies*, Rome and Bari: Laterza.

(1997), 'No longer a 'party state'? Institutions, power and the problems of Italian reform', pp. 34–53, in Martin Bull and Martin Rhodes (eds.), *Crisis and Transition in Italian Politics*, London and Portland, OR: Frank Cass.

(2000), *La transizione a parole*, Bologna: il Mulino.

(2005a), 'Democrazia, partiti, primarie', paper presented to the conference organised by the Società Italiana di Studi Elettorali on 'Le primarie in Italia: selezione dei candidati o legittimazione della leadership', Florence, 2 December.

(2005b), 'Populism and Democracy', paper presented to the 55th Annual Conference of the UK Political Studies Association, University of Leeds, 5–7 April.

(2008), 'The political context 2001–2006', pp. 15–32, in James L. Newell (ed.), *The Italian General Election of 2006*, Manchester: Manchester University Press.

Pederzoli, Patrizia (2005), 'La riforma dell'ordinamento giudiziario', pp. 185–203, in Carlo Guarnieri and James L. Newell (eds.), *Politica in Italia: i fatti dell'anno e le interpretazioni*, Bologna: il Mulino.

Peterson, John (2001), 'US and EU in the Balkans: "America Fights the Wars, Europe does the Dishes?"', European University Institute: EUI Working Paper RSC No. 2001 /49.

(2006), 'Is the wolf at the door this time? Transatlantic relations after Iraq', *European Political Science*, vol. 5, no. 1, March, pp. 52–61.

Piacentini, Valeria (2003), 'La politica estera italiana, i paesi arabi e il mondo musulmano', pp. 219–41, in Massimo de Leopardi (ed.), *Il Mediterraneo nella politica estera italiana del secondo dopoguerra*, Bologna: il Mulino.

Piason, Frank J. (1986), 'Italian foreign policy: the Achille Lauro affair', pp. 146–63, in Robert Leonardi and Raffaella Y. Nanetti (eds.), *Italian Politics: A Review*, vol. I, London: Frances Pinter.

Piattoni, Simona (1998), 'Clientelismo virtuoso: una via di sviluppo nel Mezzogiorno?', *Rivista Italiana di Scienza Politica*, vol. 23, no. 3, December, pp. 483–513.

Pizzigallo, Matteo (2003), 'Diplomazia parallela e politica petrolifera nell'Italia del secondo dopoguerra', pp. 141–55, in Massimo de Leopardi (ed.), *Il Mediterraneo nella politica estera italiana del secondo dopoguerra*, Bologna: il Mulino.

Pizzorno, Alessandro (2001), 'Perché si paga il benzinaio: per una teoria del capitale sociale', pp. 19–45, in Arnaldo Bagnasco, Fortunata Piselli, Alessandro Pizzorno and Carlo Trigilia, *Il capitale sociale: istruzioni per l'uso*, Bologna: il Mulino.

Pizzorusso, Alessandro (1990), *L'organizzazione della giustizia in Italia: La magistratura nel sistema politico e istituzionale*, Turin: Einaudi.

(1996), *La Costituzione: i valori da conservare, le regole da cambiare*, Turin: Einaudi.

Pochet, Philippe (2005), 'The open method of co-ordination and the construction of social Europe: a historical perspective', pp. 19–33, in J. Zeitlin and P. Pochet (eds.), *The Open Method of Coordination in Action: The European Employment and Social Inclusion Strategies*, PIE-Peter Lang: Brussels.

Politi, Marco (2006), 'Il Papa: no ai Pacs. Ed è lite a sinistra', *la Repubblica*, 13 January, p. 11.

Procacci, Giuliano (1973), *History of the Italian People*, Harmondsworth: Penguin.

Putnam, Robert (1993), *Making Democracy Work: Civic Traditions in Modern Italy*, Princeton, NJ: Princeton University Press.

Pye, L. (1995), 'Political culture', pp. 965–9, in S. Lipset (ed.), *The Encyclopaedia of Democracy*, London and New York: Routledge.

Pyke, Frank and Werner Sengenberger, 'Introduzione', pp. 15–23, in Frank Pyke, Giacomo Becattini and Werner Sengenberger, *Distretti industriali e cooperazione fra imprese in Italia, studi e informazioni*, no. 34, Florence: Banca Toscana.

Ratti, Luca (2002), 'Continuity and Consensus in Italian Foreign Policy', paper presented to the 52nd Annual Conference of the UK Political Studies Association, University of Aberdeen, 5–7 April.

Regini, Marino and Ida Regalia (1997), 'Employers, unions and the state: the resurgence of concertation in Italy?', pp. 210–30, in Martin Bull and Martin Rhodes (eds.), *Crisis and Transition in Italian Politics*, Portland, OR and London: Frank Cass.

Rémond, René (1999), *La secolarizzazione: religione e società nell'Europa contemporanea*, trans Michele Sampaolo, Rome and Bari: Laterza.

Rhodes, Martin (1997), 'Financing party politics in Italy: a case of systemic corruption', pp. 54–80, in Martin Bull and Martin Rhodes (eds.), *Crisis and Transition in Italian Politics*, Portland, OR and London: Frank Cass.

Robson, Mark (2000), *Italy: Liberalism and Fascism 1870–1945*, London: Hodder and Stoughton.

Romano, Sergio (2002), *Guida alla politica estera italiana: da Badoglio a Berlusconi*, Milan: Rizzoli.

Roncarolo, F. and M. Belluati (2008), 'Surfing and trying to keep afloat: the political communication process in a highly fragmented coalition led by a "Great Mediator"', *Modern Italy*, vol. 13, no. 3, 333–48.

Rosenberg, Alexander (1988), *Philosophy of Social Science*, Boulder, CO: Westview Press.

Rossi, Salvatore (2000), *La politica economica italiana 1968-2000*, Rome and Bari: Laterza.
(2004), 'Economia italiana: perché la deriva non si muti in declino', *il Mulino*, no. 4, pp. 639–49.

Russo, Federico and Luca Verzichelli (2009), 'A different legislature? The parliamentary scene following the 2008 elections', pp. 211–27, in James L. Newell (ed.), *The Italian General Election of 2008: Berlusconi Strikes Back*, Basingstoke: Palgrave.

Sacchi, Stefano and Francesca Bastagli (2005), 'Italy – striving uphill but stopping halfway: the troubled journey of the experimental minimum insertion income', pp. 84–140, in Maurizio Ferrera (ed.), *Welfare State Reform in Southern Europe: Fighting Poverty and Social Exclusion in Italy, Spain, Portugal and Greece*, Milton Park: Routledge.

Sadeh, Tal (2002), 'The establishment of the European Monetary System: on the role of leadership and reciprocity in cognitive evolution', paper presented to the annual meeting of the International Studies Association, New Orleans, 24–27 March, www.isanet.org/noarchive/Isa01.pdf.

Saiu, Liliana (2005), *La politica estera italiana dall'Unità a oggi*, Rome and Bari: Laterza.

Salazar, Carmela (2002), *La magistratura*, Rome and Bari: Laterza.

Salerno, Giulio M. (2002), *I nostri diritti*, Rome and Bari: Laterza.

Salvadori, Massimo L. (1994), *Storia d'Italia e crisi di regime*, Bologna: il Mulino.

Santino, Umberto (1994), 'La mafia come soggetto politico. Ovvero: la produzione mafiosa della politica e la produzione politica della mafia', pp. 118–41, in Giovanni Fiandaca and Salvatore Costantino, (eds.), *La mafia, le mafie: tra vecchi e nuovi paradigmi*, Rome and Bari: Laterza.

Santoro, Carlo Maria (1994), 'La politica estera', pp. 634–6, in Paul Ginsborg (ed.), *Stato dell'Italia*, Milan: il Saggiatore.

Sartori, Giovanni (1995), *Come sbagliare le riforme*, Bologna: il Mulino.

Scalfari, Eugenio (2006), 'The terapia che vuole dissolvere la sinistra', *la Repubblica*, 18 January, www.repubblica.it/2006/a/sezioni/politica/versoelezioni4/tera/tera.html.

Sciolla, Loredana (2003), 'Cultura civica e "carattere nazionale": il caso italiano in prospettiva comparata', pp. 81–116, in Gaspare Nevola (ed.), *Una patria per gli Italiani: la questione nazionale oggi tra storia, cultura e politica*, Roma: Carocci Editore.

Seton-Watson, Christopher (1967), *Italy from Liberalism to Fascism 1870-1925*, London: Methuen and Co.

Signorini, Federico L. and Ignazio Visco (2002), *L'economia italiana*, 3rd edition, Bologna: il Mulino.

Stone Sweet, A. (2000) *Governing with Judges: Constitutional Politics in Europe*, Oxford: Oxford University Press.

Tarchi, Marco (2003), *L'Italia populista: dal qualunquismo ai girotondi*, Bologna: il Mulino.

Tarrow, Sidney (1977), *Between Center and Periphery: Grassroots Politicians in Italy and France*, New Haven, CT, and London: Yale University Press.

Thomas, Clive S. (2001), 'Studying the political party-interest group relationship', pp. 1–23, in Clive S. Thomas (ed.), *Political Parties and Interest Groups: Shaping Democratic Governance*, Boulder, CO and London: Lynne Rienner.

Thompson, John B. (2000), *Political Scandal: Power and Visibility in the Media Age*, Cambridge: Polity Press.

Toniolo, Gianni (2004), 'L'Italia verso il declino economico?', pp. 7–29, in Gianni Toniolo and Vincenzo Visco, (eds.), *Il declino economico dell'Italia*, Bruno Mondadori.

Torchia, Luisa (2000), 'Il nuovo ordinamento dei ministeri: le disposizioni generali (articoli 1–7)', pp. 125–44, in Alessandro Pajno and Luisa Torchia (eds.), *La riforma del governo: commento ai decreti legislativi n. 300 e n. 303 del 1999 sulla riorganizzazione della presidenza del consiglio e dei ministri*, Bologna: il Mulino.

Trento, Sandro (2003), 'Stagnazione e frammentazione produttiva', *il Mulino*, no. 6, pp. 1093–1102.

Trigilia, Carlo (1995), 'A tale of two districts: work and politics in the Third Italy', pp. 31–50, in Arnaldo Bagnasco and Charles Sabel (eds.), *Small and Medium-Size Enterprises*, London: Pinter.

  (2001), 'Capitale sociale e sviluppo locale', pp. 105–31, in Arnaldo Bagnasco, Fortunata Piselli, Alessandro Pizzorno and Carlo Trigilia, *Il capitale sociale: istruzioni per l'uso*, Bologna: il Mulino.

Trupia, Piero (1989), *La democrazia degli interessi: lobby e decisione collettiva*, Milan: il Sole 24 Ore.

Tsebelis, Goerge (1999), 'Veto players and law production in parliamentary democracies: an empirical analysis', *American Political Science Review*, vol. 93, no. 3, pp. 591–608.

  (2002), *Veto Players: How Political Institutions Work*, Princeton NJ: Princeton University Press-Russell Sage Foundation.

UNIDO [United Nations Industrial Development Organisation] (2005), 'The UNIDO Cluster/Network Development Programme: The Italian experience of industrial districts', www.unido.org/en/doc/4310.

Vandelli, Luciano (2005), *Il governo locale*, Bologna: il Mulino.

Varese, Federico (2000), 'Pervasive corruption', www.colbud.hu/honesty-trust/varese/pub01. PDF.

Vassallo, Salvatore (2005), 'The constitutional reforms of the center right', pp. 117–35, in Carlo Guarnieri and James L. Newell (eds.), *Italian Politics: Quo Vadis?*, New York and Oxford: Berghahn.

Vecchi, G. G. (2008), '"Di Pietro nel Pd? Certi deliri non mi riguardano"', *Corriere della Sera*, 15 February, p. 13.

Veltroni, Walter (2007), *La nuova stagione*, Milan: Rizzoli.

Verderame, Francesco (2006), 'Il pressing del Cavaliere su Mastella', *Corriere della Sera*, 24 January 2004, www.corriere.it/Primo_Piano/Politica/2006/01_Gennaio/24/mastella. shtml.

Verzichelli, Luca (1999), *La legge finanziaria*, Bologna: il Mulino.

Verzichelli, Luca and Maurizio Cotta (2002), 'Still a central institution? New patterns of parliamentary democracy in Italy, 1992–2002', paper presented at the workshop, 'A Renewal of Parliaments in Europe? MPs, behaviours and action constraints', ECPR Joint Sessions of Workshops, Turin, 22–27 March 2002.

Visco, Vincenzo (2005), 'Spesa pubblica e procedure di bilancio', *il Mulino*, no. 4, pp. 698–705.

Walston, J. (2008), 'La politica estera: il difficile perseguimento di un ruolo influente', pp. 151–71, in M. Donovan and P. Onofri (eds.), *Politica in Italia: i fatti dell'anno e le interpretazioni*, Bologna: il Mulino.

Waters, M. (1996), *Globalization*, London and New York: Routledge.

Index

Note: Page numbers in *italic* refer to Figures; those in **bold** refer to Tables and Appendix; those in ***bold italic*** refer to Boxes